T0168822

ANTHROPOLOGICAL PAPERS OF
THE UNIVERSITY OF ARIZONA
NUMBER 75

Potters and Communities of Practice

Glaze Paint and Polychrome Pottery in the American Southwest, A.D. 1250 to 1700

Linda S. Cordell and Judith A. Habicht-Mauche,
Editors

CONTRIBUTORS

Eric Blinman	Kelley Hays-Gilpin
Jeffery J. Clark	Cynthia L. Herhahn
Diane Curewitz	Deborah L. Huntley
Tom Dickerson	Rosemary A. Joyce
Jennifer Boyd Dyer	Patrick D. Lyons
Suzanne L. Eckert	Barbara J. Mills
Thomas Fenn	David A. Phillips, Jr.
Hayward H. Franklin	Ann F. Ramenofsky
Dennis Gilpin	Kari L. Schleher
Sheila Goff	David H. Snow
Ibrahim Gundiler	Noah Thomas

THE UNIVERSITY OF
ARIZONA PRESS
TUCSON

THE UNIVERSITY OF ARIZONA PRESS

© 2012 The Arizona Board of Regents
All Rights Reserved

www.uapress.arizona.edu

Library of Congress Cataloging-in-Publication Data

Potters and communities of practice : glaze paint and polychrome pottery in the American southwest, a.d. 1250 to 1700 / Linda S. Cordell and Judith A. Habicht-Mauche, editors.

    p. cm. — (Anthropological papers of the University of Arizona ; v.75)
 Includes bibliographical references and index.
 ISBN 978-0-8165-2992-6 (pbk. : alk. paper) 1. Indian pottery—Southwest, New—Themes, motives. 2. Indian pottery--Southwest, New—Classification. 3. Indian pottery—Southwest, New—Design. 4. Glazing (Ceramics)—Southwest, New. 5. Polychromy—Southwest, New. 6. Southwest, New—Antiquities. I. Cordell, Linda S. II. Habicht-Mauche, Judith A., 1959–
E78.S7P66 2012
738.0979—dc23

                    2012014751

Manufactured in the United States of America on acid-free, archival-quality paper processed chlorine free.

18 17 16 15 14 13 12   6 5 4 3 2 1

About the Editors

LINDA S. CORDELL is Professor Emerita at the University of Colorado, Boulder, a Senior Scholar at the School for Advanced Research on the Human Experience in Santa Fe and an external faculty member at the Santa Fe Institute, Santa Fe. She is a member of the National Academy of Sciences (2005) and the American Academy of Arts and Sciences (2007). In 2001, Cordell received the A. V. Kidder Award for Eminence in American Archaeology from the American Anthropological Association and in 2009 a Lifetime Achievement Award from the Society for American Archaeology. Cordell received her B.A. in Anthropology from George Washington University (1965), her M.A. in Anthropology from the University of Oregon (1967), and her Ph.D. in Anthropology from the University of California, Santa Barbara (1972). She specializes in Southwest archaeology and archaeological method and theory. Her field research has focused on fourteenth- and fifteenth-century Ancestral Pueblo sites in the Rio Grande region.

JUDITH A. HABICHT-MAUCHE is Professor of Anthropology at the University of California, Santa Cruz, where she joined the faculty in 1990. She earned her B.A. in Anthropology from the College of William and Mary in Virginia (1981) and her M.A. (1984) and Ph.D. (1988) in Anthropology from Harvard University. Her research interests include the organization of production and exchange of ancient pottery in the American Southwest and Southern Plains. She is an expert in applying mineralogical, chemical, and isotopic techniques for sourcing artifacts and reconstructing ancient trade routes. In 2009, the Society for American Archaeology presented Prof. Habicht-Mauche with its Award for Excellence in Archaeological Analysis for her innovative research that has significantly impacted the discipline. This award highlighted Prof. Habicht-Mauche's specific contributions to the field of ceramic materials analysis.

Cover

The graph plots the lead isotope ratios ($^{207}Pb/^{206}Pb$ by $^{208}Pb/^{206}Pb$) for southern Rio Grande glaze paints. This plot is discussed in Chapter 2 by Deborah L. Huntley, Thomas Fenn, Judith A. Habicht-Mauche, and Barbara J. Mills

The ceramic is a Nine Mile Polychrome, Gila Variety bowl from the Curtis site (AZ CC:2:3[ASM]), Catalog No. 7623CS. Photograph by Patrick D. Lyons, reproduced courtesy of Eastern Arizona College. This vessel is discussed in Chapter 3 by Patrick D. Lyons and Jeffery J. Clark.

Contributors

Eric Blinman	Office of Archaeological Studies, Museum of New Mexico, Santa Fe,
Jeffery J. Clark	Archaeology Southwest, Tucson, Arizona
Diane Curewitz	Department of Anthropology, Washington State University, Pullman,
Tom Dickerson	Artist, Santa Fe, New Mexico
Jennifer Boyd Dyer	Department of Anthropology, University of New Mexico, Albuquerque
Suzanne L. Eckert	Department of Anthropology, Texas A&M University, College Station
Thomas Fenn	School of Anthropology, University of Arizona, Tucson
Hayward H. Franklin	Maxwell Museum of Anthropology, University of New Mexico, Albuquerque
Dennis Gilpin	PaleoWest Archaeology, Phoenix, Arizona
Sheila Goff	Colorado Historical Society, Denver
Ibrahim Gundiler	New Mexico Bureau of Geology and Mineral Resources, New Mexico Institute of Mining and Technology, Socorro
Kelley Hays-Gilpin	Northern Arizona University and the Museum of Northern Arizona, Flagstaff
Cynthia L. Herhahn	US Bureau of Land Management, Albuquerque, New Mexico
Deborah L. Huntley	Archaeology Southwest, Tucson, Arizona
Rosemary A. Joyce	Department of Anthropology, University of California, Berkeley
Patrick D. Lyons	Arizona State Museum and School of Anthropology, University of Arizona, Tucson
Barbara J. Mills	School of Anthropology, University of Arizona, Tucson
David A. Phillips, Jr.	Maxwell Museum of Anthropology, University of New Mexico, Albuquerque
Ann F. Ramenofsky	Department of Anthropology, University of New Mexico, Albuquerque
Kari L. Schleher	Crow Canyon Archaeological Center, Cortez, Colorado
David H. Snow	Independent Researcher, Albuquerque, New Mexico
Noah Thomas	School of Anthropology, University of Arizona, Tucson

Contents

FIGURES

TABLES

Preface

This volume contains revised and expanded papers that were presented on April 23, 2009, at the 74th Annual Meeting of the Society for American Archaeology (SAA) in Atlanta, Georgia. The full morning session, titled "Technology as Practice: Polychrome and Glaze-Painted Pottery in the Late Prehispanic Southwest," consisted of 15 presentations and remarks by the symposium discussant, Rosemary A. Joyce. Fourteen of the papers and Dr. Joyce's discussion are included here. One paper, "18th Century Pueblo Polychromes in Spanish Colonial Contexts," by Heather Atherton of Columbia University, examining pottery from the Middle Rio Grande site of San Jose de las Huertas, was withdrawn by the author so she could address other commitments.

The 2009 SAA symposium was meant to follow up on continuing research that developed out of work presented in 2002 at the 67th Annual SAA Meeting in Denver, Colorado, and subsequently published as *The Social Life of Pots: Glaze Wares and Cultural Dynamics in the Southwest, AD 1250–1680* (Habicht-Mauche and others 2006). Like its predecessor, this volume includes a mix of research conducted by graduate students, recent PhDs, and more experienced archaeologists. Although this volume grew out of lively discussion and debate reviewed in *"The Social Life of Pots,"* it departs from its predecessor in a number of ways. Nearly all of the papers in this book are collaborative efforts among scholars working at different institutions, sharing data, and providing insights gained from different analytical techniques and perspectives. These joint efforts are a direct result of contributors moving a research agenda forward. The effort was enhanced by some of the contributors to this volume participating in the workshop, "New Statistical Approaches to Southwest Archaeology," hosted by Douglas H. Erwin at the Santa Fe Institute on January 17–18, 2006, in Santa Fe. Unlike its predecessor, this volume expands thematically to include polychrome pottery, rather than focusing exclusively on glaze-paint decorated ware. The volume also expands temporally to examine both the origins of these pottery wares in the late prehispanic period and the decline and disappearance of glaze-painted pottery in the context of the Spanish colonial period in the Greater Southwest.

We view the chapters in this book as a series of working papers. As such, they focus on explaining and providing data that support different analytical approaches, and they work toward amplifying a new theoretical perspective that combines practice theory and situated learning theory. Their emphasis is on the social network contexts within which polychrome and glaze-decorated pottery were introduced and produced in the Greater Southwest. There is less here on the functions of these vessels in their diverse social contexts or the archaeological contexts of their ultimate deposition and recovery. These papers are very much works in progress.

We thank T. J. Ferguson for encouraging us to submit this volume to the Anthropological Papers of the University of Arizona and all of our contributors for their timely responses to our requests. Graphic artist Helen Cole redrafted a number of the figures for this volume and we appreciate her professionalism and talent, which greatly enhanced the artistic quality of our book. June-el Piper provided invaluable assistance with a number of editorial tasks, including collating and formatting the bibliography. We gratefully acknowledge the helpful comments of our anonymous reviewers, and we thank the editorial staff of The University of Arizona Press.

Linda S. Cordell and Judith A. Habicht-Mauche
January 2011

Practice Theory and Social Dynamics among Prehispanic and Colonial Communities in the American Southwest

Linda S. Cordell and Judith A. Habicht-Mauche

From an archaeological perspective, one of the most important trends in social theory over the past quarter-century is a revival of interest in the concrete materiality of social life (Appadurai 1986; Bourdieu 1977)—a recognition that "social worlds are as much constituted by materiality as the other way around" (Miller 1998). However, as Miller (1998) points out, if we are to understand how various "artefacts, commodities, and aesthetic forms" are implicated in social dynamics, then we need to move beyond a general theory of material culture to a more detailed analysis of the specificity of particular material domains. We need to move from a discussion of "why things matter" to one of "why some things matter" a lot in particular places and times.

BACKGROUND, HISTORY, AND THEORY

The researchers whose work is highlighted in this volume are concerned with events in the Greater Southwest that occurred between about A.D. 1250 and 1700. The events begin with large-scale population movements and are marked by redistributions of population on the landscape, formation of very large settlements, and production and exchange of polychrome and glaze-paint-decorated pottery. The period ends in the turbulence of the early Spanish colonial period, around the time of the Pueblo Revolt of 1680, and is marked by a massive decline in Pueblo population, further reorganization of population, new kinds of settlements (missions, Hispanic villages), demands on Pueblo labor, and cessation of production of glaze-painted pottery, although matte-painted yellow and polychrome pottery types continued to be produced among both Eastern and Western Pueblo groups.

New ceramic styles that were first made in the late thirteenth century used color, texture, and iconic imagery in innovative ways that do not appear to have had precedents in the earlier regional corpus of decorated pottery. A central premise of this volume is that this new pottery—polychrome and glaze-paint-decorated pottery—mattered a lot in the context of the specific social dynamics of the late prehispanic and early colonial periods. Further, we believe that through detailed study of polychrome and glaze-paint-decorated pottery we can deepen our understanding of the changing social dynamics of this period. Polychrome pottery and glaze-paint-decorated pottery are compositionally and technologically complex. Their production, distribution, and use involved activating multiple social networks at various scales. These networks can be thought of as "communities of practice" that both encompassed and cross-cut various social groups and boundaries and, thus, can effectively be studied using a practice theory approach (Habicht-Mauche 2006; Stark 2006).

The contributors to this volume investigate these networks by mining various ethnographic, historical, and archaeological archives and by using a variety of archaeological, archaeometric, ethnoarchaeological, and experimental techniques to trace patterns of raw material acquisition, to reconstruct production techniques and sequences, to define and compare local and regional technological and decorative styles, and to begin to model local and regional patterns of distribution and consumption. We view these material practices as cultural performances that were both constituted in and constitutive of social life during this particularly dynamic period in the history of the Greater Southwest.

The chapters that follow are working papers by researchers actively engaged in a number of independent and collaborative projects throughout the Southwest. The chapters break new ground in linking innovative methods of analysis and characterization to processes of social change. They therefore tie advances in anthropological method and theory to advances in materials analysis. One focus of the chapters in this volume is on reconstructing, in exacting detail, the technologies, techniques, and canons of style that characterized specific local and regional traditions of polychrome and glaze-painted pottery in various parts of the Greater Southwest, from the latter half of the thirteenth century through the seventeenth century. Another focus of this volume is on how these various technologies, techniques, and canons of style were learned, transmitted, perpetuated, and ultimately changed or lost through interactions or the breaking of interactive ties between and among communities of potters. These studies allow us to trace the movement of materials, technologies, and ideas, and, in some instances, even people across the dynamic landscape of the Southwest. In turn, they facilitate our understanding of the ways the complex flows of materials, people, things, and ideas shaped and were shaped by crosscutting and interrelated social networks that were activated in different contexts and that functioned at varying scales of local and regional interaction.

In brief overview, the period of interest in this volume begins in about A.D. 1300, when the Mesa Verde region, Four Corners, and San Juan Basin were largely depopulated. By about 1400, most of the Western Pueblo regions, with the exception of the Hopi, Zuni, and Acoma areas, were no longer permanently occupied (Adams and Duff 2004:3–4). After 1300, the "clear cultural pattern of Hohokam dissipates especially in the uplands north of Phoenix and east and south of Tucson" (Adams and Duff 2004:5), and in these southern Arizona areas, Puebloan immigrants settled among indigenous groups. Although vast areas of the Mogollon highlands and the Mimbres Valley also saw population loss by the early fourteenth century, there was population increase in northern Chihuahua with the development of Paquimé (Casas Grandes). The shift of the center of gravity for Ancestral Pueblo populations from the north and west to the south and east is shown by increased Ancestral Pueblo settlement in the northern Rio Grande region, in the Galisteo Basin, and east to Pecos and the Salinas area. How many people left the north and west, and over precisely what interval the south and east became densely occupied, continues to engage archaeological scholarship. Nevertheless, by the time of the

Spanish *entradas*, beginning in 1540, the Pueblo world extended from Taos to El Paso, with many villages in the Galisteo Basin, the Salinas District, and in the vicinity of Zuni and the Hopi Mesas. Large areas of northern Chihuahua, including Paquimé, were depopulated. Following the entradas and subsequent Spanish settlement and missionization, Pueblo populations were decimated and many villages forcibly removed (Barrett 1997; Riley 1995; Schroeder 1979:254).

At the early end of the period of interest, the demographic turmoil of the thirteenth and early fourteenth centuries was accompanied by the formation of aggregated communities. Settlements grew in size beyond any previous period, surpassing both those of Chaco Canyon and the Pueblo III centers of the northern San Juan/Mesa Verde area (Adams and Duff 2004:4; Varien and others 1996). Some, if not many, of these new, very large settlements incorporated peoples from different ancestral localities. Social heterogeneity in these villages would have required new forms of within-settlement integration. Just as important, placement of numerous, very large settlements in areas that previously had been sparsely inhabited would have entailed reformulating regional social landscapes in entirely new ways so as to realign access to people and resources.

Following Patricia Crown's (1994) groundbreaking study of the Salado polychromes, a number of scholars have interpreted the new, brightly colored, glaze-paint-decorated and polychrome pottery as being related to region-wide belief systems and public ritual performances, particularly feasting, that are thought to have played key roles both in attracting migrants to emerging aggregated villages and village-clusters and in serving to integrate these new, larger, and initially more socially heterogeneous communities (Eckert 2008; Habicht-Mauche 1995; Huntley 2008; Neuzil 2008).

As Crown (1994) suggested and others subsequently demonstrated (Duff 2002; Spielmann 2004a), the use and long-term efficacy of these material, ideational, and performance strategies varied regionally and over time. For example, Spielmann (2004a) contrasts settlement clusters in which heterogeneous pottery traditions are maintained with those in which one pottery tradition unites the cluster, noting that the latter are generally larger and persist for a longer time. We do not suggest that the production and use of polychrome and glaze-painted pottery constituted a single social dynamic or even a class of closely related dynamics where they occurred. Rather, demonstrating how and why this pottery mattered in different local and regional contexts is a focus of many of the chapters in this volume.

Ever since Anna O. Shepard's groundbreaking petrographic work, first at Pecos (Kidder and Shepard 1936) and then elsewhere in the Northern Rio Grande (Shepard 1942, 1965), archaeologists have known that not all households or communities in the Greater Southwest produced their own pottery. Various degrees of household and community specialization in pottery production and exchange probably characterized most times and places in the Southwest. Various lines of evidence appear to indicate that the intensity and scale of this specialization and exchange increased significantly after A.D. 1300 (Crown 1994; Duff 2002; Habicht-Mauche 1993; Huntley 2008; Shepard 1942)

More than just finished pots moved through these networks of interaction. Potters needed to acquire raw materials from diverse sources, including clay, temper, slip, and pigment for paint. And while clay and temper were probably obtained close to the potter's village by the potter herself or members of her household (Arnold 1985), other raw materials, such as slips and pigments, may have been acquired from more distant sources, and their acquisition may have been "embedded in" other social networks of interaction (see Huntley and others, Chapter 2; and Thomas, Chapter 13). The dynamics of migration and demographic collapse that characterized the late precontact and early postcontact periods in the Greater Southwest opened up new lines of communication and interaction and facilitated the flow of people between communities and regions in the Southwest. In other cases, these processes cut off longstanding networks of interaction and led to the loss of specialized technical, social, and ideological knowledge.

Since the time of Kidder and Shepard (1936), research on the polychrome and glaze-painted pottery traditions in the Southwest has moved in two important directions, both of which are critical to advancing our broader understanding of how these traditions are linked to multiple and diverse scales of social interaction. The first direction, which derives directly from Shepard's (1942) pioneering research, is the development of new and increasingly sophisticated laboratory methods for characterizing the composition of ceramic materials and for reconstructing technologies of production. Characterization studies include the continued use of petrography, as pioneered by Shepard, as well as other methods not generally available in Shepard's time, such as instrumental neutron activation analysis (INAA), which

allow researchers to trace the material constituents of pots back to their source areas and to follow their movements across the landscape. In the case of glaze paints, techniques such as lead isotope analysis now allow researchers to routinely identify the source of ores used in paints, thus tracing the acquisition of this raw material through networks that are distinctly different from those that facilitated the movement of whole pots (Nelson and Habicht-Mauche 2006; Huntley and others, Chapter 2). Other techniques, such as use of the scanning electron microscope and the electron microprobe, have allowed researchers to reconstruct actual paint "recipes" (see Blinman and others, Chapter 11; and Schleher and others, Chapter 10). When combined with experimentation and replication (as in Blinman and others, Chapter 11), such characterization studies allow us to gain a better understanding of how raw materials were acquired, handled, mixed, and processed. The chapters by Deborah Huntley and others (Chapter 2), Eric Blinman and others (Chapter 11), and Kari Schleher and others (Chapter 10) present us with a glimpse of the "state of the art" in this area of research. A notable feature of all these chapters is their collaborative nature. In each case, independent researchers working on different projects have combined expertise and information to produce large, integrated data sets that are revolutionizing our understanding of technological practice on a regional and inter-regional scale.

The second major research focus reflected by the chapters in this volume is the development of new approaches to and applications of social theory to the study of pottery technology and pottery production and exchange in the Greater Southwest. While paths toward understanding the problem of why polychrome and glaze-painted pottery "mattered" are diverse and tackle the issue at a variety of different scales using multiple lines of evidence and analytic methods, most of the contributions to this volume reflect consideration of pottery technology from a practice theory perspective (Bourdieu 1977; Ortner 1984; Pauketat 2001). As pointed out by Rosemary Joyce (Chapter 15), practice theory allows us to focus on the actions of potters as people embedded in diverse networks of social interaction. One observation based on the research presented here is that for each of our case studies, the authors identify various and diverse "communities of practice" that are implicated in the production, distribution, and use of polychrome and glaze-painted pottery. Further, these communities of practice intersect through various individuals, as Joyce suggests in Chapter 15. Paying attention to these intersections allows recognition of what Joyce terms constellations of practice. Such constellations go beyond communities of practice related to pottery making or use. For example, Huntley and others (Chapter 2) and Gilpin and Hays-Gilpin (Chapter 5) suggest constellations of communities of practice that include those engaged in making textiles and painting ritual objects, as well as potters.

Production of novel pottery types required finding and developing new raw material sources (for glaze paint and colored paints and slips), development of new production techniques (such as the formulation of glaze paints), and adopting new firing regimes. These innovations entailed major transformations in specific techniques and whole technological systems of ceramic production. Technology is more than a material act; it is an embodied form of cultural practice (Mauss 2006). The specific techniques, gestures, and production sequences required to make a pot must be taught through combinations of demonstration, verbal instruction, critique, and at times physical guidance of gestures that move the apprentice toward replication of the standards that characterize a local group of producers and that conform to the preferences of local consumers (Gosselain 1992). In this sense technology can be said to have "style"; that is to say technology entails a set of choices and those choices are socially defined and constrained (Lechtman 1977; Lemonnier 1986). It is the emphasis on choices made at various stages of pottery production, distribution, use, and ultimate discard that is beginning to provide threads that we can follow through the diverse socially constructed networks that we argue constitute multiple "communities of practice" at different scales.

The contributors to this volume emphasize multiple communities of practice mobilized in pottery production rather than distribution and use of vessels. In part, this is a result of the availability of analytic techniques that inform about the geographical or geological provenance of source materials used in pottery making. The emphasis on production has amplified theoretical perspectives based on practice theory by adding notions derived from situated learning theory, presented in this volume by Patrick Lyons and Jeffrey Clark (Chapter 3), and also explored by Rosemary Joyce (Chapter 15). Situated learning theory (Wenger 1998) addresses negotiated relationships between teachers and apprentices in communities of practice. Different modes of apprenticeship can either contribute to the stability of a tradition or encourage innovation, and relationships between

apprentice and teacher can involve negotiated sequestering or sharing of information. Situated learning theory focuses attention on the social dynamics within communities of potters and future potters.

Another important distinction made by situated learning theory that is relevant to the polychrome and glaze-paint pottery traditions explored in this volume is that different communities of practice can be bridged by "boundary objects" and "brokers," which are, respectively, objects or technologies that are sources of practice, such as tools or recipes, and people who introduce elements of practice from one community to another (Lyons and Clark, Chapter 3; Minar and Crown 2001). Situated learning theory helps us to consider the negotiated relationships among individuals who learned (and taught others) how to recognize clays, ores, and tempering materials; how to produce pastes, slips, and paints; and how to form and fire vessels. The theory also helps us understand how completed artifacts might serve as boundary objects for some but not all of the processes of pottery production. The combination of perspectives offered by practice theory and situated learning theory produce a hybrid theory that provides richer explanatory power than either theory by itself. This hybrid theory enables Lyons and Clark to elucidate the dynamics among migrant Kayenta potters living in diasporic communities in south-central Arizona. The hybrid theory is also useful to Suzanne Eckert's (Chapter 6) discussion of identity among ancestral Zuni potters, and to Schleher and others (Chapter 10) in addressing differential standardization of glaze-paint recipes versus paste composition and slip colors of pottery made at San Marcos Pueblo. Joyce (Chapter 15) provides further insight from situated learning theory concerning instances of technology loss, such as the end of glaze production in the Rio Grande as described by David Snow (Chapter 12), who ascribes the cessation of glaze painting in part to loss of knowledgeable individual mentors.

These new methods and approaches draw our attention to how the production, circulation, and consumption of polychrome and glaze-painted pottery were implicated in the formation of networks of interaction at different scales. For example, compositional studies of ceramics have shown that communities of practice in raw material acquisition were often spatially very broad, on the order of regions (such as use of Cerrillos Hills lead by potters on the Pajarito Plateau). At the same time, potting groups were probably localized within single settlements, although they may have involved several households, specialists, or "many hands," as Crown (2007a) suggests. Communities of ideology, manifest in shared symbols on pottery, may or may not be spatially extensive (Crown 1994), and may or may not be isomorphic with communities of materials procurement or production. For example, some apparently iconic design motifs are found on different pottery types, even different wares (Fenn and others 2006; Graves and Eckert 1998).

ORGANIZATION OF VOLUME

The chapter by Huntley and others (Chapter 2) follows this introduction because it provides the foundation for the analyses and interpretations presented in the case studies that follow. This chapter discusses the most recent chemical and isotopic data on late prehispanic glaze pigments, giving readers an understanding of how, and with what precision, archaeologists are discovering the sources of the constituents of glaze paint. The authors also explore pigments in other media, such as wooden objects and wall paintings, and ask if glaze paint procurement was embedded in the general procurement of pigments. While they suggest answers, they also make a point that is reiterated in many other contributions to the volume—that there were likely many communities of practice, operating at different scales, in the procurement and making of pigments.

The following chapters are arranged in three general chronological groups. The first concerns the origins of polychrome and glaze paint traditions and consists of chapters by Lyons and Clark (Chapter 3) and David Phillips (Chapter 4). Lyons and Clark argue for the origin of the Salado polychromes among enclaves of Kayenta migrants to central and southern Arizona. Their notion is intriguing, and their argument may be compelling, but it is not the only source area suggested, as is seen in the chapter by Phillips, who reminds us that a critically important potential source area for the Pueblo polychrome and glaze paint tradition may be in northern Mexico, among the pottery types and wares ancestral to Ramos Polychrome of Casas Grandes. Lyons and Clark also provide an important discussion of situated learning theory that gives insight into the social processes of technology transfer and offers an addition to our original statement about communities of practice. Phillips points out that in northern Mexico, styles of polychrome painting on vessels follow particular artistic canons that may be effective in allowing recognition of communities

of practice and changes in communities of practice in ceramic production over time.

Chapters in the second section are case studies that explore the spread of polychrome and glaze paint traditions within the Greater Southwest, especially from the Zuni region to the Rio Grande. The contributions by Gilpin and Hays-Gilpin (Chapter 5) and by Eckert (Chapter 6) are keystone contributions in the eventual architecture of fourteenth- and fifteenth-century polychrome pottery in the Southwest because they represent the strong Hopi and Zuni traditions as they emerge. In these chapters, the archaeological record supports oral traditions of identity formation, including migration and gathering of clans.

Reconstructing communities of practice by recognizing color and design elements to signal identity at different scales, as Eckert does, provides insight into how and why certain canons of design may persist. Subsequent movement of pottery out of the Hopi and Zuni areas traces differentially expanding networks and signals different kinds of interactions over very large areas, for example from the Hopi Mesas to the Rio Puerco of the East and from Zuni to the Cerrillos Hills lead sources. These chapters ask us to consider the nature of the networks of communities of practice into which Hopi and Zuni pottery spread. Lyons and Clark argue that the Kayenta immigrants to the Hohokam area moved into regions that had no previous widespread production of painted pottery. Clearly this was not the case in the Rio Grande, where painted pottery traditions were long in place.

Shepard (1942, 1965) argued that the glaze paint tradition was introduced into the Rio Grande from the Western Pueblos, most likely Zuni, and both Shepard (1942) and Helene Warren (1969a) proposed that glaze-painted ware was first introduced from the west into the Albuquerque Basin. Eckert's discussion of the sources of lead for Zuni glazes, which incorporates Huntley's (2006, 2008) previous work, provides some insight into how that process might have been carried out. However, until now, little information has been available about the area over which early Rio Grande glaze paint ware was made and what social networks are implied by this particular instance of technology transfer. The chapters by Hayward Franklin and Schleher (Chapter 7), Diane Curewitz and Sheila Goff (Chapter 8), Ann Ramenofsky (Chapter 9), and Schleher and others (Chapter 10) illuminate these issues.

The Montaño Bridge site, discussed by Franklin and Schleher, provides a glimpse of the richness of the ceramic inventory at one of the Albuquerque Basin glaze sites. At the Montaño Bridge site the diversity of ceramic types is huge and very different from that manifest at Pottery Mound on the Rio Puerco and at contemporary sites on the Pajarito Plateau and in the Galisteo Basin. In this chapter, the Albuquerque Basin is seen to have been a place of active exchange and movement, perhaps more like the southern Rio Grande and Gran Quivira regions.

Curewitz and Goff provide the first petrographic and isotopic demonstration that glaze-painted pottery was made in the northerly sections of the Pajarito Plateau, and that the lead ores for the paint on this pottery likely derived from the southern Cerrillos Hills source. Use of this source, which is near San Marcos Pueblo, suggests that potters on the northern Pajarito Plateau either had a special relationship with San Marcos or that San Marcos did not maintain exclusive access to this source (Nelson and Habicht-Mauche 2006). Since Shepard's (Kidder and Shepard 1936) work with the pottery of Pecos, it has been assumed that the earliest glaze ware at Pecos came from the Galisteo Basin pueblos. While this ultimately may be correct, the work of Curewitz and Goff suggests an alternative source on the Pajarito Plateau, and the Pajarito Plateau is also the source of the Biscuit Ware found at Pecos. Curewitz and Goff make it clear that various communities of practice were involved in the production and distribution of this Pajaritan glaze ware.

San Marcos Pueblo is one of the largest of the Galisteo Basin pueblos, one that was almost certainly a glaze production center and one of the few that has benefited by recent restudy (Ramenofsky and others 2009). Here, Ramenofsky demonstrates that at San Marcos Pueblo, the frequency of Glaze A Yellow does not vary over time. Ramenofsky's observation is crucial. By separating out the different communities of practice at San Marcos Pueblo, she shows that the frequency of Glaze A Yellow does not vary with the frequencies of the other glaze types. Rather than seeing a regular progression of glaze types, for Glaze A Yellow we may be seeing alliance reconfigurations, the comings and goings of craft specialists, or the presence of sodalities. Schleher and her colleagues demonstrate the remarkable consistency of the glaze paint recipe from San Marcos over time. This may reflect a specific type of apprenticeship discussed by Lyons and Clark (Chapter 3) that may have been involved in paint production. The community of practice reflected in the glaze paint production at San Marcos may, of course, not be the same as those involved

in forming, painting, or distribution of these pots over time. Schleher and her colleagues also demonstrate production at the source beyond household needs. This is critical because San Marcos, close to the Cerrillos lead source, may have supplied pottery to other Galisteo Basin pueblos, perhaps as far as Pecos.

Chapters in the third group, by Blinman and others (Chapter 11), David Snow (Chapter 12), Noah Thomas (Chapter 13), and Jennifer Dyer (Chapter 14), concern Rio Grande glaze-painted pottery during the Spanish colonial period and should be read as a unit. While these ostensibly focus on the "end of glaze production" in the Rio Grande, which occurred within the context of Spanish conquest, the early colonial period, and the Pueblo Revolt, they also highlight three areas that need additional research. These are (1) identification of indigenous and Spanish metallurgical practices, including the sources of lead used by each group, how lead and copper minerals were prospected for, and how and why glaze paint became a lost art in the Rio Grande area; (2) an appreciation for the differential destruction of communities of practice and the disruption of networks of alliances and information exchange by the Spaniards; and (3) the importance of Puebloan population loss and the expropriation of Pueblo labor by the Spaniards. These studies also show different analytic approaches (experiment, analysis, use of historic documents) and reflect on the deep clash of cultures when ideologies, alliances, communities of practice, and learning are torn asunder.

Rosemary Joyce (Chapter 15) gives us an insightful discussion of the implications of looking for communities of practice, the potters, their societies, and their creations in broader contexts. Specifically, following Bruno Latour (2005), she advocates considering networks of communities of practice as evidence of past assembly of "the social." Joyce carefully links both continuity and change to individual choices made actively and largely consciously. Finally, by introducing the notion of "schema" to incorporate Phillips's discussion of artistic canon, she hints at the conceptual bonds that likely unified constellations of communities of practice throughout the prehispanic Puebloan Southwest over five centuries.

SUMMARY

Recent methodological developments in the areas of ethnoarchaeology, experimental archaeology, and material science studies have greatly enhanced our ability to study technological behavior in considerable detail, and in a greater variety of social contexts and arenas, at both finer and broader scales than had previously been possible. The chapters in this volume reflect a diverse range of these new methodological developments and approaches and highlight their impacts on the study of polychrome and glaze-painted pottery. For example, these new methods have gotten us to a place where we can identify and trace quite specific forms of knowledge, ways of using materials (that is, material "recipes"), and production sequences whose circulation across community and regional boundaries can probably only be explained in part by the actual movement of knowledgeable and skilled practitioners. These methods potentially provide us with a very robust and precise means of tracking the actual migration of specific groups of people (or at least potters) from one community to another across the very dynamic demographic landscape of the Greater Southwest.

Having begun with the activation of various communities of practice in the context of the period of the introduction of the novel polychrome and glaze-paint-decorated pottery, we followed these interaction networks into the Spanish colonial period. Various matte-painted yellow and polychrome pottery types were produced through the colonial period, but glaze-paint-decorated types ceased to be made around the time of the Pueblo Revolt of 1680. With their understanding of the various scales at which communities of practice were integrated in the production, distribution, and use of glaze-paint-decorated pottery, several researchers in this volume explore the different technologies and communities of practice implemented by Spanish colonial institutions in the production, distribution, and use of lead, primarily for ammunition and armaments. These studies provide information that reveals the social contexts in which the use of glaze-paint-decorated pottery came to an end. Finally and importantly, the archaeological contexts within which matte-paint yellow and polychrome pottery were made and used among variously constituted indigenous and Spanish colonial communities (missions, Spanish colonial settlements, and Pueblos occupied in Spanish colonial times) are explored. These provide a means by which we can begin to appreciate another set of complex negotiations of social identity and community expression, when some of the same materials—these things—mattered a lot in very different contexts.

CHAPTER TWO

Embedded Networks?

Pigments and Long-Distance Procurement Strategies in the Late Prehispanic Southwest

Deborah L. Huntley, Thomas Fenn, Judith A. Habicht-Mauche, and Barbara J. Mills

The concepts of "technological style" (Dietler and Herbich 1998; Hegmon 1998; Lechtman 1977, Lemonnier 1986) and "communities of practice" (Lave and Wenger 1991; Stark 2006) have both been important in recent works on Southwest ceramics, especially those that address glaze-decorated pottery (Habicht-Mauche and others 2006). Both ideas are powerful tools for understanding the different ways that people practiced their craft, and their use in tandem has much potential for looking at different scales of learning within communities, social identities, and regional-scale interaction and migration. The concepts are largely drawn from studies of apprenticeship or "situated learning" (Lave and Wenger 1991) that focus on the social contexts in which learning was practiced, especially the learning involved in the production of different goods (Crown 2001; Duwe and Neff 2007; Haas 2006; Lyons and Clark, Chapter 2, this volume; Minar and Crown 2001; Stark 2006; Wallaert-Pêtre 2001; Wendrich 2012).

Many applications of this hybrid approach in archaeology have focused on the production process, as we do in this chapter with the analysis of paint recipes. Yet, we think that an important part of the production process has been left out—the communities of practice engaged in the actual procurement of the raw materials, which we do not assume are the same. Each of the materials used in ceramic production has its own biography, all of which intersect in the finished vessel. Thus, there are many potential hands in the procurement process, each of which could be a member of a different community of practice. This is especially true of materials, which are used in multiple kinds of practices. For example, pigments are frequently considered in terms of their spatial qualities or their provenance, rather than their social qualities. Pigments, however, had many uses besides decorating pots (see Shepard 1965; Solometo 2008; Thomas 2008, and Chapter 13), particularly in the Greater Southwest where paint also decorated wood, textiles, stone, ritual architecture, and people.

Because of the social importance of multiple contexts for the use of pigments we think that their procurement for glaze production should be considered within communities of practice that minimally crosscut or are embedded within other communities and other fields of practice—not just those for ceramic production. This is particularly relevant to the acquisition of lead ores in the Southwest, some of which are clearly procured at great distances from settlements where pottery was made. We also suggest that thinking about embedded or overlapping networks of situated learning and communities of practice can contribute to broader methodological and theoretical discussion about how practices are learned and transmitted (such as Lyons and Clark, Chapter 3; Stark and others 2008) and expand upon the somewhat rigid social boundaries that a strict reading of "communities of practice" might promote. Communities of practice should overlap in many different ways; one that we discuss here concerns the networks that are involved with different parts of a material's life history.

In this chapter we address two spatial and social scales of lead ore use for glaze-decorated ceramic production in the Eastern and Western Pueblo areas. First, we build on existing databases for glaze-decorated ceramics and lead ores to demonstrate where the ores were procured and the diversity of sources by region. We argue that in some areas, the diversity of sources and their distances from pottery production loci make it likely that ores were embedded within other procurement systems, such as the acquisition of paints for a range of socially charged objects. Second, we introduce the possibility that lead ores may have been made "ready" or useful for household pottery production. This aspect of our chapter is more speculative and deserves a more thorough treatment elsewhere, but we think that if different communities of practice used pigments, then raw ore may have been transformed when it entered the household or work group.

GLAZE WARE CONTEXT OF PRODUCTION AND USE

During the late thirteenth century, Ancestral Puebloan potters in the American Southwest began using glaze paints to decorate red-slipped pottery. As many researchers have noted (Blinman and others, Chapter 11; Herhahn 2006; Huntley 2008; Schleher and others, Chapter 10), glaze paint represents a technological innovation in that well-vitrified glazes can only be made by using certain combinations of ingredients under a limited range of firing conditions. Once a basic glaze mixture was achieved, potters had some flexibility in the proportions of fluxes and colorants they used to produce distinctive glaze recipes. Indeed, such variation characterizes distinct regional and local glaze paint traditions identified through chemical compositional analysis and replication studies (Blinman and others, Chapter 11; Bower and others 1986; De Atley 1986; Fenn and others 2006; Hawley 1938; Herhahn 2006; Huntley 2008; Huntley and Herhahn 1996; Huntley and others 2007; Shepard 1942, 1965). Regional recipes differ mainly in their proportions of lead, copper, iron, and manganese.

The conventional wisdom is that glaze technology originated along the Mogollon Rim around A.D. 1250 or 1275, quickly spreading to the Little Colorado and Zuni regions and then to the Rio Grande by about 1300 (Fig. 2.1). The rapid adoption of glaze paint technology throughout much of the Ancestral Puebloan Southwest within about a generation suggests far-reaching social networks and population movements. Knowledge of raw materials and techniques of glaze paint production may have moved east with Western Pueblo immigrants to the Rio Grande (but see Phillips, Chapter 4; and Snow 1982 for alternative models). Rio Grande potters then quickly developed their own high-lead recipe, which they continued to use through the 1600s. Glaze-painted ceramics ceased to be made in the Zuni and Mogollon Rim areas by the middle to late 1400s but were revived at Zuni during the Mission period, only to end again during the Pueblo Revolt (Mills 2002; Schachner 2006).

In some cases, such as at Pueblo San Marcos (Schleher and others, Chapter 10), skilled individuals or communities specialized in glaze ware manufacture and produced vessels beyond the needs of the household for exchange. Elsewhere in the Southwest we lack evidence that decorated pottery production was organized beyond the level of the household (Habicht-Mauche 1993, 1995; Mills and Crown 1995; Shepard 1942, 1965; Triadan and others 2002; Warren 1969a, 1979a). Historically, Pueblo women produced most pottery (Bunzel 1972; Crown and Wills 1995; Guthe 1925; Hays-Gilpin 2000; Mills 1995, 2000), and archaeologists tend to assume that this was also true for glaze-decorated ceramics in prehistory. There is evidence, however, for diversity in the organization of pottery production steps among Southwestern groups; for example, men or children may paint pots they did not form (Brody 1977; Crown 2001; Hegmon and Trevathan 1996). Thus, household production may have involved multiple family members in various production steps rather than a single designated potter (Crown 1999, 2001). Although glaze-decorated pottery likely was used in everyday household contexts, ritual use at least partially fueled the demand for its production (see Graves and Spielmann 2000; Mills 1999, 2000; Spielmann 1998).

GLAZE PAINT RECIPES AND SOURCING

Minerals used in glaze paint manufacture, particularly lead ores, have somewhat limited distributions on the landscape. One well-known source is the Cerrillos Hills near Santa Fe. Although Cerrillos is famous for its turquoise mines, this area also contains major deposits of lead and copper that have been mined for hundreds of years (Bice and others 2003; Schroeder 1979; Warren and Mathien 1985; Warren and Weber 1979). Figure 2.1 shows the location of Cerrillos and other New Mexico and Arizona ore sources.

Stable lead isotopes provide indirect evidence for lead ore procurement patterns in the Ancestral Pueblo world. Geological deposits of lead and lead-based materials can be "fingerprinted" using the ratios of four stable isotopes of lead (^{204}Pb, ^{206}Pb, ^{207}Pb, ^{208}Pb). These ratios are a result of differences in the composition of the source material in which the lead mineralized and the age of the deposit. Thus, lead isotope ratios from different districts tend to form distinct trends or "evolution lines," which reflect the process of lead ore mineralization within the specific parent material through time.

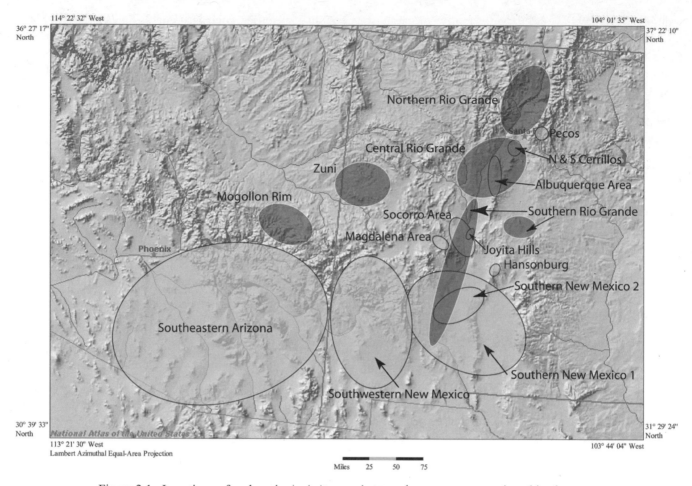

Figure 2.1. Locations of archaeological sites, regions, and ore sources mentioned in chapter.

As part of various individual and collaborative projects (Fenn and others 2006, 2012; Habicht-Mauche and others 2000, 2002; Huntley 2008; Huntley and others 2007; Nelson and Habicht-Mauche 2006), we collectively have analyzed hundreds of lead ore samples from mining districts throughout New Mexico and Arizona, as well as more than 600 samples of glaze paint from nearly a dozen late prehistoric to early contact period archaeological sites in New Mexico and eastern Arizona. The New Mexico ore and glaze samples were analyzed at the University of California, Santa Cruz using a Finnegan MAT ELEMENT high-resolution magnetic sector inductively-coupled plasma mass spectrometer (Hr ICP-MS). The Arizona ore and glaze samples were run on an isoprobe multi-collector inductively-coupled plasma mass spectrometer (MC-ICP-MS) in the Department of Geosciences, University of Arizona. We have also included a few additional ore and lead samples

published by other lab groups using older analytical techniques (such as ICP-MS and thermal ionization mass spectrometry [TIMS] instruments). Because all of the data from all of the labs have been corrected using NIST standard lead, the results are generally comparable. However, isotopic fractionation issues and instrumental error in some older analyses make them somewhat less reliable.

We have compiled a master isotope database that includes additional published ratios (Blenkinsop and Slawson 1967; Bouse and others 1999; Ewing 1979; Pingitore and others 1997; Slawson and Austin 1960, 1962). This chapter represents the first synthesis of all the New Mexico and Arizona data, including new data on sources of raw materials. We compare ore data to glaze paints on White Mountain Red Ware, early Zuni Glaze Ware, and Rio Grande Glaze Ware, including probable Rio Grande copies of Western glaze-decorated types. All were made between A.D. 1275 and 1700, with the Western Pueblo sample largely predating A.D. 1400.

Blinman and others (Chapter 11) argue that most of the ore used to make glaze paint was in the form of galena (lead sulfide) because it would have been the most accessible form of lead ore in the Southwest and the easiest to identify, transport, and process. Shepard (1942:224) suggested that glaze-paint potters may have used either galena or cerrusite. Most of the ores analyzed by our lab group and others have been galena, but we have also analyzed samples of cerrusite and other lead-bearing minerals. These analyses indicate that different lead ore types from the same district all plot along the same evolution line. This is to be expected since the different ores within specific deposits, whether primary or secondary minerals, all formed from the same source materials.

Figure 2.2 shows a plot of the lead isotopic ratios for most of the Arizona and New Mexico lead ores we have analyzed. For visual comparisons the ratio data are plotted in graphs using two or three ratios: $^{207}Pb/^{206}Pb$ for the x-axis, and $^{208}Pb/^{206}Pb$ or $^{208}Pb/^{207}Pb$ for the y-axes. The use of the same ratio for the x-axis on two graphs provides a three-dimensional perspective on data plotted in two dimensions in the two graphs. The choice of these particular ratios is based on issues related to comparison with existing published lead isotopic ratios from Southwestern ores. Although ^{206}Pb, ^{207}Pb, and ^{208}Pb are typically normalized to ^{204}Pb in most geological applications, much of the existing published lead isotopic ratio ore data were generated with instruments that had isotopic mass fractionation problems typically resulting in under-representation of ^{204}Pb concentrations. These lower concentrations of ^{204}Pb result in artificially high values for ratios utilizing ^{204}Pb in the denominator. However, ratios utilizing the other three ratios of lead only (that is, ^{208}Pb, ^{207}Pb, and ^{206}Pb) typically have fewer mass fractionation problems and thus are likely to be closer representations of the true isotopic ratios of the analyzed ores. Therefore, to avoid potential interpretation problems in comparisons utilizing existing published ore data ratios, graphic representations of the lead isotopic data were made with ratios excluding ^{204}Pb. We use these isotopic ratios to define geologically distinct ore "fields" onto which we plot glaze samples in subsequent figures. In some cases these isotopic fields may overlap or intersect, but the overall trends for specific ore districts are usually distinct.

In some cases overlap in isotopic lead signatures of different mining districts makes it difficult to precisely identify lead sources in individual glaze paints. More systematic sampling of the southern mining districts and use of other isotopic systems, such as strontium, to characterize ore sources might resolve this issue. Nonetheless, trends in the data from particular groups of glazes reveal distinct patterns and preferences of resource use by local and regional communities of potters who shared common practices and techniques. Taking a closer look at regional trends, the Mogollon Rim glazes (Fig. 2.3) plot in the area of overlap among eastern Arizona, Cerrillos, and Magdalena area ores. With the exception of two samples, though, the group corresponds well to the eastern Arizona field, and this makes sense archaeologically. Turquoise was mined in the area just below the Mogollon Rim at Canyon Creek (Welch and Triadan 1991), and copper and lead ores occur in association with these deposits, as in the Cerrillos area. A large number of Early Zuni glaze paints (Fig. 2.4) form a tight cluster in the area of source overlap on the plot. Huntley (2008) has argued that many of these correspond to the Cerrillos source, although it also seems plausible that some of these could be attributed to eastern Arizona or southern New Mexico sources. Later Zuni glaze paints are much more spread out along the southern New Mexico evolution line. With few exceptions, northern and central Rio Grande potters in the Galisteo Basin, Santo Domingo, Pajarito, and Santa Fe districts selected galena from the Cerrillos Hills to make glaze paints (Fig. 2.5; see also Curewitz and Goff, Chapter 8; Habicht-Mauche and others 2000, 2002; Nelson and Habicht-Mauche 2006). Early copies of Western glazes from the Albuquerque and Rio Puerco areas appear fairly diverse (Fig. 2.5). Salinas and Socorro area potters tended to favor the use of southern New Mexico lead ores with some use of Cerrillos ores as well (Fig. 2.6; Huntley and others 2007).

There are also regional and temporal trends in coefficients of variation for isotope ratios (Table 2.1). Notable in this table are the overall low values for CVs: all are well under 10 percent and most are less than 5 percent. Within districts, early and late glaze samples show few differences in isotopic variability. Nonetheless, there appears to be an overall reduction in isotopic variability over time. In some areas, such as the Salinas pueblos, the reduction is rather dramatic. As discussed below, we interpret this as evidence for variability in the scales of ore procurement networks and targeting specific resources. Reduction in isotopic variability also has implications for increasing specialization over time.

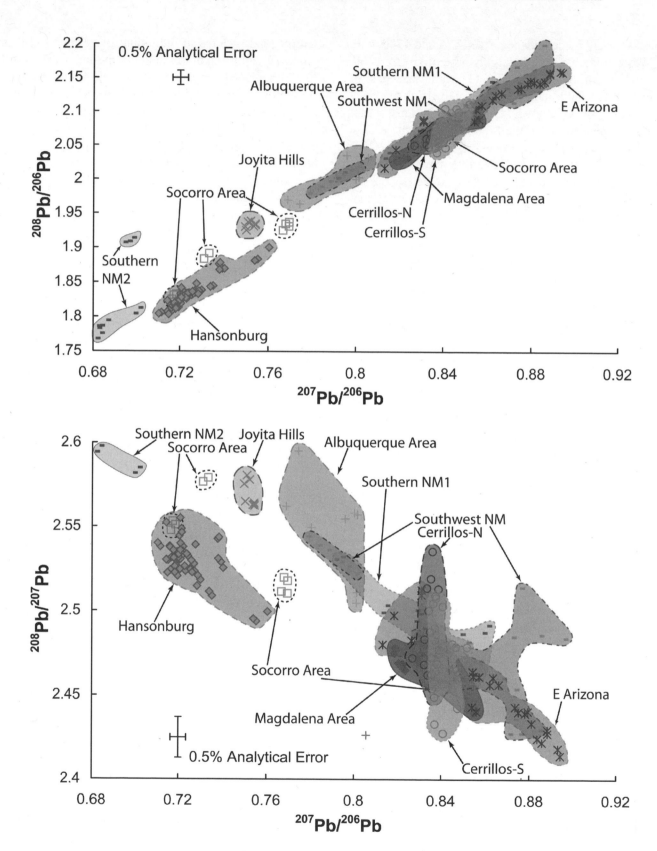

Figure 2.2. Plot of lead isotope ratios (207/206 by 208/207 and 208/206) for selected Arizona and New Mexico lead ores.

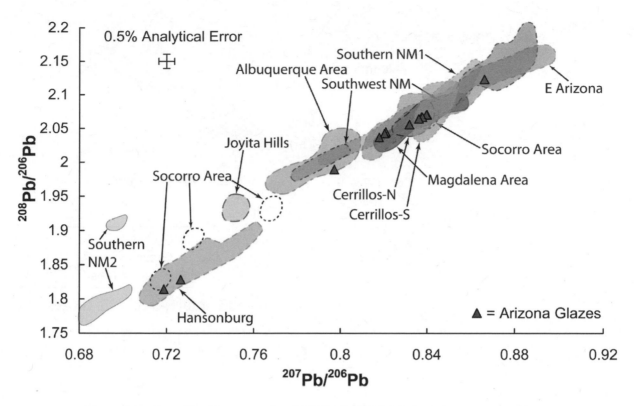

Figure 2.3. Plot of lead isotope ratios (207/206 by 208/206) for Arizona glaze paints.

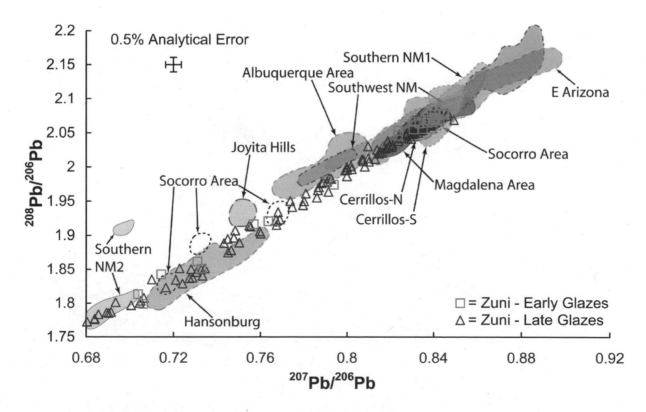

Figure 2.4. Plot of lead isotope ratios (207/206 by 208/206) for Zuni region glaze paints.

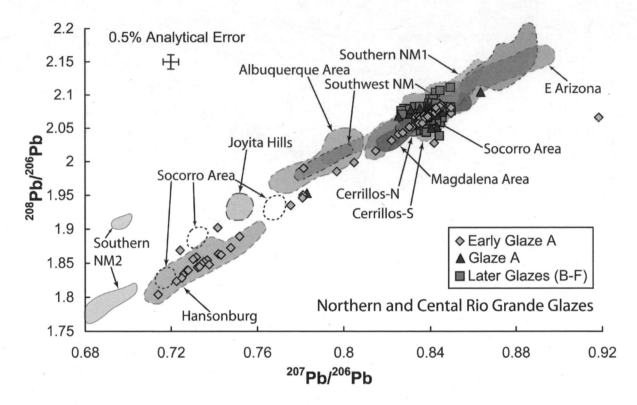

Figure 2.5. Plot of lead isotope ratios (207/206 by 208/206) for northern and central Rio Grande glaze paints.

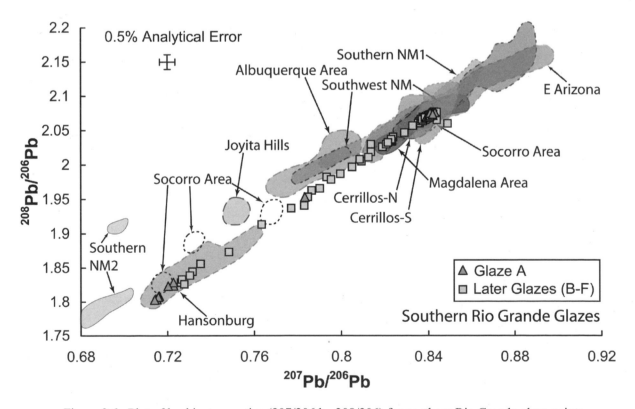

Figure 2.6. Plot of lead isotope ratios (207/206 by 208/206) for southern Rio Grande glaze paints.

Table 2.1. Isotopic Ratios for Glaze Paints by District and Time Period

District	Time Period	$^{207}PB/^{204}PB$ CV	n	$^{206}PB/^{204}PB$ CV	n
Silver Creek	Early	0.01	16	0.05	16
Zuni	Early	0.01	251	0.07	251
Rio Puerco	Early	0.02	10	0.06	10
Tijeras	Early	0.01	22	0.07	22
	Late	0.01	2	0.02	2
Santo Domingo	Early	0.06	38	0.07	38
	Late	0.02	20	0.02	20
Santa Fe	Early	0.02	20	0.07	20
	Late	0.01	6	0.01	6
Galisteo	Early	0.03	10	0.03	10
	Late	0.02	49	0.02	49
Salinas	Early	0.01	25	0.09	25
	Late	0.00	117[1]	0.04	117
Socorro	Late	0.02	5	0.05	5

[1] Highly unusual; no variation even though there is a large sample size (but see early Zuni).

PROCUREMENT NETWORKS

We know very little about the specifics of lead procurement because ethnographically known pueblos do not make lead glazes. Nonetheless, we can look to Pueblo ethnography to understand lead ores as part of a larger class of pigments and other minerals. These had many uses, including body paint and the painting of masks and hides (Cushing 1979; Parsons 1966; Shepard 1965; Thomas 2008, Chapter 13). For many of these items, the opportunities to procure them may have been limited, either because they were rare or far away, or both, or because others controlled access to them. Certainly this was the case for turquoise, salt, and particular clays (Ellis 1981). This is not to say that potters or their family members did not collect their own clays, pigments, and other materials; a large body of anthropological literature demonstrates otherwise (Arnold 1985). But under certain circumstances, such as when the materials are at a great distance, we need to think carefully about how this might have been practiced.

Although we do not directly equate pottery paints, including glazes, with ritual paraphernalia like masks and kiva murals, it is interesting to note that a similar range of minerals is used in the creation of all these items (see Odegaard and Hays-Gilpin 2002; Plog 2003). For ritual paraphernalia, use of minerals carries certain proscriptions. In Pueblo society, members of particular religious societies (usually men) may control access to precious minerals. For example, Bunzel (1984) reports that members of Zuni medicine societies traditionally control access to paints used to decorate katsina masks, and ceremonies often accompany mask production. As recounted by Pueblo ethnographers (Bunzel 1984; Parsons 1966) and outlined in detail by Solometo (2008), restricted paints are commonly referred to as "valuable" (see Thomas 2008 and Chapter 13 for a discussion of Pueblo mineral valuation). Brandt (1985:13) reports that knowledge concerning the locations of important mineral resources, as well as the procurement of these materials, was limited to members of appropriate ritual societies.

Considering lead ore procurement as a practice embedded in or overlapping with larger-scale networks of resource procurement and exchange seems reasonable for Zuni and Mogollon Rim potters given the relatively long distances involved in ore acquisition (see Figure 2.1). We use a slightly different definition of embedded procurement than that coined by Binford (1979:259) as the acquisition of raw materials "incidentally to the execution of basic subsistence tasks." For long-distance ore sources, acquiring ores was unlikely entirely "incidental" but may have been part of a suite of resources that were targeted in various locations across the landscape as part of larger resource acquisition or trading missions, or both. Traditional Zuni and Hopi resource collection territories and trail systems, for example, provide clues as to the spatial scale and possible constituents of these networks (Ferguson and Hart 1985). One of these trail systems linked the Zuni, Hopi, Acoma, Navajo, and other groups to Zuni Salt Lake and to each other (Stevenson 1904). Minerals and other long-distance resources as diverse as obsidian, marine shell, turquoise, and salt were circulated within trade networks that crisscrossed the Pueblo world (Snow 1981). The Zuni collected turquoise from the Cerrillos Hills (Ferguson and Hart 1985:127; Hart 1984; Riley 1975), and particular Zuni religious societies obtained galena and copper minerals from the Sandia Mountains (Ferguson and Hart 1985:125). Riley and Manson (1983) argue that copper minerals from the Jerome area were traded during prehistoric and historic times along a route that crossed the Zuni region (see also Ferguson and Hart 1985: Map 19). Copper ores also may have come from the San Francisco Peaks of northern Arizona (Hart 1995). Archaeological examples of lead in transportable form include galena "pencils" from the Rabid Ruin (ASM specimen #A-47537), where powdered galena was packed into tubes of reed or other cylindrical organic material (David Killick, personal communication, 2009). A utility ware jar filled with galena crystals was also found near a small jacal structure north of Socorro (Weber 1999).

For Zuni and Mogollon Rim populations, lead ores may be significant by virtue of their association with Cerrillos (and Eastern Arizona) turquoise, which was circulated throughout the Southwest. They may have served as symbolically charged "pieces of places" (Bradley 2000) that are important because they tie networks of people to places (see also Spielmann 2004b). This may help explain why local lead sources often were bypassed for more distant sources both in the West and the East.

The concept of an embedded network does not work as well for the Rio Grande region, particularly the pueblos in the Galisteo Basin and Socorro area that are closer to ore sources than other settlements. As noted above, potters in the northern and central Rio Grande region obtained lead for glaze paint production almost exclusively from the Cerrillos Hills (Habicht-Mauche and others 2000, 2002; Nelson and Habicht-Mauche 2006). While this source was not always the closest available to any given glaze-producing pueblo, it was usually within an easy one- or two-day walk of most villages. In the case of San Marcos Pueblo in the Galisteo Basin, potters would have been able to see the Cerrillos Hills from the roofs of their houses. Thus, it is difficult to imagine that the symbolic or ritual value of lead pigment was linked to its exotic, long-distance origin for people in this region. However, the co-occurrence of lead and ritually important turquoise within the Cerrillos Hills may have been significant and may explain why this source was favored over others in the region. In this sense, lead acquisition in the northern and central Rio Grande might be seen as "embedded" within a broader ritual or cosmological system, if not physically embedded within long-distance procurement networks per se.

How lead procurement in the southern Rio Grande might have been embedded in larger social, economic, or cosmological networks is less clear. However, as with the Galisteo pueblos, towns in the Socorro area may have been able to exert some control over access to local lead sources and thus insert themselves into broader regional networks of interaction that facilitated the flow of people, materials, and ideas between the Eastern and Western Pueblo regions, especially during the fourteenth and fifteenth centuries.

Lower overall CVs in later glazes, together with increased homogeneity in glaze recipes through time (see Table 2.1), may be evidence for increasing uniformity in resource acquisition in the protohistoric period. We can think of several reasons why this might have occurred. First, increasing specialization in glaze paint production, perhaps simply a reduction in overall number of potters, would have promoted less variability. Increased packing of larger populations in the Rio Grande region after A.D. 1300 may have reduced the availability of Cerrillos ores outside the Galisteo Basin, particularly if San Marcos or its neighbors restricted access to this source. During the Protohistoric period (A.D. 1450–1700), long-distance travel may have become less safe, especially along the eastern frontier of the Rio Grande, because of increased raiding by nomadic groups such as the Apache. In addition, the Spanish missionization and settlement program may have constrained how far Pueblo people could travel to acquire ores or other resources in their procurement networks.

TRANSFORMATION

Operating differently but overlapping with ore procurement networks was a network of knowledge concerning glaze ware manufacture. This interaction network implies a different type and frequency of movement and different contacts than entailed by procurement networks. Here we are talking about potters, many of whom were probably women, who migrated, intermarried, or visited kin, and who thus interacted with one another, often in domestic contexts. Potters moving between communities could bring certain practices with them, leading to similarities in approaches (shared communities of practice) over quite distant areas. Use of a high-lead "Zuni" glaze recipe in the Rio Grande (see Herhahn 2006; Huntley 2006) is one likely example of this phenomenon.

One of the implications of the presence of embedded networks for pigment procurement is that at some point lead ores move from the community of practice engaged in the acquisition of these socially charged materials to the community of practice engaged in pottery production. As discussed above, minerals and pigments were used for various things, and the manufacture or use of many of these things required esoteric knowledge or particular social positions in Pueblo society. Given that, was some sort of transformation of raw lead ore required to make it suitable for use as paint on pottery that is used in both domestic and ritual contexts? Did transformation, perhaps through roasting as discussed by Blinman and his colleagues (Chapter 11), move the raw ore into the household realm, altering proscriptions on who can handle it? Note that we are not arguing that transformation to an element of decoration decreased the material's power or significance, because at least some glaze-decorated wares likely were socially and ideologically important. Nor do we minimize the potentially significant role of potters in creating glaze paints and glaze-decorated vessels that served important social needs. But even though glaze-decorated ceramics were not necessarily mundane objects, we argue that there is a qualitative difference between materials that might be placed on a katsina mask, for example, versus those painted on a vessel—even if some of the images painted were katsina representations. Certainly masks and pottery were made using different production processes—masks were not fired, for example. A more important difference may be that masks were inalienable objects but ceramic pots moved much more freely throughout Pueblo society, by means of either gifting or exchange (Mills 2004).

Nonetheless, production of glazes may have had ideological connotations stemming from the ability to transform a raw material (galena) into a vitreous decoration. Helms (1993:19) discusses the importance of the transformation of matter through crafting. She argues that the production process itself, whereby a raw material is transformed into a finished state, may be considered a powerful and dangerous activity. A transformable raw material, such as lead ore, is considered more symbolically powerful if it is perceived as exotic (Helms 1993), and this was probably the case for ores from distant sources.

CONCLUSIONS

In conclusion, we identify at least two kinds of practice associated with glaze paint production. The first is the practice of ore procurement, whether embedded in larger regional acquisition networks or not. The people residing in the different regions or districts we examined appear to have maintained their own independent but probably intersecting networks through which ore was obtained. This practice may have carried significantly different kinds of social significance in different areas. Pueblos located near ore sources must have approached procurement in a different way than pueblos that were several hundred miles from ore sources. Nevertheless, even ores obtained locally may have been charged with powerful cosmological significance, which may have embedded their procurement within broader social networks.

The second kind of practice is the act of transformation through which glaze paints are created from raw ores. We speculate that roasting of the raw ore (Blinman and others, Chapter 11) may have facilitated its transfer from the realm of a distant and potentially ritually charged activity to the realm of the local, that is, household production. This transformation may or may not have entailed a gender- or ritual-based division of labor. No doubt transformation, if connected to the power of distant sources, was more important in the Zuni and Mogollon Rim areas than along the Rio Grande, particularly the Galisteo pueblos residing near the Cerrillos source. However, even in the Rio Grande the connection between lead and turquoise procurement may have linked glaze-paint production to cosmologically charged places on the landscape. As Mary Helms (1988) notes, cosmological and physical distance is often conflated within Native American systems of meaning. Thus, while Rio Grande potters may have procured ore locally from the Cerrillos Hills or Magdalena Mountains, it still may have been conceived as coming from a distant or exotic realm. Thomas's (2008, Chapter 13) analysis of changing value systems under Spanish colonialism sheds a different light on ore transformation and suggests a possible impetus for the demise of glaze ware production.

Acknowledgments

Funding for the various analyses synthesized in this chapter came from many sources: the Academic Senate Committee on Research and the Social Sciences Division, UCSC; Arizona State University; the National Geographic Society; the National Science Foundation; the SAA Fred Plog Fellowship; the University of Arizona; and the Wenner-Gren Foundation for Anthropological Research. Several New Mexico ore samples were provided by David Hill, Homer Milford, Virginia McLemore, and Robert Weber. We are grateful for the hard work of research assistants Cicely Amato, Ryan Dean, Sarah Ginn, Stephen Glenn, Sarah King, Deirdre Morgan, Rachel Ramirez, and Mara Ranville at UCSC. Joaquin Ruiz, Dean of Sciences, and John Chesley, Department of Geosciences, facilitated access to UA sample preparation and analysis facilities. At UCSC, Bruce Tanner, Dan Sampson, and Rob Franks in Earth and Marine Sciences provided valuable technical assistance. The methodology used for lead isotope analysis at UCSC was pioneered by A. Russell Flegal in the Department of Environmental Toxicology. We also wish to thank the organizers and participants of the 2009 SAA Symposium "Technology as Practice: Polychrome and Glaze-Painted Pottery in the Late Prehispanic American Southwest," as well as discussant Rosemary Joyce, for an eye-opening early morning session!

CHAPTER THREE

A Community of Practice in Diaspora

The Rise and Demise of Roosevelt Red Ware

Patrick D. Lyons and Jeffery J. Clark

This volume addresses a research focus central to the social sciences in general and to anthropological archaeology in particular: cultural transmission. Over the past thirty years, theory and method for documenting and understanding cultural transmission have increasingly incorporated the concept of practice. Researchers now regularly proceed from two key premises: (1) it is through the dialectic of structure and agency that individual identities are constructed and society is reproduced, and (2) a particular item of material culture can passively reflect and, at the same time, actively signal different aspects of social identity.

We have long been convinced that understanding archaeological evidence of cultural transmission requires distinguishing the residues of exchange, emulation, enculturation, and ethnicity (Clark 2001; Lyons 2003). This approach has guided our research on ancient migration, which we pursue in two phases: first documenting the presence of immigrants (based on evidence of distinct traditions of material culture), and then investigating interaction between immigrants and local groups. Much of our work over the past decade has been driven by a desire to better understand the Salado phenomenon and, more specifically, Roosevelt Red Ware ("Salado polychromes")—a widespread Southwestern pottery tradition that appeared, spread, and disappeared in the context of unprecedented demographic upheaval between A.D. 1275 and 1450.

In this chapter, we review Patricia Crown's (1994) inferences regarding the origin and dissemination of the Roosevelt Red Ware tradition and provide a sketch of our model of the Salado phenomenon as material traces of Kayenta-affiliated groups in diaspora (Fig. 3.1). We then examine aspects of the process of diaspora relative to situated learning theory (Lave and Wenger 1991;

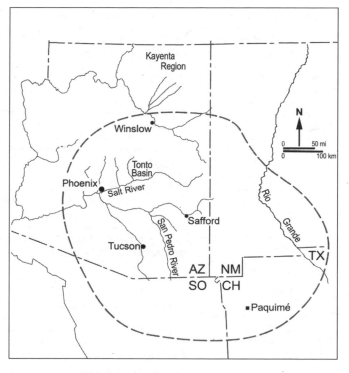

Figure 3.1. Map of Arizona and portions of New Mexico, Sonora, and Chihuahua showing the maximum spatial distribution of Roosevelt Red Ware (after Crown 1994: Figure 3.1). This area is associated with Gila and Tonto Polychrome; earlier and later types were limited to smaller areas.

Wenger 1998), and combine aspects of these two models of cultural transmission to evaluate our interpretations of the available data. We conclude by considering changes through time in Roosevelt Red Ware decoration in the context of macroregional trends in vessel surface color and paint colors (Phillips, Chapter 4; Carlson 1982).

SALADO

An influx of immigrants from the north was a key ingredient in the first models accounting for the dramatic changes in ceramics, architecture, and treatment of the dead that marked the shift from the pre-Classic to the Classic period in southern Arizona—changes eventually lumped under the rubric of Salado (Gladwin 1928; Gladwin and Gladwin 1929, 1930, 1931, 1935; Hawley 1928; Schmidt 1927, 1928). By the 1930s, archaeologists had inferred connections between Tusayan and Kayenta ceramics, specifically, and Roosevelt Red Ware (Gladwin and Gladwin 1935; Haury 1945) (Table 3.1, Figures 3.2 and 3.3).

With the accumulation of more data, however, it is now clear that many of the traits early workers insisted arrived in the Hohokam region from the north as a complex instead developed locally at different times and at different rates (Doyel 1974, 1981; Steen 1965; Wasley and Doyel 1980; Weaver 1972, 1973, 1976). In addition, many researchers call attention to variability among "Salado" sites and components, noting that the

Table 3.1. Roosevelt Red Ware Types, Dates (all A.D.), Summary Descriptions, and References

Type (Date)	Summary Description	References
Los Muertos Polychrome (1390–1450)	bowls, jars, mugs; red used as paint (alongside black paint) on white slip.	Lyons and Neuzil 2006; Neuzil and Lyons 2006
Dinwiddie Polychrome (1390–1450)	recurved bowls only; exterior: decoration like Gila or Tonto Polychrome jars, interior: smudged.	Lyons and Neuzil 2006; Mills and Mills 1972; Neuzil and Lyons 2006
Cliff White-on-red (1390–1450)	recurved bowls only; exterior: white paint on red slip, interior: smudged.	Lyons and Neuzil 2006; Mills and Mills 1972; Neuzil and Lyons 2006
Phoenix Polychrome (1375–1450)	recurved bowls only; exterior: decoration like Gila or Tonto Polychrome jars, interior: slipped red.	Lyons and Neuzil 2006; Neuzil and Lyons 2006
Nine Mile Polychrome (1375–1450)	recurved bowls only; exterior: decoration like Gila or Tonto Polychrome jars, interior: slipped red except for band of black paint on white slip near rim.	Lyons and Neuzil 2006; Neuzil and Lyons 2006
Whiteriver Polychrome (1360–1450)	incurved and hemispherical bowls only; exterior: decoration like Gila or Tonto Polychrome jars, interior: slipped red.	Lyons 2012b
Cliff Polychrome[1,2] (1360–1450	recurved bowls only; interior: two black-on-white design fields (one at rim and one below) separated by banding line, exterior: slipped red.[3]	Harlow 1968; Lyons 2004a
Cliff Black-on-red (1360–1450)	recurved bowls only; interior: two black-on-red design fields (one at rim and one below) separated by banding line, exterior: slipped red.	Arizona State Museum Collections
Pinto Black-on-red (1280–1330	bowls only; interior: black paint on red slip (lacks wide, black, banding line at rim), exterior: slipped red.	Gifford 1980:36–37
Tonto Polychrome (1340–1450	jars, bowls, mugs, ladles; bowl interior: panels or meandering ribbons of black paint on white slip surrounded by red slip, bowl exterior: slipped red;[3] jar exterior: (1) single design field comprised by panels or meandering ribbons of black paint on white slip surrounded by red slip, (2) separate design fields for neck and body, each comprised by panels or ribbons of black paint on white slip surrounded by red slip, or (3) separate design fields for neck and body: one comprised by panels or ribbons of black paint on white slip surrounded by red slip, the other consisting of horizontal band of white slip with black paint.	Colton and Hargrave 1937:90–91; Gladwin and Gladwin 1930:8–9; Haury 1945:63–80

only characteristic that ties them all together is Roosevelt Red Ware (Lindsay and Jennings 1968; Nelson and LeBlanc 1986).

Regardless of problems inherent in the original model of Salado, evidence of links between Kayenta immigrants and Roosevelt Red Ware has continued to accumulate over the past several years. Indeed, Crown (1994:203–209), who has made—by far—the most significant contributions to understanding Roosevelt Red Ware, has demonstrated that these pottery types were developed by Kayenta potters. She argues, however, that

production of the ware quickly spread beyond the immigrants who developed it, in the context of a regional cult.

Southwesternists have increasingly recognized Kayenta immigrant enclaves throughout central and southern Arizona, identified on the basis of unique architectural and ceramic traits and other indicators (Lyons 2003, 2004b; Neuzil 2008; Woodson 1999). A consistent association has been observed in many parts of the Southwest between the local production of Roosevelt Red Ware and the local manufacture of other pottery types, such as the Maverick Mountain Series, and particular vessel forms,

Table 3.1. (Continued)

Type (Date)	Summary Description	References
Gila Polychrome [1,2,4] (1300–1450	bowls, jars; bowl interior: black paint on white slip (usually wide, black, banding line at rim), bowl exterior: slipped red; jar exterior: (1) single horizontal band of white slip and black paint, jar base (below black-on-white zone) slipped red, or (2) multiple, horizontal stripes of white slip and black paint separated by stripes of red slip.	Colton and Hargrave 1937:88–90; Gladwin and Gladwin 1930:6–7; Haury 1945:63–80
Gila Black-on-red (1300–1450)	bowls, jars; bowl interior: black paint on red slip (usually wide, black, banding line at rim), bowl exterior: slipped red; jar exterior: black paint on red slip.	Wendorf 1950:123–24
Pinto Polychrome [1,2,4] (1280–1330)	bowls only; interior: black paint on white slip (lacks wide, black, banding line at rim), exterior: slipped red.	Colton and Hargrave 1937:87–88; Gladwin and Gladwin 1930:4–5
Pinto Black-on-red (1280–1330)	bowls only; interior: black paint on red slip (lacks wide, black, banding line at rim), exterior: slipped red.	Gifford 1980:36–37

NOTES:

[1] Includes "salmon varieties," e.g., Pinto Polychrome: Salmon Variety, Gila Polychrome: Salmon Variety (Di Peso 1958:100; Haury 1931:70-71, 1934:135; Lindsay and Jennings 1968:9; Lyons 2012a). Salmon variety vessels (all bowls) exhibit a pink interior surface. Most have been slipped with a pink-firing rather than a white-firing clay, although some appear to be unslipped, i.e., the interior surface is the oxidized color of the clay used to build the vessel. In both cases, the color of the interior contrasts with the red slip applied to the exterior.

[2] Includes "Tucson varieties," e.g., Gila Polychrome: Tucson Variety (also known as Pinto-Tucson Polychrome and Gila-Tucson Polychrome; see Di Peso 1958:100; Franklin 1980:66; Gerald 1958; Lindsay and Jennings 1968:12). Such vessels (all bowls) exhibit Roosevelt Red Ware technology (including black, carbon paint) and decoration on the inside and Maverick Mountain Series technology (specifically, that associated with Tucson Polychrome—solid geometric elements in brownish, mineral paint outlined in white; see Lindsay 1992) on the outside.

[3] Bowl exteriors may be slipped red and lack painted decoration or, instead, may bear decoration characteristic of Gila Polychrome (e.g., Cliff Polychrome: Gila Variety) or Tonto Polychrome (e.g., Cliff Polychrome: Tonto Variety) jars.

[4] Some Gila and Pinto Polychrome bowls bear banded (rather than radial) interior designs similar to those seen on the exteriors of Gila Polychrome jars. Such vessels sometimes exhibit a circular, unpainted area of red slip in the center of the design field. More rarely, black, painted decoration is applied to this area of red slip. In cases such as the latter, the vessel's layout often consists of concentric bands of black painted decoration (some on white slip and some on red slip).

[5] Maverick Mountain Black-on-red is often mistakenly identified as Pinto or Gila Black-on-red.

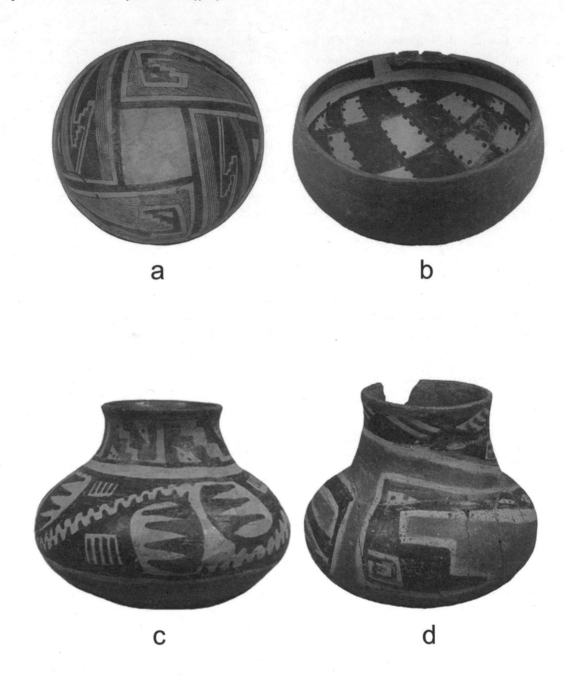

Figure 3.2. Roosevelt Red Ware types: (a) Pinto Polychrome from Hilltop House/East Ruin (AZ V:9:68[ASM]), Catalog No. 85-82-22; (b) Gila Polychrome from Bead Mountain Pueblo (AZ V:9:67[ASM]), Catalog No. 16898; (c) Gila Polychrome from Gila Pueblo (AZ V:9:52[ASM]), Catalog No. GP8702; (d) Tonto Polychrome from Gila Pueblo, Catalog No. 82-45-85. Photographs by Mathew A. Devitt, reproduced courtesy of the Arizona State Museum, University of Arizona.

a

b

c

d

e

f

Figure 3.3. Newly defined, late Roosevelt Red Ware types: (a) Cliff Polychrome from Hilltop House/East Ruin (AZ V:9:68[ASM]), Catalog No. 74-87-30; (b) Nine Mile Polychrome: Gila Variety from the Curtis site (AZ CC:2:3[ASM]), Catalog No. 7623CS; (c) Phoenix Polychrome: Tonto Variety from the Nine Mile site (AZ CC:15:1[AF]), Catalog No. 443; (d) Dinwiddie Polychrome: Gila Variety from the Kuykendall site (AZ FF:2:2[ASM]), Catalog No. 1385K; (e) Los Muertos Polychrome: Gila Variety from Las Colinas (AZ T:12:10[ASM]), Catalog No. A-37258; (f) Cliff White-on-red from the Dinwiddie site (NM S:14:1[ASM]), Catalog No. 6148D. Photographs by Mathew A. Devitt (a) and Patrick D. Lyons (b-f), reproduced courtesy of the Arizona State Museum, University of Arizona (a, e), and Eastern Arizona College (b-d, f).

Figure 3.4. Perforated plate from Hilltop House/East Ruin (AZ V:9:68[ASM]), Catalog No. 17078. Photograph by Mathew A. Devitt, reproduced courtesy of the Arizona State Museum, University of Arizona. This vessel was most likely produced in the Globe-Miami area, based on the results of petrographic analysis (Ownby 2012).

such as perforated plates (Fig. 3.4), that mark the presence of Kayenta immigrants (Crown 1994:204–206; Lyons 2003, 2012a). We therefore argue that Roosevelt Red Ware production remained closely tied to northern immigrants and their descendants rather than quickly and easily spreading to local host groups.

For this reason, we believe that the Salado phenomenon is best viewed as the material residue of Kayenta groups that maintained a shared identity in diaspora (Lyons, Clark, and Hill 2011; Lyons, Hill, and Clark 2011). We also believe that viewing the spread of Roosevelt Red Ware through the lens of situated learning theory supports our alternative model and helps to frame interesting and important questions for future research. Before illustrating the interpretive value of the diaspora concept and addressing the role of situated learning theory in generating possible explanations for archaeological patterns, we present an overview of the theory and method we employ in tracking ancient migrations.

This material is introduced first because, for us, it is the foundation upon which inferences about population movement are built, and this logically precedes any discussion of the effects of migration on immigrants and host groups.

TRACKING ANCIENT MIGRATIONS

We proceed from the premise that style—including technological style (Lechtman 1977; Lemonnier 1986)—is multifaceted and multifunctional. Thus, some aspects of style may be "active" while others may be latent or "passive" (Carr 1995a, 1995b; David and others 1988; Friedrich 1970; Hegmon 1992). Indeed, latent (Sackett 1982) and active (Wiessner 1983, 1984; Wobst 1977) messages may be combined in the same medium or even in the same object, with each corresponding to one or more aspects of technology, design structure, or decorative execution (Carr 1995a).

Because different processes—exchange, emulation, ethnicity, and migration—can result in similar material culture in different places, we prioritize distinguishing their residues. Although some archaeologists may be uncomfortable with discussing ethnicity as a process, this is an important point of theory for us (Clark 2001; Lyons 2003; Lyons and Clark 2008). We view ethnic identity as an emergent property that is practiced through the interplay of structure and agency. Thus, ethnicity is not something one has (an essentialist perspective), but something one does (a social constructionist perspective) (Jenkins 1997).

Compositional analyses allow researchers to either identify or exclude exchange as the process responsible for a given pattern. If exchange has been ruled out, effort can be focused on disentangling the traces of emulation, ethnicity, and migration. We approach migration by documenting and tracing the origins of different patterns of enculturation and describe these in terms of learning frameworks (Hayden and Cannon 1984) resulting in distinct pottery and architectural traditions. Following Carr (1995a, 1995b; also see Wobst 1977), we link the purposeful communication of identity (through the process of ethnicity or emulation) to objects, and attributes thereof, that have high physical and contextual visibility, and suggest that latent signaling of identity (as a result of enculturation) is reflected generally in objects and attributes that have low physical and contextual visibility.

Patterns produced as a result of emulation and ethnicity are purposeful, unstable, and conditional, whereas those associated with enculturation are relatively stable and unconscious. High-visibility objects and attributes are easily emulated and can be distributed widely without migration. Low-visibility objects and attributes have less messaging potential and are thus more static, less subject to careful scrutiny and reflection, and less likely to be imitated. Similarities in low-visibility objects and attributes reflect a common enculturative background, whereas differences are the result of stylistic or cultural drift. For these reasons, differences attributable to enculturation can be used to detect ancient immigrants.

These tenets have been tested through a cross-cultural analysis of ethnographically and ethnoarchaeologically recorded population movements. Based on sixty-one cases spanning five continents, the most useful indicators for tracking immigrants are domestic spatial organization, foodways, and technological styles reflected in the nondecorative production steps of pottery vessels, textiles, walls, and domestic installations (Clark 2001:18; Crown 1996; Gosselain 2000; Wallaert-Pêtre 2001:489; compare with Gosselain 2008:170–171). That said, cultural differences of any kind might become the raw material for constructing ethnic boundaries (Gosselain 2008:170; Jenkins 1997; Lyons and Clark 2008).

Some aspects of more physically and contextually visible artifacts, however, such as the layouts of painted designs on pottery vessels, are also well suited to study within this framework. Many discussions of ceramic decorative and technological style assume that assemblage-scale stylistic patterns are created as a result of the differential transmission of information among potters (Carlson 1970:109; Hill 1970; Longacre 1970; Washburn 1977). Hardin's (1984; Friedrich 1970) work suggests that some aspects of decorative style are passive reflections of socialization.

According to Hardin (1984; Friedrich 1970), styles are learned, stored, viewed, and transmitted in terms of group-specific mental stylistic "grammars." Such grammars, Hardin (1984:592) suggests, represent significant "barriers to visual communication" with outsiders. Hardin argues that styles or elements thereof may be borrowed and manipulated, but the act of manipulation usually entails reference to the borrower's repertoire (also see Washburn 2001). This, she insists, is because styles are cognitively based and are analyzed differently by different groups. Hardin (Friedrich 1970) notes that design elements or configurations may be transmitted from potter to potter or from pot to potter with a minimum of interaction, but their specific, "precisely correct" uses

and the decorative division of space are not easily transferred (also see Van Keuren 2006).

Social boundaries are marked by differences in the organization of decorative space, much in the same way that such boundaries are often marked by differences in the organization of domestic space. Hardin (1984; Friedrich 1970) and Washburn (1977, 1978) specifically suggest that group membership will be reflected in the rules of design composition. It seems wise, then, to conceive of the rules of decorative division of space, or layout, as reflective of the process of enculturation (Lyons 2003). This is an especially powerful approach when coupled with fine-grained knowledge of ceramic production, distribution, and recovery context (Montgomery and Reid 1990; Shepard 1985:336–347, Table 11; Triadan 1997:60–78, 80–81; Zedeño 1994:18–21, Table 3.1). Of course, multiple lines of converging evidence, such as exotic foodways, foreign traditions of architecture, pottery manufacture and decoration, and stone tool production and use, strengthen an argument and provide additional context within which to explore interactions between immigrants and locals (Lyons and others 2008).

A suite of material markers, including plain ware perforated plates, Maverick Mountain Series painted pottery, room block architecture, entryboxes, and kivas, have been used to identify dozens of Kayenta immigrant enclaves (Di Peso 1958; Haury 1958; Lindsay 1987; Lyons 2003, 2004b; Lyons and Lindsay 2006; Neuzil 2008; Woodson 1999). These enclaves were present in nearly every major settlement cluster occupied between A.D. 1250 and 1450 in the eastern half of Arizona, bounded on the north by the Little Colorado River Valley and on the south by the border between the United States and Mexico (Fig. 3.5). This pattern of spatial dispersion has led us and other researchers to consider the utility of examining population movement from the Kayenta region, and its social consequences, in terms of the concept of diaspora (Lyons, Clark, and Hill 2011; Lyons, Hill, and Clark 2011; Mills 2011).

DIASPORA

From an anthropological perspective, the key elements of the process of diaspora are population dispersal, preservation of identity, and a network of connections among dispersed enclaves and between these enclaves and the homeland (Clifford 1994; Cohen 1997; Gilroy 1997; Hall 1990; Safran 1991, 1997, 2004; Sheffer

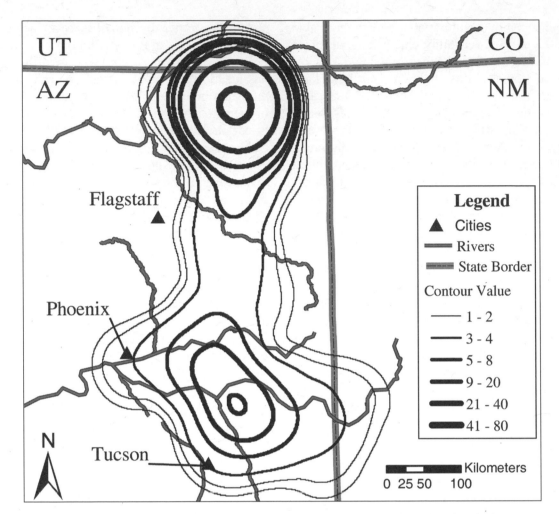

Figure 3.5. Map of portions of Arizona, New Mexico, Utah, and Colorado showing the known distribution of sites having yielded perforated plates. Contours represent numbers of sites with perforated plates per 100 km2 (minimum = 1; maximum = 80). Graphic produced by Marina Sergeyeva.

1986). In some cases, the homeland no longer exists in the same form as it did before dispersal, or it is more broadly conceived than in the past. Diasporic networks allow cooperation on a large geographical scale, moving information, goods, raw materials, and ritual specialists (Sökefeld 2002, 2004; Vertovec 1994; Wellmeier 1998).

In diaspora, a distinct group identity is often preserved through language and religion (Baumann 1995; Safran 2004). It is important to note that this identity survives through hybridity and syncretism (Clifford 1994; Gilroy 1997; Hall 1990). The process of choosing which traditions to maintain and which to discard, repeated by different groups of immigrants among different host populations, is the source of variability among diasporic cells that originated from the same homeland (Clifford

1994; Gilroy 1997; Tölölyan 1996). The ethnographic literature specifically tells us to expect the development of new ritual practices involving revival, invention, or reinvention of traditions (Parekh 1994; Sökefeld 2002, 2004; van der Veer and Vertovec 1991; Vertovec 1991, 1994).

Economic specialization is also associated with diaspora (Cohen 1997). The ethnographic record shows time and time again that immigrants find economic niches to exploit among host populations, including specialized craft production. Evidence of three key elements of diaspora—dispersal, network, and economic specialization—has been marshaled to link the depopulation of the Kayenta region with the development of the Salado phenomenon.

SALADO AS THE
KAYENTA IN DIASPORA

Kayenta immigrants mixed with disparate host groups under different local economic, demographic, and political circumstances, and this led, over generations, to varied, partially shared expressions of group identity (Lyons and Clark 2008; Lyons and others 2008; Neuzil 2008). In some places, such as the San Pedro Valley and the Safford Basin, immigrants were allowed, at least initially, to reestablish their northern homeland almost entirely. In others, such as the Tonto and Phoenix basins, they had to deemphasize certain practices that distinguished them from locals.

Contact between immigrant enclaves is easily demonstrated. Before Kayenta immigrants arrived in the San Pedro Valley, obsidian was extremely scarce. After the immigrant influx, obsidian became much more common in the valley and most abundant in sites yielding traces of northerners. Obsidian was obtained through exchange between Kayenta groups in the Safford Basin and the San Pedro, and this material was then moved to local groups in the San Pedro (Clark and Lyons 2012; Lyons and others 2008).

Sustained contact with a broadly conceived northern homeland is indicated as well. Government Mountain obsidian from the Flagstaff area is found in immigrant enclaves in both the San Pedro Valley and the Tonto Basin. In the San Pedro Valley, there is also palynological evidence of beeweed, which was used for pottery paint, moving through the diasporic network from the plateau or the mountains to the desert (Gerald 1975; Schoenwetter 1965).

The genesis of Roosevelt Red Ware, in and of itself, is evidence of the diasporic network because it represents widespread immigrant exploitation of an economic niche through craft specialization. Dispersed enclaves chose virtually simultaneously to shift from Maverick Mountain Series pottery to Roosevelt Red Ware and to exchange Roosevelt Red Ware with local host groups. Crown (1994:90) documents consistency in vessel forms and painted decoration across a huge geographical expanse, and over generations, and this indicates frequent interchange among diasporic cells.

Ancient potters would have faced difficulties in transmitting Roosevelt Red Ware technological and decorative style from the community of immigrant potters who developed it to potters among disparate local groups, each with a distinct set of ceramic traditions. We find situated learning theory, and the concept of communities of practice in particular, useful for framing this discussion.

SITUATED LEARNING THEORY AND COMMUNITIES OF PRACTICE

The key theorist associated with situated learning theory and communities of practice is Etienne Wenger (Lave and Wenger 1991; Wenger 1998; Wenger and others 2002; also see Li and others 2009), and his concepts have been employed in one form or another by many ceramic ethnoarchaeologists (Bowser and Patton 2008; Gosselain 2008) and Southwestern archaeologists (Crown 2001, 2002, 2007b; Duwe 2005; Eckert 2008; Habicht-Mauche and others 2006; Huntley 2008; also see Bamforth and Finlay 2008). Situated learning is the notion that learning entails practice, both in terms of actually performing tasks and in the sense of the interplay between structure and agency associated with practice theory (Bourdieu 1977; Giddens 1979, 1984; Ortner 1984; Sewell 1992). This perspective is clearly both constructionist and constructivist, in that it focuses on the production and reproduction of communities of practitioners—a process that involves the negotiation (and continuing renegotiation) of meaning, as well as individual and group identity.

Communities of practice consist of co-participants with a shared history of learning, which implies social relations and issues of power, legitimacy (competency), and access to knowledge. Thus, identities are constituted through the relations of participation. Wenger (1998; Wenger and Snyder 2000) defines three core characteristics of communities of practice—mutual engagement, joint enterprise, and shared repertoire:

- "Mutual engagement" refers to "sustain[ed,] dense relations . . . organized around" an activity in which the members of a group co-participate (Wenger 1998:73–77).
- "Joint enterprise" means that there is a negotiated regime of mutual accountability (Wenger 1998:77–82).
- A "shared repertoire" is defined as resources for practice that reflect a history of mutual engagement; this would include laws, tools, procedures, and stories (Wenger 1998:82–84). This concept

overlaps somewhat with the notion of "funds of knowledge" (Vélez-Ibáñez 1988; also see Vélez-Ibáñez and Greenberg 1992) and Sinclair's (2000) "constellation of knowledge."

Wenger (1998) describes a "centripetal" process through which novices become journeymen and then masters as they shift from "legitimate peripheral participation" to "full participation" (see also Bowser and Patton 2008; Lave and Wenger 1991). It is through this dynamic that the identities of participants change and, as they move to mastery, the shared repertoire changes through innovation by influential participants. Situated learning theory, which flows from the premise that social relations are in constant renegotiation, forces researchers to view long-term continuity (rather than change) as unexpected, as something that requires explanation (Wenger 1998:90-98).

Wenger (1998:103–121) and his colleagues (Lave 1996:16; Lave and Wenger 1991:100–109) explicitly address latent and actively maintained boundaries or barriers to communication and learning, both within (peripheral versus full participants) and between communities of practice (participants versus nonparticipants). Such boundaries, they argue, are the result of co-participation and reification, which create "detailed and complex understanding," of tools and techniques in cultural context (Wenger 1998:104; Lave and Wenger 1991:101). Wallaert-Pêtre (2001), using concepts developed by Leplat (1988) and ethnoarchaeological examples from Cameroon, illustrates how different modes of apprenticeship can either contribute to the stability of a tradition or foster innovation. The social factors that reinforce stability are also considered by Gosselain (2008).

Boundaries between communities of practice, as noted by Van Keuren (2006:92), are reflected by examples of "failure to learn" (Lave 1996:16), evident in the form of clumsy emulation rather than faithful reproduction of a shared template. Sequestration, a concept used by Wenger (1990; Lave and Wenger 1991:21, 100–105, 109), captures the notion of boundary in terms of limiting access to the activities shared within a community of practice. Such boundaries can be internal as well as external. The sequestering process generates differences in practice between people on either side of a boundary (Bradley 2004:346; Kanes and Lerman 2007:310; Marshall 1972; Vare 2008:136).

According to Wenger (1998:105–110), different communities of practice can be bridged by "boundary objects" and "brokers." Boundary objects (as reifications) are resources for practice, such as tools, procedures, jargon, and recipes, that are shared between or among different communities of practice and can facilitate understanding across boundaries (Minar and Crown 2001:375; Washburn 2001; Wenger 1998:58–61, 105, 108). Brokers introduce elements of practice from one community to another, engaging in translation, if necessary (Wenger 1998:105, 108–110). A relevant example for this chapter would be two communities of practice composed of ancient potters using similar (but not the same) raw materials and sharing some (but not all) pottery-making techniques. Such boundary objects would give potters common ground upon which to begin sharing each other's distinct practices. This process might begin with a broker or brokers—perhaps immigrant potters who have recently been accepted into a host-group village.

Incorporating situated learning theory into the study of ancient migrations is beneficial because it focuses attention on the social context of transmission within and between groups. Particularly salient issues include the effects of boundary objects and brokers, correlations between different modes of transmission (including specific forms of apprenticeship) and receptiveness to innovation, and the possibility of links between modes of transmission and the organization of production.

Wallaert-Pêtre (2001, 2008) and Crown (1999, 2001, 2002, 2007b) have made important contributions to understanding transmission within and between groups. Wallaert-Pêtre associates "open-ability" apprenticeships with learning by trial-and-error and extensive verbal instruction, showing that open-ability learners easily adapt to new situations and are open to innovation. In contrast, "closed-ability" apprenticeship entails learning by observation and imitation, with little verbal instruction, resulting in reduced adaptability and resistance to innovation.

Crown (2001, 2007b) builds on this foundation, examining differences among ancient potting traditions in hands-on involvement by adults in instruction and the approximate age at which novice potters begin working. In this way, Crown is able to characterize the Hohokam pottery tradition as a closed-ability system and the Mimbres tradition as an open-ability system. Data from her various studies seem to indicate a correlation between a high level of adult involvement (measured in terms of relative frequencies of different kinds of multi-authored vessels, such as those exhibiting cooperative painting) and open-ability systems (Crown 1999, 2001, 2002, 2007b). The converse, of course, would be a link between relatively low investment by master potters in the training of novices and closed-ability systems. Given this framework and Crown's data pertaining to Roosevelt Red Ware vessels made by novices, the potters who made Roosevelt Red Ware learned their craft in a closed-ability system. This is consistent with the ware's unusual technological and stylistic homogeneity over time and across space (Crown 1994:90).

Anthropological models of the process of diaspora, and a large portion of work conducted in the situated learning paradigm, focus on change from generation to generation, literally or figuratively. Recent ethnoarchaeological and archaeological studies have illuminated apprenticeship within individual social groups and the ways we can examine learning by children. In the context of trying to understand the spread of Roosevelt Red Ware, we consider two related questions: What are the implications for sharing between communities of practice based on modes of apprenticeship? What does learning by children tell us about learning by adults?

THE RISE OF ROOSEVELT RED WARE

Did producers of Roosevelt Red Ware represent a community of practice? Wenger (1998:73–84) would require evidence of mutual engagement, a joint enterprise, and a shared repertoire. He would therefore expect, more specifically (Wenger 1998:125–126):

- sustained mutual relationships,
- mutually defining identities,
- the ability to assess the appropriateness of the actions and products of co-participants,
- specific tools and other shared resources for practice, and
- styles recognized as evidence of membership.

Crown (1994:3, Figure 4.1, Table 4.1) analyzed 779 Roosevelt Red Ware vessels from 77 sites in four subregions: Hohokam (the Phoenix and Tucson basins), the Tonto Basin-Globe Highlands area, Mogollon Rim-Anasazi (the Little Colorado River Valley, Silver Creek, the Sierra Ancha, Kinishba, and the Zuni area), and Borderlands (southeastern Arizona, southwestern New Mexico, and northern Mexico). She found that:

[t]he Salado polychrome assemblage examined is remarkably uniform. Despite the wide area over which these vessels were manufactured, the vessels reflect a narrowly defined tradition with similar trajectories of change throughout the area of manufacture . . . [This] suggests that potters in all areas shared a common template of how vessels should be made and what they should look like. The pottery was made using a suite of techniques and shaped into a narrow range of forms that recur wherever we find the pots. Specific designs, layouts, and motifs also recur throughout the range of manufacture. . . . The fact that the pottery styles evolved in essentially the same manner in all four subregions indicates a continuing sharing of information among these potters throughout the period of Salado polychrome production. . . . [R]egardless of the area in which they worked, all Salado polychrome potters drew from a common pool of knowledge concerning how to make and decorate the pottery [Crown 1994:90].

As previously discussed, Crown argues that this widespread sharing of knowledge was made possible by a regional cult uniting potters from *different* cultural backgrounds. We suggest, instead, that the diasporic network of connections among scattered enclaves of Kayenta immigrants fostered the development of a spatially dispersed community of practice among potters with a *shared* cultural background. To weigh the merits of these two models, we consider the general social and economic contexts into which immigrant potters moved, and the effect that a lack of boundary objects may have had on the spread of Roosevelt Red Ware technology and decorative styles to local groups in the southern Southwest.

SOCIAL AND ECONOMIC CONTEXT

Central and southern Arizona had relatively little painted pottery compared to northern Arizona, particularly in the Hohokam region, and production was much more concentrated. In the north, between A.D. 1100 and 1300, painted pottery regularly accounts for between 30 percent (by sherd count) and slightly more than half of the ceramic assemblage at a site (Anderson 1969; Beals and others 1945; Blinman 1989; Lindsay and others 1968; Ward 1975). In the Phoenix Basin (the heart of the Hohokam region), between A.D. 1100 and 1450, painted pottery at most sites ranges from 3 percent to 6 percent (Abbott 1994, 2000; Peterson 1994). Although, before 1100, proportions regularly totaled as much as 20 percent. Decorated pottery percentages in the San Pedro Valley, before the arrival of Kayenta immigrants about A.D. 1300, ranged on average between 5 and 10 percent. In the Tonto Basin, decorated pottery was similarly scarce. Before the appearance of Roosevelt Red Ware in the Tonto Basin, the only locally produced painted ceramic type seen in any substantial quantity was Salado White-on-red, most likely produced by Puebloan immigrants (Heidke 2004; Stark and Heidke 1995; Vint and Clark 2004).

Salado White-on-red (Colton and Hargrave 1937:64–66; Gladwin and Gladwin 1930:10–11), distinct from Cliff White-on-red, is not a Roosevelt Red Ware type, despite the fact that eminent researchers (Colton 1955:8, 1965:12–13) have placed it in this category. Salado White-on-red is an obliterated-corrugated type characterized by a smudged interior and a red-slipped exterior that bears white painted decoration. The available information suggests its makers were immigrants from the Mogollon highlands or the southern Colorado Plateau. Prior to the emergence of Salado White-on-red about A.D. 1250 during the Roosevelt phase, the inhabitants of the Tonto Basin obtained their decorated pottery primarily from groups located to the southwest (Middle Gila Buff Ware) and the northeast (Cibola White Ware, Little Colorado White Ware, and Tusayan White Ware).

In the Kayenta region, direct on-site evidence of pottery production is relatively common, and includes raw materials, tools (perforated plates, polishing stones, potsherd scrapers), and unfired vessels (Ambler 1983; Anderson 1969; Beals and others 1945; Blinman 1989; Crotty 1983; Gallagher 1986; Guernsey 1931; Judd 1930; Ward 1975). Perforated plates are particularly important to our research because these pottery-making tools (base molds and potters' turntables) are ubiquitous in Kayenta sites by A.D. 1150, and they are a key marker of Kayenta immigrants in the southern Southwest (Christenson 1991, 1994; Lyons and Lindsay 2006). Available data strongly suggest that production of Kayenta decorated and utilitarian pottery (Tusayan White Ware, Tsegi Orange Ware, and Tusayan Gray Ware) involved household specialization: potters were present in all parts of the region and in most settlements, but not all households.

Before A.D. 1100, in the Phoenix Basin, pottery production was spatially concentrated, especially in the case of painted types. Abbott and his colleagues have shown that during the Sedentary period (about A.D. 950–1100) all of the red-on-buff pottery in the region was manufactured by the inhabitants of a tight cluster of sites adjacent to outcrops of a key raw material, the micaceous schist used for temper (Abott 2000, 2006, 2008; Abbott and others 2001; Abbott, Smith, and Gallaga 2007; Abbott, Watts, and Lack 2007; Cogswell and others 2005).

Although the organization of production of Casa Grande Red-on-buff, the Classic period painted buff ware type, is not well understood, a number of important facts are known. First, Casa Grande Red-on-buff, like earlier types in the sequence, was manufactured using micaceous schist, and experts believe the temper source remained the same. Second, red-on-buff painted bowls disappeared from the Phoenix Basin pottery assemblage, and Casa Grande Red-on-buff only appears in jar form. Third, the percentage of painted pottery at each site dropped from an average of 20 percent to an average of 5 percent. Painted buff ware vessels, in particular bowls, were replaced by unpainted but slipped red ware and Roosevelt Red Ware polychrome vessels. The unpainted red ware was made by community specialists, principally those inhabiting a small cluster of settlements near the South Mountains (Abbott 2000).

There is also evidence of concentrated production in Hohokam red-on-brown pottery in the Tucson Basin (Heidke 1996a, 1996b). In the San Pedro Valley, a local version of red-on-buff pottery was made by the inhabitants of a small cluster of sites surrounding an outcrop of phyllite and circulated to people throughout the valley. Later, a locally produced, phyllite-tempered red-on-brown type (San Carlos Red-on-brown) and slipped red ware were produced at these sites exclusively (Lyons 2012a).

We argue, given the relatively low number of pottery producers relative to consumers in the Phoenix Basin and other places below the Mogollon Rim, the presumably high number of potters among Kayenta immigrants, the large number of sites identified as immigrant enclaves, and the association between evidence of immigrants and evidence of local production of Roosevelt Red Ware, that Kayenta newcomers quickly out-competed local specialist producers of painted pottery. This would have been especially easy in the Phoenix Basin, where, as previously discussed, red-on-buff painted bowls had been dropped from the local repertoire. Bowls constitute approximately 69percent of Crown's (1994: Table 4.8) Roosevelt Red Ware sample from the Hohokam region. A focus for future research is how reduced transport costs affected transactions between consumers, who formerly obtained painted vessels from distant suppliers, and who now had easy access to this commodity due to the presence of immigrant potters.

BOUNDARY OBJECTS

Taking a cue from situated learning theory, we ask: Were there any boundary objects to facilitate sharing between immigrant and local potters? The short answer is that there does not seem to have been much in the way of common ground. In all places where Roosevelt Red Ware appeared, it represented the introduction of a radically different paint technology and a new firing technology. Indeed, among the people of the mountains, there was no locally produced decorated pottery (except for painted corrugated) until the arrival of immigrants. For centuries, these groups had obtained their painted ceramics from producers on the Colorado Plateau. In most places, the introduction of Roosevelt Red Ware also meant introducing a new forming technique (coil-and-scrape versus paddle-and-anvil thinning) and new vessel shapes.

Given the lack of boundary objects and the low likelihood of direct interaction between immigrant potters and local potters who made painted ceramics (aside from those inhabiting the southern edge of the Colorado Plateau), we wonder how Roosevelt Red Ware technology and decoration could have been transmitted to local potters in such as way as to produce the "remarkably uniform" assemblage described by Crown (1994:90). It seems more parsimonious to suggest that production remained closely associated with immigrants, providing them an economic advantage. We think that when intermarriage with locals inevitably occurred, the closed-ability learning system associated with Roosevelt Red Ware and the diasporic network of communication helped to maintain the community of practice.

Additional evidence supports the inference that production did not spread to local host groups. Crown (1994:76–78, Table 5.15) evaluated the quality of the execution of painted decoration on the vessels in her sample, using a scale from 1 to 5, with 1 being "excellent." She found that, overall, more than 86 percent rated a 2 or a 3, and that in each of the four subregions between 80 percent and 90 percent of the specimens were worthy of a 2 or a 3. We would not expect such consistently competent execution across all subregions if Roosevelt Red Ware had been adopted by groups who

lacked potters altogether or who only had among them very few skilled potters experienced in painting vessels. Conversely, one might argue that immigrant potters invested heavily in teaching members of host groups.

THE DEMISE OF ROOSEVELT RED WARE

New data indicate that in the context of the collapse of the Hohokam regional system during the late 1300s and early 1400s, Kayenta immigrants and their descendants born in diaspora attempted to maintain widespread connections between dispersed enclaves, in part by developing a feasting tradition (Lyons, Hill, and Clark 2011). This is marked by the appearance of a class of extremely large Roosevelt Red Ware bowls with prominent exterior decoration and very little or no interior decoration (see Figure 3.3b, c, d, and f).

As regional population continued to decline, the remaining inhabitants coalesced into increasingly fewer and larger settlements, creating large unoccupied zones. By about A.D. 1390, the Roosevelt Red Ware community of practice split in two, and an eastern tradition (Dinwiddie Polychrome and Cliff White-on-red) and a western tradition (Los Muertos Polychrome) had emerged. We attribute this schism to the breakdown of the diasporic communication network. As Wenger might argue, it became too difficult or costly, given low population and huge no-man's lands, to sustain (1) relationships, (2) mutually defining identities, (3) the ability to assess the appropriateness of the actions and products of co-participants, (4) specific shared resources for practice, and (5) styles recognized as evidence of membership in the group.

CONCLUSION

Since the 1920s, researchers have linked the emergence and spread of Roosevelt Red Ware to an influx of immigrants from the north. Work over the past several decades has resulted in abundant evidence of Kayenta immigrant enclaves throughout the southern Southwest and also robust indications that these groups were responsible for developing Roosevelt Red Ware. More importantly, the strength of these inferences has improved as archaeological theory and method have evolved.

Crown (1994) argued that immigrants quickly disseminated knowledge of Roosevelt Red Ware technology and decoration to their local host groups in the context of the spread of a regional cult. We infer, however, that production stayed tightly bound to immigrants and their offspring. This leads us to argue that the Roosevelt Red Ware tradition was maintained across a large geographical space and over many generations through the network of ties that connected dispersed Kayenta enclaves to each other and to the homeland in the north.

The body of theory and method we use to track ancient immigrants focuses on distinguishing different processes of cultural transmission, including exchange, emulation, ethnicity, and enculturation. This dovetails well with practice-theory-based concepts designed to illuminate learning, as well as continuity and change in craft traditions. Particularly important points of overlap include the notion of boundaries between and within traditions, the concept of boundary objects, and the idea that modes of apprenticeship may promote or constrain transmission among communities of practice. Such concepts allow researchers to model past processes in a richly complex fashion. They remind us that pottery traditions were not moving around the landscape in isolation; these practices constituted and yet were themselves embedded in rich matrices of meaning. We believe that viewing the available data in the context of situated learning theory strengthens our inferences and generates new and important questions.

Looking back at Crown's (1994) study of Roosevelt Red Ware, we see that in the process of building her explanation, she excluded a model of Roosevelt Red Ware as a marker associated with an immigrant ethnic group. Crown may be correct about links between Roosevelt Red Ware painted decoration and a pan-Southwestern religious movement, but this notion need not exclude the diaspora model presented here, or the possibility that a distinct ethnic identity was maintained among producers. Rather, we should continue to explore the relationship between diaspora, religion, and craft production.

One interesting and potentially fruitful way to begin this endeavor would be to compare and contrast on a macro-regional scale the histories of decorative patterns and the social contexts of changes in practice. An example would be the shift from the "Babícora rule" (red and black paint do not touch) to the "Ramos rule" (red paint must be outlined in black), as discussed by Phillips (Chapter 4) in reference to the Chihuahuan Polychromes. Although it is clear, as Phillips observes, that one cannot derive either of these patterns from White Mountain Red Ware, and polychrome Rio Grande

Glaze Ware thus may reflect Chihuahuan Polychrome canons, it is also clear that the specific rules characteristic of early Roosevelt Red Ware cannot be traced to the Chihuahuan Polychromes.

There are three main, temporally overlapping Roosevelt Red Ware rules. These are presented in order, from the oldest, beginning about A.D. 1280, to youngest, beginning about A.D. 1390. The first is the Pinto rule—red is complementary or opposed to white and black. This rule also applies to Gila Polychrome, Cliff Polychrome, Nine Mile Polychrome: Gila Variety, Phoenix Polychrome: Gila Variety, and Dinwiddie Polychrome: Gila Variety. Second is the Tonto rule—red surrounds white and black. This rule applies to all Tonto Polychrome vessels, as well as all Tonto Varieties of other types. Third is the Los Muertos rule—red is applied on top of white, alongside, but not "outlined" by, black.

The Pinto rule and the notion of red and white complementarity are perhaps traceable on the Colorado Plateau as far into the past as Lino Black-on-gray bowls with fugitive red pigment applied to their exteriors. This rule makes sense in the context of the Salado-as-Kayenta-diaspora model presented here, as well as Hays-Gilpin's (2008a, 2010; also see Gilpin and Hays-Gilpin, Chapter 5) recent suggestion that thirteenth-century Kayenta potters expressed the complementary of earth and sky, baskets and cotton textiles, and female and male ritual responsibilities through Tsegi Orange Ware bowls and Tusayan White Ware jars. Hays-Gilpin also argues that Sikyatki Polychrome, which appeared about A.D. 1385, juxtaposes, in individual vessels, elements of earth and sky, this world and the underworld, and references to the two halves (agricultural and ceremonial) of the year. Crown (1994:163–173) long ago considered the possibility that Roosevelt Red Ware vessels expressed similar dualities.

Los Muertos Polychrome, which is defined by the co-occurrence of red paint and black paint on a white background, is dated in part based on its association with Sikyatki Polychrome. Los Muertos Polychrome is arguably one of many local expressions of a late prehispanic stylistic horizon that includes Kinishba Polychrome, Matsaki Polychrome, and other yellow ware types (Carlson 1982; Phillips, Chapter 4). As noted by Crown (1994) and others (VanPool and others 2006), horned or plumed serpent imagery is part of this symbolic complex, which may reference Quetzalcoatl. This complex may ultimately derive from Mesoamerica, and it may or may not have been transmitted to communities of practice in the southwestern United States via makers of Ramos Polychrome (Mills and Ferguson 2008; Lange 1992). In fact, it is conceivable that Quetzalcoatl-related concepts are quite old in the southwestern United States, representing boundary objects of a sort, and that the late prehispanic constellation of pottery types bearing red and black paint on a yellow or white background relate to processes of revitalization that unfolded in Postclassic Mesoamerica (Boone 2003:211–212).

As Phillips wisely reminds us, archaeologists can no longer be satisfied with the use of the term "influence" to describe such instances of cultural transmission as the Pinedale Style horizon, the Salado Phenomenon, or the Pueblo IV yellow ware horizon (Carlson 1970; Crown 1994; Lyons 2003). Different processes can be responsible for similar patterns in material culture, and we believe that the theory and method presented here can be used to help disentangle them.

CHAPTER FOUR

The Northwest Mexican Polychrome Traditions

David A. Phillips, Jr.

For I remember stopping by the way
To watch a potter thumping his wet clay
And with its all-obliterated tongue
It murmured "Gently, Brother, gently, pray!"
—Rubaiyat, tr. E. Fitzgerald, 5th ed., Quatrain 37

For many years, Rio Grande Glaze Ware was linked to a specific narrative: as local potters switched from black-on-white to polychrome designs, they took their cues from the White Mountain Red Ware tradition to the west. The prototype local glaze ware, Los Padillas Polychrome, was a variant of Heshotauthla Polychrome, a White Mountain Red Ware. After White Mountain Red Ware became the Acoma-Zuni glaze series, the western wares served as further inspiration to Rio Grande potters. The latter continued making glaze wares until A.D. 1700, when the Spaniards cut off access to the critical glaze ingredient—lead. In response, local Pueblo potters adopted a matte black paint for their polychrome tradition.

As we now realize, this narrative is too simple. Habicht-Mauche and Ginn (2004) argue, for example, that the supposed local prototype vessels were imports, while Spielmann (1998:253) states that early local glaze ware designs reflect "the design styles on indigenous Rio Grande black-on-white ceramic types." Recent studies have explored temporal and spatial variability in paint recipes, as well as their potential social implications. The goal of this chapter is to further complicate the narrative by suggesting that the polychrome traditions of Northwest Mexico influenced those of the Rio Grande region. I use the term "polychrome tradition" in addition to "ware" because the named polychrome types in each culture area fall within both a ware and a polychrome tradition, and a given polychrome tradition can be expressed in more than one ware. I suggest lines of influence among the northwest Mexican polychromes, including from the Mimbres culture and Mesoamerica. To develop those arguments, I invoke concepts of practice, summarize the polychrome traditions of Northwest Mexico, and use paint recipes and painting rules to tease out larger relationships in the Pueblo IV world. Let the reader be aware, however: data on Northwest Mexican polychrome pottery (and especially on its technology) are sparse, forcing me to render my arguments with a very broad brush.

The word "influence" in the previous paragraph serves to remind us of a time when cultural transmission was treated as self-explanatory. Today, "influences" are no longer simply invoked but must be placed in contexts of identity, practice, and belief. The essay thus serves as an illustration of theoretical issues reviewed by Lyons and Clark in Chapter 3.

HABITUS, CANONS, AND PRACTICE

By now, archaeologists do not need an extended introduction to the concept of *habitus*. In *The Logic of Practice,* Pierre Bourdieu defined habitus as involving

principles which generate and organize practices and representations that can be objectively adapted to their outcomes without presupposing a conscious aiming at ends or an express mastery of the operations necessary in order to attain them. . . . [T]hey can be collectively orchestrated without being the product of the organizing action of a conductor [Bourdieu 1990:53].

In his next sentence, however, Bourdieu (1990:53) adds that "the responses of the habitus may be accompanied by

Table 4.1. Author's Chronological Framework for the Casas Grandes Culture

Period	Dates (A.D.)	Comments
Pre-Viejo	pre-600?	Plainware only; hypothetical period possibly present in Swallow Cave (Lister 1958); see also Stewart and others (2004:235).
Viejo	600?–1200	Red-on-brown pottery; at end, polychrome pottery following the Babícora rule.
early	600?–1000	Predates Mimbres Black-on-white. Corresponds to Larkin's (2006) "Viejo" in the southern zone of the Casas Grandes culture, and to the pre-Perros Bravos phase occupation (Di Peso 1974; Di Peso and others 1974) in the northern zone.
late	1000–1200	First local production of polychromes. Imported Mimbres Black-on-white pottery. Corresponds roughly to Larkin's (2006; Larkin and others 2004) "Transitional" period in the southern zone, and to the Perros Bravos phase (Di Peso 1974; Di Peso and others 1974) in the northern zone.
Medio	1200–1450	Babícora and Ramos Polychrome, related polychrome types. Phase distinctions at Paquimé (Di Peso 1974; Di Peso and others 1974) cannot be extended to other sites. No Tardío period (Phillips 2008; Phillips and Carpenter 1999).

a strategic calculation tending to perform in a conscious mode the operation that the habitus performs quite differently [to bring about] an expected objective." One way to address "strategic calculations" and "conscious modes" is to speak of explicit principles, or canons. In this regard, I use "canon" in its original sense (a formal rule) rather than in the sense of a corpus of exemplary art. Regional ceramic traditions were heavily but not entirely based on habitus, so we must also consider canons in studies of ancient artistic practice.

THE CASAS GRANDES POLYCHROME TRADITION

The first Northwest Mexican pottery—meaning that of Sonora and Chihuahua—was brown ware, and much of the pottery from the northern Sierra Madre Occidental and its flanks is easily classified as Mogollon. Very early on, red-slipped and red-on-brown variants were also produced (Carpenter and Sánchez 2008; Di Peso and others 1974 [vol. 6]). In northwest Chihuahua, a typical painted vessel of a thousand years ago had a corrugated neck and red painted designs, the latter extending down from the corrugated area, and often over the corrugation as well (Fig. 4.1). At some point (Table 4.1), potters began adding lines of black paint to their red-on-brown corrugated vessels, creating polychromes (Fig. 4.2).

The new Chihuahuan polychromes were quite unlike the early polychromes in the White Mountain area. In the latter area, potters created their new polychrome vessels by adding white to black-on-red bowls. It's safe to say that the Casas Grandes and White Mountain polychrome traditions evolved independently.

The first named example of the new northwest Chihuahua traditions is Mata Polychrome, which occurs in Pilón and Perros Bravos phase contexts (Di Peso and others 1974[6]:75). Based on the presence of Mimbres Black-on-white (Di Peso and others 1974[4], Figure 328-4), Mata dates from A. D. 1000 to 1150–1200. Northwest Chihuahua potters continued to make corrugated polychromes during the Medio period

Figure 4.1. Fragments of a Viejo period red-on-brown neck-corrugated vessel. The transition from the corrugated neck to the smooth-walled body can be seen at the top of the fragments. From Ch-180 in the Babícora Basin; found by the Proyecto Arqueológico de Chihuahua (see Kelley 2008: Figure 1.6). Image reproduced by permission of Jane Kelley.

Figure 4.2. Dublán Polychrome jar, Medio period. This vessel follows the Babícora Rule, in that the red paint (lighter) and black paint (darker) do not touch. On the upper, obliterated corrugated portion of the vessel a red zigzag line is framed by black zigzag lines. Maxwell Museum of Anthropology, University of New Mexico, Catalogue No. 65.24.5. Photograph by the author.

Figure 4.3. Two sherds of Santa Ana Polychrome. Top: below the broad red area is a series of alternating black and red (here, gray) lines that do not touch. Bottom: a more typical example, in which the lines are less carefully drawn and thicker relative to the intervening spaces. Both sherds follow the Babícora rule. Top image reproduced by permission of Jane Kelley. Bottom image reproduced by permission of Karin Burd Larkin.

(1200–1450), but their standard background for such designs was now an entirely smoothed surface. One can leap directly from the textured polychromes of the Viejo period (pre-1200) to the squatter, smooth-bodied polychromes of the Medio period (1200–1450). Potters simply left off the textured necks and built rims directly on the smooth vessel bodies.

In west-central Chihuahua (the southern part of the Casas Grandes area), the polychromes emerged along a different path. Here as well, the polychromes began between A.D. 1000 and 1200, when black paint was added to an existing red-on-brown pottery tradition. In this case, however, the polychrome design often appeared on smooth-walled vessels, a combination known as Santa Ana Polychrome (Larkin 2006; Larkin and others 2004) (Fig. 4.3).

Whether on a corrugated vessel or a smoothed one, the earliest Chihuahuan polychromes have two signatures. First, the red and black paint do not touch. Second, spaces between painted lines are often narrower than the lines themselves. The exceptions are mostly due to sloppy execution.

In the southern Casas Grandes area, the transition from Viejo to Medio polychrome painting is seamless. Over a dozen or more generations the locally dominant Medio period type, Babícora Polychrome (Fig. 4.4), shows a tendency toward finer and more widely spaced lines, while the potters become much better at creating a dynamic balance between red and black, and between painted and unpainted space. As is the case for all of the Viejo period polychromes, Babícora Polychrome continues the artistic canon that red and black paint do not touch. I refer to this canon as the "Babícora rule."

Figure 4.4. Babícora Polychrome. The red (here, gray) and black paint do not touch. Maxwell Museum Catalogue No. 65.24.35. Photographer: B. Bernard. Image used by permission of the Maxwell Museum, University of New Mexico.

Other major types of the Medio period conform to the Babícora rule. Unlike Babícora, where the paint is applied directly to a smoothed vessel wall, Villa Ahumada is first slipped over most of the vessel with a whitish clay (most likely to provide a lighter background than the local potting clays allow). Carretas Polychrome, which is not slipped, is made with local clays that fire more orange than those used for Babícora. In addition, the black paint on Carretas often looks more like a subglaze paint than its counterpart on Babícora.

When Carretas is slipped, it becomes Huérigos Polychrome. Most examples of these types are variations on the Babícora theme. In other words, the Babícora rule was allied with a habitus of considerable time depth and geographic extent, which should be viewed as the "main stem" of the Chihuahuan polychrome tradition.

To be so enduring and widespread, the Babícora rule most likely reflected, and was backed by, some strong belief. It's a good example of technology as practice: nothing in the polychrome technology requires the

Figure 4.5. Ramos Polychrome. The red paint (here, gray) is enclosed by black lines. Maxwell Museum Catalogue No. 68.13.33. Photographer: B. Bernard. Image used by permission of the Maxwell Museum, University of New Mexico.

Babícora rule. Instead, it represents a culture's selective expression of the technology available to it.

Until now I have not mentioned Ramos Polychrome, the "classic" (Sayles 1936:54) or "quintessential" (Heckman and others 2000:114) Casas Grandes polychrome. Like Babícora, Ramos involves red and black paint applied to a smoothed, non-slipped vessel wall. Unlike most Chihuahuan polychromes, Ramos applies a new artistic canon: when red paint is present it must be outlined in black (Fig. 4.5). The exceptions (such as framing lines and vessel lips) preserve the intent of the rule. I refer to this new canon as the "Ramos rule." Although the finest examples of the Casas Grandes polychrome tradition are all Ramos Polychrome, its defining attribute is a conscious break with the tradition's most obvious canon. Moreover, while Ramos Polychrome partly continues the regional habitus (for example, paint is usually applied on a polished but unslipped surface),

Figure 4.6. Mimbres Polychrome. The "red" (typically a limonite yellow) is in the triangular portion of the design (lighter gray) and is outlined by fine black lines. Maxwell Museum Catalogue No. 40.4.92. Image used by permission of the Maxwell Museum, University of New Mexico.

design layouts often break with that habitus, most notably by emphasizing twofold rotational symmetry (and thus duality) over other n-fold rotational symmetries. It is therefore not surprising to learn that many vessels in the new tradition were produced by specialists, and that Ramos Polychrome production was spatially uneven (Sprehn 2003; Woosley and Olinger 1993).

If the Ramos rule did not spring from the Viejo period polychromes, where did it come from? The obvious source is Mimbres Polychrome (see Carlson 1982:211–216) (Fig. 4.6). The Mimbres potters never achieved a consistent red on their polychromes, but the yellow-to-red they settled for is always outlined in black. The connection between Mimbres Polychrome and Ramos Polychrome is plausible given the historical connections between the two cultures. From A.D. 1000 to 1150, the Mimbres villages served as ceremonial centers where visitors watched, feasted, and received Mimbres bowls as presents (Shafer 1999:128–130). As one result of this pattern, the Mimbres world included a halo of non-Mimbres sites with occasional Mimbres black-on-white potsherds. The halo extends well into Chihuahua (Brand 1935:302; Di Peso and others 1974[6]; Larkin and others 2004:185–186; Whalen and Minnis 2001), suggesting that many Viejo period villages were home to someone who attended Mimbres ceremonies.

There is also iconographic continuity between Mimbres and Casas Grandes pottery. Both show horned serpents and individuals with horned serpent headdresses (for example, VanPool 2003; VanPool and others 2008). Robert Leonard's (2001) cluster analysis further suggests continuity between the two ceramic traditions. I suspect that the transfer of the Ramos rule from Mimbres Polychrome to Ramos Polychrome was part of a reshuffling of patron-client relationships following the Mimbres collapse of the middle A.D. 1100s. To put it differently, within two or three generations of that collapse the northern Casas people revitalized the Mimbres ritual system, with themselves as the new hosts. Alternately, Larkin (2006:293–299) suggests that Mimbres people emigrated to the Casas Grandes area, which would have fostered the process of southward ceremonial transfer. In either case, the process of transfer was uneven. The southern zone of the Casas Grandes culture held back from the new, Paquimé-centered patron-client system, as shown by its limited use of Ramos Polychrome and the near-lack of northern Casas style exotic goods (Kelley 2009:94–96).

These suggestions bear on long-standing arguments for ideological continuity between the Pueblo world and Mesoamerica (Brew 1943; Parsons 1933; Schaafsma and Taube 2006) and Polly Schaafsma's (1994; Schaafsma and Schaafsma 1974) thesis that the Rio Grande katsina movement originated to the south, not to the west. To the extent that Mesoamerican-inspired priestly offices or beliefs passed to the Pueblos, they may have first been reinvented in the Mimbres villages and then in the Casas Grandes world.

The exact temporal relationship between the gradual emergence of Babícora and the possibly sudden appearance of Ramos remains unclear, but most scholars have leaned toward Babícora starting before Ramos (Amsden 1928; Brand 1935; Carey 1931; Larkin and others 2004; Rakita and Raymond 2003; Sayles 1936). Some early views, in which Babícora entirely predates Ramos, were too simple, but it would not be surprising to find that Babícora (as opposed to Santa Ana) was first made before Ramos.

THE TRINCHERAS POLYCHROME TRADITION

Northwest Mexico was home to a second polychrome tradition, which centered on the Altar Valley of northwest Sonora. The two local types within the tradition are Altar (or Trincheras) Polychrome, which is unslipped, and Nogales Polychrome, which is slipped (following Heckman and others 2000) (Fig. 4.7). Both types involve red and not-quite-black paint on a lighter background and date very roughly from A.D. 700 to 1150 (see Haury 1950:352–353, Heckman and others 2000, McGuire and Villalpando 1993, and O'Donovan 2002 for discussions of types and the murky Trincheras chronology). Both are outgrowths of Trincheras Purple-on-red. Despite its outlandish name, Trincheras Purple-on-red is not far removed from the red-on-brown pottery of the Mogollon, in that a dark reddish ("purple") paint contrasts with an already fairly dark (slipped or unslipped) background.

McGuire and Villalpando (1993:43) see Trincheras pottery as part of Desierto Brown Ware, which extends along the coast of Sonora. There seems to be a close relationship between the Sonora-Sinaloa and Mogollon brown wares, however (Carpenter and Sánchez 2008), and Mogollon pottery may have derived from early Sinaloa-Sonora brown wares rather than spreading north from Durango.

The Trincheras polychromes are more reminiscent of Babícora than Ramos, in that the red and not-quite-black designs are mostly contrasted by spatial arrangement, not by a rule of enclosure. The Trincheras polychromes are clearly different from Babícora Polychrome and its variants, however, being separated by space, time, and specific decorative approaches. Nonetheless, given the estimated temporal priority of the Trincheras polychromes (about three centuries), Trincheras potters may have provided artistic inspiration and technical guidance for the early polychromes of the Casas Grandes tradition.

After A.D. 1150, the Trincheras polychrome tradition died out in the Altar Valley, being replaced by unpainted pottery. I see a survival of the tradition in two later types in southern Arizona, Babocomari and Santa Cruz Polychrome (see also Heckman and others 2000:40–41). While overall designs on Babocomari and Santa Cruz can be inspired by Casas Grandes design layouts, the habitus of those two types suggests a link to the Trincheras polychromes (consider the light slip background,

Figure 4.7. Trincheras Polychrome. The three pieces at lower left are Altar Polychrome, in which the painted design is applied to an unslipped surface. The remaining pieces are Nogales Polychrome, which includes a white slip. Photograph by Janelle Weakly; used by permission of the Arizona State Museum, University of Arizona.

the spatial arrangements of the contrasting paint colors, the use of crosshatching in lieu of solids, and the looseness of the line work). Even so, by 1450 at the very latest, the Trincheras polychrome tradition was extinct. In particular, the not-quite-black paint of the Trincheras tradition is an unlikely ancestor of Puebloan lead-based paints (however, proof of that assertion awaits chemical analysis of Trincheras paint recipes).

ANCESTORS AND DESCENDANTS

Although the Trincheras polychromes could have inspired the first Casas Grandes polychromes, an alternative possibility is that both traditions were inspired by a common artistic ancestor. The best candidate for that common ancestor is Early to Middle Chametla Polychrome of southern Sinaloa, initially documented by Sauer and Brand (1932) and more thoroughly described by Isabel Kelly (1938; see also Scott and Foster 2000:111–112 and Figures 8.5 and 8.6). Chametla dates

roughly from A.D. 250–300 to 700–750 (Kelley and Winters 1960; Kelly 1938). In other words, the Casas Grandes and Trincheras polychrome traditions may both derive from frontier Mesoamerica (Snow 1982).

The changing northwestern frontier of Mesoamerica is discussed by Braniff (1974) and Schaafsma and Taube (2006: Figure 1) provide a map of the frontier at 1200.

The "Ramos rule" is, incidentally, widespread in northwest Mesoamerica (Kelly 1938; Sauer and Brand 1932). The enclosed color is not limited to red, but red is the most common color being enclosed. The frontier Mesoamerican polychromes may have been the inspiration for Mimbres Polychrome, just as I suspect they were for the Casas Grandes and Trincheras polychrome traditions.

The reason to bring up the Northwest Mexican polychromes, in this particular context, is what happened once the Northwest Mexican polychrome traditions were in place. The Trincheras polychromes had a good run—generations of potters made them—but these polychromes died without issue. In contrast, the effect of the Casas Grandes polychrome tradition can be found among the polychromes of the Rio Grande Pueblos. (Carlson [1982:215] states the thesis more broadly, viewing the Chihuahua polychromes as inspirations for the "yellowware horizon of Pueblo IV.") The connection is plausible for two reasons. The timing is right: when the Rio Grande glaze polychromes began, slightly after A.D. 1300, the Medio period had been underway for a century and Paquimé was one of the region's great centers. Also, the continuity between the Medio period and late prehistoric Pueblo culture is striking—the Medio period was, in effect, the south end of the Pueblo world. Since this volume is about pottery, I turn to two technical aspects of the Casas Grandes polychromes that may have carried over to the modern Pueblo world: paint recipes and artistic canons.

PAINT RECIPES

For pots fired in an oxidizing atmosphere, red is an easy color. Iron compounds turn (or remain) red and are widely available. Black is the trick; any reduced iron exposed to oxygen converts to iron oxide, while any exposed carbon converts to carbon dioxide. For Rio Grande potters the answer was, famously, to use lead-based paint (Bower and others 1986; Habicht-Mauche and others 2000; Huntley and others 2007; Jones 1995; Shepard 1942, 1985; Warren 1979b). In true lead glazes the lead serves as a flux for silica but by itself typically results in a clear glaze, so color is provided by other minerals. In the Southwest, copper, manganese, and iron minerals all served as colorants. The silica and alumina also needed for vitrification are principal constituents of clay.

The first potters to make Rio Grande Glaze Ware turned to White Mountain Red Ware for recipes as well as inspiration. As Habicht-Mauche and others (2000:709) state, "Although glaze-paints have been identified on some of the earliest decorated pottery from the Four Corners area, the technique apparently was reinvented by Pueblo potters during the thirteenth century and spread eastward to the Rio Grande Valley of New Mexico by A.D. 1300." Other authors have addressed the polychrome paint recipes in the Southwestern United States far more competently than I can, so I restrict myself to a quick review of the literature.

Most early White Mountain black paint is characterized by far more copper than lead, as Fred Hawley (1938) determined from studies of St. Johns, Pinedale,

and Fourmile Polychrome. A few years later, Anna Shepard (1942:222) reported the same pattern, based on samples of Pinedale and Fourmile Polychrome. Later, De Atley (1986) examined multiple samples from a single site, Fourmile Ruin, and complicated the issue by demonstrating the existence of multiple paint recipes. More recently, Huntley (2008: Table 4.1) reported means of 7 percent lead, 18 percent copper, and 5 percent iron (oxides by weight) in a sample of 70 St. Johns Polychrome sherds. She further reports that in half her samples, lead constituted less than 1 percent of the oxides by weight (Huntley 2008:47). Huntley (2004, 2008) describes a bimodal distribution, however, suggesting that two recipes were being used, one of which emphasized lead.

Later White Mountain black paints show more far more lead than copper, "a gradual development characterized by experimentation with lead-based glaze recipes at the late end of the White Mountain Red Ware Series and the early end of the Zuni Glaze Ware sequence" (Huntley 2006:109–110). Huntley (2008: Table 4.1) found that in a sample of 153 Heshotauthla Polychrome sherds, the means were 27 percent lead and 13 percent copper. In a sample of 90 Kwakina Polychrome sherds the means were 27 percent lead and 12 percent copper (again, by weight). In this case as well, there appear to be two different recipes, one of which emphasized lead (Huntley 2004, 2006, 2008). In summary, White Mountain potters took two broadly different approaches to black paint, but through time, high-lead recipes grew in popularity at the expense of low-lead recipes. Huntley's (2008: Table 4.5) analysis also identified minor usage of manganese oxide as a black pigment.

Shepard (1942, 1965) found that, as a whole, Rio Grande Glaze Ware sherds include increasingly high percentages of lead (from 20 to 60 percent) through time (see also Bower and others 1986:312). Based on current research (Herhahn 2006; Huntley and others 2007), it is now clear that Rio Grande potters used several recipes for black paint, involving mixes of lead, copper, and manganese, but that standardization of recipes increased through time, based on a lead-manganese formula developed in the Galisteo Basin in the A.D. 1400s (Herhahn 2006; Huntley and others 2007:1145). Still, "standardization" is relative. Working on a finer scale, Jones (1995) found three minor glaze paint recipe variations at Quarai during Glaze E and F times, possibly relating to the specific mineral sources being used by three different groups of village potters.

In summary, the White Mountain potters used multiple, changing recipes involving copper, lead, and manganese. The Rio Grande potters also had multiple recipes, based on the same basic ingredients, albeit one recipe eventually predominated. It will be interesting to see what paint recipes emerge as research continues. Meanwhile, the presumed connection between the White Mountain and Rio Grande areas remains eminently plausible. But is it the only connection?

Although the cornerstone reference on Chihuahua ceramic types (Di Peso and others 1974[6]) is a typological rather than technological analysis, it includes a few details on paint recipes. Red paint "was consistently an iron pigment." Black paint from Paquimé was "typically a copper paint, usually with a major amount of lead as well," but samples from CHIH:D:9:14 "usually had major quantities of iron" and one Villa Ahumada sherd had "traces of copper and lead and intermediate amounts of iron, barium, and manganese" (Di Peso and others 1974[6]:93). This information is extracted from a summary of a chemical analysis performed for the Joint Casas Grandes Expedition. Di Peso notes that "Spectroscopic analysis of . . . paints was done by Robert T. O'Haire of the Arizona Bureau of Mines, The University of Arizona" (Di Peso and others 1974[6]:5), but I was not able to locate a copy of O'Haire's report.

It appears that the Casas Grandes potters were familiar with the basic lead-copper recipe for black paint intended for oxygen-rich firings. It also seems that, like potters to the north, they had more than one recipe, and were aware of manganese as an option. As Rio Grande potters perfected lead-based black paints, they had southern sources of information to consult, not just western ones. Snow (1982:239–243) takes the argument a step further, citing appropriate sources of glaze paint recipes in West Mexico (in which case the Casas Grandes potters could have served as intermediaries between the people who resided in West Mexico and the Southwestern United States. Until we have more information on Casas Grandes paint recipes, however, I am reluctant to press the issue.

PAINTING RULES

Earlier in this chapter I identified two painting rules. One of them, the Ramos rule, appears in the Rio Grande area (where Eckert [2006:57] calls it a "paint combination") on Cieneguilla Polychrome, first made about A.D. 1325. In other words, use of the rule began about the same time as local production of glaze ware pottery or, at most, a generation later. Pottery made according to the rule continued even after Rio Grande Glaze Ware production ceased about 1700—as can be seen, for example, in vessels illustrated by Harlow (1973).

There is no way to derive the Rio Grande version of the rule from White Mountain Red Ware, "a red-slipped pottery with painted black or black-and-white decorations" (Carlson 1970:1). Use of the rule therefore either was an independent invention of the Rio Grande potters or came from some tradition other than White Mountain Red Ware. Given that the Ramos rule appeared in northwest Chihuahua a century before it did in the Rio Grande area, I propose that a key artistic canon of Rio Grande Glaze Ware pottery is derived from the Casas Grandes culture. It may also be that the minor Casas tradition of life forms, which most likely has its roots in Mimbres naturalistic painting, similarly inspired the life forms sometimes found on Pueblo IV pottery.

The Ramos rule also appears on ancestral Western Pueblo pottery types such as Kechipawan, Matsaki, and Hawikuh Polychrome in the Acoma-Zuni area and on Sikyatki Polychrome and its variants in the Hopi area. In those areas, the rule appears later than it does in the Rio Grande Valley: about A.D. 1375 in the Acoma-Zuni area and about A.D. 1400 in the Hopi area. One may therefore argue that the rule spread from the Medio period villages to their counterparts on the Rio Grande, and from there to the Western Pueblos. The second leg of this spread, from east to west, runs counter to the oft-claimed flow of plaza-oriented religious practices, and specifically the katsina movement, from the Little Colorado River basin to the Eastern Pueblo country. The spread of the Ramos rule indicates that in Pueblo IV times, the east-west corridor of U.S. pueblos was a two-way street.

CLOSING REMARKS

The Pueblo IV polychrome tradition is best known from the U.S. Southwest, but the tradition is also found in Chihuahua, where it has ancient roots. Some of those roots may lead us to the Mimbres area of southwest New Mexico, to northwest Sonora, and even to Mesoamerica. As soon as our curiosity about such wide-flung connections moves beyond an exercise in trait diffusion, polychrome ceramic design becomes entangled with religious practice.

The notion that the Pueblo IV regional ceramic changes were linked with religion is not a new one (Crown 1994;

Graves and Eckert 1998; Huntley 2006:121; Spielmann 1998). My only contribution is to extend the search for such links across today's international border. As contributions go, it's not original: a quarter-century ago, Dave Snow asserted that "The glaze-paint tradition in the late prehistoric and early historic Southwest can be traced to technological innovations in Mesoamerica" (Snow 1982:237–238).

One of those ultimately Mexican traditions may be linked, through the Ramos rule, to the Rio Grande glaze polychromes—and through them, to the Western Pueblo and modern Pueblo polychromes. Any such spread did not include the "big bowl" pattern linked to feasting (Eckert, Chapter 6; Spielmann 1998), however. Casas bowls are quite small. This suggests an important difference in food distribution during Pueblo IV ceremonies at Casas Grandes versus Rio Grande communities.

Given the known iconographic continuity between the Casas Grandes and modern Pueblo cultures, such as horned serpents (Phillips and others 2006), we are seeing more than the spread of an arbitrary painting rule. Instead, I suspect, the Ramos rule marks the spread of beliefs from what must have been, between A.D. 1200 and 1450, the most impressive religious center in the Pueblo world. The Ramos rule allows us to tentatively connect the dots between the Mimbres villages (or Mesoamerica, if you prefer!) and late prehistoric Pueblo iconography, through the intermediary of Medio period Casas Grandes.

These assertions have implications for future research. The pressing need is for multiple chemical studies of Northwest Mexican and frontier Mesoamerican paint recipes, for comparison with the known paint recipes in the Southwestern United States. More generally, I urge anyone who studies the polychrome pottery of the Southwestern United States to also work with the polychrome types of Mesoamerica's northwest frontier. Until they take those steps, they are looking at only part of the puzzle. Once they take those steps, they can judge for themselves where the connections are likely to lie.

Meanwhile, given the present state of knowledge in Northwest Mexico, there is a real danger of "thumping" our ceramic data too much. Like the clay for the pots themselves, the data cry "Gently, Brother, gently, pray!" I therefore temper (sorry) my previous remarks by admitting that they are a series of hypotheses. Nonetheless, they are hypotheses we should not ignore. To fully understand the rich and tangled roots of Pueblo culture, we must take the broadest possible view of regional polychrome development.

Acknowledgments

My thanks to Jean Ballagh, Linda Cordell, Judith Habicht-Mauche, and the Press's reviewers for their comments on drafts of this paper, and to Michael Conway, Eric Kaldahl, and Jan Rasmussen for archival assistance.

CHAPTER FIVE

Polychrome Pottery of the Hopi Mesas

Dennis Gilpin and Kelley Hays-Gilpin

The Hopi Mesas today are home to about 12,000 people living in 12 villages. Many still speak Hopi, a Uto-Aztecan language, as well as English. Many members of Tewa village speak Tewa, their ancestors having arrived on First Mesa around A.D. 1700, in the latest wave of many migrations that characterize Hopi history. Even today, many Hopis identify themselves first as "clan people." More than 40 matrilineal clans comprise Hopi communities (see Bernardini 2009 for explanation of Hopi clan migrations as they relate to archaeology and history). Each former village site that is today identified as a Hopi ancestral place probably housed a changing array of migrants for varying lengths of time, especially during the 1200s and 1300s, which are remembered today as the "migration period" that preceded the "gathering of the clans" in the vicinity of the Hopi Mesas beginning sometime in the 1200s. As a result, polychrome pottery traditions in the Hopi area show stylistic and technological influences from many directions.

In this chapter, we summarize the history of the Hopi polychrome pottery tradition as we see it from the archaeological evidence available in a region spanning all of northeastern Arizona from the Mogollon Rim to the San Juan River, and from the San Francisco Peaks (Flagstaff) to the Chuska Mountains (roughly the New Mexico state line). We approach this history in terms of how different communities of potters contributed to the development of Hopi polychrome pottery.

Practice theory examines how the behaviors of everyday life result in expectations or rules for social behavior. Archaeological studies that use practice theory investigate the regularities and variability in the material manifestations of everyday life. Communities of practice are the groups of people whose regular, though not necessarily daily, interactions lead to these expectations or rules for social behavior. Communities of practice reflect different scales, modes, intensities, and types of interaction, which can be identified through the study of everyday life. Scales of interaction can vary widely, from regional settlement systems to individual site organization, different areas within a single site, and households.

This chapter focuses on ceramic production and exchange as a mode of interaction at a regional scale and addresses the intensities and types of interaction entailed in the production and distribution of polychrome pottery in northeastern Arizona. The current state of knowledge about production and distribution of polychrome pottery in northeastern Arizona, based largely on survey data with limited information from excavation, allows analysis of regional interactions between site clusters and sites within site clusters. The best-reported excavations at sites with polychrome pottery in the region are those at St. Michaels Pueblo (Andrews 1978), Wide Reed Ruin (Mount and others 1993), Puerco Ruin (Burton 1990), the Homol'ovi sites (Adams 2002), and Awat'ovi (Smith 1971), but existing analyses of the pottery from several of these projects are outdated or incomplete. Notably, most of the polychrome pottery at Wide Reed Ruin was classified as St. Johns Polychrome, but it appears to us to be mostly Kintiel or Klagetoh Polychrome, which was made several generations later. The only pottery from Awat'ovi that has been analyzed in detail is that from the Western Mound (Smith 1971), which was occupied only until about A.D. 1375.

In reconstructing the communities of potters (if not communities of practice) that produced polychrome pottery in northeastern Arizona, we can sometimes discern variability in forming, painting, and firing within wares and types. We emphasize geographical and chronological transitions between wares and types across the region, and cautiously use those wares and types as proxies for strong temporal and geographic patterns of technological and stylistic choices. To some extent, we track choices about color, surface finish, vessel form, iconography, and other attributes that are easily observed in archaeological records and collections. We refer to communities of potters rather than communities of practice because we do not have the level of detail needed to examine evidence for motor patterns and other details of production that would allow us to identify scales and kinds of interaction at or below the village level—at the level of "regular interaction" necessary to define a community of practice. That said, the patterns we observe *are* the results of decisions made by individuals working in communities of practice, so we are interested in innovation and variation as well as broad, regional patterns.

Prior to A.D. 1300, northeastern Arizona was characterized by a geographically undifferentiated expanse of Puebloan settlement (Wilcox and others 2007: Figures 12.6, 12.7). In the 1300s, settlement clusters formed, separated by distances requiring more than one day of travel. Settlements were clustered in the Hopi, Flagstaff, Anderson Mesa, Homol'ovi, Rio Puerco of the West, and upper Little Colorado River areas. By the 1400s, settlement in northeastern Arizona was restricted to the Hopi Mesas.

Even prior to the 1300s, though, when settlement was not geographically clustered, potters produced distinctive regional styles, each of which manifests a community of potters making more or less consistent patterns of choices at each production step. The exchange of pottery between different regions prior to 1300 indicates communication among different communities of potters. The pre-1300 pottery exchange, necessitating both familiarity with and cooperation between members of different communities, may have facilitated the migration of populations into increasingly clustered settlements after 1300. Once these migrants became concentrated within more-compact settlement clusters (and ultimately only one settlement cluster, at Hopi), potters increasingly incorporated iconography and design layout from different traditions and ultimately created a single new synthetic community of potters, evident in the Sikyatki style.

Specifically, we see potters in this region developing parallel red ware and white ware traditions from about 1000 to the early 1300s, with a dramatic decrease in white ware by 1300, followed by the replacement of red ware

with yellow coal-fired pottery in the early 1300s. Potters created Hopi polychrome pottery apparently by combining elements from White Mountain Red Ware (Carlson 1970) and Tsegi Orange Ware (Colton 1956) traditions. The distinct color combination of late Hopi polychrome pottery—Sikyatki Polychrome, with its massed red outlined by black on a buff to yellow ground—reminds us of Ramos Polychrome and follows Phillips's "Ramos rule" (Phillips Chapter 4). Yet Ramos layouts and vessel forms are very different from Sikyatki, suggesting connections as far south as Paquimé were not mediated by long-distance exchange of pottery but by some other medium. In this case, we do not see evidence for interactions between two communities of practice; the communities of potters were too distant from each other for interaction or observation that might lead to emulation. Rather, we may be seeing results of partial emulation of designs and color schemes (but not vessel forms and layouts) via painted textiles or other media.

Sikyatki Polychrome, the most elaborate expression of Hopi Polychrome pottery, is the result of increasing decorative complexity in the yellow ware trajectory. This change may have involved a fusion of earlier red ware and white ware traditions or a radical replacement of the earlier pattern by innovation or by influence from other media, such as mural paintings and painted textiles. Sikyatki Polychrome probably represents shifts toward craft specialization, and elaboration of katsina iconography that reflected or even helped to catalyze new kinds of community identities.

BICHROME BEGINNINGS

Early northeastern Arizona red wares (Woodruff/Forestdale Red and Tallahogan Red) were plain red wares that appear to have had little effect on later painted pottery types. The red ware traditions that did seem to affect later painted pottery types were Puerco Valley Red Ware (also known as Showlow Red Ware), Tsegi Orange Ware, and White Mountain Red Ware, all of which began about A.D. 1000, at a time when most communities in the region were organized along the Chacoan model, with a great house or great kiva, or both, surrounded by dispersed small houses (Judge 1989; Stein and Fowler 1996).

Potters began to produce Puerco Valley Red Ware about 1000 by adding a red slip to Woodruff Brown. Puerco Valley Red Ware (Hays-Gilpin and Van Hartesveldt 1998:140–161) had a very restricted production area, from the Petrified Forest to the present-day New Mexico state line. Potters used similar clays and a variety of treatments to make white ware, gray ware, and brown ware pottery as well as red ware. Showlow Black-on-red is dated to about 1030–1200. This type is probably ancestral to Roosevelt Red Ware (Crown 1994), which includes the well-known Salado polychrome types, Pinto, Gila, and Tonto polychrome; these types were produced over a very wide area in the 1300s.

Tsegi Orange Ware was made with Chinle Formation clays in the greater Kayenta area (Zedeño 2002:79). The earliest bichrome began as local copies of Deadmans Black-on-red, a red-slipped San Juan Red Ware type made in southeastern Utah and widely traded during the 900s and early 1000s (Breternitz and others 1974). Sometime in the mid-1000s, potters began to emulate the Chaco-centric hatched Gallup style of decoration, producing Tusayan Black-on-red. Potters in the same area used a different clay source (probably iron-poor Cretaceous clays of Black Mesa) to produce Tusayan Gray Ware and White Ware (Colton 1955). Painted decoration on red wares at this time was very much like designs on black-on-white pottery—for example, Tusayan Black-on-red and Dogoszhi Black-on-white both bear hatched designs.

White Mountain Red Ware (Carlson 1970) had the largest production area. The earliest White Mountain Red Ware, Puerco Black-on-red (1030–1150), was produced in western New Mexico and perhaps in northeastern Arizona. Designs are similar to Puerco Black-on-white pottery made in the same area.

EARLY POLYCHROMES

Polychrome pottery began about A.D. 1125, when the Chacoan influence in the region was at its peak, although transitional or post-Chacoan great houses, or compound-style buildings (after Stein and Fowler 1996:117), began to replace Chacoan community organization.

Puerco Valley (Showlow) Red Ware remained mostly unchanged, and potters of the Rio Puerco Valley did not develop a polychrome type at this time. Makers of Tsegi Orange Ware and White Mountain Red Ware did develop polychrome types in this era, but the two wares were characterized by different design styles.

To make the earliest Tsegi Orange Ware polychromes, Citadel Polychrome (1125–1200) and Tusayan Polychrome (1150–1300), potters used the naturally orange color of source clays to set off designs of broad red ribbons with black outlines (Fig. 5.1, upper left) and hachures. Designs diverge from contemporaneous black-on-white pottery at this time (Flagstaff and Tusayan black-on-white), with Tsegi Orange Ware polychrome designs apparently referencing plaited baskets, and white ware designs referencing loom-woven cotton textiles (Hays-Gilpin 2008b; see Tanner 1976:30, 82–88 for examples of designs). No life forms were depicted in either style.

The earliest White Mountain Red Ware polychromes had black-on-red interiors with white-on-red exteriors (Carlson 1970; Hays-Gilpin and Van Hartesveldt 1998:166–171). Wingate Polychrome has black-on-red interior designs rendered in the interlocking solid and hatched geometric Reserve style, with white painted or unslipped exterior with bold red designs, which sometimes include life-forms such as hands and birds. Wingate Polychrome was antecedent to St. Johns Polychrome, which has black-on-red interior designs in the Tularosa design style (Carlson 1970) and white-on-red broad line designs (Fig. 5.1, middle left), sometimes including life forms, such as parrots. St. Johns Polychrome was probably produced in a broad area of western New Mexico and eastern Arizona and was apparently widely traded. This is the first polychrome pottery type to be circulated through a very broad region.

POLYCHROMES DIVERSIFY

In the A.D 1200s, true Pueblo villages (large enough to have constituted endogamous communities) became the most common community type, and polychrome pottery became much more diverse. Diversity apparently peaked in the late 1200s, as aggregation into large pueblos increased and depopulated hinterlands formed between settlement clusters. Four primary centers of production for gray ware and white ware pottery (Kayenta, Hopi Buttes, Puerco Valley, and Defiance Plateau) and five centers of production for polychrome pottery (the Tsegi Canyon area, Hopi Mesas, Homol'ovi, Puerco Valley, and Defiance Plateau) represent different communities of potters at this time. More than one village in each cluster probably produced pottery, and thus each settlement cluster would have comprised more than one community of practice.

In the Kayenta region (including northern Black Mesa and the plateaus to the north of Black Mesa), Tsegi phase buildings formed the core of communities. These multistoried Tsegi phase buildings (such as

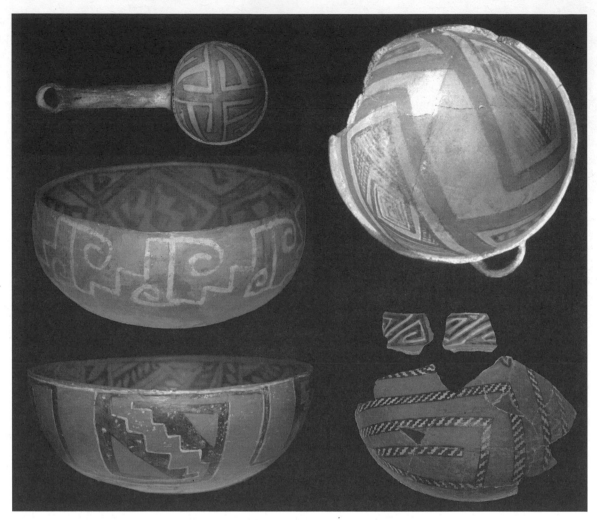

Figure 5.1. Tsegi Orange Ware and White Mountain Red Ware vessels. Upper left: Tusayan Polychrome ladle (Museum of Northern Arizona catalog number A336. Photo by Kelley Hays-Gilpin). Upper right: Kayenta Polychrome bowl with characteristic strap handle (Museum of Northern Arizona catalog number A1106. Photo by Ryan Belnap). Middle left: St Johns Polychrome bowl from Foote Canyon Pueblo (Field Museum catalog number 258140. Photo by Matt Peeples). Middle right: Kiet Siel Polychrome pitcher (Museum of Northern Arizona catalog number A1083. Photo by Ryan Belnap). Lower left: Pinedale Polychrome bowl from Foote Canyon Pueblo (Field Museum catalog number 258154. Photo by Matt Peeples). Lower right: Zuni glaze polychrome jar fragments with a design that is more characteristic of Tonto Polychrome, from Atsinna Pueblo, El Morro National Monument (National Park Service, ELM0 606. Photo by Kelley Hays-Gilpin).

Long House in the Long House Valley and Red House, Yellow House, and Guardian Pueblo at Navajo Mountain) were constructed of parallel walls of core-veneer masonry forming a corridor that was subdivided into rooms with simple masonry walls abutted to the parallel walls (Dean and others 1978; Lindsay 1969; Lindsay and others 1968). Around 1250, Kayenta potters began to add white outlines to create three- and four-color geometric designs. In Kayenta Polychrome (Fig. 5.1, upper

right), the black designs of Tusayan Polychrome were outlined in white; in Kiet Siel Polychrome (Fig. 5.1, middle right), the black designs of Tusayan Black-on-red were outlined in white (Colton 1956). Pinedale-style (Lyons 2003:49–52) elements and cotton textile-derived designs also appear at this time.

At about the same time, in the late 1200s, some Mogollon Rim and Zuni area potters began to use white outlines on Pinedale, Heshotauthla, and Kwakina polychromes (Carlson 1970; Woodbury and Woodbury 1966) (see Figure 5.1, lower left and right). We do not yet know where this stylistic innovation originated or how it spread. Other stylistic changes in late Tsegi Orange Ware polychrome suggest influence from, or at least interaction with, potters in the Mogollon Rim area. Many archaeologists have proposed a Kayenta migration to the Rim area in this time period to account for similarities (Clark 2001; Di Peso 1958; Haury 1958; Lindsay 1987; Lyons 2003; Wilcox and others 2007:182; Woodson 1999). Although we think there is some evidence for that, a one-way migration scenario does not account for style changes in the Kayenta "source" area, and we propose that mobility and interaction in both directions is likely.

Accretional pueblos were also constructed at Homol'ovi, in the middle Little Colorado Valley. Locally produced utility ware pottery here seems to be a late version of Little Colorado Gray Ware (Colton 1955), but a surprising amount of Alameda Brown Ware was imported from the Flagstaff and Anderson Mesa areas (Colton 1958). White ware pottery was imported from the Hopi Buttes, Mogollon Rim, and Kayenta areas, and red ware was equally diverse. Locally produced Winslow Orange Ware seems to have fused styles from many directions. The Winslow Orange Ware tradition included both red-slipped and unslipped orange pottery with black designs and white outlines (Colton 1956; Hays-Gilpin and others 1996; Lyons 2003; Lyons and others 2001). Use of white exterior designs is very rare in the Homol'ovi area. Ceramics thus support Hopi oral traditions that this was a place where people from many areas came together.

The accretional pueblos constructed in the Hopi Buttes are associated with Little Colorado White Ware and Gray Ware, locally made pottery. Communities in the Hopi Buttes never produced polychrome pottery.

Puerco Valley people from Petrified Forest east to the Lupton Cliffs aggregated into a line of at least 15 accretional and planned pueblos, some of which produced Puerco Valley Gray Ware, White Ware, and Red Ware, including Pinto Polychrome (A.D. 1280–1300+). Pinto Polychrome is the earliest polychrome type in the Roosevelt Red Ware, and may have been locally produced using the Showlow Red Ware paste, slipping the interior with a white slip, and painting Pinedale-style designs. Accretional and planned pueblos in the area from the west slope of the Defiance Plateau to perhaps as far east as Manuelito Canyon, New Mexico, including Kintiel, produced Cibola Gray Ware and White Ware, Kintiel Black-on-orange and Polychrome, and Klagetoh Black-on-Yellow and Polychrome. Some White Mountain Red Ware, such as St. Johns Polychrome and Pinedale Polychrome, may have also been produced in this region (Hays-Gilpin and Van Hartesveldt 1998:172–175). Kintiel and Klagetoh red, yellow, and polychrome pottery pose two issues: first, should these be classified as one type or two, and, second, should they be considered a variant of Jeddito Polychrome, as proposed by Smith (1971:472–473), or a localized expression of White Mountain Red Ware? Either way, their unique combination of technological and stylistic features is specific to a particular time and place—a signature of separate, yet connected, communities of potters. These issues are not strictly typological because they address questions of production and, potentially, identity. We tend to see this type (or these types) as a local variant (or variants) of White Mountain Red Ware. Like St. Johns Polychrome, these southern polychromes are characterized by bowls with broad white line designs on their exteriors, and Pinedale-style solid and hatched designs on their interiors. Mesa Verde elements such as thick-thin banding lines, flat rims, and occasional rim ticking appear in Ganado area pottery (Hays-Gilpin and Van Hartesveldt 1998:172). More work needs to be done on the pottery of the Kintiel–Klagetoh community.

On southern Black Mesa (the Hopi Mesas), people aggregated into accretional pueblos with no distinctive public buildings. Hopi Mesas potters produced Tusayan Gray Ware and White Ware (as in the Kayenta region) but developed their own polychrome styles. Jeddito Black-on-orange and Polychrome have Pinedale-style bichrome interior designs, but their exteriors sometimes have broad white outlines like St. Johns and Kintiel Polychromes from the south and east (Smith 1971). Other ceramics are essentially locally produced Hopi versions of Kayenta and Kiet Siel polychromes made to the north. Rare use of white paint in two contrasting styles suggests influences from both northern and southern pottery traditions.

The easternmost of the Hopi Mesas, Antelope Mesa, had an unusually robust population in the late 1200s. Thanks to the Harvard Peabody Museum's Awatovi Expedition of the 1930s (Montgomery and others 1949; Smith 1971), we know quite a lot about sites in this area, particularly Awat'ovi and Kawàyka'a. Pottery assemblages of the late 1200s contain not only Kayenta and locally produced white ware and polychrome pottery but also white ware and slipped red ware from the Ganado area. Klagetoh Black-on-white's mineral paint contrasts with locally produced organic-painted white ware types. As noted above, Kintiel Black-on-orange and Polychrome and Klagetoh Black-on-yellow and Polychrome are an intergrade between Jeddito Orange Ware and White Mountain Red Ware, and even exhibit Mesa Verde influences. This fusion of regional styles and wide circulation of pottery from different production areas is consistent with both archaeological understanding of thirteenth-century population aggregation and Hopi understanding of the "gathering of the clans."

By the last decades of the thirteenth century and the early decades of the fourteenth century, white ware pottery declined (Smith 1971). Orange ware pottery dominated the ceramic assemblages of large and small pueblo sites occupied on and around the Hopi Mesas at this time

At one small site in Petrified Forest National Park, we noticed typical black-on-orange pottery from about A.D. 1300 with no white ware present. A small proportion of pottery there had a bright yellow, fine paste with very little visible temper, a red slip (varying from thin to quite thick), and black Pinedale-style designs. Apparently coal-fired, this type, Kokop Black-on-orange, is the earliest yellow-paste pottery from the Hopi area. This type also occasionally bears white outlines on black interior designs (Kokop Polychrome).

YELLOW WARE BEGINS

After A.D. 1300, peoples of greater Hopiland initiated a major shift in settlement and pottery production. Population aggregated onto the Hopi Mesas, Hopi Buttes, Homol'ovi, and the Puerco Valley, all relatively well-watered areas (Adams 2002, 2004; Duff 2002).

Once ancestral Hopi potters began coal-firing their local iron-poor clays in the early decades of the fourteenth century, it was a small step to omit the red slip and produce black-on-yellow pottery. The latest white ware type in the Hopi sequence, Bidahochi Black-on-white, would, however, be a yellow ware if it were fired at a higher temperature (Goff 1993) and in an oxidizing atmosphere, so yellow ware may come out of the white ware tradition. Thus, Hopi yellow ware can be viewed as fusion of both traditions—iron-poor clay of the white ware tradition combined with the oxidizing firing and mineral paint of the red ware tradition.

The earliest yellow ware type, Awatovi Black-on-yellow, bears Pinedale-style designs that are not very

different from earlier orange and white ware designs (including designs on Jeddito Black-on-orange, Kokop Black-on-orange, and Bidahochi Black-on-white). Occasionally white outlines were added to create Bidahochi Polychrome (Colton 1956; Lyons and others 2001). White outlining, which comes out of Kayenta and Kiet Siel Polychrome, is not very striking in appearance and never constitutes a very large percentage of assemblages. White outlines do not show up very well on light yellow paste, and perhaps for this reason, Bidahochi Polychrome is neither dominant nor long-lived. Black-on-yellow bichrome pottery—especially Jeddito Black-on-yellow of the late 1300s—dominates Hopi pottery assemblages during the 1300s (Fig. 5.2, top row). For almost a century, then, polychromes were not very important in the region. This changed when Sikyatki Polychrome (Fig. 5.2, bottom row) burst onto the scene.

Distributions of Jeddito Yellow Ware, Roosevelt Red Ware, Winslow Orange Ware, White Mountain Red Ware, and Zuni Glaze Ware among the major settlement clusters in the region illustrate patterns of production and exchange in the region from about A.D. 1300 to 1400 (Table 5.1) (see also Duff 2002).

Obviously, Hopi was the major production area and supplied most of the painted pottery in the region. The Homol'ovis were a secondary production area but relied on Hopi for most of their painted pottery (perhaps owing to paucity of wood available for firing in the arid Homol'ovi landscape). The people who lived in the Hopi Buttes area, including Bidahochi pueblo, produced no painted pottery at this time, so far as is known, and imported virtually all of their painted pottery from Hopi. The Puerco Valley pueblos were highly variable. Puerco Ruin imported much of its painted pottery from Hopi. Wallace Tank imported most of its painted pottery from the Homol'ovis, or made it locally. Stone Axe imported most of its painted pottery from Zuni. Oddly, Stone Axe potters seem to have practiced an eclectic pottery tradition that freely mixed paint recipes, slips, and design styles from Hopi, Zuni, Homol'ovi, and Salado traditions. Salado polychrome pottery (primarily Gila Polychrome) appears at all these sites.

SIKYATKI POLYCHROME DEBUTS

After A.D. 1350, almost all the people who remained in northeastern Arizona apparently moved to the Hopi Mesas, although some people in the Puerco area might

Figure 5.2. Jeddito Yellow Ware vessels. Upper left: Jeddito Black-on-yellow bowl from Chavez Pass with geometric designs on interior and exterior (Museum of Northern Arizona catalog number OC239). Upper right: Jeddito Black-on-yellow bowl depicting a katsina painted by a less-than-competent painter (Museum of Northern Arizona catalog number A1340). Lower left: Sikyatki Polychrome bowl with spattered paint, from Kokopnyama (Museum of Northern Arizona catalog number OC307). Lower right: Late style Sikyatki Polychrome jar with white as well as red paint; also called Kawaika-a Polychrome (Museum of Northern Arizona catalog number OC1820). Provenience unknown except where indicated. Photos by Kelley Hays-Gilpin.

have gone to Zuni. Among the last pueblos to be occupied away from Hopi were Homol'ovi II, occupied until 1380 or 1400, and Stone Axe, occupied into the 1400s.

Sikyatki Polychrome—black-on-yellow pottery in the Jeddito style with added blocks of massed red paint (Fig. 5.1, lower left)—appeared sometime between 1380 and 1400, but the Sikyatki *style* did not appear until about 1400 or even 1450, shortly after all of the population in

the region aggregated into nine or ten pueblos on the Hopi Mesas: Orayvi (Oraibi), Musangnavi (Old Mishongnovi), Songòopavi (Old Shungopovi), Qotsaptuvela (Old Walpi), Kookopngyama (Kokopnyama), Nesuftanga, Tsakpahu (Chakpahu), Kawàyka'a (Kawaika'a or Kawaoiku), and Awat'ovi (see also Adams and others 2004).

As a pottery type meant to communicate the date range and place of origin to researchers, the definition

Table 5.1. Percentages of Selected Wares Relative to Total Pottery at Each Site (remainders are corrugated and other types)

	Jeddito Yellow Ware	Winslow Orange Ware	White Mountain Redware	Zuni Glaze Ware
Awatovi (W. Mound)	60.3	0.5	0.4	0.4
Bidahochi	27.5	1.3	1.8	2.7
Homol'ovi	38.3	30.0	10.8	3.0
Puerco (Upham)	36.0	22.0	3.0	7.0
Puerco (Vint and Burton)	18.8	10.4	0.2	0.7
Wallace Tank	18.9	49.0	17.2	5.7
Stone Axe	22.9	12.6	8.0	24.1

NOTE: Data for Awatovi and Homol'ovi from Upham 1982: Table 29. Data for Bidahochi from Fowler 1988. Data for Puerco Ruin from two different studies on the same site: Upham's 1982 reporting of Jennings's 1965 excavations, and Vint and Burton 1990. Data for Wallace Tank and Stone Axe from in-field analysis by Hays-Gilpin.

of Sikyatki Polychrome is a bit sloppy. Harold Colton's initial definition (Colton 1956) offers a date range of 1400 to 1625, but today we can do much better than that, though not as well as we would like. At the moment, we can offer the following phases in the development of Sikyatki Polychrome:

1. Jeddito-style designs with red outlining in the late 1300s

2. Jeddito-style designs with red solids, from about 1385 to the mid-1400s (Fig. 5.1, lower left)

3. Sikyatki-style designs ("flamboyant" Sikyatki, described below; Figure 5.1, lower right), from 1400 or 1450 to 1500

4. Very late Sikyatki (new vessel forms and very densely painted vessel exteriors), from 1500–1630

The development of both Sikyatki Polychrome and the Sikyatki style appears to have occurred relatively suddenly at Hopi. Archaeologists have hypothesized several sources for Sikyatki style, and there may be some influence from all of these: Mimbres Polychrome, Ramos Polychrome, Fourmile Polychrome, Gila and Tonto Polychromes, Winslow Orangeware polychromes, Zuni Glaze and Matte Paint pottery, and Rio Grande Glaze A and B. Each of these may have contributed to Sikyatki Polychrome and the Sikyatki style in some ways, but the pottery and the style were developed on the Hopi Mesas.

Early Sikyatki style is clearly homegrown—Jeddito Black-on-yellow with red paint. But sometime after 1400, a rapid and dramatic stylistic shift took place. Watson Smith (1971) called this late Sikyatki style "flamboyant." It is characterized by asymmetrical designs that include bird and feather elements, elongated curved elements, katsinas, flowers, brocade-like textile designs, stylized dragonflies, and naturalistic butterflies. Rim treatments are varied. Engraving and spattering are fairly frequent in this style. At some point in the sequence, white paint was occasionally used to fill in solid areas, a variant Colton (1956) called Kawaika-a Polychrome. Sometimes more than one shade of red or orange paint was used. On some vessels, red and orange elements lacked black outlining. This style is always stratigraphically above the Jeddito style at Awat'ovi and Kawàyka'a and is the only style present at Sikyatki. Bowls in this style are usually larger than earlier Sikyatki Polychrome bowls, and they apparently were not as widely distributed. Sikyatki-style Sikyatki Polychrome is rarely found off the Hopi Mesas, although it does occur in small quantities at Pottery Mound and Hawikku. A cache of vessels in Canyonlands National Park and occasional sherds in Canyon de Chelly and elsewhere suggest that late Sikyatki Polychrome vessels, sherds, or both sometimes traveled with Hopi pilgrims, Utes, Paiutes, and perhaps early Navajos.

A very late style appears only at Awat'ovi and not at other Antelope Mesa sites. "Very late" Sikyatki-style Sikyatki Polychrome vessels have red or black painted rims, high density of painted design, bowls with very elaborate exterior designs, usually simple interior designs such as spattered paint, and a strongly recurved bowl shape one might call a bowl-jar for lack of a better term. This very late style must have appeared sometime after 1500 because it does not appear at Kawàyka'a, whose last tree-ring dates are in the late 1400s. Awat'ovi is the only site with data for this time period. We lack data on pottery for the villages on First, Second, and Third mesas that were occupied between 1500 and 1700. This strongly recurved rim shape is also frequent on Rio Grande Glaze polychrome pottery (Glaze D and E), suggesting interaction between potters of the Hopi Mesas and the Rio Grande that was not mediated by other media (or only by other media), such as textiles and murals.

SIKYATKI STYLE IN OTHER MEDIA

Some motifs in Sikyatki Polychrome and the Sikyatki style also occur in rock art, but rarely, and rock art and Sikyatki Polychrome do not overlap significantly in repertoire. Many kiva murals, however, contain Sikyatki motifs, and some kiva murals are in the Sikyatki style (Hibben 1975; Hays-Gilpin and LeBlanc 2007; Smith 1952). Murals at Pottery Mound on the Rio Puerco of the East, west of Albuquerque, depict textiles decorated (probably painted) in the Sikyatki style (Hays-Gilpin and LeBlanc 2007), but no actual textiles in the Sikyatki style are known.

PRODUCTION

At least some Sikyatki Polychrome vessels may have been produced by craft specialists. The level of skill demonstrated in forming and finishing large vessels with unusual shapes (effigies, "flying saucer" jars) is unsurpassed. Many Sikyatki Polychrome bowls are thin, well polished, and symmetrical, and even complex recurved rim shapes are well executed. However, all vessels were not produced by master potters (Fig. 5.1, upper right, lower left). Every woman perhaps made her own pottery, and highly skilled potters and their families may have produced a surplus for trade. Because so much detailed ritual iconography appears on some of this pottery, it seems plausible that much of it was painted by male sodality initiates; by older women who had ritual knowledge and responsibilities; by women potters who had specialized craft production and "non-feminine"

ritual roles, such as Nancy of Zuni, who wore men's clothes and danced katsina (Roscoe 1991:26–27); or by males who did some women's work in addition to special ritual roles, such as We'wha, a Zuni *lhamana* (male-bodied woman), who was expert in pottery-making and weaving, both traditionally feminine activities at Zuni (Roscoe 1991:29–73).

ICONOGRAPHY

Elsewhere Hays-Gilpin (2008b) has suggested that Kayenta potters in the thirteenth century made orange ware bowls and white ware jars to express complementary alternating dualities between earth and sky, baskets and cotton textiles, and women's and men's ritual responsibilities. Sikyatki Polychrome brings together earth and sky in the same vessels, particularly birds of the upper world and water of the underworld, along with colors and sounds that evoke katsinas and the agricultural half of the ceremonial year.

SIKYATKI'S DEMISE: SAN BERNARDO POLYCHROME

Perhaps one of the most interesting questions about the Hopi polychrome pottery tradition is what effects the Spanish entrada had on Hopi potters. To what extent did European diseases and Rio Grande refugees impact Hopi potters even before the missions were founded? The mission period brought disease, oppression, and hardship. Colono wares are readily identifiable in the form of plates, candlesticks, and ring-base vessel forms. Spanish and Rio Grande Pueblo motifs appear alongside older Hopi designs. Colton described mission-period polychrome pottery as "crudely executed" (Colton 1956: Ware 7B Type 12). San Bernardo Polychrome, named for the mission founded at Awat'ovi in 1629, tends to be thicker, softer, and more crudely painted than its Sikyatki predecessor. Its paste is siltier, suggesting different clay sources or less clay processing (Capone 1995).

Potters seem to have stopped painting katsina faces on pottery during the mission period, understandable as doing so might have resulted in death or dismemberment. But flowers, butterflies, dragonflies, and other icons of the katsina religion persisted, although flowers took on Spanish and Rio Grande shapes. Persistence of these icons and other features of San Bernardo Polychrome pottery may constitute evidence of covert resistance to Spanish oppression.

CONCLUSION

Prior to about A.D. 1400, widely dispersed communities of potters emphasized their distinct identities in their red ware polychrome traditions, even as they exchanged vessels and the concepts and practices incorporated in those traditions. When the population of the region coalesced on the Hopi Mesas, potters created a striking new style—Sikyatki Polychrome. Sikyatki Polychrome's yellow and red colors; images of flowers, birds, and butterflies; and the bell-like sounds that ring out from its hard, coal-fired paste all evoke the flowery world of the katsinas who danced in the plazas of Pueblo communities (Hays-Gilpin and others 2010:122). In Western Pueblos, practice of katsina religion is open to and binds together community members who nonetheless maintain their own diverse family migration histories. These diverse histories are literally documented in the pottery traditions of the region, whose traces Pueblo people consider to be the footprints of the ancestors on their ancestral landscape.

CHAPTER SIX

Choosing Clays and Painting Pots in the Fourteenth-Century Zuni Region

Suzanne L. Eckert

In this chapter, I focus on the development of Zuni Glaze Ware to argue that the earliest polychromes within this ware reflect two communities of identity within a single community of practice. I show that very little difference exists between the two most common fourteenth-century Zuni Glaze Ware types in terms of vessel size, technological and compositional attributes, regional distributions, design attributes, or exterior slip color. However, interior slip color on the two types is dramatically different. I interpret these findings as reflecting two social groups that had at least two centuries of residency within the Zuni region. I speculate—based on modern Zuni oral tradition and archaeological investigations of Zuni origins—that these two social groups had identities grounded (at least in part) in migrations that occurred generations earlier.

COMMUNITIES OF PRACTICE AND COMMUNITIES OF IDENTITY

Communities of practice are social networks in which potters share a technological tradition. Ethnographically, this tradition is passed down from one generation of potters to another but does not necessarily correspond to a specific type of social unit, such as a village, a culture, or an ethnic group (Stark 2006:25). Multiple communities of practice may exist within a single village, and a single community of practice may exist across multiple villages. Archaeologists working in the American Southwest have linked communities of practice to glaze paint compositions (Huntley 2006), sequence of paint application when decorating a vessel (Van Keuren 2006), suites of technological attributes (Eckert 2008), and suites of technological and decorative attributes (Lyons and Clark, Chapter 3). Often, these variables

are considered to carry "inherent messages about social identity and experience that are not intended by their producers" (Van Keuren 2006:92), and these messages allow archaeologists to identify the social networks in which potters learned their craft.

Communities of identity are social networks in which potters share a group identity (Eckert 2008). Communities of identity are nested, overlapping, and sometimes contradictory. As individuals move between different social situations, they may emphasize membership in the community of identity that most benefits them within a particular social context (Bowser 2000). Further, some social contexts may require an individual to affirm membership in multiple communities of identity simultaneously. Over time, the communities of identity in which an individual belongs may change as the individual moves through life-cycle events or experiences new social situations. Whereas membership in a community of practice often corresponds to unconscious decisions made throughout the production process, membership in a community of identity corresponds to conscious production decisions that would have helped to emphasize or deemphasize group membership within specific social contexts.

The community of practice outlined in Lyons and Clark's discussion of Roosevelt Red Ware in Chapter 3 seems to have also reflected a community of identity based upon ancestral immigration from the Kayenta region. However, there need not be such a perfect correspondence between the two. Multiple communities of practice can exist within a single community of identity, or vice versa. For example, one possible implication of Gilpin and Hays-Gilpin's examination of Sikyatki Polychrome in Chapter 5 is the presence of potters from multiple communities of practice that developed a pottery style that helped to integrate disparate groups into a single community of identity as they settled together onto the Hopi Mesas. In this chapter, I argue for yet another possible social combination as reflected in the earliest Zuni Glaze Ware types: that potters from the same community of practice belonged to multiple communities of identity.

THE ZUNI REGION IN THE FOURTEENTH CENTURY

The prehispanic Zuni region (Fig. 6.1) is commonly defined as the area composed of the modern-day Zuni reservation, the El Morro Valley, and the Jaralosa Draw (Huntley and Kintigh 2004). During the early and middle 1200s, potters throughout the Zuni region produced St. Johns polychrome and bichrome bowls. At about A.D. 1275, local potters developed a Zuni Glaze Ware tradition out of this preceding White Mountain Red Ware tradition (Carlson 1970). This chapter focuses on the social dynamics reflected by the two earliest ceramic types in this glaze ware tradition, Heshotauthla Polychrome and Kwakina Polychrome. These two polychrome types dominated the decorated bowl assemblage in the Zuni region from approximately A.D. 1275 to 1375. The development of the Zuni Glaze Ware tradition occurred in conjunction with a demographic shift, in which residents of the region moved from aggregated room block settlements to large, often planned, nucleated pueblos (Kintigh 1994, 2007).

Researchers working in the Zuni region do not find evidence of a large migration into the area during the thirteenth and fourteenth centuries. Kintigh (2007) argues that settlement patterns from the 1100s through the 1300s suggest only limited immigration into the area over time. Although he does not doubt some immigration occurred into the Zuni region, he states that at the beginning of the 1300s "it is far from clear that migrants made up a large component of the Zuni population" (Kintigh 2007:375). Similarly, Duff (2002) argues that the relatively small amount of pottery moving in or out of the Zuni region during the fourteenth century reflects the population's self-containment during this time. Numerous researchers argue that the strongest evidence for a large migration into the Zuni region is in the early 1400s with the appearance of cremations and the production of Matsaki Buff Ware (Eckert 2005; Kintigh 2000; Mills 2007a; Rinaldo 2008; Schachner 2006; Smith and others 1966). The production of Matsaki Buff Ware—a matte-painted polychrome—quickly replaced the production of Zuni Glaze Ware throughout the Zuni region and represents a major technological break in ceramic production (Schachner 2006).

Within the framework of little to no immigration into the Zuni region prior to the early fifteenth century, I consider how the production of polychrome vessels during the late thirteenth and early fourteenth centuries was informed by, and helped inform on, the development and maintenance of a regional identity in the Zuni area. On the one hand, polychrome pottery was common throughout much of the prehispanic Pueblo world during the thirteenth and fourteenth centuries; on the other hand, residents of the Zuni region developed their own polychrome tradition. Ultimately, our understanding of what it means to have eventually become Zuni within the larger social landscape requires, at least in part, an understanding of the social dynamics behind the origins of Zuni Glaze Ware.

HESHOTAUTHLA POLYCHROME AND KWAKINA POLYCHROME

Following the Woodburys' (Smith and others 1966) descriptions combined with observations made by various colleagues and myself (Eckert 2006) over the years (see also Reed 1955 and the Seventh Southwestern Ceramic Seminar 1965), Heshotauthla and Kwakina Polychrome bowls found in the Zuni region can be summarized as having the following characteristics: (1) both types are tempered with sherds, and both normally have gray or buff pastes; (2) on the exterior, both types are slipped red or orange-red; (3) on the interior, Heshotauthla Polychrome has a red or orange-red slip while Kwakina Polychrome has a white slip; and (4) both types usually have interior bowl designs painted with a glaze or subglaze paint, and exterior designs painted in white paint. Heshotauthla has a glaze-on-red variant and a polychrome variant; the variants are distinguished by the lack of white lines on the exterior of the former and the presence of white lines on the exterior of the latter. I am focusing on the polychrome variant here, as it is by far the more common variant in the Zuni region. The characteristics outlined here describe those that are "typical" of Heshotauthla Polychrome and Kwakina Polychrome. The goal of my analysis is to understand the variation between these two types in terms of attributes that reflect communities of practice and communities of identity present in the fourteenth-century Zuni region. In examining such

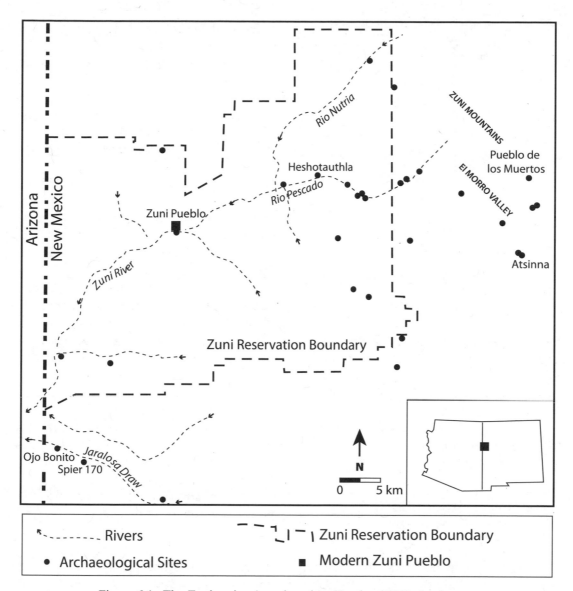

Figure 6.1. The Zuni region (map based on Huntley 2008). Jaralosa
Draw area is in the southwestern portion of the region, modern Zuni
is in the central portion, and El Morro Valley is in the eastern portion.

attributes, I rely primarily on data collected by Andrew Duff (1999, 2002) and Deborah Huntley (2004, 2008) in the course of their dissertation work.

Vessel Size

Prior to examining technological and decorative attributes, I analyzed bowl size to determine if Heshotauthla Polychrome and Kwakina Polychrome bowls could have been used for similar purposes. Combining data from Huntley (2004) with my own work, I examined rim diameters for Kwakina Polychrome and Heshotauthla Polychrome bowls (Fig. 6.2). The two types have similar size distributions, with both types having a majority of bowl diameters that are greater than 24 cm. This pattern follows a similar one in other regions of the Southwest during the early fourteenth century (Mills 2007b; Spielmann 1998), with red-slipped bowls being relatively larger than contemporaneous or previous white-slipped bowls found in the same region. It has been argued that these large bowls were used as serving vessels during feasting events (Graves and Spielmann 2000; Mills

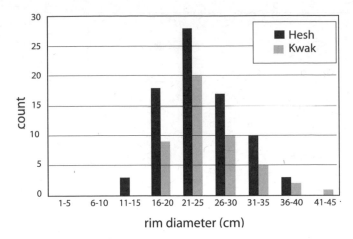

Figure 6.2. Bowl rim diameters for Heshotauthla Polychrome and Kwakina Polychrome sherds recovered in the Zuni region.

2007b; Spielmann 1998), which may have become a more prominent ritual practice as communities across the Pueblo Southwest aggregated into large villages during the thirteenth century and then nucleated in the fourteenth century. Since vessel size and settlement patterns in the Zuni region follow this pattern, I argue that both Heshotauthla Polychrome and Kwakina Polychrome were used in feasting events.

Technological Attributes and Compositional Data

Technological attributes are associated with decisions made during the production process and reflect the Pueblo potter's community of practice. Decisions such as how to choose and prepare clay or what tempering material to use are learned by young apprentice potters from experienced women within groups of potters who routinely work together or regularly watch each other work. And once learned, these techniques are normally conserved throughout the lifetime of the Pueblo potter, regardless of whom she may marry or what village she may reside in. Although potters producing Heshotauthla Polychrome and Kwakina Polychrome in the Zuni region had a range of clays to choose from (Mills 2007a), they consistently chose clays that refire to lighter hues. There are no differences between the two ceramic types in terms of how well the clays were processed or how the clays were tempered. Petrographic examination shows that both types were produced using

well-mixed, well-cleaned clays and that they were tempered with sherd-tempered sherd.

Compositional analyses relying on Instrumental Neutron Activation Analysis (INAA) confirm the similarities observed in the technological attributes. Although focused on slightly different regions and samples, Duff (1999, 2002) and Huntley (2004, 2008) were able to define compositional groups within their INAA data and then argue that there were at least four ceramic production loci within the Zuni region. Although Duff and Huntley looked at numerous pottery types over time, here I focus only on their data for the Heshotauthla Polychrome and Kwakina Polychrome found in the Zuni region. Using the same suite of statistical techniques that they used, I recreated their compositional groups. My results were consistent with their analyses of larger datasets, and I was able to define four compositional groups. However, there is no separation by type (Fig. 6.3). Both ceramic types were produced over the entire Zuni region, including all the production loci as defined by Duff and Huntley.

Another way to consider these data is through regional distributions. If regional distribution is considered in terms of production loci, it becomes clear that both Heshotauthla Polychrome and Kwakina Polychrome were made and moved across the Zuni region, but in different proportions (Fig. 6.4).

Potters not only learn how to prepare clay for ceramic production from other potters, they also learn paint recipes within their community of practice (Huntley 2006). After examining glaze paint composition data from glazes in St. Johns and Heshotauthla glaze-on-red and polychrome and Kwakina Polychrome, Huntley (2008) argues that, over time, potters in the Zuni area changed from a relatively high copper glaze paint to a relatively high lead glaze paint (Huntley 2008). She further argues that, for the time period examined here, there are "no indications that distinctive glaze paint recipes developed among potters residing at particular pueblos" (2008:59). Using her electron microprobe data for only Heshotauthla Polychrome and Kwakina Polychrome, I performed k-mean cluster and principal components analyses (Fig. 6.5). Examination of bivariate plots of all oxide combinations reveal with the same results: Heshotauthla Polychrome and Kwakina Polychrome do not separate by glaze paint composition. In other words, the glaze paints on both types use the same basic recipe across the Zuni region.

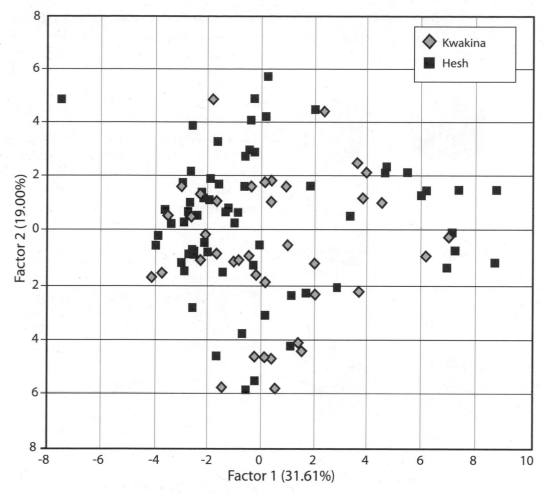

Figure 6.3. PCA factor scores for INAA paste compositional data from Heshotauhtla Polychrome and Kwakina Polychrome sherds recovered in the Zuni region.

Decorative Attributes

While technological attributes reflect communities of practice, many decorative attributes are associated with communities of identity. Through decoration, a prehispanic Pueblo potter could have chosen to emphasize or deemphasize membership in one, or more, communities of identity. These decisions would have been conscious aspects of the production process but may have changed over the life of the potter. When considering decorative attributes, it is important to realize that some decoration may better serve to emphasize specific types of messages than other decoration. Bowser (2002; Bowser and Patton 2004) found that women potters in Conambo, Ecuador, paint exterior designs on a vessel made for use in a public setting so as to be visible across the space

of that public area, whereas they paint interior designs on a vessel to be visible specifically to the individuals using the vessel. I would add that Pueblo potters could have used slip color (Crown 1996), as well as size and placement of painted designs, to emphasize specific messages. With these differences in decorative attributes in mind, I consider the decoration on the exterior and interior of Heshotauthla Polychrome and Kwakina Polychrome bowls.

The exterior decoration on Heshotauthla Polychrome and Kwakina Polychrome is similar, consisting of red slip that often includes geometric banded designs painted in thin white lines. However, sometimes a black glaze line is incorporated with the thin white lines, or there is no exterior design. Rarely, on Kwakina Polychrome, there is a polychrome unit design such as a

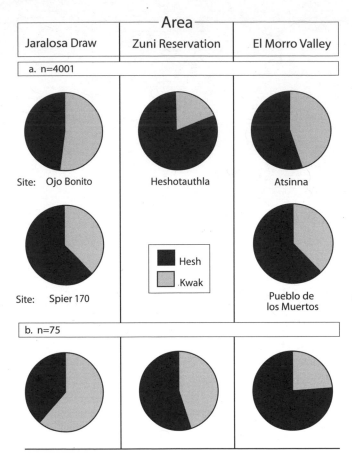

Figure 6.4. Regional distributions of (a) where Heshotauthla Polychrome and Kwakina Polychrome have been recovered and (b) where Heshotauthla and Kwakina Polychrome were produced based on INAA paste compositional data.

butterfly (if this design were to occur on a Heshotauthla Polychrome bowl, it would be typed as Pinedale Polychrome). Three separate analyses of sherd collections by Huntley (2004), Kelly (2009), and myself suggest that there is some subtle variation in exterior decoration. The white lines on the exterior of Kwakina Polychrome bowls have a broader range of thickness; exterior design elements vary more on Kwakina Polychrome than on Heshotauthla Polychrome; and Kwakina Polychrome is more likely to incorporate black glaze on the exterior. Kelly (2009) has argued that there is a temporal component to some of this variation, with Kwakina Polychrome being more diverse earlier in its production sequence. I have observed that there may be a spatial component to some of this variation, with black glaze on the exterior of vessels being more common in the El Morro Valley. How this variation was meaningful to those using and viewing the bowls is difficult to say, especially without a more systematic study of whole vessels. I have no doubt that the exterior design elements were meaningful to those viewing the vessels. However, what is important here is whether or not the exterior design would inform on the interior design, and I would currently argue that it did not. Despite the trend toward more variation in Kwakina Polychrome, I argue that there are very few whole vessels or sherds that an archaeologist could identify by type from the exterior alone, and I suspect that this was also true when the vessel was in use. From a distance, what archaeologists call Heshotauthla Polychrome and Kwakina Polychrome could not have been distinguished.

The interiors of Heshotauthla Polychrome bowls are normally decorated in a banded layout (Eckert 2006). This band is often divided into quarters, and sometimes in thirds and fifths. A paneled layout, rather than a band, has also been observed. Designs are geometrical, often incorporating solid fill (as opposed to hatching), "eyes," lightning, and stepped motifs. In comparison, the interiors of Kwakina Polychrome bowls often have similar layouts and motifs as Heshotauthla Polychrome bowls. However, casual examination of whole vessels suggests that the interiors of Kwakina Polychrome bowls were decorated in a greater variety of layouts (see Figures 39–42 in Smith and others 1966), while sherd data collected by Kelly (2009), Huntley (2004), and myself show a wider variety of motifs on Kwakina Polychrome than on Heshotauthla Polychrome. Overall, then, although Heshotauthla Polychrome and Kwakina Polychrome share a majority of stylistic elements, Kwakina Polychrome seems to have a broader suite of stylistic variability in terms of interior design layout and motifs. This wider variability in Kwakina Polychrome requires more systematic research before it can be properly interpreted.

The one striking difference between Heshotauthla Polychrome and Kwakina Polychrome is interior slip color: the interior of the former is always slipped red or orange-red, whereas the interior of the latter is always slipped white, although some late-fourteenth-century Kwakina Polychrome sherds have a portion of their interior surface slipped red. I discuss the meaning of this one striking difference in decoration in the next section.

Summary

Heshotauthla Polychrome and Kwakina Polychrome were made throughout the Zuni region by potters who

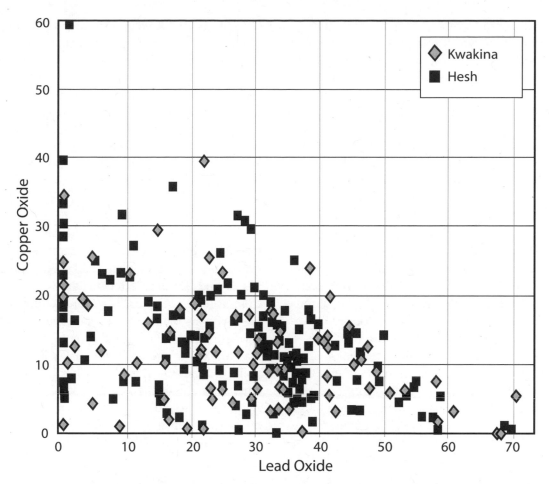

Figure 6.5. Bivariate plot of lead oxide and copper oxide for electron microprobe glaze paint compositional data from Heshotauthla and Kwakina Polychrome sherds recovered in the Zuni region.

had access to the same set of clay resources, knowledge of the same glaze paint recipes, and who shared a tradition of sherd-tempering and clay preparation. Combined, these data point to a shared community of practice among the producers of both types of pottery. Vessel size suggests bowls of both types were used in the same social settings, including probable feasting contexts. I further argue that the similarity of exterior designs suggests a conscious attempt by the painters of these bowls to make the two types indistinguishable from one another when viewed from a distance in these social contexts. Overall, I argue that this suite of data points toward a shared community of practice among potters in the Zuni region, and a conscious attempt at a shared identity as reflected by exterior bowl slip color. Because both pottery types were used in the same social settings, but were slipped differently on the interior, I

assume that the potters who made and presumably decorated Heshotauthla Polychrome were not the same potters who made and decorated Kwakina Polychrome. Further, despite similarities in production tradition and exterior designs, the dramatic difference between these two types in terms of bowl interior slip color suggests that at least two communities of identity were living together in the fourteenth-century Zuni region.

DISCUSSION

Recently, much thought has been given to "Zuni origins" through consideration of the relationships between the Zuni and Mogollon regions (Gregory and Wilcox 2007). Although the connections between these two areas are undeniable, the timing and social nature of such connections are far from clear. In an analysis specifically concerned with the relationship through time between pottery types in the Zuni and Mogollon regions, Mills (2007a:235) found that Mogollon influence on Zuni region pottery is "nearly imperceptible" by A.D. 1000. Rinaldo (2008:132) argued that Zuni region pottery from the Chaco period through the production of Zuni Glaze Ware is a "relatively homogenous craft" with a strong Puerco-Chaco character. Heshotauthla Polychrome and Kwakina Polychrome, then, developed out of a more than 200-year long tradition of pottery production within the area. These types were produced by potters from a shared community of practice as reflected by their similarity in terms of technological attributes and compositional data. Further, as discussed, researchers working in the Zuni region argue that no large migration occurred into the Zuni region until the early fifteenth century, around the time that Heshotauthla Polychrome and Kwakina Polychrome ceased to be produced.

So what were the fourteenth-century residents of the Zuni region doing prior to this fifteenth-century immigration? They were nucleating into villages, producing Heshotauthla and Kwakina Polychrome bowls, and using these bowls in feasting activities at villages throughout the area. Because these two ceramic types look basically identical from a distance, I argue that publicly these vessels were being used to emphasize a shared community of identity. This identity may have been based in a shared language, a shared religion, or a shared social and geographic landscape. The movement of Kwakina Polychrome and Heshotauthla Polychrome between villages throughout the region and over time suggests that residents from different villages participated in semi-regular feasting events that helped reaffirm this community of identity.

However, communities of identity can be situational, nested, overlapping, and even contradictory. Despite a shared community of identity that may have been emphasized in public spaces during feasting events, the residents of the Zuni region also divided themselves into social groups that had their own historical traditions. Considering the importance placed on migration histories and the role such histories play in identity among modern Pueblo peoples (Naranjo 1995), it is not unreasonable to suppose that prehispanic identity in the Zuni region could have been based in part on traditions explaining how different groups originally arrived in the area (even if this arrival was centuries earlier). These different ancestral migration stories would have been an important component of identity. Because Heshotauthla

Polychrome and Kwakina Polychrome were slipped differently on the interior, I argue that these bowls were used to reaffirm different heritages with slip color. Color would have served this purpose better than other design elements on the interior (Crown 1996), as motifs may have been obscured by bowl contents, whereas even a brief glimpse of the interior slip color would have been immediately recognizable.

Colors among modern Pueblo groups are often associated with cardinal direction. As Cushing observed (1896:370), "the north is designated as yellow with the Zunis. . . . The west is known as the blue world. . . . The south is designated as red . . . and for an obvious reason the east is designated white." Interior slip color in prehispanic Zuni region may have had a similar significance.

Cushing (1896) asserted that the Zuni were descended from at least two (possibly more) cultures and argued that one was indigenous to the region while the other was intrusive. Although this notion of "indigenous" may make sense to archaeologists discussing a certain point in time, the Zuni's own origin narratives do not emphasize any of their people emerging in the modern Zuni region. Rather, Zuni oral traditions outline multiple migration pathways from the emergence in the Grand Canyon (Ferguson 2007). Eventually, most of the Zuni reunited at the Middle Place, located at the modern village of Zuni. Although some Zuni made it to the Middle Place before others, Ferguson (2007) has pointed out that the Zuni are far more concerned with tracing movement across the landscape than with determining calendar dates for specific migration events.

To clarify this point, I am not arguing for two immigrant communities living together in the Zuni region in the early fourteenth century. The majority of potters making Heshotauthla Polychrome and Kwakina Polychrome were associated with a single pottery tradition that had developed in the area for two centuries or longer. I am arguing for a situation that is reflected more in modern Zuni identity: a people who share a community of identity, and who view themselves as descended from ancestors who emerged in the Grand Canyon. Clans and religious societies may have traveled along different migration routes to get to the Middle Place, but they were always Zuni. Nested within this community of Zuni identity are communities of identity based in different migration histories—recent or in the distant past, archaeologically detectable or not. And although I am not suggesting a one-to-one correlation with modern Zuni, I am suggesting that archaeologists often fail to recognize that an individual can have synchronous—and possibly contradictory—identities.

In this volume, Lyons and Clark (Chapter 3) discuss a specific type of community of identity—a diasporic community—in which people share an identity based on history, but not space. They argue that Roosevelt Red Ware reflects a community of practice and a community of identity over a broad spatial scale, and that this identity was based upon ancestral origins in a common homeland. Modern Zunis would not consider themselves a diasporic community. Diaspora infers a shared homeland from which the community relocated. The Zuni emerged in the Grand Canyon but then split and several groups followed different routes to their eventual homeland in the Middle Place. Conversely, Hill and his colleagues (2004) discuss coalescent communities, in which people of different cultural backgrounds live within proximity to one another, sharing an identity based on space but not history. They argue that the highly nucleated settlements in the Hohokam region during the fourteenth century reflect such communities. Coalescent community as discussed by Hill and his colleagues infers different ethnicities. Although modern Zuni have social subgroups such as clans and religious sodalities, they all view themselves as being Zuni. Further, they share a similar history in that they all emerged in the Grand Canyon and then migrated to the Middle Place. It is simply the migration pathways that differ.

While my argument for the communities of identity in the fourteenth-century Zuni area share characteristics with both diasporic communities (identities across a region based on origins elsewhere) and coalescent communities (people living within a village but with different migration histories), I argue that, from an *emic* perspective, neither model correctly reflects the social dynamics of the fourteenth-century Zuni region. One problem is that neither model recognizes that potters could have had nested and overlapping identities. Potters producing Heshotauthla Polychrome and Kwakina Polychrome shared an identity, possibly based on language, religion, or a history of two centuries or more of living in the region, which they expressed on the exterior of their vessels. At the same time, they had separate identities, possibly based on different oral traditions about ancestral migrations, which they expressed on the interior of their vessels. In some social situations, individuals may have had to resolve tensions related to having synchronous identities that contradicted one

another. However, on a daily basis, the social reality of overlapping identities would have helped to define an individual's privileges and obligations in the complex social landscape of nucleated village life.

The situation would have changed during the late fourteenth century as immigrant groups began to move into the region. As discussed, numerous researchers in the Zuni region argue that the production of Matsaki Buff Ware is one marker of the arrival of immigrant groups into the region (Smith and others 1966; Kintigh 2000; Eckert 2005; Schachner 2006; Mills 2007a; Rinaldo 2008). If Heshotauthla Polychrome and Kwakina Polychrome correspond broadly to two groups with different historical traditions—such as "ancestral migration from the east" and "ancestral migration from the south"—these broad social divisions may have created a way to integrate newly arrived immigrants into the established social order while still allowing them to hold onto their migration heritage. Zuni historical tradition has multiple clans and religious societies taking several migration pathways, possibly at different times. And, again, although I am not suggesting a one-to-one correlation with modern Zuni, I believe that archaeologists focused on identifying immigrants and indigenous peoples living in a region sometimes forget that newly arrived immigrants stepped into a social situation where the local residents had already been divided into groups. These local groups quite possibly divided themselves based on historical migrations that may have occurred much earlier but were still a strong component of identity. At Zuni, newly arrived immigrants "from the south" could have had immediate social obligations and privileges among local descendants of other immigrants "from the south."

With the onset of Matsaki Buff Ware production, the production of Zuni Glaze Ware quickly declined (Eckert 2006). It is interesting to note that Matsaki Polychrome shares many of the decorative characteristics of Sikyatki Polychrome (Gilpin and Hays-Gilpin, Chapter 5) and seems to have developed within a similar social environment of settlement nucleation and immigration. Given these similarities, it is possible that Matsaki Polychrome was produced by potters from numerous communities of practice and used in social contexts that helped to integrate disparate groups into a single community of identity as they settled together along the Zuni River. This transition from Zuni Glaze Ware-dominated assemblages to Matsaki Buff Ware-dominated assemblages may reflect not only the fluid nature of identity but also a different suite of nested and overlapping identities as potters negotiated their new social landscape.

CONCLUSIONS

Much recent attention has been given to migration in the prehispanic Southwest. Communities of identity, especially nested and overlapping communities of identity, have two implications for these studies. First, archaeologists too often ignore the realities of social identity when trying to interpret material culture. A potter may have been recognized as particularly skilled in her craft, of a certain gender, a mother, a descendant of immigrants from another region, a resident in a specific village, and as a member of certain religious sodalities all at the same time. These multiple social roles would have reflected the overlapping, nested, and contradictory identities such an individual would have had in her daily life, and these identities would have served to define her behavior within different social settings. Any or all of these identities could have been reflected in the material culture produced and used by an individual. Interpreting such information is difficult but it provides us with a richer insight into past social dynamics.

Second, while recent studies of migration in the Southwest have helped us understand the dynamic nature of the prehispanic social landscape, an unfortunate result of these studies is that the "indigenous" population is often treated as a homogeneous social group. In reality, the dynamics between groups within an indigenous population would have had bearing on the political and social landscape into which the immigrants stepped. Further,

we seem to have forgotten that a population referred to as "indigenous" may also have descended from immigrants. Such social histories would have helped characterize the dynamics between newly arrived immigrants and existing populations. Most of the potters living in the fourteenth-century Zuni area and producing Heshot-authla Polychrome and Kwakina Polychrome were probably descendants of potters who had lived in the Zuni area for two centuries or more. On the one hand, these potters may all have recognized themselves as belonging to one people, but on the other hand, this shared identity does not mean that these potters did not continue to honor and recognize their different migration pathways and historical traditions. One way to do this would have been to decorate their bowls in a manner that created reminders of their heritage for others to see. In our search for tracing migrations and identifying immigrant groups in the archaeological record, we need to remember that the time line that drives our assumptions may not be the same time line that was used by the peoples we are attempting to understand.

Acknowledgments

Many thanks to Helen Cole, who did an excellent, last-minute job redrafting all of my figures. I am indebted to Andrew Duff and Deborah Huntley, who were willing to share and discuss the finer points of their datasets with me. Judith Habicht-Mauche, Linda Cordell, David Snow, and Brenda Bowser also provided many thoughtful insights on various drafts of this manuscript that helped to greatly clarify my arguments.

CHAPTER SEVEN

On-ramps to the Glaze Ware Interstate

Ceramic Trade at Pottery Mound Pueblo and Montaño Bridge Pueblo, New Mexico

Hayward H. Franklin and Kari L. Schleher

Many of the chapters in this volume reflect "communities of practice" (Stark 2006) encoded in the production of pottery and the learning framework in which information about how to successfully manufacture pots is transmitted (Blinman and others, Chapter 11; Huntley and others, Chapter 2; Schleher and others, Chapter 10). This chapter, however, focuses on a broader scale of analysis—regional exchange networks. A regional scale of analysis complements studies that focus on local communities of practice in several ways. First, it is necessary to distinguish nonlocal products in order to accurately characterize local practices of pottery production. Secondly, nonlocal pottery may influence local production in different ways. Influence may take the form of simple imitation of some characteristics of imported vessels (Eckert 2008) or be expressed in more complex patterns of mixture of local and imported traits. Most importantly for the current research, regional scale analysis may be an indicator of differences in social ties between communities. These social phenomena can only be understood within a broader context. In summary, in order to fully understand local practices, it is necessary to place them within their broader, regional context.

The archaeological study of the pots that were not made within the local community of practice allows us to reconstruct how communities were linked together in exchange networks. Here we examine imported ceramics, and their corresponding areas of origination, to reconstruct differences in the exchange networks for two sites in the Middle Rio Grande region: Pottery Mound Pueblo (LA 416) and Montaño Bridge Pueblo (LA 33223). We argue that these two contemporary, nearby sites participated in different exchange networks that received imports from different sources, a pattern that has been identified by others elsewhere prehistorically

in the Southwestern United States (Harry and others 2002).

FOCUS OF THIS STUDY

At a typological level, the characteristics of Northern Rio Grande Glaze Ware types are well known. Defined and mapped by Kidder and Shepard (1936) and Mera (1933, 1935, 1940), the glaze ware sequence has been described by the Eighth Southwest Ceramic Seminar (Honea 1966), Snow (1982), Wilson (2005), and Eckert (2006). Because the same glaze ware types are manufactured at many sites, technological or geochemical techniques are essential to parse out location of origin within glaze ware type. At the raw materials level, efforts to delineate production "districts" began with the pioneering work of Anna O. Shepard (1985), who outlined methodology to source pottery to its origin. She also applied this theory to specific Southwestern subregions, including the Rio Grande (Shepard 1936, 1942, 1965). Utilizing optical mineralogy, archaeologists are now able to identify constituent paste and temper materials with increasing confidence, and to trace these back to geographical and geological sources with varying degrees of accuracy. We are able to recognize pottery traded out of its manufacturing area based on the nature of the clays, tempers, or typological characteristics. With an expanding database for comparison, these efforts are increasingly successful.

In this paper, we focus on the exchange of finished pottery and identification of its origins. Our analysis is based on ceramics recovered from two archaeological sites in the Middle Rio Grande area, Pottery Mound (LA 416) and Montaño Bridge (LA 33223). The non-local ceramic assemblages from these contemporary Pueblo

IV (Classic) period sites are compared and contrasted here to elucidate differences in the exchange networks represented.

BASIS FOR COMPARISON

The two archaeological sites used in this comparison are alike in many respects, but different in two notable ways: size and location. Pottery Mound and Montaño Bridge are situated about 72 km apart (Fig. 7.1).

Located on the banks of the lower Rio Puerco, a tributary of the Rio Grande, Pottery Mound is at the southern end of the Middle Rio Grande district (Shepard 1942). Pottery Mound has been the focus of extensive ceramic research through the years, and we now have considerable knowledge of the chronology and typology of its pottery (Brody 1964; Eckert 2003, 2007, 2008; Franklin 2007; Hibben 1955, 1975; C. Schaafsma 2007; Voll 1961). We also are gaining important knowledge about the raw materials used in pottery production at Pottery Mound and about the quantity of glaze ware and utility pottery brought to the settlement from distant production centers (Eckert 2003, 2008; Franklin 2010a; Garrett 1976; Schleher 2010b). Pottery Mound has four dendrochronological dates and three AMS radiocarbon dates (Franklin 2008), dating the occupation to A.D. 1325–1500.

Montaño Bridge Pueblo was a multicomponent site, including a substantial Pueblo IV component, on the west side of the Rio Grande in Albuquerque. Before it was destroyed by bridge construction, Montaño Bridge Pueblo was excavated during several archaeological investigations in the 1980s. Today, the site is under the west-bank approach to the bridge. Earlier research at the site revealed a long occupational history, going back to Basketmaker III times (Gossett and Gossett 1988). More recently, this site has been the subject of a large-scale analysis effort (Raymond 2010). A major locus within the site was a Pueblo IV village, consisting of two or three room blocks (about 20 rooms), and at least one kiva. Although not as extensive as at Pottery Mound, the excavations yielded abundant glaze ware and utility pottery (Franklin 2010b). Judging by the ceramic types, stratigraphic information, and two recent AMS dates from the Pueblo IV occupation, this component also belonged to the Rio Grande Glaze A to D production period, between about A.D. 1300 and 1500.

In summary, these two sites are contemporaneous and both have large samples that were collected under controlled field conditions. Both produced Glazes A to

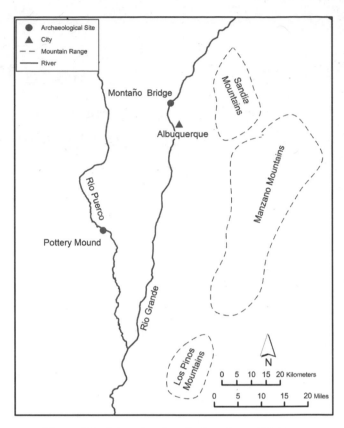

Figure 7.1. Map showing the location of Pottery Mound and Montaño Bridge pueblos.

D, and date to the A.D. 1300 to 1500 period. The sites differ in two respects: first, Montaño Bridge Pueblo was a smaller settlement and may have been a satellite of the nearby Piedras Marcadas, a large Pueblo IV town. Another (and perhaps a more important) difference is that they lie on opposite ends of the Middle Rio Grande cultural zone, raising the question of whether they participated in the same exchange network.

DATA AND METHODS

The Pottery Mound sample consists of sherds recovered from a stratigraphic test in a midden area excavated during the 1979 University of New Mexico field school directed by Linda Cordell (Cordell and others 2008). This collection has also been studied by Suzanne Eckert (Eckert 2003, 2008). Franklin (2010a) analyzed the entire collection of more than 38,500 sherds, recording pottery type, temper, vessel form and portion, and rim dimensions. Temper was identified under a binocular microscope for the majority of the assemblage.

In another project, the nearly 15,000 sherds from Montaño Bridge were studied in the same manner by Franklin (2010b). The Montaño Bridge sample consists of all the ceramics recovered from the Pueblo IV portion of the site during earlier excavations (Gossett and Gossett 1988; Raymond 2010). The recorded variables and methods were the same as for Pottery Mound.

Schleher conducted petrographic analysis on selected samples from both sites (Schleher 2010a, 2010b). A sample of 40 sherds from Pottery Mound and 50 sherds from Montaño Bridge was selected, representing examples from all dominant pottery types and all recognized temper categories. The mineralogical composition of each was noted, and photomicrographs were taken. Petrographic analysis has been demonstrated as a useful means to refine and confirm temper groups identified through binocular analysis (Eckert 2003, 2008; Habicht-Mauche 1993).

Nonlocal ceramics were identified in two ways: typological and compositional. Many intrusive trade pieces can be recognized at the level of pottery type. For example, in some cases, such as the Jeddito and Sikyatki Hopi pottery appearing at Pottery Mound, recognition of an imported vessel is quite straightforward. However, in situations where the trade is "within-type," analysis of paste and temper combinations is required to identify trade wares. For example, recognition of imported utility wares tempered with micaceous schist from sites in the Sandia or Manzano mountains requires microscopic examination of sherd cross-sections to separate it from the local product, which is similar in appearance. Recognition of variability at the sub-type analytical level is essential for identification of ceramic exchange that occurred within the geographical range of a given pottery type or series (such as the Rio Grande Glaze Ware district).

Separation of local from imported specimens was accomplished with confidence in most cases. It is significant that some ceramics that appear "Western" in style may be locally produced copies. Eckert documents this occurrence at Pottery Mound (Eckert 2003, 2008). In this analysis, we have identified these wares as locally made through temper and paste identification. These ceramics are not included in the imported sample.

For many intrusive ceramics, a specific, or at least general, origin was identified through comparison with other published data. In other instances, however, similarity of paste-temper characteristics did not allow a definitive assignment. Specifically, the degree of internal exchange in glaze ware within the Albuquerque Basin is difficult to measure owing to the use of nearly identical red pastes and basalt tempers at many sites. Their separation will require a finer level of analysis by future studies.

Results from typological and technological analyses were tabulated and integrated in order to assess the extent of imported pottery, and the probable sources of the nonlocal ceramics. Large sample sizes allowed us to derive patterns of imported pottery at each site. In addition, source-area reconnaissance for clays and tempers in the vicinity of both sites revealed matches between prehistoric ceramics and natural deposits of clays and tempers in the vicinity of these settlements (Eckert 2003, Franklin 2010a).

QUANTITY AND VARIETY OF CERAMICS

The most obvious characteristic of both assemblages is the overall quantity of ceramics, as well as the diversity of the types and varieties present. At Pottery Mound 38,500 sherds were collected from a 5 m by 5 m test, whereas about 15,000 sherds came from two room blocks and a kiva at Montaño Bridge. The diversity is also large; 38 pottery types have been identified at Pottery Mound, with 22 types at Montaño.

CERAMIC RESOURCES

Potters in the Albuquerque Basin and surrounding areas used a variety of rock materials as temper. Most often, they preferred igneous rocks, either volcanic or plutonic in origin. Petrographic studies have revealed their mineralogical composition in some localities. Variation in these igneous rocks occurs in different parts of the region. Their identities and locations have been recorded geologically by Kelley (1977) and Northrup (1959), and illustrated by the New Mexico Geological Society (1982). Archaeologically, numerous studies have documented use of these rocks as pottery tempers across at least part of the broad area. Based on petrographic analysis of ceramics, areas of production have been documented by numerous researchers (Habicht-Mauche 1993; Nelson and Habicht-Mauche 2006; Shepard 1936, 1942, 1965; Warren 1969a, 1970, 1976, 1979b, 1980).

Present knowledge of temper materials is detailed for some sites and districts but lacking in others. Tempers used by potters at some sites and in some areas have been studied intensively, including Tonque Pueblo (Warren 1969a), San Marcos Pueblo (Nelson and Habicht-Mauche 2006; Schleher 2010c), and the Cochiti areas (Warren 1976, 1979b). However, use of basalt temper across much of the Rio Puerco and central Rio Grande Valley makes separating out production locales for basalt-tempered ceramics more difficult (Eckert 2003, 2008; Schleher and Boyd 2005).

Current information suggests the following about Classic period ceramic production:

1. The central Rio Grande Valley contains red and tan clays, although they remain poorly studied. Volcanic flows immediately to the west of the river were used for basaltic tempers. Sand and mixed rock fragments are available along the river and major tributaries; these were used as temper occasionally.

2. The Lower Puerco contains abundant clay. In the Pottery Mound vicinity, these clays are mainly brick-red, but localized yellow, tan, and olive clays were also used as slips. Here too, volcanic outcrops were used for temper, and a range of vesicular to diabase basalts has been identified in the pottery. Harder basaltic rocks used as temper have been identified as intergranular, diabase, gabbro, and olivine basalts. Other basalts include vesicular (vitric), appearing as either red or black (Eckert 2003, 2008; Franklin 2010a; Garrett 1976).

3. Large Pueblo IV villages in the vicinity of Galisteo Basin made use of red-, buff-, or yellow-firing clays, with the light colors preferred for slips. Tempers are again crushed intermediate igneous rocks, mainly from diorites, monzonites, and latites that outcrop in the area. The hornblende latite ash notable from Tonque (Warren 1969a) and the weathered augite monzonite from San Marcos Pueblo (Nelson and Habicht-Mauche 2006; Schleher 2010c) are well-studied examples.

4. The mountainous area of the Sandia and Manzano mountain ranges to the east of the Rio Grande valley contain veins of micaceous schist, which were valued as pottery temper from Pueblo IV to Historic times. The use of micaceous schist temper, especially in utility ware, is a diagnostic marker. Warren (1980, 1981a) suggested that micaceous schist temper may have been used as a tempering material by potters at Tijeras Pueblo. Clays may be red- or tan-firing, and clays are located near major settlements at Tijeras and Pa'ako.

5. The Bandelier-Pajarito region contains buff-firing pastes and abundant volcanic tuff and pumice that make ideal tempers. These materials are diagnostic markers in the Biscuit Wares (Wilson 2005).

6. Hopi ware from the mesas of northern Arizona was produced with yellow paste and fine sand/sherd (or untempered) (Colton 1956; Fewkes 1973).

7. Acoma and Zuni Glaze Ware are frequently indistinguishable as small sherds. The glaze ware of these pueblos is noted by fine white paste and sherd-sand and finely crushed igneous rock temper (Harlow 1965; Huntley 2008; Seventh Southwestern Ceramic Seminar 1965).

Some clays and tempers lack geographic specificity. Potsherd temper is universally available; it is typical of Acoma and Zuni and in some of the earliest Rio Grande Glaze Ware types. Sand is likewise ubiquitous and was used occasionally by Pueblo IV potters. In other cases, the widespread distribution of desirable materials makes it difficult to pinpoint origins. The use of basalt, primarily vesicular, was commonplace during the Pueblo IV period from the Cochiti area south to the Lower Rio Puerco at Pottery Mound. Separating these basaltic tempers remains a daunting and unresolved issue, which is a promising direction for future research.

IMPORTS AT POTTERY MOUND

Results of recent analyses at Pottery Mound have revealed several facts. First, potters at Pottery Mound produced massive quantities of glaze ware ceramics. Use of red-firing body clays, varied hues of slip clays, and local basalt tempers provided a basis for production. Body clay was obtained from extensive deposits at the village, while the Hidden Mountain lava flow 8 km away was the source for ground stone implements and pottery temper (Eckert 2003, 2008; Franklin 2010a). Both

Table 7.1. Locations of Origin and Quantities of Decorated Imported Pottery

Area of Origin	Pottery Mound		Montaño Bridge	
	n	%	n	%
Glaze ware from Galisteo and Tonque	2	0.3	2271	98.3
Sandia-Manzanos (Tijeras?)	1	0.2	18	0.8
Rio Grande B/w (carbon-painted)	47	7.5	20	0.9
Hopi	222	35.5	0	0.0
Acoma	353	56.5	2	0.1
Total	625	100.0	2311	100.0

the dense diabasic basalt and vesicular basalts were employed as pottery tempers. One slip, a chalky white, is not available locally and had to have been imported, possibly from Acoma or Tijeras trade partners. Major local glaze ware types include Agua Fria Glaze-on-red, Cieneguilla Glaze-on-yellow, San Clemente Glaze Polychrome, Kuaua Glaze Polychrome, and Pottery Mound Glaze Polychrome.

Most imported pottery at Pottery Mound came from the west. Trade orientation was predominantly with Acoma, Zuni, and Hopi pueblos. The strong ceramic connections may also imply a population connection and possibly origin in the Western Pueblos, as has been proposed by other investigators (Brody 1964; Eckert 2003, 2008; Voll 1961). One indication of this influence is the local production of "imitations" of glaze wares from the west. Specifically, certain examples of San Clemente and Kuaua Glaze polychrome employ chalky white slips, slip patterns, and rim forms which had precedence in the West. Resemblances to the Zuni and Acoma Kwakina and Pinnawa types have been noted by Eckert (2003), and again in this study. However, such "copies" contain the typical red pastes and basalt tempers of Pottery Mound production. These local copies of western types are not included in the "imported" category of this study, which is restricted to ceramics of nonlocal manufacture.

White Mountain Red Ware (Carlson 1970), in the form of St. Johns Polychrome, arrived in the Middle Rio Grande in some quantity during the preceding Coalition phase prior to A.D. 1300. The succeeding Classic period pueblos all seem to have small amounts of this type in their earliest levels; Pottery Mound and Montaño are no exception.

The 1979 test collection includes 575 painted sherds from the west, including 353 from Acoma or Zuni

(similar to each other ceramically), and 222 from the Hopi villages (Table 7.1). Acoma-Zuni types recovered at Pottery Mound include Kwakina Polychrome, Pinnawa Glaze-on-white, and some Kechipawan Polychrome. From Hopi came Jeddito Black-on-yellow followed by Sikyatki Polychrome. All these types are contemporary with Pottery Mound, dating to A.D. 1325–1500. The distinctive Hopi pottery is so recognizable that many researchers have noted it. However, the Acoma-Zuni pottery is numerically more common. The surface slips and paints of the Acoma-Zuni types can so closely resemble the local Pottery Mound equivalent glazes that some specimens cannot be correctly identified except by paste and temper identification. The white pastes and sherd and fine-grained-rock tempers of the Acoma-Zuni imports are a clear indicator of imported ware. The green glaze (as opposed to local dense black) of some of the western imports is also indicative of the imported pieces.

The black-on-white types that are second in frequency are either earlier Pueblo III pottery or the continuation of production of white ware into the early glaze ware production period. Socorro Black-on-white, common in the Pueblo III pit houses of the Lower Rio Puerco, appears consistently in the lower strata of Pottery Mound. Imported white wares include Puerco-Escavada, Gallup, and Cebolleta Black-on-white in small quantities. These trade wares from the San Juan Basin and Acoma areas appear at many sites in the Middle Rio Grande region and suggest that ties with the western production centers were strong in the Pueblo II and Pueblo III periods, as well as in the later Pueblo IV glaze ware period.

Abiquiu Black-on-gray and Bandelier Black-on-gray (the Biscuit Wares) are evidence of trade with the large proto-Tewa towns on the upper Rio Grande-Chama drainages (Habicht-Mauche 1993; Mera 1935). There,

Table 7.2. Locations of Origin and Quantities of Imported Utility Pottery

Area of Origin	Pottery Mound		Montaño Bridge	
	n	%	n	%
Tonque and Galisteo Basin	0	0.0	1677	46.2
Sandia-Manzanos (Tijeras?)	29	30.9	1951	53.8
Acoma-Zuni and Hopi	65	69.1	0	0.0
Total	94	100.0	3628	100.0

large towns produced abundant carbon-painted white ware that shows up in small amounts in the glaze ware villages to the south. However, surprisingly little of this pottery reached Pottery Mound; only 42 sherds were found. The small amounts of these types come as a surprise, since large amounts were being made as close as 95 to 130 km to the north. This contrasts with much larger amounts of Western Pueblo pottery arriving from as far as 400 km to the west.

Imports from another production area, the Galisteo Basin, are likewise minor. A few pieces of Largo and Espinoso bichromes and polychromes were seen, but only a handful. The distinctive buff pastes and hornblende latite and augite monzonite tempers appear only rarely at Pottery Mound. Here again, production centers to the north are not well represented in the imported collection at Pottery Mound.

Several painted Casas Grandes sherds have been identified at Pottery Mound (David Phillips, personal communication). Together with a copper bell and macaw depictions on kiva murals, these give evidence of contact with northern Mexico.

Finally, internal trade between the closer pueblos of the Middle Rio Grande must also have brought ceramics to Pottery Mound. Surely trade with Valencia (Franklin 1997) and other nearby Pueblo IV villages on the Rio Grande must have been frequent. Unfortunately, use of similar red-firing clays matched with basalt tempers makes identification of these imports difficult at this time.

Utility pottery at Pottery Mound underwent the area-wide transition from corrugated styles to obliterated coils to plain gray surfaces. Locally, red clays were mixed with several basalts and mixed sands or sandstones in utility ware production. Nevertheless, ceramic importation is apparent here also (Table 7.2); 4 percent of the utility assemblage is nonlocal. Distinctive schist-tempered utility ware was brought from Tijeras or other mountain villages to the east. Schist-tempered

utility pottery represents only 3 percent of all utility wares, however. No verified utility ware imports from the Galisteo Basin or the Biscuit Ware regions have been identified. The major painted ware trade with the west is also mirrored by imports of utility wares from the same districts. Some 48 Acoma-Zuni plain and corrugated, and 17 Hopi, utility sherds are identified. As with the decorated imports, Acoma-Zuni utility outnumbers the Hopi wares. The arrival of utility as well as painted wares from these distant locations implies that all kinds of pottery arrived, not simply the "pretty" ones.

IMPORTS AT MONTAÑO BRIDGE

The Montaño collection also yielded the typical glaze ware types of the Middle Rio Grande area. The Agua Fria, Cieneguilla, and San Clemente types found there are all locally produced, either at the village or in other nearby riverine pueblos. However, little San Clemente and no Kuaua or Pottery Mound Polychrome is seen at the Montaño Bridge Pueblo. In addition to the ubiquitous Glaze A red and yellow slipped bichromes, Montaño revealed some classic Glaze B (Largo series) and Glaze C (Espinoso Polychrome). These types are scarce at Pottery Mound, but frequent at Montaño. This suggests strong ties with settlements to the northeast in the Galisteo Basin, where these types were popular.

Local production at Montaño is marked by red-firing clays and basalt tempers, similar to Pottery Mound. Abundant basalt lies less than 3.2 km to the west at the lava escarpment, and clays were available under the Santa Fe gravels of the West Mesa (Kelley 1977). Sand and sand-sherd tempers likewise may be local, or are non-specific. No major sources of schistose rock or intermediate igneous rocks are currently seen in the vicinity.

More than 99 percent of all painted pottery at the site falls within the Rio Grande Glaze Ware series, but that does not imply that it was all produced locally. Therefore, glaze ware imports are identified at Montaño using temper and paste rather than pottery type. Binocular microscopy initially revealed that a substantial portion of the glaze ware, and some of the utility ware as well, contained intermediate igneous rocks. Some were clearly hornblende latite ash, distinctive and traceable to Tonque Pueblo (Warren 1969a). Further examination via petrography refined this group and revealed specific identifications of augite latite, augite monzonite, hornblende latite, and hornblende latite ash (Schleher 2010a). These rock types are generally typical of the Galisteo Basin pueblos and Tonque Pueblo, and specific examples can be traced petrographically to San Marcos and Tonque pueblos.

While local basalt- and diabase-tempered glaze ware remained popular, constituting 43.9 percent of the glaze wares at the Montaño Bridge Pueblo, significant amounts of other tempers are present. A few glaze-on-red examples contain mica flakes and sherd temper and may have come from Tijeras Pueblo or other villages near the Sandia Mountains to the east. Equally small amounts of mixed sand or rock fragments could be local or could have come from anywhere. Nearly 50 percent of the glaze ware sherds contained clays and tempers traceable to Tonque and the Galisteo Basin area (Table 6.1). Petrographic identifications by Schleher indicate that some sherds were traceable to San Marcos Pueblo, with 9.6 percent identifiable as being from Tonque Pueblo. Although it is not possible to specifically identify the pottery made at every Galisteo Basin pueblo in this group, it is clear that glaze ware from several major towns in that area are included. The fact that up to half of the glaze ware contains tempers typically associated with pueblos to the north and east is remarkable.

In sum, imported decorated ceramics at the Montaño Bridge Pueblo consist almost exclusively of Rio Grande Glaze Ware types. Almost 50 percent of the total glaze ware sample (2,271 sherds) have paste and temper signatures suggesting manufacture elsewhere. Some of these sherds are identified as pottery made at Tonque or San Marcos, with the remainder likely from other Galisteo Basin towns. Aside from this, decorated imports are very rare. Only four Biscuit Ware sherds were found, despite the proximity of Biscuit Ware-producing centers to the north. The paucity of these types echoes the pattern at Pottery Mound. Also, as at Pottery Mound, the persistence of minor amounts of Socorro and Santa Fe Black-on-white, together with small amounts of Cibola White Ware, are interpreted as evidence of earlier occupation at Montaño, since pre-Pueblo IV components exist at this site. Notably absent, however, are trade wares from the west; essentially no Acoma, Zuni, or Hopi wares reached Montaño.

Utility ware at Montaño consisted of late corrugated and plain-surfaced Pueblo IV jars used for cooking and transport. Typically, these were made with red- or tan-firing clay tempered with basalts, reminiscent of the local glaze ware and the practices at Pottery Mound already noted. Sand and mixed rock makes up 12 percent of Montaño utility temper, and a few have sherd temper. These are non-specific and may or may not have been made locally.

However, 16.3 percent of utility ware sherds contain intermediate igneous rocks of several kinds, reflecting their popularity in the glaze ware. At least some of these tempers are traceable to sources at Tonque and the Galisteo Basin area. The import of substantial amounts of utility pottery from the same sources as the decorated intrusives is indicted (Table 7.2). Trade was not confined to painted wares only.

The other striking feature of the Montaño utility assemblage is the large amount of pottery tempered with micaceous schist, or schist and rock combinations. Nearly 2,000 sherds (19.5 percent of all utility ware) have mica schist as the dominant temper. It is readily identifiable with the binocular scope, and often with the naked eye. No schistose rock is available in the Montaño vicinity, and these utility vessels are massively tempered with this rock so they must be imported. Again, the most likely known source is Tijeras Pueblo, about 80 km away (Cordell 1980, Warren 1980). Although only a few glaze ware sherds seem to have come from this area, large quantities of utility ware were brought from the Sandia Mountains or Tijeras. In this unusual case, utility ware imports greatly exceed decorated imports from a given source. The presence of schist-tempered utility has been noted at other Pueblo IV glaze ware sites in the Albuquerque Basin (Warren 1981b), and the subject requires further study because there may be sources other than Tijeras Pueblo.

Therefore, most utility, as well as glaze ware, was made from local materials. But 16.3 percent contained intermediate igneous rocks typical of the general Galisteo-Tonque area. In addition, nearly 20 percent of all utility ware contained a distinctive schist temper referable to Tijeras Canyon or other Sandia or Manzano mountain sites. No Montaño Bridge Pueblo utility ware was identified as imported from the Biscuit Ware region or the Western Pueblos.

Table 7.3. Montaño Bridge Temper Usage by Slip Color and Time (Expressed as Percentage)

Glaze Period	Pottery Type	Intermediate igneous rock	Hornblende latite	All basalt	Other	Total %
A	Agua Fria Glaze-on-red	43	1	45	11	100
A	Cieneguilla Glaze-on-yellow	66	0	32	2	100
B	Largo Glaze-on-yellow	69	14	17	0	100
B	Largo Glaze Polychrome	43	43	14	0	100
C	Espinoso Glaze Polychrome	24	64	12	0	100

CONCLUSIONS

Pottery Mound and Montaño Bridge Pueblo were occupied concurrently in the A.D. 1300–1500 period. Glaze ware manufacture at both towns started with Glaze A production and ceased early in the Glaze D production period. Many of the local pottery types are the same, especially during the Glaze A production period, suggesting there was a basic cultural cohesion early in the Pueblo IV period. Thereafter, the indigenous glaze ware types deviated increasingly across the Middle Rio Grande culture area. Types popular in the Socorro-Pottery Mound area to the south began to differ from those made in the northern area, especially as the dominance of the Galisteo Basin pueblos increased during Glaze B and C production periods at Montaño Bridge.

Ceramics at Pottery Mound as Compared to Montaño Bridge Pueblo

Despite their similar general cultural identities, it is clear that Pottery Mound and the Montaño Bridge Pueblo participated in different exchange systems. Aside from the common glaze types made in identical ways, the imported trade wares seem to be drastically different. The divergent directions and quantities of imported ceramics are summarized in Tables 7.1 and 7.2. Only the imported ceramics, and their sources, are shown in these two tables.

Decorated imports at Pottery Mound derive mainly from the west, including Acoma-Zuni (56.5 percent) and Hopi (35.5 percent) sources (Table 7.1). In total, 575 pieces (92 percent of all decorated imports) arrived from the Western Pueblos. Small amounts of Biscuit Ware also appear, but only tiny amounts of glazed pottery from the Galisteo Basin or Tonque region. Clearly, trade orientation was much more powerful to the west

than to the north. Western influence affected not only ceramics, but also kiva art (Crotty 2007; Hibben 1975; P. Schaafsma 2007).

Montaño, on the other hand, has imports that are recognizable mostly at the variety rather than pottery-type level of analysis. Differing in paste-temper attributes, these glaze wares originate almost totally from the Galisteo-Tonque centers to the northeast. Based on temper-paste identification, as many as 2,271 glaze sherds may have come from this general region. This represents 50.7 percent of total decorated ware, or 98.3 percent of imported painted pottery (Table 7.1). As with Pottery Mound, surprisingly small amounts of Biscuit Ware were imported. Only a few glaze ware sherds were tentatively assigned to Tijeras Pueblo or other Sandia Mountain sources, and almost none to Western Pueblo origins.

Based on glaze ware rim forms, import of ceramics from the northeast increased through time. Table 7.3 shows temper type by chronological rim form at Montaño. The Glaze A though Glaze C rims indicate there was a definite increase in hornblende latite and hornblende latite ash tempers through time. This corresponds to the increasing size and influence of population centers of the Galisteo-Tonque region during this period. It also reflects the decline of Tijeras Pueblo, which occurred after A.D. 1425 at the end of the Glaze A period (Cordell 1979, 1980).

The paucity of Biscuit Ware at Pottery Mound and the Montaño Bridge Pueblo may reflect a general lack of import of this series into the Albuquerque Basin. Although large towns in the Pajarito Plateau-Bandelier area produced this carbon-painted ware at this time, very little of it reached the glaze ware villages to the south. Cultural or linguistic barriers may have restricted ceramic trade.

The extent of glaze ware trade within the immediate Albuquerque production zone remains uncertain, as do connections to the Salinas pueblos. Future research should focus on finer degrees of materials separation between sites sharing the same pottery types and even the same temper-paste categories.

Most utility ware was produced with basalt tempers at both centers. However, the nonlocal utility assemblage again shows a contrast (Table 7.2). Pottery Mound received only 94 utility sherds from sources outside the immediate vicinity. Most ($n = 65$) came from Western Pueblo sources, along with the abundant glaze ware imports from that area. A smaller number ($n = 29$) contained mica schist indicative of Tijeras Pueblo or other mountain sites origin. None was definitely assigned to the Galisteo region, in accordance with the general lack of glaze ware intrusives from there.

At the Montaño Bridge Pueblo, however, a different pattern emerges. Here, large amounts of utility ware were brought in, comprising Galisteo and Tijeras area corrugated and plain wares. A total of 1,677 sherds (16.3 percent of all utility ware or 46.2 percent of imported utility ware) arrived from the Galisteo-Tonque region. Even more was brought from Tijeras or other mountain pueblos. Some 1,951 sherds (19.2 percent of all utility or 53.8 percent of intrusive utility) contain micaceous schist typical of that district. In all, nearly a third of all utility ware was imported from external sources. The data illustrate that trade in utility pottery was common at both sites, although it is especially evident in the case of the Montaño Bridge Pueblo.

Large quantities of utilitarian pottery were transported to distant population centers that made the same kind of vessels. This raises the question of whether items carried in these vessels may have been the desired objects, rather than the pottery itself. Bringing essentially the same kinds of utilitarian vessels to a village that already produced them would not seem to offer any advantage. But, the transport of pinyon nuts or other products from different environmental zones might have been the major motivation. Trade in perishables must have accompanied trade in ceramics alone, but we are left with only the ceramic part of the story. Exchange of goods between high and low elevation zones may have played an important role (Cordell 1979).

Distance Considerations

Finally, the extensive ceramic trade took place over great distances. Some of these distances are illustrated from Pottery Mound in Table 7.4. Some pottery at Pottery Mound was imported from distances as much as 600 km. The Hopi Mesas and Paquimé are the most distant locations represented in the collection. On the other hand, olivella shells arrived from the Gulf of California, an equally long distance. Interestingly, the quantity of imports is not related directly to distance. Hopi pottery from 415 km away arrived at Pottery Mound consistently over time, but only a few sherds of Biscuit Ware come from major population centers only 100 km to the north. A model of "distance-decay," in which trade item quantities would decrease in relation to distance, clearly does not apply here. Social ties and possible cultural origins played a larger role in trade routes than sheer distance.

At the Montaño Bridge Pueblo, the strong links to Sandia Mountain villages and the Galisteo Basin, over distances of 80 to 175 km, is remarkable. Large amounts of pottery were brought from both areas. The lack of Western Pueblo contact stands in contrast to the situation at Pottery Mound. Here again, though, essentially no Biscuit Ware was imported, even though those sources are no farther away than the ones involved with consistent trade with Montaño. Clearly the communities of exchange in which residents at Pottery Mound and the Montaño Bridge Pueblo participated were more related to social obligations and networks than they were to convenience or distance.

Summary

These results lead us to several conclusions:

1. Origins and quantities of imported pottery may differ dramatically between contemporary Pueblo IV towns, even in the same geographical district. Pottery Mound and the Montaño Bridge Pueblo, both located in the Middle Rio Grande District, yet on different river drainages, have substantially different imported pottery assemblages. Harry and her colleagues (2002:106) have documented a similar pattern, with differences in ceramic exchange networks demonstrated for sites within the same Hohokam community.

2. Movement of pottery was not confined to decorated ceramics; it involved utility ware as well. There was import of utility pots at both Pottery Mound and Montaño Bridge pueblos.

Table 7.4. Approximate Distances from Pottery Mound to Major Trading Centers via Modern Roads

Modern town	Ceramic Wares	Miles	Kilometers
Acoma Pueblo, NM	Acoma glazes	67	108
Zuni Pueblo, NM	Zuni glazes	179	289
Hopi (Second Mesa), AZ	Hopi yellow wares	257	415
St. Johns, AZ	White Mountain Red Ware	235	379
Tijeras, NM	Glaze A wares	50	81
Santa Fe, NM	Glaze A-D wares	90	145
Galisteo, NM	Galisteo Basin glazes	110	177
Espanola, NM	Biscuit Ware	115	185
Casas Grandes, Mexico	Paquimé ceramics	381	615

3. Other goods undoubtedly traveled with, or in, such containers, especially when crosscutting environmental zones.

4. The direction and intensity of trade is not directly related to distance. Instead, the strength of social or preexisting cultural ties between settlements determined the direction of contacts. Ties with the west, as suggested by Eckert (2003, 2008) for ceramics, and by Crotty (2007) and P. Schaafsma (2007) for kiva murals, may be related to ancestral ties, and continued trade with those areas for residents at Pottery Mound.

The exchange networks for Pottery Mound and the Montaño Bridge Pueblo are dramatically different for two sites within the Middle Rio Grande District. Social ties for Pottery Mound are almost exclusively with the west, while Montaño residents interacted most closely with villages to the north and east. It may be that networks along watersheds and drainages are more significant than simple spatial proximity. This comparison suggests few similarities in exchange partners at the two sites examined here.

Research Directions

These conclusions suggest related lines of inquiry. Although we have measured import of ceramics, the export of locally made ceramics from these two sites to other areas is unknown. Pottery Mound Polychrome, for instance, seems to be a specialized local product of that site, with almost no export to other towns.

Likewise, import of ceramic raw materials remains an untested possibility at both sites. Although prehistoric mining and distribution of glaze paints is a subject of much interest currently (Huntley and others, Chapter 2), the specific origin of the glaze paints at these two sites remains unknown. Similarly, slip clays, often limited in geologic distribution, are also likely to have been exchanged. For example, the use of nonlocal white slip clays by Pottery Mound potters may indicate import of rare slip materials, perhaps from Acoma or Tijeras Pueblo. Furthermore, the routes and social networks associated with the transport of these raw materials may not have been the same ones along which finished pottery traveled.

Finally, the precise routes and mechanics of this trade remain elusive. Were there major organized routes with "on-ramps" at each town or village? Or did the exchange travel over a web of less-organized routes in an informal fashion? Such questions remain for further research.

Acknowledgments

We wish to acknowledge the assistance of the Maxwell Museum for access to collections, and funding for the petrographic analysis. Thanks also to Audrey Salem, who made the map for this chapter.

CHAPTER EIGHT

The Right Ingredients

Southern Cerrillos Hills Lead in Paint on Pajarito Plateau-Produced Glaze-Painted Pottery

Diane Curewitz and Sheila Goff

The development of glaze paint during the late thirteenth century for use in pottery decoration was a significant transition in ceramic technology in the Southwestern United States, especially in the northern and middle Rio Grande, Little Colorado, and Zuni regions. Its widespread production, exchange, and use most likely played an important role in constructing and maintaining social, economic, and ritual interactions among diverse individuals, households, and communities coming together in large aggregated pueblos during this period (Cordell 1997, 2006; Crown 1994; Futrell 1998; Graves and Eckert 1998; Habicht-Mauche 1993, 1995, 1998; Nelson and Habicht-Mauche 2006; Snow 1981; Spielmann 1998).

According to Stark (2006:23), "potters do not make their goods in a cultural void, nor do consumers use pots in a social vacuum." As do other authors in this volume, we find the concept of communities of practice helpful in understanding the dynamics of ceramic production. In our case, we are interested in ceramic production on the Pajarito Plateau in the northern Rio Grande during the Classic period (A.D. 1325 to 1600 or 1700). Lave and Wenger (1991:98) characterize communities of practice as a set of relations among persons, an activity, and the world over time and in relation to other tangential and overlapping communities. Participants in particular communities of practice share common meanings of activities and artifacts.

In the northern and middle Rio Grande during the Classic period, multiple and overlapping communities of practice emerged with respect to glaze ware production; some centered on choice of slip color or decorative elements in the manufacture of glaze-painted pottery while others were formed around acquisition of raw materials, such as lead for use in glaze paint or a particular temper

to add to clay. Communities of practice varied in size, and their members consisted of individuals with diverse culture histories.

Our collaborative research contributes to this volume in two ways. First, we provide new petrographic and stable lead isotopic data from Pajarito Plateau sites (Fig. 8.1) that strongly support our hypothesis of local production and exchange of Classic period glaze paint ware by prehispanic potters. These new data shed light on the communities of practice to which potters on the Pajarito belonged. Second, our research demonstrates that Parajito potters had ties with communities in the Galisteo Basin. Shortly after glaze-paint technology appeared in the middle and northern Rio Grande Valley, some Pajarito potters chose to be part of the larger community of practice. They adopted the new tradition, produced glaze-painted pottery, and exchanged it with residents on and off the Plateau, including those in the Galisteo Basin. These Pajarito potters appear to have preferred the use of lead ore from the southern Cerrillos Hills in their glaze paint recipes. In choosing this particular source of lead ore, they became part of another, overlapping, community of practice. This aspect of social interaction for the Pajarito Plateau has not been previously established.

GLAZE PAINT WARE PRODUCTION AND EXCHANGE IN THE MIDDLE RIO GRANDE REGION

Glaze-painted pottery was first produced in the Zuni and Little Colorado region as early as A.D. 1275 (Huntley 2006) before spreading to the Rio Grande pueblos around A.D. 1300 as imports or copies. Eckert (2006) presents the most recent chronology of glaze-painted

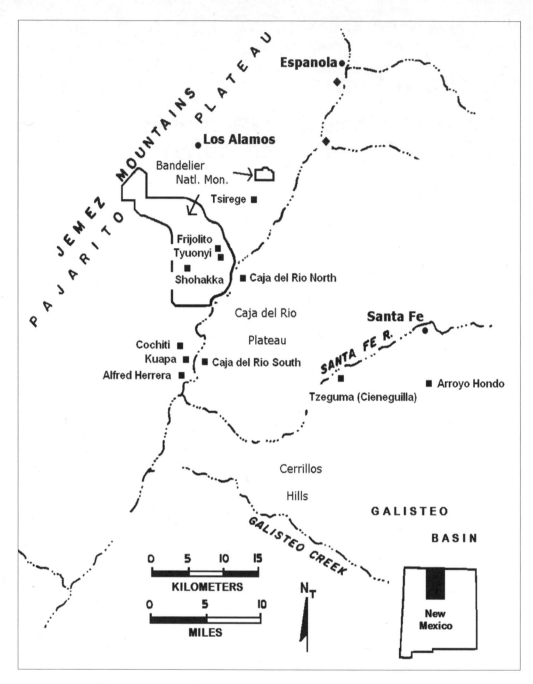

Figure 8.1. Location of archaeological sites discussed in chapter.

pottery production and suggests production may have started somewhat earlier. Within a generation or two, however, it became the dominant serving ware in some areas, almost completely replacing black-on-white wares. Potters in the Zuni region appear to have stopped producing glaze-painted pottery in the 1400s (Huntley 2006), whereas the Rio Grande potters continued production well into the 1600s or 1700s (Schachner 2006).

Shepard's (1942) study of Rio Grande glaze paint ware, focusing on temper characterization, demonstrated trends over time in production locations and exchange. Early Glaze A and Glaze B were first produced in the Albuquerque, Zia, and Santo Domingo areas. Intermediate Glaze C and Glaze D were produced mainly in the Galisteo Basin pueblos, and late Glaze E and Glaze F production was decentralized, occurring at numerous pueblos throughout the Rio Grande region. Subsequent studies have increased our understanding of production and exchange, and petrographic studies specifically suggest a greater number of early glaze-painted pottery production centers than Shepard realized (Crown 1994; Eckert 2003; Futrell 1998; Graves and Eckert 1998; Habicht-Mauche 1993, 1995, 1998; Habicht-Mauche and others 2006; Snow 1981; Spielmann 1998; Warren 1969a, 1970, 1979b). Within Shepard's trade districts, specific villages such as San Marcos (LA 98) or Tonque (LA 240) may have dominated glaze-painted pottery production and possibly distribution of raw materials, such as the lead used in the paint (Habicht-Mauche and others 2000; Nelson and Habicht-Mauche 2006; Warren 1969a, 1979b).

Glaze-painted pottery played an important role in social dynamics during the Classic period as migration and reorganization altered the social landscape (Habicht-Mauche and others 2006). These ceramics appear to have been an important component of community feasting, facilitating social interaction and integration (Spielmann 1998), and they were more extensively exchanged than earlier black-on-white wares (Habicht-Mauche 1993). Travel for the purposes of feasting and exchange of goods or raw materials may have been an integral part of the ceremonial system, giving ritual a role in redistribution of goods, the social integration of producer and consumer groups, the spread of ideas and technology, and the reinforcement of interaction patterns and ritual celebration.

Eckert (2003) and Spielmann (1998) used the higher proportion of serving ware to cooking or storage ware and an increased percentage of large bowls to demonstrate that feasting was well established by the Classic period, when an increase in feasting is thought to have integrated social groups above the household level. At the large towns in the northern Rio Grande, as in other areas of the Southwest, we see evidence of ritual architecture in the form of enclosed and partially enclosed plazas containing small and large kivas, as well as very large cooking and serving vessels. Increased communal feasting required food preparation and serving vessels that met performance, and possibly ideological, requirements (Dietler 2001; Graves 1996; Hayden 2001; Mills 2007b; Potter 1997a, 1997b, 2000; Snow 1981; Spielmann 1998, 2002). Goods required in the expression of a new ideology and transmission of ritual knowledge, including glaze-painted pottery, could have become necessary and valuable (Mills 2003; Spielmann

2002). The expansion of the communal feasting system during the Classic period would have conferred added social value on the serving and cooking vessels used during these occasions, increased demand for them, and stimulated increased production.

The adoption of glaze-painted pottery throughout much of the Rio Grande region created a large community of practice made up of people with different culture histories living together in large aggregated settlements. The members of this community of practice understood and shared the technological and decorative attributes of ceramic production and use. Community members devised ways to participate in the glaze paint tradition, while at the same time maintaining and signaling their individual cultural identity (Bernardini 1998; Duff 1998; Eckert 2003; Futrell 1998; Graves and Eckert 1998; LeBlanc 1998; Spielmann 1998; Triadan 1998).

The reorganization that swept the Rio Grande Valley impacted the Pajarito Plateau as well, as population increased and the aggregation begun in the Coalition period continued. This reorganization included the production and exchange of glaze-painted pottery. Shepard (1942), building on previous work by Kidder (1915) and Mera (1940), identified two Pajarito glaze ware production districts: the Southern Pajarito and the Northern Pajarito. The southern district included Frijolito (LA 78), Yapashi (LA 250), San Miguel/Ha'atsi (LA 370), Kuapa (LA 3444), and Cochiti (LA 295). The northern district included Rainbow House/Rito de las Frijoles (LA 217), Tyuonyi (LA 82), Puye (LA 47), Tsankawi (LA 211), and Tsirege (LA 170). At the latter two sites, however, Biscuit Ware, a black-on-white ware produced during the Classic period, dominates. This ware is one of a suite of diagnostics often used to distinguish a second cultural group living on the Pajarito (Futrell 1998; Graves and Eckert 1998; Kidder 1915). Glaze ware found at Biscuit Ware sites is most likely the result of trade (Powers and Orcutt 1999).

Early studies of glaze-painted pottery on the Pajarito focused on the late production period, at Puye in particular, when Shepard (1942) identified large amounts of Glaze E and F with a distinctive temper sourced to the Pajarito that she called devitrified tuff. More recent studies (Capone 2006; Nelson and Habicht-Mauche 2006; Orcutt 1999; Preucel and Capone 2002; Vint 1999; Warren 1979b) provide evidence for glaze paint ware production at other Pajarito sites, such as San Miguel/Ha'atse, Yapashi, Kuapa, Rainbow House/Rito de los Frijoles, Cochiti, and Tyuonyi during the early and intermediate production periods as well. Tyuonyi, in the central part of the Pajarito, appears to have been not only a production center for glaze paint ware throughout the Classic period but also a center of exchange and interaction. Both glaze-painted pottery from the Galisteo Basin and Biscuit Ware from northern Pajarito and Chama sites were imported into Tyuonyi. Our research, reported below, provides additional evidence that Pajarito potters in Frijoles Canyon at Shohakka Pueblo (LA 3840), Tyuonyi Annex (LA 60550), Caja del Rio South (LA 5137), and Caja del Rio North (LA 174) made glaze paint ware early in the Classic period and used the same southern Cerrillos Hills lead in their glazes as potters at Galisteo Basin sites.

IMPORTANCE OF SOURCING LEAD IN GLAZE PAINT

The identification of the sources of the lead used in glaze paint recipes allows us to examine the movement and acquisition of lead, or pigment containing lead, throughout the glaze paint ware production region. This provides an avenue for understanding production and exchange of Classic period glaze-painted pottery in the middle and northern Rio Grande (Habicht-Mauche and others 2000, 2002; Huntley 2006; Nelson and Habicht-Mauche 2006). Judith Habicht-Mauche and colleagues (2000, 2002) developed a technique for identifying lead from specific areas, using Inductively Coupled Plasma Mass Spectrometry (ICP-MS) to determine its stable isotopic composition. Lead from each source has a distinct stable isotopic "fingerprint," which is not affected by firing or weathering of the glazes. Stable lead isotopic studies (Habicht-Mauche and others 2000, 2002; Huntley 2006; Nelson and Habicht-Mauche 2006) have determined that lead used in the early glazes from the Zuni region (Heshotauthla and Kwakina Polychromes and their precursor, St. Johns Polychrome) most likely came from the southern Cerrillos Hills in the Galisteo Basin near San Marcos Pueblo and was transported up to 320 km west to the Zuni region. Zuni-region potters used Cerrillos lead for about 100 years but they eventually modified their glaze recipes and lead sources, and later stopped glaze paint ware production altogether (Huntley 2006).

Habicht-Mauche and others (2000, 2002) studied the intermediate glazes in the Rio Grande pueblos, finding that the lead in the glaze paint from various Galisteo Basin sites also came from the southern Cerrillos Hills,

even though a source in the northern Cerrillos Hills was closer. The source of lead used in the glaze paint from the Pajarito Plateau, including Kuapa, near Cochiti, was investigated by Nelson and Habicht-Mauche (2006). They found that the lead in the glazes thought to have been produced at Kuapa also came from the southern mining district in the Cerrillos Hills, although ore deposits in the northern Cerrillos would have been closer. Nelson and Habicht-Mauche concluded that potters' preferences and the resulting networks were more important than ease of procurement. San Marcos Pueblo, in the Galisteo Basin, may have controlled, but not restricted, access to these preferred lead sources.

The potters who procured lead from the southern Cerrillos Hills for use in their glazes constituted a community of practice nested within the larger community of practice that produced glaze paint ware. Echoing questions posed by Cordell and Habicht-Mauche (Chapter 1), we ask why choosing a lead source matters. The decision may have been for technological reasons because a particular lead was known to produce successful glazes. The choice may also have been ideological. Ethnographic data and oral traditions indicate that the Cerrillos Hills are sacred to the Zuni, the first producers of glaze-painted pottery (Ferguson and Hart 1985), and raw materials from a sacred area often take on a similar significance (Cordell 2006). Additionally, veins of galena near the surface in the Cerrillos Hills are found in proximity to turquoise mines, which were significant in the Pueblo world (Judge 1989; Mathien 1985, 1997, 2001; Plog 2003; Weigand and Harbottle 1993). Finally, the ideological significance of lead may have dated to earlier times. Galena cubes from as-yet-unidentified sources have been found in numerous ritual contexts at Pueblo I sites in the northern San Juan and Chaco Canyon (Judd 1954, 1959; Mathien 1985; Morris 1939; Pepper 1996; Windes and Ford 1992; Yunker and Wilshusen 2000). Power relationships between San Marcos and other pueblos may have been another reason for the use of this particular lead.

PAJARITO PLATEAU GEOLOGY

Our first task was to determine that the glaze-painted pottery used in our study had been produced on the Pajarito Plateau. This required understanding the geologic history and surficial geology of the northern Rio Grande, particularly the Pajarito Plateau and the Galisteo Basin. The Pajarito Plateau is bounded by the Jemez Mountains on the west, the Rio Grande on the east, Santa Clara Canyon on the north, and Cochiti Canyon on the south. This land form was created by the generation of the Rio Grande Rift, beginning about 35 million years ago, and the volcanism of the Jemez Mountains, beginning about 16 million years ago (see Broxton and others 2008).

Basalts from the Pliocene Cerros del Rio volcano system on the east side of the Rio Grande form the basal layer of the Pajarito Plateau (Broxton and Reneau 1996). A range of volcanic eruption types is exposed close to the Rio Grande at the lower end of Frijoles and Los Alamos canyons, including tuff deposits, maar deposits, and fine-grained rhyolites, andesites, and basalts. The red and black scoria found in ceramics made in Frijoles Canyon and Cochiti Pueblo are cited by Warren (1979b) as evidence of glaze ware production on the Pajarito Plateau.

During Pliocene eruptions, the Rio Grande was periodically dammed by the Cerros del Rio basalt flows, creating large lakes where alluvial clay deposits formed. These clay deposits were subsequently exposed when the basalt dams broke. The dam breaks also created huge debris flows that brought sand, gravel, cobbles, Pedernal cherts, and boulders of granites, quartzites, andesites from the Puye Formation deposits of the Espanola Basin to the north. These deposits were later exposed by canyons cutting into the Bandelier Tuff (Reneau and Dethier 1996; Reneau and others 1996).

The Bandelier Tuff deposits were formed in several eruptions from the Jemez Caldera during the formation of the Jemez Mountains. The Otowi Member or Lower Bandelier Tuff was produced during the first major eruption, beginning about 1.6 million years ago. The second major eruption, about 1.2 million years ago, produced the Tshirege or Upper Bandelier Tuff. Each eruption began with ashfall pulses that spread east and west, depending on the wind direction. Deposits up to 3 m thick are found as far as 20 km from the Jemez Caldera, and a deposit 10 cm thick has been found 300 km away in Socorro (Dunbar 2005; Self and others 1996). These deposits are rhyolitic tuffs that have varying concentrations of feldspars and hornblende in some units, which can be distinguished through chemical analysis (Stimac 1996). Eruptions of ignimbrite, or tuff, followed the initial Plinian ashfall events. The Lower Bandelier Tuff is approximately 180 m thick and the Upper Bandelier Tuff is 250 m thick.

The Galisteo Basin, about 30 km south of Santa Fe, lies to the east of the Rio Grande between the Sangre de Cristo Mountains to the northeast and the Sandia Mountains to the southwest. There are three different geologic zones within the basin. The upper watershed drains the Sangre de Cristo Mountains and consists of shallow alluvium, exposed Precambrian rocks, and Triassic rock outcrops. The central portion of the basin, eastward from La Bajada, consists of sedimentary formations with intruding volcanic rocks, including the Ortiz Mountains and the Cerrillos Hills. The lower watershed, along the Galisteo Creek, consists largely of sands, gravels, clays, and silts of the Santa Fe Group (New Mexico Energy, Minerals, and Natural Resources Department 2008:36–37). Intermediate igneous rocks are found east of the Rio Grande in the Espinaso Formation of the Galisteo Basin. These include granitic monzonite and volcanic latite, both of which contain augite (a pyroxene) and hornblende (an amphibole).

METHODOLOGY

We conducted two types of analyses to better understand the communities of practice to which Pajarito glaze-painted potters belonged. The geologic history and composition of the Pajarito Plateau and the Galisteo Basin were used to determine the production locale for sherds recovered at Pajarito Plateau sites. First, we conducted petrographic thin-section analysis of Rio Grande glaze ware ceramic pastes found in the sherds. Tempers were identified, described, and compared with rock samples collected on the Pajarito by Curewitz (2008) from outcroppings located within a reasonable distance of possible production sites, such as Tyuonyi, Frijolito, Caja del Rio North, and Caja del Rio South (Arnold 1985).

An initial temper characterization study suggested Glaze A, C, D, and E were produced on the Pajarito Plateau (Goff 2009). All of the samples in that study were submitted for stable lead isotopic analysis to determine the source of the lead used in the paint recipes. These studies were conducted by Sarah Ginn and Judith Habicht-Mauche (2005) at the Ceramic Material Research Laboratory at the Department of Anthropology at the University of California, Santa Cruz. In additional studies, Curewitz (2008) matched the Glaze A and C sherds (Eckert 2006; Mera 1933) that were tempered with red or black scoria to geologic deposits on the Pajarito, and determined that those ceramics were produced there. A subset of this ceramic sample was submitted to Garret Hart at the Geoanalytical Laboratory at Washington State University for lead isotope studies, following the method established by Habicht-Mauche and colleagues (2000, 2002). Habicht-Mauche has developed a large database with the distinct lead isotopic signatures of the Southwestern lead sources available to prehispanic potters. By comparing the signatures with those in our sample, we were able to determine the source of lead in our samples.

We did not include sherds tempered mainly with other types of extrusive igneous rocks, such as fine crystalline, vesicular, or intergranular basalt. Basalts are found from the Pajarito Plateau south to the Lower Puerco in the Rio Grande Valley, and sourcing them can be challenging. Warren (1968:192), working at the Alfred Herrera site (LA 6455) near Cochiti, pointed out that "basalt flows and dikes are widespread throughout the upper Rio Grande region, so that many sources were available to the prehistoric potters." Basalt textures vary, and multiple textures can be found within a particular flow. We limited our subsample to sherds tempered mainly with red and black scoria exhibiting the same texture and mineral inclusions as Frijoles Canyon geologic samples to increase confidence in the results of our petrographic studies.

Scoria is "a pyroclastic rock that is generally highly vesicular or cellular, dark in color, and partly glass and partly crystalline" (Warren 1968:191). Shepard (1942) included scoria and cinders in her category "vitrophyric basalt." In sherds, the fragments are irregular to angular and dull or slightly glassy. Fine vesicles can be seen with a binocular microscope or hand lens. Both red scoria and black scoria are found in glaze ware sherds in the northern Rio Grande. Scoria and various basalts are often found together in these sherds, suggesting that the different textures may be found in the same outcrop. Several sherds show particles where scoria grades into vesicular basalt, as Warren (1968:191) noted at Cochiti.

PRELIMINARY TEMPER AND LEAD STUDIES FOR PAJARITO PLATEAU GLAZE-PAINTED POTTERY

Goff (2009) initially analyzed ten Glaze A, C, D, and E sherds from Frijolito and Tsirege, the two Pajarito sites that were part of Shepard's (1942) extensive Rio Grande glaze ware study (Table 8.1). Shepard (1936), using Kidder's system, had originally classified these sherds as types I, III, IV, and V. The sherds are curated in the Anna O. Shepard Collection at the University of Colorado Museum of Natural History. Petrographic analysis of sherd and rock in these sherds determined that eight of them could be matched with geologic deposits on the Pajarito Plateau. Four sherds, all Glaze A, contain distinctive basalts found at Bandelier National Monument. A coarse intergranular basalt found east of Tyuonyi occurs in one sherd from Frijolito and another from Tsirege. A vesicular basalt or scoria from Lower Falls, farther east on the Frijoles Canyon Trail, is also found in one sherd from Frijolito and another from Tsirege. Four others (one Glaze A, two Glaze D, and one Glaze E) contain the distinct tuff temper specific to the Pajarito. The final two sherds contain an augite porphyry (Glaze C) and a hornblende porphyry (Glaze D). Based on our understanding of the geological environment, we think these deposits are found on the Pajarito Plateau, although this remains to be confirmed through chemical analysis.

The composition of tempers in this sample suggests that Pajarito potters at Frijolito produced glaze-painted pottery from the early period of production through the late period. Because Tsirege is currently considered to be a Biscuit Ware production site, the glaze-painted sherds in the sample recovered at Tsirege most likely arrived there through exchange (Powers and Orcutt 1999).

In order to establish ties between Pajarito producers of glaze paint ware and the larger network of glaze paint ware producers in the Rio Grande Valley, Goff had lead isotopic studies conducted on paint from the ten voucher sherds from Shepard's collection (Fig. 8.2). The stable lead isotopic analysis of this sample indicated that the measured isotopic ratios of glaze paints from the Pajarito sherds were "remarkably uniform" and that the southern Cerrillos Hills, near San Marcos Pueblo, was the "most likely source of the ore favored by these Pajarito potters to produce glaze paints" (Ginn and Habicht-Mauche 2005). There was some overlap with the Magdelena District signature, prompting additional analyses. These verified that the ores most closely matched the lead evolution line associated with the southern Cerrillos ore source.

ADDITIONAL STUDIES OF PAJARITO PLATEAU GLAZE-PAINTED POTTERY

With funding from the New Mexico Archaeological Council, we submitted 29 additional glaze-painted sherds from Pajarito Plateau sites to the Geoanalytical

Table 8.1. Temper Characterization for Sherds from Pajarito Sites (Goff)

Sample	Frijolito (LA 78)	Tsirege (LA 170)
Intergranular Basalt (1002-19) Glaze A	1	1
Intergranular Basalt (1002-19) Glaze C)	1	1
1002-18 (Red Scoria)	-	-
Augite Porphyry Glaze C	-	1
Devitrified Tuff Glaze A	-	1
Devitrified Tuff Glaze D	-	2
Devitrified Tuff Glaze E	-	1
Hornblende Porphyry Glaze D	-	1
Total	2	8

Laboratory at Washington State University for ICP-MS analysis of the lead isotope ratios to confirm these findings and determine the extent to which southern Cerrillos Hills lead was used in Pajarito glazes (Table 8.2). The sample consisted of 24 scoria-tempered Glaze A bowl rim sherds and 5 scoria-tempered Glaze C bowl rim sherds. Temper studies comparing geological samples taken from volcanic deposits at Bandelier National Monument with lithic inclusions in pottery found at Bandelier and nearby sites strongly support local production and long-distance exchange of glaze-painted ware by Pajarito Plateau potters (Curewitz 2008).

Garret Hart prepared the samples and conducted the analysis following the procedure developed by Habicht-Mauche and others (2002). The samples are mainly from Tyuonyi at Bandelier National Monument. Samples were included from two other sites at Bandelier (Shohakka Pueblo and the Tyuonyi Annex), two sites directly across the Rio Grande from Bandelier (Caja del Rio South and Caja del Rio North), and one site on the northern edge of the Galisteo Basin (Tzeguma or Cieneguilla [LA 16]). All sherds contained either red or black scoria or a combination of the vesicular basalt and scoria found within a kilometer of Tyuonyi at Bandelier. Most sherds from this sample contained some vesicular basalt in addition to scoria, as the two are often found in the same deposit. In a few cases, the vesicular basalt dominated, with lesser but significant amounts of scoria.

Hart obtained results from 28 of the samples (the twenty-ninth sample returned a signal too low to measure). The results for the Glaze A and Glaze C samples generally cluster very tightly within the parameters that define southern Cerrillos Hills lead (Figures 8.3 and 8.4). One outlier, however, resembles an archaeological sample of galena ore found at Quarai Pueblo southeast of Albuquerque. In addition to providing support for the initial results obtained by Goff (2009), the inclusion of Glaze C samples in this analysis shows that the use of lead from the southern Cerrillos Hills in the paint on vessels made on the Pajarito Plateau persisted through time and across space.

Curewitz (2008) examined the mechanical and design attributes of local and nonlocal Glaze A ($n = 287$) and Glaze C ($n = 43$) bowl rims at five Pajarito sites and one large northern Galisteo Basin site. She then correlated these attributes with production locale using temper type. Glaze-painted bowls tempered with scoria from local deposits are assumed to have been produced on or very near the Pajarito Plateau, whereas basalt-tempered vessels may have come from many different locations in the northern Rio Grande; those containing monzonite and latite are assumed to have come from production sites near the Espinaso volcanic deposits in the Galisteo Basin. Chi-square analysis indicates a significant and moderately strong association between area and temper for Glaze A rim sherds *(df* = 2; $x^2 = 71.983$; *p* = < 0.0001; *V* = 0.5043). The majority of Glaze A rims found at Pajarito sites contain local scoria, while the majority at Tzeguma contain intermediate igneous rock from the Galisteo Basin.

The mechanical attributes include bowl sizes, sherd thickness, and rim form. The research showed that mechanical attributes of Glaze A produced on the Pajarito do not vary considerably from Glaze A produced in the Galisteo Basin.

Design attributes show additional differences associated with temper type. Design attributes include slip color, design elements, and framing line width and placement. These differences strongly suggest that scoria-tempered Glaze A sherds with red slip on both interior and exterior surfaces were made on the Pajarito Plateau and exchanged to Galisteo Basin sites such as Tzeguma.

For instance, chi-square analyses show significant but not strong associations between color, temper, and geographic area. Red-slipped rims in both areas are most often tempered with scoria, whereas yellow-slipped rims at Pajarito sites are most often tempered with scoria and those at Tzeguma most often contain intermediate igneous rock. In addition, the exchange of vessels with these different color combinations was asymmetrical: a larger proportion of red-slipped, scoria-tempered bowls moved from the Pajarito Plateau to the Galisteo Basin than yellow-slipped, latite- or monzonite-tempered bowls moved in the other direction.

The width of framing lines on Glaze A bowls also supports production differences. Scoria-tempered Glaze A bowl rims have the lowest framing-line variability (below 30%). Basalt-tempered bowl rims, which were probably made in a large number of locations, have the highest (above 40%). Rims containing monzonite and latite fall in between.

Fewer Glaze C vessels were made on the Pajarito Plateau, but these were also red-slipped and almost none of them moved to Tzeguma. In contrast, many yellow-slipped Glaze C vessels containing latite and monzonite temper are found on the Pajarito Plateau. Temper in Glaze C sherds is associated with area (Fisher's Exact $p = 0.0208$), but only exterior color is associated with temper type in any significant manner ($p = 0.0120$). Glaze C has different dominant slip color combinations than Glaze A. Yellow-slipped interiors dominate both Pajarito sites and Tzeguma, but exteriors at Pajarito sites are more likely to be red-slipped, while exteriors at Tzeguma are more likely to be yellow.

Exterior designs and framing lines, which are rare on Glaze A, appear on Glaze C. At the same time, exterior designs also appear on Biscuit Ware, another ceramic tradition that is sometimes used to distinguish a second linguistic or cultural group inhabiting the Pajarito Plateau at this time. Rim figures, which are common on

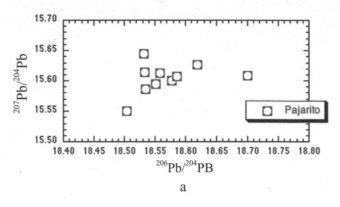

a

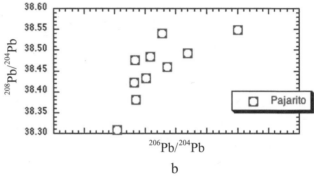

b

Figure 8.2 (a) Stable lead isotope ratios from glaze paint on sherds from the Pajarito Plateau, $^{207}Pb/^{204}Pb:^{206}Pb/^{204}Pb$ (Goff). (b) Stable lead isotope ratios from glaze paint on sherds from the Pajarito Plateau, $^{208}Pb/^{204}Pb:^{206}Pb/^{204}Pb$ (Goff).

both early and later Biscuit Ware, are also more common on Glaze C than on Glaze A. These changes in decorative style, and particularly the use of exterior decoration, suggest that large Glaze C bowls were used by larger groups at ceremonial feasts, where the visibility of designs would be critical in conveying ritual identity (Mills 2007b).

DISCUSSION

In the Southwestern United States, the Classic period was a time of great change. It has been suggested that the formation of new and multiple communities of practice allowed people to more easily negotiate these changes. A variety of communities of practice developed in association with the production of glaze-painted pottery, and these were focused on shared manufacturing techniques, raw material acquisition and exchange, and shared use of color and decorative elements.

Studies reported in this chapter indicate the participation of some Pajarito potters in two of these communities

Table 8.2. Temper Characterization for Sherds from Pajarito Sites (Curewitz)

Sample	Tyuonyi (LA 82)	Shohakka (LA 3840)	Tyuonyi Annex (LA 60550)	Caja del Rio South (LA 5137)	Caja del Rio North (LA 174)	Tzeguma (LA 16)
Intergranular Basalt (1002-19) Glaze A	-	-	-	-	-	-
Intergranular Basalt (1002-19) Glaze C	-	-	-	-	-	-
Vesicular Basalt/Scoria (1002-04) Glaze A	2	-	-	-	-	1
Vesicular Basalt/Scoria (1002-04) Glaze C	1	-	-	-	-	0
Red Scoria (1002-18)	10	4	1	1	2	3
Red Scoria (1002-18) Glaze C	3	-	-	-	-	1
Total	16	4	1	1	2	5

of practice, and demonstrate ties between Galisteo Basin potters and Pajarito Plateau potters. Pajarito potters participated in a large community of practice that employed standard manufacturing and decorative techniques to produce, use, and exchange glaze-painted pottery that demonstrated their identity. At the same time, Pajarito potters belonged to a second, smaller community of practice that used southern Cerrillos Hills lead in their glaze paint.

Production and exchange of finished ceramics, as well as raw materials, need to be situated within the context of the larger social and political system of the time. The model that most closely describes what we see is that of Bohannon (1967), in which multiple exchange networks operate at different levels of organization (termed multi-centric), with no one person or group controlling exchange transactions.

Habicht-Mauche (2000:217) suggests that most northern Rio Grande Classic-period economic decision making probably occurred at the household level. In no case is there evidence of regional managerial entities, central control, or the conspicuous consumption that is a hallmark of prestige and power. Communal feasting in the northern Rio Grande probably functioned primarily to strengthen alliances and cooperation within and between communities, rather than to promote economic gain or sumptuary display (see Hayden 2001: Figure 2.1). Certain imported goods were socially necessary, and were used to signal community membership. A diversity of goods would allow people to demonstrate membership in a number of crosscutting social groups. In the situations of "rapid social and political change" (Smith 1999:109–110) that often precede an increase in social complexity, membership in multiple groups increased the potential for survival and reduced risk. The desire for diverse goods would stimulate the production of exchange items, and this contributed to social complexity.

CONCLUSIONS

Curewitz's (2008) temper studies provided additional evidence supporting production of glaze-painted pottery on the Pajarito Plateau. They also demonstrated that vessels were exchanged between production locales within the northern Rio Grande: large and small Glaze A glaze-painted bowls containing intermediate-igneous rock temper moved from the Galisteo Basin to the Pajarito Plateau, while large scoria-tempered Glaze A bowls moved in the opposite direction. Glaze C bowls—mainly large—moved from the Galisteo to the Pajarito, while small Glaze C bowls were made on the Pajarito but not exchanged.

The aspect of social interaction we have discussed here—the exchange of raw materials for ceramic production—has not been previously established for the Pajarito Plateau. Goff's (2009) sourcing study of the lead in glaze-painted sherds from the Pajarito Plateau, supplemented with our study of a larger sample of sherds from additional sites, provides evidence of the role of exchange in maintaining and creating networks among large Pueblo villages in the fourteenth and fifteenth centuries. Our research supports the role of Rio Grande glaze paint ware as an integrative element during the Classic period social reorganization.

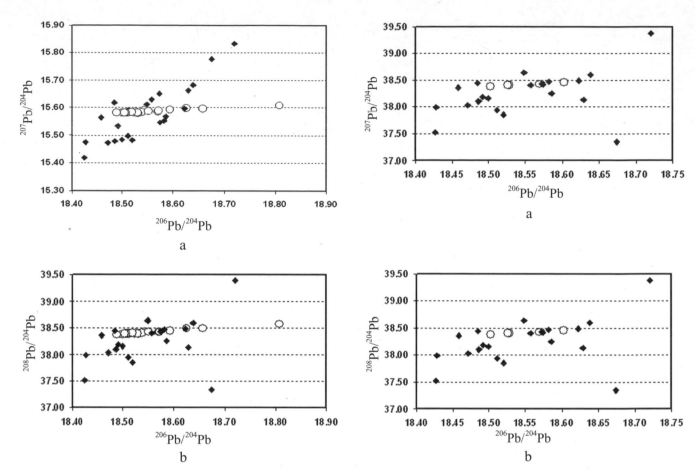

Figure 8.3   (a) Stable lead isotope ratios from Glaze A sherds from the Pajarito Plateau, $^{207}Pb/^{204}Pb:^{206}Pb/^{204}Pb$ (Goff and Curewitz). (b) Stable lead isotope ratios from Glaze A sherds from the Pajarito Plateau, $^{208}Pb/^{204}Pb:^{206}Pb/^{204}Pb$ (Goff and Curewitz). In both plots, black diamonds represent southern Cerrillos Hills ores; open circles represent Pajarito glazes.

Figure 8.4   (a) Stable lead isotope ratios from Glaze C sherds from the Pajarito Plateau $^{207}Pb/^{204}Pb:^{206}Pb/^{204}Pb$ (Goff and Curewitz). (b) Stable lead isotope ratios from Glaze C sherds from the Pajarito Plateau $^{208}Pb/^{204}Pb:^{206}Pb/^{204}Pb$ (Goff and Curewitz). In both plots, black diamonds represent southern Cerrillos Hills ores; open circles represent Pajarito glazes.

Our results demonstrate the use of southern Cerrillos Hills lead in glaze paint on the Pajarito Plateau. This strongly suggests that Pajarito ceramic producers were part of a network of potters who considered paint containing lead from this source to have social, ritual, and economic significance. The initial use of lead from the southern Cerrillos Hills, and its persistence over time, may have been based on technological, traditional, or ritual reasons that indicate shared belief systems among glaze paint ware producers in the Rio Grande Glaze Ware region.

It is significant that Pajarito potters chose to and were able to obtain southern Cerrillos Hills lead from a distance of 60 to 80 km, rather than using lead from other, closer sources. It indicates that these Pajarito potters were part of a larger community of potters who accessed this particular lead either directly or through exchange.

The potential for temper and lead isotopic studies on glaze paint ware from Pajarito sites to tease out finer details concerning production and exchange networks between sites on the Pajarito and between the Pajarito and other areas of the Rio Grande Valley should be obvious. Glaze paint ware and the importance of southern Cerrillos Hills lead in its production clearly are central to understanding the dynamics of the Classic period of reorganization.

CHAPTER NINE

Cieneguilla Glaze-on-Yellow

Temporal Measurement and Learning Traditions at San Marcos Pueblo, North-Central New Mexico

Ann F. Ramenofsky

In American culture history, tradition and horizon are the largest scale concepts that integrate time and space and that demonstrate cultural continuity (Willey and Phillips 1958). Both concepts rely on design styles to group archaeological expressions into larger cultural units. Horizons link styles spatially, and traditions link them temporally. Although vastly different than the recent community of practice framework, they share an underlying principle. Culture historians assume that stylistic similarity within traditions is due to shared cultural learning (Van Hoose 2008), and community of practice is shared learning. Theorists employ the framework to explain some of the causes of sharing (Habicht-Mauche and others 2006; Huntley and others, Chapter 2). Technologies have style (Lechtman 1977), and if a technology persists, artisans are choosing to produce that particular technology. For artifacts such as metal or ceramics with complex production sequences, the steps typically require direct learning.

This discussion weaves together the traditional concept of style with community of practice in the analysis of one form of the glaze paint ceramic tradition, Cieneguilla Glaze-on-yellow. I employ frequency seriation, a touchstone of chronology building in culture history, to determine the temporal behavior of Cieneguilla Glaze-on-yellow at one source location, San Marcos Pueblo (Schleher and others, Chapter 10).

San Marcos is culturally aligned with the other Galisteo Basin towns, but it is not located in the basin. It is geographically situated just west of the basin on the Santa Fe Plateau, within 8 km of the Cerrillos Hills (Fig. 9.1). The occupation of San Marcos began in the fourteenth century and terminated with the Pueblo Revolt of 1680. The long time span makes it possible to assess the temporality of Cieneguilla Glaze-on-yellow in relation to the other glaze-painted types from the pueblo. Throughout the occupation of San Marcos, potters at the pueblo were players in the glaze paint story, producing and exporting their products. Galena from the Cerrillos Hills was the flux San Marcoseños employed in their glaze paint recipes (Curewitz and Goff, Chapter 8; Herhahn 2006; Huntley and others 2007, and Chapter 2; Nelson and Habicht-Mauche 2006; Schleher and others, Chapter 10).

Seriation is a useful archaeological method for assessing the temporal or stylistic behavior of Cieneguilla Glaze-on-yellow. It is ordinal in scale and based on a model that requires all types in a single seriation to conform to some part of a unimodal curve. If a type does not conform to that model, then it has a different temporality than the other types in the seriation. It is not temporally sensitive at the same scale as the other types.

In the San Marcos case, I show that Cieneguilla Glaze-on-yellow does not meet the requirements of the seriation model (Dunnell 1970; Ford 1962). It does not seriate, meaning that the temporality of Cieneguilla Glaze-on-yellow is different than the other glaze paint types in the seriation. On the other hand, because the type persists through multiple episodes of abandonment and reoccupation at the pueblo, it is a significant indicator of the learning networks with embedded social meaning through the many generations of potters of San Marcos.

From the onset of research on the glaze paint wares, culture historians believed that the glazes were temporal types that represented a single regional ceramic tradition. The technology of producing glaze paint ceramics was transferred from the skilled to the unskilled across multiple pueblos up and down the Rio Grande.

Based on his work at Pecos Pueblo, Kidder (1917; Kidder and Shepard 1936) defined the glaze typology

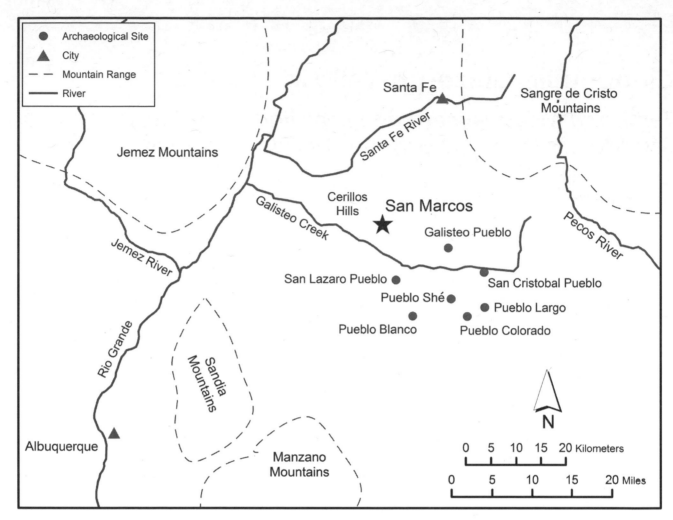

Figure 9.1. Aggregated pueblos in the Galisteo Basin.

as composed of six glaze types (I–VI) (Schleher and others, Chapter 10). He assumed that one type replaced another in an uninterrupted sequence that began in the mid-fourteenth century and continued until the Pueblo Revolt in the late seventeenth century (Ramenofsky and Feathers 2002). Mera (1933), working in the Rio Grande corridor with glaze ceramics from many more settlements, modified Kidder's classification into Glaze types A through F. He subdivided these into smaller units based on rim shape, slip color, and design. Cieneguilla Glaze-on-yellow was defined as one form of the earliest-produced glaze paint type, Glaze A. Like Kidder, Mera did not question the temporality or the linear replacement of the types, but he pushed the assumptions further by associating tree-ring dates with the types. Later still, the assumptions gained further support as more tree-ring dates accumulated and were used to estimate the

duration of the glaze paint types (Breternitz 1966; Eckert 2006; Vint 1999) (Table 9.1). By the late twentieth century, the temporal order of the glaze paint types was so widely accepted that the types became index fossils. The discovery of two or more of these types during survey or excavation became a coarse-grained temporal method for estimating the age of individual structures or even sites.

The assumption of the linear sequence of one glaze type replacing another has been questioned (Ramenofsky and Feathers 2002; Snow 1997). Archaeologists working south of Albuquerque have shown that Glaze A Red (Agua Fria Glaze-on-red) was produced across the entire temporal interval of the glaze paints (Hayes and others 1981; Marshall 1987; Shepard 1942). Snow (1997) recorded Glaze A rims co-occurring with Glaze F rims at Las Humanas, suggesting the persistence of an assumed early form into the seventeenth century. Moreover, the timing of the appearance of a new glaze technology—a type—in one region may not be applicable to all regions. The technology of production is time transgressive both spatially and temporally (Creamer and others 2002).

Although this analysis is restricted to a single place, understanding the temporality of Cieneguilla Glaze-on-yellow at San Marcos is significant not only in its own right but for questions of agency and exchange. Because San Marcos potters produced and exported their glaze paint ceramics, knowing the temporal envelope of Cieneguilla Glaze-on-yellow production at San Marcos has implications for the duration of exchange and interaction outside the pueblo. Shepard (1942, 1965) showed that the San Marcoseños exported Glazes C and D; Warren (1969a, 1970, 1979b) believed that the export of San Marcos ceramics began earlier, with Cieneguilla Glaze-on-yellow and Glaze B, and that the exports were concentrated in the Galisteo Basin. If Warren is correct, and we have misjudged the temporal behavior of the ceramic at the source pueblo, then we are also wrong regarding the timing of its appearance, or the duration of exports to other Galisteo Basin pueblos.

Besides producing and exporting glaze-paint ceramics, the San Marcoseños may have played a significant role in the access and distribution of Cerrillos Hills lead within the Galisteo Basin and beyond. Given its role in glaze paint production and export, the pueblo likely had a vested interest in that resource and knew the location of various galena veins. They may have acted as the "gatekeepers" to the Cerrillos Hills generally. Alternatively, as suggested by the lead isotope analyses of Habicht-Mauche (2000; Nelson and Habicht-Mauche 2006), they may have restricted access by other communities to certain veins and locations. Following conquest, the Spanish also mined Cerrillos Hills lead. Again, San Marcos was involved, showing the Spanish miners galena locations in the Cerrillos Hills. They also were certainly involved in the extraction of lead and copper recovered from the seventeenth-century Spanish smelter at the pueblo (Ramenofsky and others 2008).

ABOUT SERIATION

Kroeber (1916) and Spier (1917, 1918, 1919) pioneered the development of seriation in the Southwest while working at Zuni during the second decade of the twentieth century. The initial enthusiasm for this method faded, however, once the temporal power of dendrochronology was discovered (Kidder 1927). With that discovery, reliance on seriation as a temporal method all but ceased in the Southwest (Beals and others 1945; Graves 1984). Only in the past decade or so have Southwesternists begun using seriation again to address temporal questions (Creamer and others 2002; Duff 1996; Eckert 2006; Rakita and Raymond 2003; Ramenofsky and others 2009; Van Dyke 1997). Nonetheless, the method continues to be underutilized.

Frequency seriation is an ordinal-scale temporal method that employs historical classes to order a set of assemblages derived from different spatial units. The goal of frequency seriation is to array the assemblages such that the classes reflect a temporal gradient. That gradient is achieved if the classes have unimodal shapes (the familiar battleship curves) (Ford 1962). It is for this reason that the classes selected for a seriation must demonstrate historicity, or reflect time more than space (Kreiger 1944). However, because time is an abstraction (Ramenofsky 1998), additional conditions are employed to insure that time is the principal gradient responsible for ordering a set of assemblages. Independent dates are important for confirming the order of assemblages.

Classes must have comparable duration. In other words, if the duration of one class is vastly different than the duration of other classes, the resulting distribution of that class will not be unimodal. The classes to be seriated must also derive from a single cultural tradition. To capture time in a seriation, space must be controlled.

All three conditions—unimodality, comparable duration, and same cultural tradition—appear supported in the San Marcos case. Dendrochronological cross-dates used to anchor the seriations suggest that all glaze paint types were manufactured across a period of approximately 350 years (see Table 9.1). San Marcos is a single place, which means that the spatial parameter is supported. Finally, all the research of San Marcos glazes points to a single learning tradition (Schleher 2010c; Dyer 2010). Current knowledge suggests that augite monzonite is a unique temper of the glaze paint ceramics at San Marcos (Dyer 2010, and Chapter 14; Habicht-Mauche 1991; Nelson and Habicht-Mauche 2006; Schleher 2010c; Warren 1979b). Recent compositional analyses by Schleher (2010c) and Dyer (2010) show that local production of glaze paint ceramics at the pueblo far outweighs glaze paint imports.

The support of the frequency seriation assumptions at San Marcos does not guarantee a successful seriation

Table 9.1. Tree-ring Cross-dates of Glaze–paint Types

Glaze Type	Kidder (1936)	Mera (1940)	Breternitz (1966)	McKenna and Miles (1991)	Eckert (2006)
Glaze I/Glaze A Red/Yellow		1350-1450	1300-1425+	1315-1425	1313-1500 (Red) 1321-1450+ (Yellow)
Glaze II/Glaze B	1425-1475	1350-1450	1300-1450	1400-1450	1410-1500+
Glaze III/Glaze C	1475-1550	1425-1575	1400-1500	1425-1490	1410-1600+
Glaze IV/Glaze D	1550-1600	1475-1550	1425-1575	1490-1515	1460-1550+
Glaze V/Glaze E	1600-1700	1550-1600	1425-1600	1515-1650/1700	1480-1630+
Glaze VI/Glaze F		1600-1700		1625-1700	1520-1700

outcome. Simply, the ultimate test of the frequency seriation model is whether the resulting order of spatial units across classes is unimodal. If this result occurs, then with the addition of independent dates, the order can be inferred to be temporal.

SERIATING SAN MARCOS GLAZE-PAINT SHERDS

The seriations reported here are the result of a large University of New Mexico project at San Marcos that I directed between 1997 and 2002. One of the goals of the project was to create a use history of the pueblo. Previous researchers (Creamer and Renken 1994; Welker 1997) had also reconstructed occupational history of the pueblo, but their methods were different than ours. Both Creamer and Welker relied on excavated sherd samples of room blocks. Creamer limited her fieldwork to the central part of San Marcos, and her reconstruction is restricted to that section of the site (presented in Welker 1997). Welker (1997) worked across the entire pueblo, and her reconstruction used Nelson's excavated collections (1912–1915) from room blocks, currently housed at the American Museum of Natural History.

The UNM project, by contrast, was a predominantly surface project that focused on the identification and collection of temporally sensitive artifacts from middens because they are rich repositories of such indicators. Because Nelson's original planimetric map of San Marcos (Fig. 9.2) did not include surface middens, the first task was to locate and then collect ceramic rims from the middens.

Over a two-year period, we located 20 surface middens adjacent to every room block at the pueblo (Fig. 9.3). We then used a systematic surface strategy to collect all decorated and plain rims from these middens in

a series of 5 m² units. At the end of that phase of fieldwork, the decorated sample of rim sherd assemblage was in excess of 7,000. The glaze paint portion of that sample was nearly 4,000 sherds (Pierce and Ramenofsky 2000; Ramenofsky 2001).

Numerous frequency seriation analyses of the systematically surface collected rim sherds from San Marcos were undertaken (Ramenofsky and others 2009). In all these iterations, middens were the spatial units and the decorated rim sherds, including both the glaze-paint and black-on-white decorated rim sherds, constituted the historical classes. The inclusion of the black-on-white wares was justified because Nelson's (1916) stratigraphic cuts in the Galisteo Basin had demonstrated that in north-central New Mexico, glaze paints replaced the black-on-white tradition.

The ceramic units in the seriations have variable membership. The San Marcos black-on-white sample collapses a number of individual types into one ceramic unit. To evaluate the temporal performance of Cieneguilla Glaze-on-yellow, Glaze A is separated into the two principal forms, Agua Fria Red and Cieneguilla Glaze-on-yellow. Glazes B through F collapse variations in slips into single units, but certain slip colors predominate within each type. More than 95 percent of the Glaze B sherds are Largo Glaze-on-yellow. Glaze C sherds are dominated by Espinosa Glaze Polychrome, Glaze D by San Lazaro Polychrome, Glaze E by Puaray Glaze Polychrome, and Glaze F by either Koyiti or San Marcos Glaze Red.

In one preliminary solution, the general unimodality of the seriation matrix is apparent, demonstrating the strong temporal signals of the types across middens (Fig. 9.4). The temporal behavior of black-on-white and Agua Fria Glaze-on-red matches the frequency seriation and the known cross-dates of these types. They appear

Figure 9.2. N. C. Nelson's planimetric map of San Marcos Pueblo.

early in the sequence and are spatially concentrated in the southwest section of the site, becoming much less frequent before the later types, Glazes C and especially Glazes E and F, are produced and become popular. The spatial circumscription of these types to the southwest corner of settlement duplicates Nelson's impressions from nearly a century ago (Nelson 1912–1915), as well as the small excavation by Reed (1954) in this section of the settlement. In addition, the later types are

concentrated in middens to the north and east of these early locations.

There are, however, two significant problems with this initial solution. The early historical types (black-on-white and Glazes A and B) reappear in middens that have a predominance of later types (Middens 3, 10, 6, and 13), suggesting that these middens are time-averaged. I do not consider the problem or its solution further here, but it is considered at length in a separate

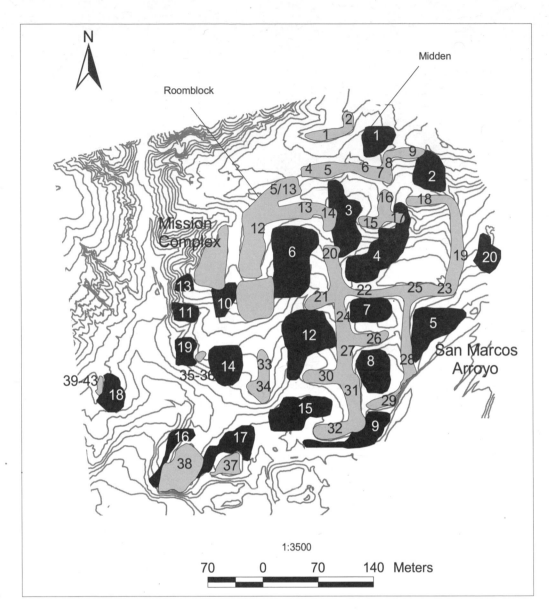

Figure 9.3. Roomblocks and middens mapped at San Marcos Pueblo in 2000.

publication (Ramenofsky and others 2009). The second problem is the temporal distribution of Cieneguilla Glaze-on-yellow. It is not unimodal. Even excluding the frequency increase in the later, time-averaged middens, the shape of the curve is minimally trimodal, with frequency peaks occurring in Middens 8, 12, and 5 before the final increase in 3.

Two explanations could account for the temporal behavior of Cieneguilla Glaze-on-yellow. First, the differential abundance of the type across the middens could be the result of taphonomic processes. In other words, erosion, the burrowing of fossorial mammals (primarily

gophers) (Pierce 1992), and human surface and subsurface alteration is differentially exposing Cieneguilla Glaze-on-yellow. Second, the duration of Cieneguilla Glaze-on-yellow is not temporal at the same scale as the other glaze-paint types.

Taphonomic processes have certainly contributed to the surface ceramics of middens. Fossorial burrowing is more common in the middens than in other locations. Approximately 22 percent of the midden surface collection units showed signs of active burrowing, while only 10 percent of non-midden units displayed comparable evidence. We also know that the Spanish built the

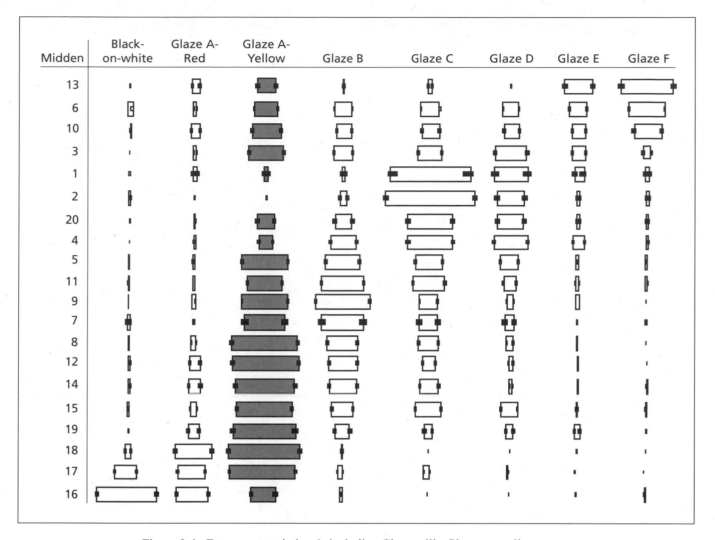

Figure 9.4. Frequency seriation 1, including Cieneguilla Glaze-on-yellow.

mission complex on top of an abandoned room block, and that they mined middens for construction of adobe brick (Pinson 2008; Thomas 2000). Finally, Nelson (1912–1915) excavated trenches across all room blocks at San Marcos without backfilling. Consequently, some of the surface debris likely derives from his excavations.

Why, however, would erosion, gophers, humans, or any other taphonomic agent target and preferentially expose Cieneguilla Glaze-on-yellow? The simple answer is they wouldn't. The most parsimonious explanation for the abundance of Cieneguilla Glaze-on-yellow on the surface is that there were simply more of these vessels, the sherds of which are both on the surface and buried. The buried sherds are migrating to the surface with all the other ceramics.

Several Spearman's ranked two-tailed correlations were used to evaluate whether taphonomic agents were acting uniformly across these early types in all middens (Table 9.2). The comparison with Glaze A types is justified because they are thought to have approximately the same temporal span (see Table 9.1). The comparison of Cieneguilla Glaze-on-yellow with Glaze B (Largo Glaze-on-Yellow, LGY) is justified because these are the two largest sherd samples from the San Marcos middens. The comparison of Agua Fria Glaze-on-red to Glaze B is included for consistency.

Despite vast differences in sample sizes (Table 9.3), Cieneguilla Glaze-on-yellow correlates with both Agua Fria Glaze-on-red and Glaze B at a *p*-value of 0.01. Simply, taphonomy cannot explain the abundance of

Table 9.2. Seriation Matrix, San Marcos Black-on-white and Glaze-Paint Sherds

Midden	Black-on-white	Glaze A-Red	Glaze A-Yellow	Glaze B	Glaze C	Glaze D	Glaze E	Glaze F	Total
13	0	4	9	1	2	0	14	26	56
6	10	13	99	76	76	65	73	148	560
10	1	10	32	16	19	16	14	30	138
3	0	4	48	26	33	43	18	12	184
1	0	1	1	1	19	8	2	1	33
2	1	0	0	5	56	17	2	2	83
20	0	1	15	15	38	22	3	2	96
4	0	3	20	35	61	44	14	3	180
5	1	4	88	66	52	33	4	3	251
11	4	7	115	147	109	42	12	8	444
9	1	13	166	198	65	24	12	0	479
7	1	0	13	14	6	3	0	0	37
8	1	7	86	41	26	9	1	0	171
12	2	12	75	33	14	5	1	0	142
14	2	14	72	34	23	4	1	1	151
15	4	17	144	56	67	41	4	3	336
19	0	7	42	11	5	5	3	0	73
18	5	31	61	1	0	0	0	0	98
17	49	61	146	12	14	3	0	0	285
16	58	30	23	2	0	0	0	1	114
Total	140	239	1255	790	586	384	178	240	3391

Cieneguilla Glaze-on-yellow at San Marcos. Higher or lower counts of Agua Fria Glaze-on-red or Glaze B in middens co-occur with higher or lower counts of Cieneguilla Glaze-on-yellow. Whatever formation processes are exposing one type are also exposing the other.

The second hypothesis, that Cieneguilla Glaze-on-yellow is not temporal at the same scale as the other types, is more likely. In the second seriation, the type is removed (Fig. 9.5), and the distributions of the remaining types approximate unimodal curves. Using the tree-ring cross-dates to bracket the temporal distribution of types in the second seriation makes possible two inferences. First, the types are temporal, and second, the order of middens, which is exactly the same in both seriations, is also temporal. The earliest middens and earliest ceramics are in the southwest section of the settlement, and the latest middens and latest types (Glazes E and F) are clustered in the vicinity of the mission and convent.

Additional information is embedded in this seriation, the most significant of which is the assumption of sequential replacement of types. The seriation does not support the assumption. As demonstrated by the presence of most types in most middens, there is considerable temporal overlap among the types, but the maximum abundance (or popularity) of particular types *is* sequential. Agua Fria Glaze-on-red and Glaze B are produced during the same temporal interval, but the popularity of Glaze B is later than that of Agua Fria Glaze-on-red. Glaze B continues to be produced at the same time as Glazes C–F, but the maximum popularity of Glazes C–F all occur in different and temporally sequential middens.

In sum, the use of the frequency seriation model to order the decorated ceramics at San Marcos has been successful in demonstrating that, at San Marcos, all types except Cieneguilla Glaze-on-yellow have strong

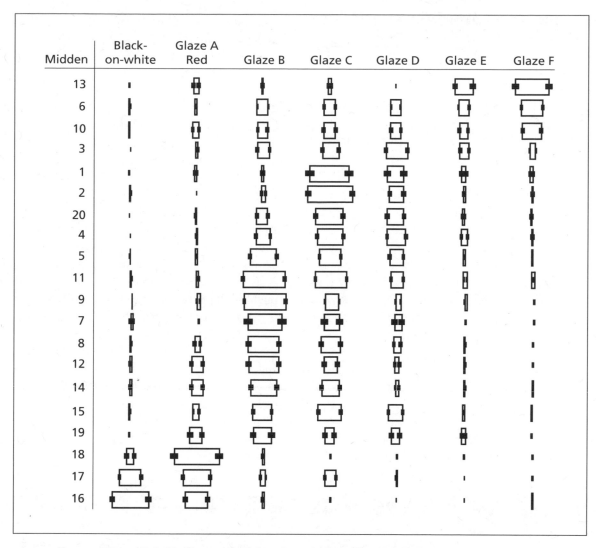

Figure 9.5. Frequency Seriation 2, excluding Cieneguilla Glaze-on-yellow.

temporal signals and are of relatively short duration. They are a single tradition. In both solutions, the midden order is maintained, suggesting a south to north temporal pattern in the use of middens. Because Cieneguilla Glaze-on-yellow could not be successfully incorporated into the frequency seriation, the temporality of the type is simply different than that of the others. It does not meet the parameters of the frequency seriation model and is not a temporal type in the context of the other types. The seriations also unambiguously demonstrate the fallacy of the linear replacement hypothesis, thereby supporting the assessment of other researchers. At San Marcos, the glaze-paint types are not discrete temporal units. The waxing and waning of glaze-paint styles is certainly a temporal process, but with considerable overlap in the production and duration of particular styles.

THE CONTINUOUS PRODUCTION OF CIENEGUILLA GLAZE-ON-YELLOW

The first frequency seriation suggests that Cieneguilla Glaze-on-yellow was produced across the entire use life of the pueblo (Fig. 9.4). What makes this inference so intriguing is that native use of San Marcos appears to be discontinuous. The San Marcoseños were not "deeply sedentary" (Lekson 1990); they practiced a form of residential mobility at the scale of 50 to 100

Table 9.3. Spearman's Rank-order Correlations

Comparisons	Rho (2-tailed)	p
AFR:CGY	0.668	0.01
CGY: LGB	0.714	0.01
AFR:LGB	0.148	Not significant

years. We documented five demographic pulses at the pueblo (Ramenofsky and others 2009), and during each residential period, the immigrants lived in certain areas of the settlement where they preferentially built and used certain middens. Throughout the entire sequence of place use, the population moved progressively north and east across the pueblo.

Although we don't know whether these periodic abandonments were complete—whether the pueblo was left unoccupied—it is clear that, despite the disruptions of leaving and returning, San Marcos potters continued to produce Cieneguilla Glaze-on-yellow. Other glaze-paint styles waxed and waned, but Cieneguilla Glaze-on-yellow persisted. The question is, why? What social, economic, or political factors can account for the long-term survival of this ceramic type? Ideas within the

literature on community of practice can contribute to understanding the temporal pattern.

Regardless of where Cieneguilla Glaze-on-yellow is found at the settlement, it is unmistakable visually. The ease of recognition, in turn, suggests great continuity in its manufacture (Fig. 9.6). The decorative style of Cieneguilla Glaze-on-yellow is simple. The bowls have straight, direct rims; the slips are thin but well applied; and the glaze paint designs are characterized by clean geometric lines, triangles and squares, and dots. Moreover, the compositional and visual data match each other. Schleher's dissertation (2010c) overwhelmingly demonstrates that San Marcos glaze paint ceramics were highly standardized and locally produced. Her petrographic analysis of 459 sherds from San Marcos showed that 81 percent of all San Marcos sherds were produced at the pueblo. The percentage of Cieneguilla Glaze-on-yellow is even higher: 97 percent of all Cieneguilla Glaze-on-yellow sherds were produced at San Marcos. Although the thin-section sample of Cieneguilla Glaze-on-yellow accounted for only 7 percent of all Cieneguilla Glaze-on-yellow bowl sherds at San Marcos, the dominance of local temper is a strong warrant that a larger sample would not produce fundamentally different results.

The continuity in manufacture and product of Cieneguilla Glaze-on-yellow over at least 200 years, as well

Figure 9.6. Cieneguilla Glaze-on-yellow bowl sherd.

as its abundance at San Marcos, suggests a ceramic conservatism with considerable significance to both the San Marcoseños and other communities. Cieneguilla Glaze-on-yellow was not simply produced for export. It was locally produced and consumed, as well as exported. These facts mean that the ceramic was desirable to both producers and consumers, prompting us to ask why Cieneguilla Glaze-on-yellow was desirable and what kind of significance potters embedded in this particular technological style. Here are several possibilities.

On the one hand, given the periodic dispersion of much of the San Marcos population, perhaps Cieneguilla Glaze-on-yellow came to symbolize the community. In this case, "community of practice" is more appropriately considered "community of identity" (Eckert, Chapter 6). Continuing to make this vessel form regardless of where potters were living was saying "San Marcos is our home" or "we come from San Marcos" (Levine 1999). Alternatively, or in addition, the maintenance of the style could have been significant within the exchange networks. Nelson and Habicht-Mauche (2006) have persuasively argued that exchange networks within the glaze paint tradition were multiscalar. Whereas Cerrillos Hills galena was widely circulated, whole vessels were traded among specific villages. Perhaps Cieneguilla Glaze-on-yellow became the vessel style that signaled social and economic connections with San Marcos regardless of whether the producers were in residence at the pueblo. If, during one or more abandonment episodes, San Marcos potters were living at one of these related pueblos, then people as well as products were moving. If all of these possibilities are correct, then the presence of one or more Cieneguilla Glaze-on-yellow bowls signaled place of origin, producer, and social identity in ways that other glaze-paint styles did not.

CONCLUSIONS

In this discussion I employed frequency seriation and practice theory to investigate the temporal behavior of Cieneguilla Glaze-on-yellow at San Marcos Pueblo, an important source pueblo for the production and exchange of this technological style. Although not typical, integration of these frameworks provided a context for a more nuanced analysis. The frequency seriation showed that Cieneguilla Glaze-on-yellow had a different temporal distribution at San Marcos than the other glaze-paint types recovered there. Current evidence suggests that Cieneguilla Glaze-on-yellow was produced across the entire temporal span of native use of the pueblo. This discovery supports the findings of others who question the duration of production of the type, and means that currently we cannot use the San Marcos form of Cieneguilla Glaze-on-yellow as a temporal marker at San Marcos or at the places to which it was exported. In other words, the traditional temporal envelope for Cieneguilla Glaze-on-yellow must be fundamentally reconsidered.

Is San Marcos unique in terms of the long-term survival of this type? Currently, we don't know, but I doubt that San Marcos is unique. San Marcos is a single place, and despite the size of the glaze paint sample, a demonstration at a single place cannot be accepted as definitive of the temporal behavior of the type everywhere. Like Glaze A Red in villages south of Albuquerque, there may be regionally variable patterns in the production and use of the type. Additional seriations from other settlements where the type was produced, such as Tonque, will either confirm the San Marcos pattern or show the duration of production at San Marcos to be anomalous. Further, bracketing the duration of the production of Cieneguilla Glaze-on-yellow with luminescence dates would be useful. Finally, although the type does not seriate, attributes of the type might be temporally sensitive. In other words, for unknown reasons, the scale of the type is too coarse-grained to capture temporal variation. Separating the type into smaller-scale analytic units and attempting to seriate these could show which attributes are temporal and which are driving the atemporality of the larger type.

Using a classic temporal method created a unique situation for considering the meaning of this technological style to producers and consumers. Addressing those meanings is complicated by our documentation of residential mobility at San Marcos. Use of the pueblo was punctuated by a series of shorter- and longer-term abandonments. Despite these abandonments, San Marcos potters continued to make, use, and exchange Cieneguilla Glaze-on-yellow. Did the ceramic signal cultural place, connection to that place regardless of where the potters were living, or social or economic connection to San Marco? For now, these questions must remain open ended but provide a road map for further investigations.

Acknowledgments

The results reported here were made possible by the support of numerous individuals and institutions, including the McCune Charitable Foundation, Standard Products, and the University of New Mexico. Christopher

Pierce co-directed the San Marcos project from 1997 to 2000. Field school students and teaching assistants made the large-scale surface investigations enjoyable. The seriation software was provided by Carl Lipo. The photograph of Cieneguilla Glaze-on-Yellow is part of Nelson's San Marcos collection curated at the American Museum of Natural History. Access to the collection was provided by David H. Thomas and Anibal Rodriguez. I am indebted to both of them. I also thank the editors, Linda Cordell and Judith Habicht-Mauche, for putting together an excellent symposium and bringing this volume together. Their comments throughout the process have been on target and extremely helpful. Errors in understanding are mine.

CHAPTER TEN

Glazed Over

Composition of Northern Rio Grande Glaze Ware Paints from San Marcos Pueblo

Kari L. Schleher, Deborah L. Huntley, and Cynthia L. Herhahn

San Marcos Pueblo, located near the Cerrillos Hills in north-central New Mexico, is often referred to as a production center for Northern Rio Grande Glaze Paint Ware (Habicht-Mauche 1993, 1995; Huntley and others 2007, Chapter 2; Mills and Crown 1995; Warren 1976, 1979b). Northern Rio Grande Glaze Paint Ware was manufactured during the Pueblo IV, or Classic, period from approximately A.D. 1300 to 1700. Glaze paint is the major defining attribute of these ceramics. Only a few other ceramic types made by Pueblo potters were ever decorated with glaze paint, and the end of this ceramic tradition marks the end of glaze paint use in the northern Rio Grande (Eckert 2006). Although much interest has focused on San Marcos as a production center, the details of how pottery production at the site was organized are not well understood. Because San Marcos is one of the closest villages to a main source of lead used in manufacturing the glaze paint, focusing on the composition of the glaze paint recipe may yield insight into how San Marcos functioned as a production center.

Given the variability in Southwestern glaze paints over time and space, we argue that potters intentionally attempted to produce certain colors, luster, and mechanical characteristics when preparing them. Composition and preparation of the paint is not the only factor that influences the final color of the glaze—firing temperature, duration, and atmosphere have significant impacts on the end result as well (Blinman and others, Chapter 11). Glaze paint production entails an intentionality and complexity that provides information about the nature of the organization of production and the community of practice for pottery manufacture at particular villages and across wider areas.

Our goals are to unravel complexities in glaze paint composition on pots produced at San Marcos Pueblo from the early A.D. 1300s to the late 1600s, and to compare the glaze paint recipe used there to recipes used by potters at other sites, including Tonque, Abó, and Quarai pueblos. In this chapter, we review previous analyses of glaze paint, present new data on glaze compositions from San Marcos, and compare these results with data produced in earlier studies of other central and northern Rio Grande sites. Finally, we discuss the implications of the longevity of the basic glaze paint recipe on San Marcos Pueblo potters' community of practice and the strikingly homogeneous community of practice of glaze paint production across the region.

BACKGROUND TO THIS STUDY

Glaze paint on ceramics in the American Southwest has been a focus of study for more than 80 years. A number of compositional analyses of Southwestern glaze paint have been conducted, including spectrographic and microchemical analysis (Shepard 1936, 1942, 1965), ICP-MS analysis (Duwe and Neff 2007), and electron microprobe analysis (Bower and others 1986; De Atley 1986; Fenn and others 2006; Herhahn 1995, 2006; Herhahn and Blinman 1999; Herhahn and Huntley 1996; Huntley 2006, 2008; Huntley and others 2007; Jones 1995). Shepard's analysis of Northern Rio Grande Glaze Paint Ware showed the major components of the glaze to be silica and lead, and this has been confirmed by all of the recent research into glaze composition on these types.

Jones (1995) examined the number of glaze recipes used at Quarai and found that they remained constant with increased production at the site, suggesting that all potting groups continued to participate in pottery production even as the volume of production changed.

Herhahn's research suggests experimentation early in glaze ware production and increased standardization of the glaze recipe by the mid-1400s throughout the Northern Rio Grande (Herhahn 2006). Herhahn and Huntley (1996) propose that increased levels of specialization were due to the increased standardization of glaze paint recipes used by potters beginning in the 1400s. Examining ceramics recovered in the Salinas District, Herhahn and Huntley found that the amount of lead in glazes with augite monzonite temper (also referred to as augite diorite [Shepard 1942]), indicating production at San Marcos Pueblo, became more standardized during the intermediate glaze period with the production of Glaze C and D ceramics.

Although the relationship between standardization and specialization is ambiguous (Arnold and Nieves 1992; Benco 1988; Costin 1991; Hagstrum 1985; Roux 2003; Schleher 2005, 2010c; Stark 1995), changes in degree of standardization may reflect changes in the organization of pottery production at a particular village. Increasing standardization in glaze paint recipes may suggest increasing routinization in paint preparation developed through repetition or a decrease in the number of individuals preparing the glaze paint (Costin 1991; Rice 1992). Applying these ideas, Herhahn and Huntley (1996) suggest that San Marcos potters may have emphasized standardization in preparation of glaze paint, perhaps by making the process more routinized. Additionally, glaze paint production may have been increasingly restricted to a few sites or to a fewer number of increasingly skilled potters. The sample size for Herhahn and Huntley's (1996) study was small, so the current research seeks to determine if these trends hold for a larger sample of vessels made at San Marcos Pueblo.

Recent innovative research by Judith Habicht-Mauche and her colleagues (Habicht-Mauche and others 2000, 2002; Huntley and others 2007) demonstrates that lead used to make Rio Grande glaze paints came from just a few locales—a dominant source being the Cerrillos Hills located just a short distance from San Marcos Pueblo. San Marcos potters seem to be exclusively using the nearby Cerrillos Hills sources for galena (Habicht-Mauche and others 2000, 2002), the lead sulfide used to make the paint (Blinman and others, Chapter 11).

These previous studies of glaze paint composition suggest that there was recipe standardization, and that San Marcos potters had easy access to, if not control over, the sources of materials needed to make glaze paint. Our current research takes these studies one step further and examines a larger sample of glaze paint made at San Marcos to identify changes in the glaze paint recipe through time and the degree of standardization attained by potters that may reflect their community of practice.

SAN MARCOS AND POTTERY PRODUCTION

San Marcos Pueblo is located on the Santa Fe Plateau, just northwest of the Galisteo Basin, in north-central New Mexico (Fig. 10.1). San Marcos, with more than 1,500 rooms (Ramenofsky 2001; Ramenofsky and others 2009), was one of the largest of the sizable, multicomponent, Pueblo IV or Classic period villages in and near the Galisteo Basin. The pueblo was occupied from the thirteenth century to the Pueblo Revolt of 1680 (Pierce and Ramenofsky 2000; Ramenofsky 2001; Ramenofsky and others 2009). Northern Rio Grande Glaze Wares were produced at the site throughout the entire occupation (Ramenofsky, Chapter 9; Schleher 2010c).

San Marcos Pueblo is frequently mentioned as a center for low-level, specialized household industry production of Northern Rio Grande Glaze Ware (Habicht-Mauche 1993, 1995; Huntley 2008; Mills and Crown 1995). Given Costin's (2001:276) definition of specialization as "fewer people make a class of objects than use it," there is definitive evidence of ceramic specialization in the Galisteo Basin and at San Marcos from the 1300s until the late 1600s. This specialization is seen in the export of ceramics from San Marcos to a number of other pueblos within northern and central New Mexico, such as the Salinas District sites of Abó and Quarai (Nelson and Habicht-Mauche 2006; Motsinger 1992, 1997; Shepard 1942, 1965; Warren 1976, 1979b). Previous researchers (Shepard 1942, 1965; Warren 1976, 1979b) argued that the volume of Glaze Paint Ware production in the Galisteo Basin and San Marcos intensified from Glaze A to Glaze C (approximately A.D. 1400 to 1500) and then decreased from Glaze D through Glaze F. The increase in the intensity of production is reflected in amount of pottery exported from the site in the fifteenth century, with a subsequent decrease in the amount of pottery exported in the later part of the glaze sequence. Although recent studies suggest a complex pattern of manufacture and exchange, they continue to support San Marcos as having been *one* of

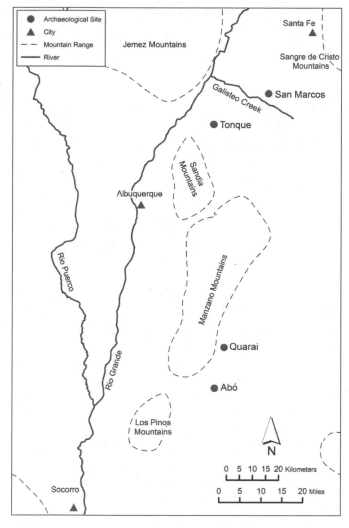

Figure 10.1. Map of north-central New Mexico showing San Marcos Pueblo, Tonque, Quarai, and Abó.

several locations producing glaze-painted pottery for export, especially during the 1400s and early 1500s when Glaze C and D types were made (Nelson and Habicht-Mauche 2006; Reed 1990). Other sites in north and central New Mexico also have evidence of ceramic production and specialization. Pottery made at Tonque Pueblo, located approximately 25 km southwest of San Marcos Pueblo, was exported in relatively large quantities (Warren 1969a). People at Abó and Quarai, in the Salinas area of central New Mexico, made pottery but they also imported pottery from San Marcos and Tonque (Herhahn 1995; Jones 1995).

Here we study San Marcos ceramic production to determine if changes in standardization of glaze paint recipes are reflected in the documented changes of

intensity indicated by the amount of pottery produced during this time period.

METHODS FOR GLAZE PAINT CHEMICAL COMPOSITIONAL ANALYSIS

Sixty-seven sherds, ten to twelve from each glaze rim type (Glaze A through F), were selected for electron microprobe analysis. The sample was selected to maximize the range of glaze colors represented for each glaze type rim form. Microprobe analysis allows for very small amounts of material to be analyzed, revealing the major, minor, and trace elements present (Rice 1987:375) if appropriate standards are used (De Atley and others 1982). To prepare samples for analysis, a small slice was removed from each sherd using a diamond saw, impregnated with epoxy in a vacuum, highly polished, and coated with a thin layer of carbon to make the surface conductive.

Microprobe analysis was conducted by the senior author using the JEOL 8200 Electron Probe Microanalyzer at the Earth and Planetary Sciences Institute of Meteoritics Electron Microbeam Facility, University of New Mexico, closely following methods outlined by Herhahn (1995, 2006), Herhahn and Huntley (1996), and Huntley and others (2007). The JEOL 8200 is equipped with five wavelength dispersive (WD) spectrometers. The microprobe uses a highly focused beam of electrons that can be narrowed to less than one micron in diameter, and it is therefore ideal for analyzing the thin layer of glaze that is visible on the cross-section of a sherd. Previous research of glaze paint composition focused on nine elements that are typically found as the major components of Southwestern glaze paints (De Atley 1986; Huntley and others 2007): silica, aluminum, iron, magnesium, calcium, potassium, copper, manganese, and lead. In this analysis, we recorded four additional elements that were detected in low levels (on average, less than 0.5 percent by weight) in a preliminary analysis: sulfur, sodium, titanium, and zinc. Abundance of each of the 13 elements was converted to oxide weight percent by the microprobe software. Up to ten individual readings were recorded for each sherd and then averaged to reduce issues with heterogeneity possible in the glaze. Weight percent was averaged for each oxide and then normalized to 100 percent. To compare data with other projects, the small concentrations of sulfur, sodium, titanium, and zinc were eliminated from the San Marcos sample and the average values were re-normalized to 100 percent.

ANALYSIS AND INTERPRETATION

Lead is the dominant element present in all glaze paints on the sherds, similar to previous analyses of Northern Rio Grande Glaze Paint Ware (Herhahn 1995, 2006). The mean weight percentage for lead oxide (PbO) for each of the glaze types ranges from 51.7 to 62.5 percent of the total concentration. Silicon dioxide (SiO_2) is the next most abundant, ranging from 23.6 to 29.4 percent, followed by alumina (AL_2O_3) and manganese oxide (MnO) (Table 10.1). Together these oxides comprise 92 to 95 percent of the total glaze paint composition. Concentrations of PbO, SiO_2, and AL_2O_3 are relatively homogeneous within each Glaze Ware rim type, with coefficients of variation ranging from approximately 8 to 28 percent (Table 10.2; Figure 10.2). PbO is at its most standardized level in Glaze C and most variable in Glaze D, but the same cannot be said for SiO_2 and Al_2O_3. The three main oxides represent the essential elements of the glaze—the PbO as flux to allow the

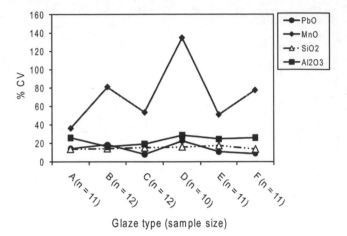

Figure 10.2. Percent coefficient of variation for the four dominant oxides by glaze type.

glaze to vitrify during low-temperature firings used by Southwestern potters, the SiO_2 to form the structure of the glaze, and the Al_2O_3 to keep the glaze from running. A successful glaze recipe would have to have relatively consistent amounts of these three materials to make the glaze "work."

Oxides that may have functioned primarily as colorants are significantly more variable than the three principal oxides (Tables 10.3 and 10.4, Figure 10.3). Although relatively low in concentration (excluding MnO), they all have relatively high coefficients of variation. Whereas the PbO, SiO_2, and Al_2O_3 coefficients of variation are largely below 25 percent, almost none of the colorants are as standardized in any of the glaze periods. The coefficients of variation for the colorant or accessory mineral oxides range from 19.8 to 161.7 percent, with most for these oxides being significantly higher than those of the three principal oxides. The coefficients of variation suggest highly variable use of particular colorants within each glaze period, and these coefficients of variation change significantly throughout the sequence. For example, the colorants in Glaze B, especially copper, have high coefficients of variation, whereas the colorants in Glaze E have relatively low and uniform coefficients of variation.

What can we make of these seemingly random and contradictory temporal patterns in glaze paint constituents? Not surprisingly, given the requirements of creating a vitrified paint, stability in the primary glaze constituents of PbO, SiO_2, and Al_2O_3 suggests continuity in the basic glaze paint composition through time. High levels of variation in minor glaze components suggest

Table 10.1. Occurrence of the Four Dominant Oxides by Glaze Type

Glaze type	PbO	MnO	SiO_2	Al_2O_3	Sum of dominant elements
	—Mean Weight Percentage—				
A (n = 11)	51.7	7.2	29.4	6.5	94.8
B (n = 12)	53.5	7.7	27.0	5.8	94.0
C (n = 12)	62.5	3.5	23.6	5.0	94.6
D (n = 10)	55.1	5.8	26.1	4.5	91.5
E (n = 11)	60.5	2.6	23.6	4.9	91.6
F (n = 11)	60.0	2.0	24.7	5.3	92.0

Table 10.2. Percent Coefficient of Variation (CV) for the Four Dominant Oxides by Glaze Type

Glaze type	PbO	MnO	SiO_2	Al_2O_3
A (n = 11)	14.1	36.0	13.4	25.7
B (n = 12)	18.2	80.7	14.0	16.1
C (n = 12)	8.0	53.2	14.9	19.2
D (n = 10)	22.6	134.3	15.9	28.3
E (n = 11)	10.4	50.8	17.2	24.3
F (n = 11)	8.6	77.1	13.3	25.8

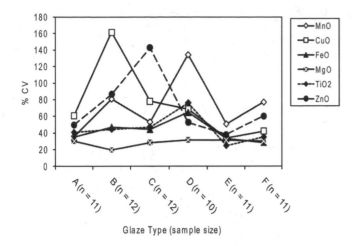

Figure 10.3. Percent coefficient of variation for the colorant oxides by glaze type.

there may be other factors at play, such as potters intentionally adding materials to modify the color of the glaze or unintentionally mixing the glaze with the underlying slip clay (Herhahn 2006). Changes in the slip color on Northern Rio Grande Glaze Ware ceramics are apparent throughout the glaze sequence at San Marcos Pueblo, with increasing variety in the slip colors through time (Schleher 2010c). However, this trend does not explain the high variability seen for the colorant oxides presented in Table 10.4. We now turn to multivariate analysis of the overall glaze paint composition.

A number of researchers have documented glaze paint recipes for groups in different sites or regions across the Southwest (Fenn and others 2006; Herhahn 1995, 2006; Huntley 2006, 2008; Huntley and others 2007). Herhahn (2006) suggests that a relatively standardized recipe was used by all potters in the Northern Rio Grande Glaze Ware production area to produce Glazes B through F.

Her research suggests there were close ties and a single, extensive community of practice in the production of the later glazes in the Northern Rio Grande region, including the site of San Marcos. To investigate this, we conducted additional analysis of the glaze paint recipe at San Marcos.

A principal components analysis (PCA) of the glaze compositional data from San Marcos (Fig. 10.4 and Table 10.5) reveals only minor differences between the glaze paint recipes used at different stages of the glaze typological sequence. Because of relatively small sample sizes, the 67 sherds analyzed from San Marcos for glaze paint composition have been grouped into early (Glaze A and B), intermediate (Glaze C and D), and late (Glaze E and F) samples. Only the first four components, accounting for 74 percent of the cumulative variation, are presented in Table 10.5. Alumina, potassium, and titanium are strongly associated with Component 1 (strong associations are indicated in bold italic in this table). These elements are present in the clay and may be introduced through mixing with the glaze during firing, rather than being added to the glaze paint by the potter (Herhahn 2006). PbO, the primary flux in the glaze, is negatively associated with Component 1. MnO, the dominant colorant, and Al_2O_3 are associated with Component 2, whereas sodium and zinc are negatively associated. In summary, early glazes have slightly higher levels of Al and Mn but slightly lower levels of Na and Zn. Late glazes have slightly lower levels of Mn and Al and higher levels of Na and Zn. The intermediate glazes fall in the middle of these two extremes, although they also overlap significantly with both the early and late glaze recipes. The higher the amount of manganese, the darker the glaze should be. This colorant is more dominant in the earlier glazes, which correlates with the prevalence of black glazes on Glaze A and B

Table 10.3. Occurrence of Colorant Oxides by Glaze Type

Glaze type	MnO	CuO	FeO	MgO	TiO$_2$	ZnO
			—Mean Weight Percentage—			
A (n = 11)	7.2	0.1	1.2	0.7	0.2	0.9
B (n = 12)	7.7	0.2	1.3	0.6	0.2	1.4
C (n = 12)	3.5	0.1	1.4	0.6	0.2	0.9
D (n = 10)	5.8	0.2	1.9	0.6	0.2	2.9
E (n = 11)	2.6	0.2	2.0	0.6	0.2	2.4
F (n = 11)	2.0	0.1	2.3	0.8	0.2	1.3

Table 10.4. Percent Coefficient of Variation (CV) for Colorant Oxides by Glaze Type

Glaze type	MnO	CuO	FeO	MgO	TiO_2	ZnO
A (n = 11)	36.0	61.0	34.9	30.3	40.6	49.9
B (n = 12)	80.8	161.7	47.1	19.8	44.4	86.7
C (n = 12)	53.2	78.2	44.2	28.5	47.1	142.8
D (n = 10)	134.3	68.7	64.5	31.7	76.1	52.8
E (n = 11)	50.8	33.7	33.2	31.5	24.8	38.1
F (n = 11)	77.1	42.2	28.7	30.1	35.0	60.4

Table 10.5. Component Matrix for the Principal Component Analysis Plotted in Figure 10.4, with Strong Associations Indicated in Bold Italic

Oxide	Component 1 Eigenvalue = 3.95, Explained Var. = 33%	Component 2 Eigenvalue = 2.38, Explained Var. = 20%	Component 3 Eigenvalue = 1.52, Explained Var. = 13%	Component 4 Eigenvalue = 1.06, Explained Var. = 9%
Al_2O_3	*0.360*	*0.242*	0.039	*-0.486*
SO_3	-0.286	-0.087	0.146	0.190
Na_2O	0.189	*-0.527*	-0.100	-0.085
MnO	0.224	*0.377*	-0.423	0.253
K_2O	*0.345*	-0.213	0.238	*0.438*
PbO	*-0.391*	-0.188	*0.401*	0.028
MgO	0.314	-0.023	0.318	*-0.503*
FeO	0.286	-0.188	-0.057	0.294
CaO	0.309	-0.366	0.246	0.010
CuO	0.036	-0.318	*-0.422*	-0.140
TiO_2	*0.385*	0.159	0.096	0.298
ZnO	-0.075	*-0.468*	-0.129	0.319

types. Alumina helps the glaze to be less runny (Rhodes 1973:79; Rice 1987:98–100), so it is not surprising that the later glazes that tend to run contain smaller amounts of this oxide. This plot shows some compositional group separation, although there is considerable overlap among the groups. We now compare these data to glaze compositional data from contemporaneous sites.

Herhahn (1995, 2006; Herhahn and Huntley 1996) and Huntley (Huntley and others 2007; Jones 1995) analyzed the glaze paint recipes used to produce ceramics at villages in the Salinas district and at a number of villages in the central and northern Rio Grande Valley. PCA of glaze compositional data from San Marcos and the Salinas District (Fig. 10.5 and Table 10.6) reveal the consistency of the glaze recipe at San Marcos throughout the glaze sequence. Figure 10.5 shows that San Marcos potters used a standardized recipe in comparison to other contemporary potters. Close examination of the graph reveals that some of the glaze paint compositions

from the Salinas sample overlap with the cluster of glaze paint compositions from San Marcos. To gain a clearer picture of the relationship between the San Marcos sample and the Salinas sample, we separate the samples by probable production locale using temper type.

Although the glaze paint composition presented in Figure 10.5 represents samples from San Marcos Pueblo and the Salinas region, similar paint recipes were likely used at a wider range of sites. Temper has been used for nearly 100 years in north and central New Mexico to identify ceramic production at particular sites or in particular areas. The temper used at some sites, including San Marcos Pueblo, Tonque Pueblo, Quarai, and Abó, has been identified through ceramic petrography (Capone 1995, 2006; Eckert 2003, 2008; Herhahn 1995; Nelson and Habicht-Mauche 2006; Schleher 2007; Shepard 1936, 1942; Warren 1969a, 1970, 1979b, 1980). Other temper types are more difficult to pinpoint, such as the wide range of basalt tempers used by central

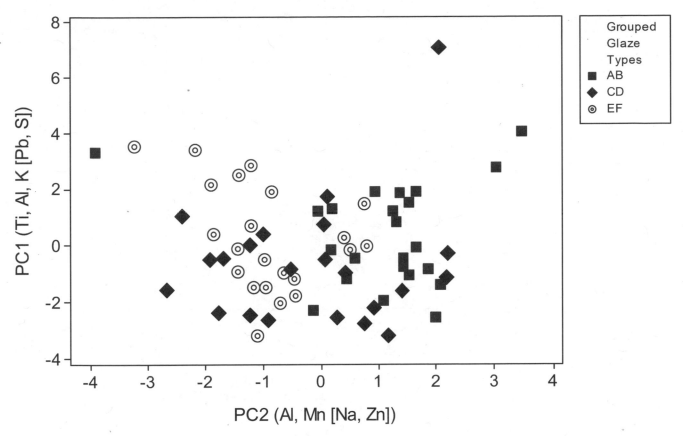

Figure 10.4. Bivariate plot of glaze paint composition principal components 1 and 2 for San Marcos sherds by grouped glaze type.

Rio Grande Valley potters, and therefore suggest only general regions of use (Eckert 2003, 2008). San Marcos pottery is characterized by weathered augite monzonite temper, Tonque pottery by hornblende latite ash, Abó by hornblende diorite, and Quarai by hornblende gneiss (Nelson and Habicht-Mauche 2006; Schleher 2010c).

Figure 10.6 shows the same PCA presented in Figure 10.5, but by temper type instead of location of recovery. This plot indicates that glaze compositions from other sites, including Tonque Pueblo and some of the Salinas area sites, overlap with the San Marcos sherds. This is significant because it supports previous claims that the glaze recipe from all of these sites is similar.

In summary, the compositional results suggest variation in colorants, with relative standardization in the main oxides used in the glaze paint at San Marcos Pueblo. There is some minor variation through time in the overall glaze paint recipe used by San Marcos potters, but when compared with glaze paint recipes at other sites the San Marcos recipe appears to be standardized and temporal differences disappear. Overall, the glaze paint

recipe used by most potters at the four sites of Tonque, Abó, Quarai, and San Marcos are remarkably similar, with similar levels of standardization at all four sites.

DISCUSSION

The glaze paint compositional data from San Marcos suggests relative stability in the basic components (PbO, SiO_2, and Al_2O_3) of Rio Grande glaze paints, but greater variability for the colorants. The relatively minor amounts of colorants suggest that they were not added intentionally at all. The interaction of the slip, clay body, and glaze during firing, and the presence of impurities such as copper in the source ore, may be major factors that introduced these other elements into the final composition we see today (Herhahn 2006). Since we know that San Marcos potters used a single lead ore source, this interpretation is plausible.

Glaze is a complex paint medium and the recipe must be taught to other practitioners before they can make a successful glaze. Thus, the temporal consistency of the

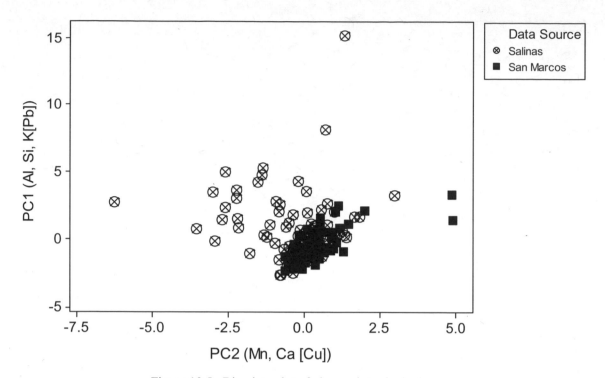

Figure 10.5. Bivariate plot of glaze paint principal components 1 and 2 for San Marcos and Salinas sherds.

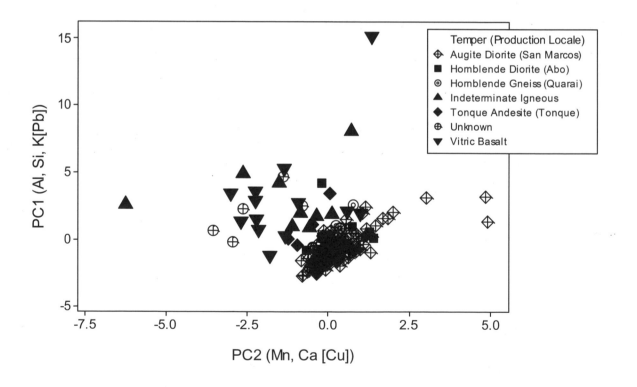

Figure 10.6. Bivariate plot of glaze paint composition principal components 1 and 2 for San Marcos and Salinas sherds plotted by temper type and likely production locale.

Table 10.6. Component Matrix for the Principal Component Analysis Plotted in Figure 10.5, with Strong Associations Indicated in Bold Italic

Oxide	Component 1 / Eigenvalue = 3.98, Explained Var. = 50%	Component 2 / Eigenvalue = 1.26, Explained Var. = 16%	Component 3 / Eigenvalue = 1.20, Explained Var. = 15%
Al_2O_3	*0.430*	-0.059	0.085
SiO_2	*0.437*	0.071	0.164
K_2O	*0.411*	0.025	-0.187
CaO	0.253	*0.339*	*-0.547*
MnO	-0.014	*0.644*	*0.583*
Fe_2O_3	0.378	-0.077	-0.247
CuO	0.180	*-0.664*	0.372
PbO	*-0.464*	-0.121	-0.304

recipe at San Marcos may reflect a teaching framework that developed to transmit the recipe to new potters. If so, the framework appears to have remained quite stable through time. Potters appear to have worked within a system that communicated information about what had to go into a glaze, but variety in colorants and experimentation in the addition of these colorants was acceptable. Similar interpretations have been made for glaze paints from the Zuni region (Huntley 2008).

The wide variation in colorants does not support the idea that prepared glaze paints were made by just a few potters and traded to others (Bower and others 1986; Habicht-Mauche and others 2000, 2002), unless that prepared glaze paint was simply crushed and roasted galena (Blinman and others, Chapter 11; see also Huntley and others 2007). We suggest that the stability in the basic glaze paint recipe (lead, silica, and alumina proportions) points to an enduring network through which new potters were taught the recipe by more experienced potters. It may have been acceptable for potters to experiment with adding small amounts of other materials to create certain colors, but either the essence of the basic glaze remained constant or mixture with the underlying slip clay accounts for some of the variation in colorants. Because of this consistency in glaze paint recipes, we infer consistency in the social networks and communities of practice that involved teaching—generation after generation of potters taught the same basic recipe to new apprentice potters at San Marcos.

In comparison with glaze paint recipes used at other sites in northern and central New Mexico, San Marcos potters followed a relatively consistent glaze recipe, and this required close communication and regular face-to-face interaction with their community of practice. The data suggest that the basic glaze recipe was passed down through generations of potters at San Marcos, yielding little variation in glaze composition on the pots they produced. This occurred even though there were major changes in the lives of residents, including increased export of pottery from the site during the Glaze C and D production periods, initial Spanish contact, and the establishment of a mission at the site. This pattern is similar to the single, stable glaze recipe documented by Jones (1995) at Quarai. In contrast, this pattern is distinctly different from the Zuni region (Huntley 2008) and the Mogollon Mountains (De Atley 1986; Fenn and others 2006), where glaze recipes were more variable or changed more dramatically through time, attesting to multiple communities of practice for the potters at these locales.

As we saw in the PCA plot of glaze recipes by locus of production based on temper, there is little difference in the basic glaze paint recipe on pots from San Marcos, Tonque, Quarai, and Abó. In addition, the standardization in the basic recipe we see at San Marcos is mirrored in standardization of the recipes at these other sites. These similarities suggest close communication between potters and, perhaps, a single pan-regional community of practice for potters throughout this wider region, as suggested by Herhahn (2006). This similarity in the glaze paint recipe is particularly notable because lead sources used throughout the community of practice varied more widely than the fired glaze paint composition (Huntley and others 2007). Lead isotopic data indicate that potters at Abó and Quarai predominantly used lead from mines near Socorro, including the Hansonburg and Magdalena mines (Huntley and others 2007), whereas potters at San Marcos, and other Galisteo Basin sites, predominantly used the Cerrillos mines (Habicht-Mauche and others 2000; Huntley and others 2007).

The similarities in the basic components of the glaze recipe throughout the glaze sequence at San Marcos, Tonque, Quarai, and Abó suggest consistency in the social networks that developed through potters teaching the recipe to other potters at distant sites. These networks may have been embedded within long-distance trading expeditions, intervillage social events, or kinship systems (see Huntley and others, Chapter 2 for a discussion of embedded networks and ore procurement). It is significant that we have evidence for exchange of pots between sites—a large number of vessels from San Marcos and Tonque have been found at Abó and Quarai. However, we do not have evidence at San Marcos of import of large amounts of pottery from Abó and Quarai (Schleher 2010c), and this suggests that San Marcos potters played a significant role in the lives of the Salinas area potters. It is possible that potters from San Marcos taught potters at other sites the basic recipe for glaze paint.

In conclusion, the glaze recipe used by potters at San Marcos changed only slightly through time, apparently having been passed down through many generations of potters at San Marcos Pueblo. A similar recipe, made using several different lead sources, was used at other sites throughout the northern and central Rio Grande Valley. We interpret these patterns as the result of close teaching and social ties and a single community of practice for producers of glaze paint throughout the central and northern Rio Grande. Although there were a number of significant changes within the northern Rio Grande during this period, including Spanish contact, establishment of missions, and changes in the decoration used on glaze paint wares, the basic glaze paint recipe remained essentially unchanged, reflecting stability in the social networks among which information about glaze recipes was transmitted. Future research should continue to analyze glaze paint recipes used by potters at other northern and central Rio Grande sites to determine the extent of the glaze paint community of practice during the Pueblo IV, or Classic, period.

Acknowledgments

Funding for the San Marcos research was provided by a National Science Foundation Dissertation Improvement Grant (BCS Proposal #0525200) and a number of University of New Mexico Graduate Research and Development grants awarded to the senior author. Funding for the Salinas research was provided by the Arizona State University Department of Anthropology, the Arizona Archaeological and Historical Society, and Sigma Xi. The electron microprobe analysis was made possible by Mike Spilde (Earth and Planetary Science, Institute of Meteoritics, University of New Mexico) and the late Jim Clark (Department of Geology, Arizona State University). Thanks also to Audrey Salem, who made the map in this chapter.

CHAPTER ELEVEN

Making a Glaze

Multiple Approaches to Understanding Rio Grande Glaze Paint Technology

Eric Blinman, Kari L. Schleher, Tom Dickerson, Cynthia L. Herhahn, and Ibrahim Gundiler

Rio Grande Glaze Ware is one of the best known of several Southwestern pottery traditions in which lead played an important role as a pigment (Fenner 1974; Huntley 2006, 2008; Shepard 1939; Waterworth 1988). The Rio Grande Glaze Ware tradition developed in the fourteenth century during a period of geographic and social reorganization of Puebloan communities. It flourished during the fifteenth-century development of large aggregated communities, and it persisted through a subsequent population decline and the initial seventeenth-century Spanish colonial transformation of New Mexico's cultural and economic landscape. During its florescence, design suites expanded from banded geometric combinations to include iconographies associated with new religious systems (Graves and Eckert 1998). In the Spanish colonial period, a decline in glaze quality presents a jarring change in appearance (Spielmann and others 2006). Glaze ware production lapsed abruptly in the early eighteenth century following the Pueblo Revolt and Spanish Reconquest, events that were associated with dramatic community relocations and new social and economic relationships between Spanish and Pueblo peoples in New Mexico.

Although there are numerous studies of Northern Rio Grande glaze paint composition (Bower and others 1986; Herhahn 1995, 2006; Herhahn and Huntley 1996; Huntley 2006, 2008; Huntley and others 2007; Jones 1995; Schleher 2010c; Schleher and others, Chapter 10; Shepard 1942), the technological details of glaze paint production remain elusive. The eighteenth-century lapse in production truncated Puebloan knowledge of the technical process, and satisfactory replication has eluded both artists and archaeologists. Our secure knowledge is that vessels were formed through coil-and-scrape techniques, the backgrounds and highlights of bichrome or polychrome designs were created with slip clays, a lead-based pigment produced lines and areas of dark glaze, and firing finished with oxidation to bring out the iron-determined red and yellow colors of the slips. Unknowns include issues as basic as the precursor lead mineral (galena, cerrusite, or both), the preparation of the pigment, roles of colorants in the glaze, and the firing regime sequences that are needed to produce the completed vessel. In this chapter, we bring a variety of analytic and experimental perspectives and expertise to the process of glaze paint production in the Northern Rio Grande. The authors have carried out studies from artisan (Blinman, Dickerson) and materials science (Herhahn) perspectives, guided by recent analytic findings (Schleher) and principles of physical chemistry (Gundiler).

The decades-long frustration of modern replicators is instructive, both in building up a substantial body of information and in demonstrating that the artists' process of glaze paint production is not self-evident. The complexity of the artists' process highlights the potential of that technical complexity for the broader study of the social and economic contexts of production. Our goal here is not to identify a community of practice but to contribute toward a technical model that can support analyses of communities of practice. Details of the production process that underlie each community of practice, such as the one presented by Schleher, Huntley, and Herhahn (Chapter 10), involve raw material selection, pigment preparation, and firing regime. Transmission and adaptation of the technological tradition across time and space can provide insight into the historical path of discovery and innovation, as well as how that knowledge spread among glaze-paint-producing villages in the northern Rio Grande.

FROM THE KNOWN TO
THE UNKNOWN

The lead-silica basis for Rio Grande Glaze Ware paint was established in 1915 (Kidder 1915:418). In the 1930s, Anna Shepard (1936, 1942) and her collaborators in the study of Pecos Pueblo pottery confirmed the basic composition of the glaze and speculated on the role of manganese colorants in the changing appearance of the glaze. Parallel work by Fred Hawley (Hawley and Hawley 1938) emphasized the variability of glaze constituents from the Western Pueblo tradition to the Rio Grande Valley, including the changing emphasis from copper to manganese as potential colorants.

Sulfide ores (galena) were identified as the most probable sources for the lead pigment (W. H. Newhouse in Shepard 1942:215), but near-surface deposits of altered minerals such as cerrusite (lead carbonate) were acknowledged alternatives. This early research also acknowledged the difficulty in sourcing lead ore bodies owing to the alteration of trace element fingerprints during the fluctuating reducing and oxidizing atmospheres of the firing process (C. R. Hayward in Shepard 1942:215–216). This difficulty results from both the selective volatilization of elements during firing and the incorporation of elements through dissolution of the underlying paste during glaze formation. In addition to complicating archaeologists' approaches to sourcing, volatilization and especially dissolution are major impediments to easy reconstruction of the glaze process from the study of final glaze composition alone, especially in regard to the question of the artists' conscious use of additives as colorants.

Modern studies of Rio Grande Glaze Paint respect the realities of the glaze formation process, interpreting compositional data as an end product of a complex chemical-physical process. Lead isotope studies by Judith Habicht-Mauche and colleagues (2000, 2002; Huntley and others 2007) take advantage of a sourcing approach that is independent of trace element transformations. Cynthia Herhahn (2006; Herhahn and Blinman 1999) has laid a foundation for the interpretation of glaze compositional variability and coloration as "recipes," with explicit acknowledgment of the confounding solubility of underlying paste components. These research efforts suggest that the lead component of the glaze pigment is derived from regional sources—Cerrillos Hills for the northern Rio Grande and the Socorro area for the Rio Abajo—but there is no clear indication of whether the potential colorants of manganese or iron are natural contaminants of the ore or are added components of an artist's mixture.

ARTIST PERSPECTIVES

The lack of an ethnographic model and the consequences of firing transformations have left us with ambiguities that can best be resolved through experiments toward replication. Tom Dickerson conducted systematic experiments in Rio Grande Glaze Ware replication beginning in the late 1960s, both as an artist and as a technical advisor to Pecos National Historical Park during an effort to reintroduce glaze technology as a Native American ceramic tradition. Building on the observations of Shepard and Hawley, Dickerson worked with galena, cerrusite, and commercial raw materials to find a combination of pigments and firing that was both relatively safe to use and effective in producing the appearance of the ancient pottery. The ultimate products of the experiments were beautiful pots, but they were accomplished only through recipes that were explicitly modern technological adaptations. Of greatest importance, however, was the generation of a large body of practical knowledge through both failures and successes.

Dickerson's observations, reinforced by the experiences of the senior author, were that the artists' processes in making glaze ware vessels were far from self-evident, despite the consistency of Rio Grande Glaze Ware pottery in both appearance and compositional qualities. Powdered galena pigment, the probable paint precursor, tended to produce matte rather than glazed designs, especially with "calm day" firings. The failure of the galena to flux consistently during wood firings appeared to be due to one or more of three factors: the strong reducing atmosphere that is maintained through the initial portion of the firing sequence, the relatively short durations of the firings, and the difficulty in reaching sufficiently high firing temperatures in wood firings that had been designed on contemporary Native American models. When glaze formation was achieved, usually during breezy days that raised firing temperatures, the finished galena-based glazes were as often transparent as dark. Whereas cerrusite melted to produce a glaze more consistently in laboratory kiln firings, this lead carbonate mineral is more difficult to recognize than galena during field collection trips (Weber in Bice and others 2003), and cerrusite continued to produce transparent rather than dark glaze lines.

One of the confusing aspects of both the experimental and analytic results has been an inconsistent correlation between the non-lead glaze components and the finished color (Schleher 2010c; Schleher and others, Chapter 10). Manganese, iron, and copper have been implicated as colorants in Rio Grande Glaze studies (Herhahn 2006; Schleher and others, Chapter 10), and especially in the Western Pueblo glazes (Huntley 2006). Schleher's on-going study of finished glaze colors and composition in Pueblo San Marcos collections reveals a relationship between manganese and the darkness of the finished color, but darkness is not reliably predicted by the presence or amount of colorant.

During glaze firing experiments, pure galena would occasionally produce the desired dark or black design areas in both uncontrolled and electric kiln firings, but as often it would result in a clear glaze. An intriguing and not uncommon failure in wood firings has been a clear glaze on one side of the vessel and a dark glaze on the other, both from the same experimental pigment (Fig. 11.1). Also, Dickerson's reconstructions required significant colorant additions to achieve consistent results. A suspicion that has developed from these observations is that coloration was as dependent, or more dependent, on the specific firing regime than on the composition of the pre-firing pigment. This is consistent with glaze principles that are taught in contemporary studio pottery texts (Green 1979:138–140).

PUEBLO SAN LAZARO

The most significant new archaeological developments in the study of glaze paint technology have been associated with San Lazaro Pueblo (LA 91 and 92) in the Galisteo Basin. Janet Orcutt encountered probable pottery firing features during systematic archaeological surveys around the pueblo in the mid-1990s. A small area of both clustered and scattered burned rock, resting on charcoal stained soil, was noted adjacent to a late-fifteenth-century portion of the pueblo (Fig. 11.2). The clusters appear to be intact firing platforms from the last use of the firing area. None of the individual features has been excavated to confirm feature function, but the platforms are surface analogs of the shallow firing basins documented for the preceding Santa Fe Black-on-white pottery by Stephen Post and Steve Lakatos (1995). The San Lazaro features, assuming they are related to pottery firing, imply the firing of only one large to three small pots at a time in a setting where the atmosphere is controlled only by fuel

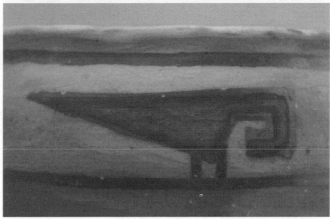

Figure 11.1. Contrasting appearance of experimental galena pigment on opposite sides of the same glaze-on-polychrome replica bowl. The bird motif has a red-slip body outlined in glaze and framed by horizontal glaze lines above and below. The glaze in the upper image is clear, whereas the lower glaze varies from relatively clear to dark.

arrangements and local air flows. The location of these features in a shallow drainage is reminiscent of Mesa Verde trench kilns where the features are situated in the paths of consistent breezes that contribute to higher firing temperatures (Blinman and Swink 1997).

A second discovery was associated with the seventeenth-century component of the site. A stone consistent with the elements of the probable firing platforms was discovered with drips of lead glaze coating its surface. Although the only provenience for the stone is the plaza area of the historic room block, this stone provides circumstantial support for the interpretations of the platforms as facilities for glaze firing, as well as evidence for the possible consistency of the firing facility through time.

Figure 11.2. Probable glaze kiln features adjacent to Building I, San Lazaro Pueblo. Two stone platforms are visible in the image, one in the foreground and one in the right background. The rocks are oxidized, and the soil beneath is stained with charcoal.

The third discovery has been residue of prepared but unfired glaze pigment adhering to the interior of a small Glaze D bowl from a San Lazaro room block that was abandoned at about A.D. 1500 (Fig. 11.3). Mistaken for slip clay by the senior author for more than a decade, the gray residue was finally analyzed by Kari Schleher as comparative data for her study of glaze pottery from Pueblo San Marcos. Test firing of a flake of the residue created a black glaze on the underlying substrate. Although this pigment discovery constitutes a sample of one, the late-fifteenth-century date for the sample is well within the period of stable glaze recipes (Schleher 2010c; Schleher and others, Chapter 10). There is no reason to believe that this sample is not representative of "standard practice" for Rio Grande glaze potters.

Schleher's analyses of the residue indicate that the precursor mineral was galena based on SEM evidence of remnant cubic crystal structure in some particles (Fig.

11.4) and the presence of sulfur within those particles (Fig. 11.5). The vast majority of the powder is lead without cubic structure and with very low levels of sulfur, indicating that the powdered pigment had been transformed into lead oxide as a preparation step. In an effort toward confirmation, a pure sample of galena was powdered and roasted. SEM analysis revealed the same pattern of remnant cubic crystals, sulfur in the crystals, and a background of lead powder with lower levels of sulfur (the presence of some lead oxide). Cerrusite, when ground, yields a light white-to-yellow powder with no cubic structure, inconsistent with both the macroscopic and microscopic appearance of the San Lazaro material.

The San Lazaro residue is a fortuitous discovery since it provides a sample of an artist's recipe and sets the stage for a very different chemical progression of glaze development during firing. The archaeological pigment includes particles enriched in manganese, iron,

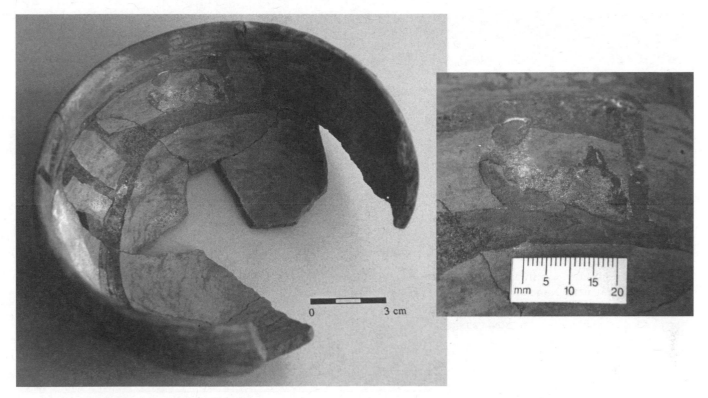

Figure 11.3. Glaze D (San Lazaro Glaze-on-red) bowl with unfired glaze pigment
residue adhering to portions of the interior surface. The bowl, recovered from
Building I of San Lazaro Pueblo, is dated to the last decades of the fifteenth century.

and zinc, which may or may not have been added independently of impurities within the galena ore source material. Also, the pigment appears to be enriched in chlorine, but whether this is a raw material or recipe characteristic or postdepositional contamination is currently unknown. The reference sample of experimentally roasted galena was a pure crystal rather than an ore. Its lack of iron, manganese, and zinc in comparison with archaeological samples leaves open the question of whether the archaeological colorants were ore contamination or artisan additions.

THE CURRENT ARTISAN MODEL

The accumulation of experimental experience, the implications of the new archaeological and analytic observations, and the application of principles of historic lead smelting processes are the foundations of the current and presumably improved model of the glaze ware production process. As it is refined and confirmed, this model will in turn have implications for how archaeologists build arguments for the linkages between glaze ware variability and the broader cultural changes within the communities of practice in the fourteenth through eighteenth centuries.

Galena is the principal precursor mineral for glaze pigment. Although cerrusite could have been used, it is rarer, more difficult to recognize in the field, and more difficult to transport over long distances without loss. The presence of small amounts of sulfur in Schleher's analyses of glaze on the majority of sherds from San Marcos Pueblo adds further support for galena as the precursor mineral (Schleher 2010c). Before firing, the galena is powdered—probably by rubbing against a passive abrader rather than being crushed and ground. This conclusion is based primarily on the fine particle size and the scarcity of cubic crystal remnants in the San Lazaro sample. Crushing and grinding experiments have resulted in generally coarser material and more abundant remnant detectable crystals. Crushing and grinding is also messy, resulting in the scattering of raw material outside of the work area. This would be detectable in the examination of the heavy fraction of flotation samples but would be difficult to detect with routine quarter-inch

20 cm

Figure 11.4. Scanning electron microscope image of unfired glaze pigment from San Lazaro Pueblo. The cubic crystal at the center of the image is unaltered galena surrounded by finely ground roasted galena particles.

screening of archaeological deposits. Rubbing evidence should be detectable through examination of archaeological galena surfaces or of residues on passive abrading surfaces.

Roasting in air at temperatures below 600–700° C drives off the sulfur, transforming the galena into lead oxide. Cooking hearth fires can provide adequate heat for the roasting process as long as there is free access to air. Dry roasting in a pottery container is probable, either slowly with no attention or more quickly with regular stirring to refresh the air-galena interface. Thorough roasting requires that the galena be finely powdered, since even long periods of roasting can fail to alter the interiors of 0.25 mm crystals.

Production steps from this point are more speculative since archaeological data are absent. Application of the roasted galena powder as pottery paint probably benefited from the use of an organic binder, such as *guaco* derived from boiled Rocky Mountain beeplant (Guthe 1925). The binder serves as a wetting agent and a carrier, insuring an even application of pigment by the brush. The binder then dries and adheres the painted design firmly to the surface of the unfired vessel. Application with water alone tends to be extremely uneven, and completion of even the most rudimentary line work is frustrating. Also, if only water is used, the dried design is extremely fragile, dusting off of the vessel surface with the lightest physical contact. This sort of design defect

(localized prefiring erasure) is not evident in prehistoric sherds or vessels. If the pigment were unroasted galena, an organic binder would also have negative chemical consequences during firing. As a reducing agent, the binder would retard the disassociation of the sulfur and would retard glaze formation during firing. When the galena powder has been prepared in advance by roasting to convert it to lead oxide, the binder's reducing effects would actually encourage the formation of lead or lead silicate during firing.

Despite the generalization of surface firings as "oxidizing" (as compared with pit firings), vessels in all wood firings are initially subjected to strong reducing atmospheres. Early in the firing, the fuel generates more combustible gasses than can be consumed by the available oxygen supply, producing a reducing chemical environment at the vessel surface. This atmosphere persists through the rise toward peak temperatures and then transitions to oxidation as volatile gasses are exhausted and combustion switches predominantly to the burning of charcoal. During the initial phases, soot (creosote) condenses on the relatively cooler vessel surfaces as a transitory process, further securing the reducing atmosphere at the vessel surface and persisting at least into the initial oxidation stages of the firing atmosphere. We assume that when these conditions are maintained through an adequate heat rise, the lead oxide in the paint is reduced and glaze formation is initiated. Threshold temperatures can be as low as 160° C in the presence of carbon monoxide, and reduction by carbon is "vigorous" by 700° C (Liddell 1945:149–159). Amendments to the roasted galena powder are unnecessary for glaze formation (silica is derived from the underlying vessel surface), but the addition of amorphous silica to the pigment cannot yet be ruled out.

Colorant issues remain confusing. The amounts of manganese, iron, or copper measured in the analytic studies could be consistent with lead ore contamination or with a conscious mixture or recipe of different raw ingredients. However, glaze colors derived from experiments with unamended galena (pure rather than ore and not roasted) have been occasionally "perfect" (black or dark brown) while yielding disappointing matte gray designs or transparent glazes in other firings. Colorants have not been derived consistently from underlying slips, as dramatically illustrated by the erasure of red slip by glaze formation in some firing experiments (the red slip is dissolved, and the color and texture of the underlying paste is visible through areas of clear glaze). Despite the

San Lazaro pigment sample

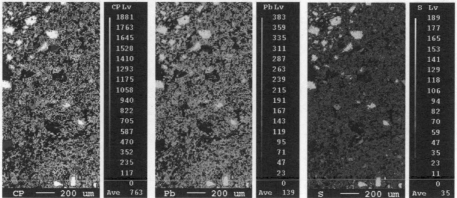

Experimentally powdered and roasted galena

Figure 11.5. Electron microprobe element maps of lead (Pb) and sulfur (S) in a sample of San Lazaro glaze pigment compared with a sample of experimentally prepared galena. The CP map is a summation of all elements detected by the instrument. In both cases, larger galena particles were unaltered by roasting, as indicated by the higher proportion of sulfur. The ancient pigment material was more thoroughly roasted than the experimental example, which retains a higher proportion of sulfur.

dissolution of the high-iron slip in these cases, there has been no effect on the color of the overlying or adjacent glaze. Similarly, dark glaze results have occurred over both low-iron and high-iron slips.

Avenues for future research include investigation of the role of carbon and even lead oxide in glaze pigmentation. Carbon is introduced through the organic binder, and under pure oxidation conditions it would be eliminated during firing. However, if glaze formation is initiated while combustion conditions are still reducing, the carbon may be trapped within the glaze. Schleher is actively pursuing this question, but the analytic characterization of carbon is relatively more difficult than the characterization of the other possible colorants. Lead oxide, uncombined with silica, can also be a colorant and would not be differentiated in the analyses conducted to date.

CHANGES IN SEVENTEENTH AND EARLY EIGHTEENTH CENTURY GLAZE TECHNOLOGY

Intriguing changes in the Rio Grande Glaze tradition took place in the seventeenth and early eighteenth centuries. Dramatically increased runniness characterizes the majority of Rio Grande Glaze Ware production by the late seventeenth century (Fig. 11.6). Characterizations of Glaze F sherds from two different San Marcos Pueblo collections resulted in "runny" frequencies of 57 and 60 percent. Some instances of runniness occur prior to the seventeenth century (one collection of pre-Glaze F sherds from San Marcos Pueblo recorded 4 percent "runny" examples), and some seventeenth- and early eighteenth-century vessels were not runny. However, the

Figure 11.6. Example of runny glaze paint on a seventeenth-century jar from San Lazaro Pueblo. The vessel was fired upside down, and the drips point upward on the finished vessel.

seventeenth-century increase in runniness is so dramatic that it appears to be technological change by one or more communities of practice rather than being an accidental phenomenon. Isotopic variation does not appear to be involved in the change (there is no evidence for changes in the ultimate source of the lead [Habicht-Mauche and others 2000, 2002]), but there are slight decreases in the concentrations of colorant elements, increases in the ratio of lead to silica, and increases in the transparency of the glaze. Equally dramatic was the end of glaze ware production. Rio Grande Glaze Ware vessels were still being made in the immediate post-Reconquest period (1690s into the early eighteenth century), but glaze vessels are nearly absent from pottery assemblages by the mid-eighteenth century.

The correlation of these changes with the history of Spanish colonial occupation of New Mexico raises the possibility of intriguing technological and cultural correlates. From the technological perspective, availability of cow manure cakes as a new firing fuel has been proposed as a mechanism of increased firing temperature (Snow 1982) or increased firing duration (Hensler and Blinman 2002). The dramatic and pervasive degradation in vessel appearance has encouraged speculation

that potters tolerated or even encouraged the runniness to obscure the symbolism of the designs from Spanish perception and repression (Spielmann and others 2006).

Based on his long experience, Dickerson proposes that the underlying change in practice is a change in the form of the lead source used by potters. The Spanish introduced smelted lead to the Rio Grande economy, and musket balls would have been available to some Pueblo communities (balls, balls still attached to sprues, and other lead objects have been recovered from the seventeenth-century room block at San Lazaro Pueblo [Fenn 2004: Plates 104, 105]). Metallic lead shavings melt rapidly, produce an extremely fluid glaze on clay surfaces, have a greater tendency for transparency, and cause frequent solution pitting of underlying vessel surfaces—all noted characteristics of runny glaze (Fig. 11.7). Lead was one of a few documented mining ventures of the Spanish colony in New Mexico, and lead was being smelted locally from the same sources that yielded the galena used by pre-Spanish Pueblo potters (hence there need not be any change in isotopic composition) (Bice and others 2003; Kessell and others 1998:125). A switch to smelted lead would have eliminated the time-consuming process of powdering and roasting galena, or

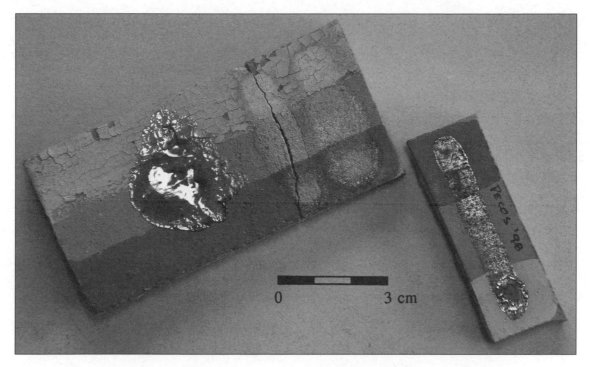

Figure 11.7. Laboratory firing of a large test tile with metallic lead filings (left), roasted galena, and cerrusite pigments. The small tile was painted with an unroasted galena preparation (right). Both tiles have areas of low- and high-iron slips as well as exposed body clay and were fired to 900° C. The lead filings resulted in "aggressive" glaze formation, including solution pitting of small areas of the underlying paste. The clear nature of the glazes was not affected by the variable iron content of the underlying substrates.

it may have been forced by Spanish appropriation of the galena mines.

If the dominance of runny glaze can be used as a proxy for the change in practice, and if that change reflects a change in the pigment precursor, at least three generations of potters employed the new technology prior to the Reconquest. Kessell (1979:316–317) reports that in 1714 Governor Flores, in order to lessen the risk of further Pueblo revolts, instituted a ban on access to guns and munitions by Pueblo populations. This coincides relatively well with the end of glaze technology. By that time, the knowledge of how to derive glaze paint from roasted galena powder may have been lost, and Pueblo potters may have found it easier to switch to other decorative technologies (matte mineral paint or organic paint).

Weaknesses in this model are noted by Snow (Chapter 12). First, Snow suggests that the frequency of runny Glaze F may be overstated. The senior author's experiences are with different sites and production locations than Snow's, and this may point to important geographic variation in seventeenth-century glaze ware practice. Second, Snow questions the importance of Spanish lead mining and smelting as competition for the use of this resource in glaze ware production. Despite the evidence of imprecisely dated (but Spanish colonial period) smelting features in the lead mine excavation near Pueblo San Marcos (Bice and others 2003), there is scant mention of local smelting of lead in surviving seventeenth-century Spanish documents. The lead bullets recovered from seventeenth-century contexts at San Lazaro Pueblo have not been analyzed for their isotopic composition, and we don't know if they represent local smelting or imported munitions from Mexico. However, Vargas's 1694 order to replenish his Reconquest munitions by mining and smelting lead from the San Marcos mines (Kessell and others 1998:125) implies that the Spanish-owned mines had been used for that purpose prior to the Pueblo Revolt. Finally, Snow notes that the transition from lead-based glaze paint technology may have preceded the Pueblo Revolt among the Pueblos of Santa Ana and Zia. This possibility reinforces the need to examine changes in artists' practice independently within the subregions of Rio Grande Glaze Ware production.

CONCLUSION

The practice of Rio Grande Glaze Ware is as dependent on knowledge of the complex alchemy of firing as it is on raw materials. The failures and successes of our production experiments reinforce the ethnographic view that firing regimes are the most conservative elements of ceramic traditions. As we continue to use pottery as a window into the social and economic systems of the past, an artist's perspective should be an important part of the definition of the community of practice, and that perspective will help sort out what is meaningful variation in our archaeological collections as well as what

that variation means. That variation may be geographic as well as temporal, especially in the seventeenth and early eighteenth centuries as potters adapted to the demands and constraints imposed by the Spanish colonial occupation of New Mexico.

Acknowledgments

Funding for the analytic portion of this research was provided by a University of New Mexico Graduate Research and Development Grant awarded to Kari Schleher and Eric Blinman. Thanks also to Mike Spilde, Earth and Planetary Sciences' Institute of Meteoritics, for assistance on the microprobe. Forrest Fenn provided the senior author access to his collections from San Lazaro Pueblo, including a wide range of pottery vessels and pottery production evidence.

CHAPTER TWELVE

Through the Glaze, Darkly

The Decline and Fall of Pueblo Glaze Ware Traditions

David H. Snow

We know in part, and we prophesy in part. . . .
For now we see through a glass, darkly;
—Corinthians 13:9–12

This paper focuses on the demise of glaze-painted ceramics among the surviving New Mexican Pueblos during the last years of the seventeenth century. The end of that tradition is frequently attributed to Spanish colonial practices that directly or indirectly prohibited potters from obtaining the necessary ore for producing glaze paint. Explanations for the decline in craftsmanship and production of glaze-painted pottery have suggested deliberate obfuscation of designs by potters who purposefully altered their traditional glaze recipes, as well as "expedient" technological practices. It also has been suggested that the abandonment of glaze production was purposeful, the result of reforging Pueblo social identities and networks following the successful return of the Spaniards in 1693. I examine here surviving historical documents that, instead, lead me to question previous explanations for the apparent sudden collapse of that nearly four hundred year tradition.

The creation of new Pueblo identities following the Pueblo Revolt almost certainly required major adjustments, not only vis-à-vis the returning Spaniards but in the face of demographic losses, migrations, and the formation of new pueblo communities and communities of practice. The forging of new social identities and interaction networks among the surviving Pueblo peoples has yet to be systematically investigated.

A historical perspective argues that demographic collapse among the glaze-producing Pueblo communities provides an alternative and adequate explanation for the disruption of Pueblo learning and production networks,

and for the final cessation of glaze-painted production shortly after 1695.

The extraction of galena and copper ores, or both, to produce a true glaze paint applied as decoration on pottery at Zuni, Acoma, and among various Rio Grande Pueblos was a significant innovation that characterizes much of the ceramic production across this broad region of New Mexico for very nearly 400 years (about A.D. 1300 to 1700) (Fig. 11.1). Although glaze paint recipes varied between Zuni and Rio Grande potters (Acoma glazes remain to be analyzed), use of those ores, together with various minerals as colorants, reflects shared technological knowledge and practice—a carefully orchestrated process from mining to finished vessel. That knowledge and the resultant processes also reflect social and economic constructs that, in turn, imply inter- and intra-regional networks of interaction, which remain to be fully elucidated.

The establishment of a permanent Spanish colony in the Rio Grande Valley of New Mexico in 1598 resulted, in a very few years, in massive redistributions and losses of Pueblo populations. The *reducción* and *congregación* strategies of Spanish authorities resulted in the founding of mission complexes in which potters from different production centers likely became situated. In addition, many Pueblo people may have retreated into territories beyond Spanish control or knowledge. It can be assumed that potters were affected by these demographic upheavals.

Seventeenth-century demands for Pueblo labor also may have affected individual potters and their apprentices, as well as the networks through which raw materials, such as clay, temper, ores, and finished products, moved. Such labor requirements can be expected to have disrupted time and travel to resource areas, and to have

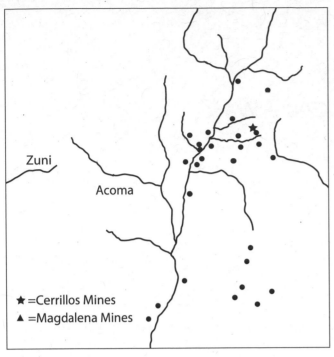

Glaze ware Pueblos about A.D. 1626

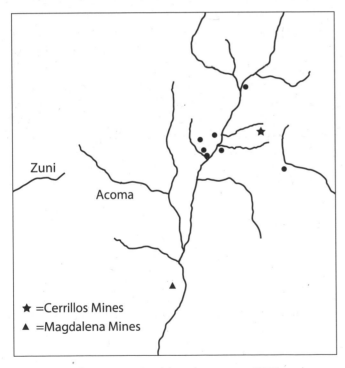

Glaze ware Pueblos about A.D. 1700

Figure 12.1. Glaze ware pueblos in the
seventeenth century (from Snow 1983).

reduced the amount of time needed for the extraction
and preparation of the raw materials and the preparation of glaze recipes. If Pueblo men were the ones who
worked the ore sources (Huntley and others, Chapter 2;
and Noah Thomas, Chapter 13), then their employment
in large numbers as auxiliaries for seventeenth-century
Spanish expeditions against hostile Apaches and Navajos, among other demands, must also have severely cur-
tailed mining activities (Kessell 2009).

In spite of such distractions, not only did traditional
glaze technology remain situated in various pueblos,
production of the late varieties of glaze ware (Glaze F;
Mera 1933) increased significantly over immediately
preceding types during the 80 or so years prior to the
Pueblo Revolt of 1680. On the surface, the persistence of
glaze paint in the face of severe disorganization and disruption is as puzzling, perhaps, as the seemingly abrupt
end of the tradition after the Revolt. That glaze-painted
ceramics were not revitalized following the reestablish-
ment of the colonial regime in the early years of the
eighteenth century, when Pueblo and Spanish relations,
presumably, had "settled down," is equally puzzling.
This paper attempts to resolve these apparent enigmas
by appealing to historical data. In short, I suggest that
the demise of glaze-paint practice resulted from the loss
of the traditional Native suppliers of lead between A.D.
1675 and 1696.

COMMUNITIES OF GLAZE
PRACTICE

Efforts to identify specific production centers of Rio
Grande glaze paint practice have, of necessity, relied
on identification of temper inclusions characteristic of
specific pueblos and districts. Following Anna Shepard's
(1936, 1942) pioneering petrographic work with Rio
Grande glaze ware sherds, subsequent investigators have
created a unique body of temper data that allows us, in
many cases, to pinpoint specific pueblos involved in the
manufacture of glaze wares (Warren 1969a, 1976). At
the same time, those studies have demonstrated a surprising range of tempering materials used in glaze ware
vessels, especially at the onset of the new technology in
the Rio Grande in the early fourteenth century.

Warren (1977a:7), for example, identified some 30
different constituent tempering materials in Glaze A
types from the Middle Rio Grande alone, and Shepard's
laboratory notes (on file at the University of Colorado
Museum, Boulder), the basis for her 1942 publication,

recorded 60 or so distinct temper combinations in the Rio Grande Glazes I–II samples. In that publication, however, Shepard (1942) grouped tempers by their major constituents only (that is, sherd, sandstone, andesite, basalt, tuff, and so on), masking what appears to have been considerable variability across the region (see Nelson and Habicht-Mauche 2006 for similar discussion of Shepard's methods). Nevertheless, Shepard and Warren both document a substantial decrease in the range of tempering materials used in the late glaze varieties (Kidder's Pecos Glaze VI, identical with Mera's Glaze F). Shepard identified only 16 major temper types in her Glaze VI category, whereas Warren's studies identified some 19 varieties in Glaze F samples. This reduction seemingly mirrors population losses and displacements and the abandonment of a number of glaze-producing pueblos during the seventeenth century.

The pueblos listed by name in the 1598 "vassalage and obedience" to the crown (Hammond and Rey 1953:345–346) represent 90 or more villages that are presumed to have been extant at the time. In a list of pueblos compiled fewer than 50 years later, about 1641 (Scholes 1944; Snow 1983:357), only 24 villages were identified in the districts described by Mera (1940) as having produced Rio Grande glaze-painted pottery (Fig. 12.1). In the Rio Abjao, the Pueblo district along the Rio Grande south of Albuquerque, were Socorro with two *visitas* (not named, but possibly Senecu and Alamillo). To the east, beyond the Manzano-Sandia mountains, were Abó with two *visitas* (Tabira and Las Jumanas, or Gran Quivira), Chilili, Tajique, Cuarac, and "San P——" (not identified further, but probably San Pedro Paa-ko). Among the former Southern Tiwa pueblos, only Sandia with one visita (Puaray), Alameda, and Isleta were occupied. The Keres pueblos consisted of Santo Domingo with one visita (Cochiti), San Felipe, San Marcos with one visita (La Cienega), and Zia with one visita (Santa Ana). Further east, in the Galisteo Basin, was Galisteo with one visita (not named, but either San Cristóbal or San Lazaro), and beyond was Pecos Pueblo.

Mera (1940) did not recognize Picuris or San Juan as glaze-producing pueblos (see Dick 1965; Shepard 1942; and Dyer, Chapter 14), so the total should be 26 or possibly 28, since the 1641 list also failed to include either San Cristobal or San Lazaro—the latter, at one time, reportedly a visita of San Marcos. Thus there might have been 28 pueblos producing glaze-painted pottery about 1641. However, only nine or ten seventeenth-century Rio Grande communities have been directly linked to

glaze paint production on the basis of their use of distinctive tempering materials: Picuris, San Juan, Cochiti, Zia-Santa Ana, Galisteo-San Cristobal, San Marcos, possibly San Lazaro, Pecos, Quarai, and Abó. Acoma presumably produced glaze paint pottery during the seventeenth century, but ceramics from that area have been poorly studied. At Zuni, only four of the original six villages seen by Coronado in 1540 remained occupied in 1604, and those are reported to have been "almost completely in ruins although inhabited" (Hammond and Rey 1953:1013–1014). Glaze paint production at Zuni, which ceased around A.D. 1400, was not revitalized until after missions had been established around A.D. 1629–1630, possibly by refugee potters from the Rio Grande (Mills 2002).

Recent studies of the Southwestern glaze paint traditions have focused on determining glaze recipes, and on sourcing the galena used by various pueblos (De Atley 1986; Habicht-Mauche and others 2000, 2002; Herhahn 2006; Huntley and others 2007; Nelson and Habicht-Mauche 2006). Huntley's (2008) studies indicate that early Zuni potters initially obtained much of the lead for their glaze paint from the Cerrillos Hills, switching to sources near Socorro (Magdalena and Hansonburg mining districts) around the middle of the fourteenth century. Lead isotope analyses by Habicht-Mauche and her colleagues (2000, 2002; Huntley and others 2007, and Chapter 2) have sourced lead in the glaze paints from a variety of sites in the Rio Grande to the Cerrillos Hills and the Magdalena and Hansonburg (Sierra Oscura) districts. In general, it appears that glaze ware potters in the north-central Rio Grande favored the Cerrillos source, while potters in the Salinas district favored the more southerly Magdalena and Hansonburg sources. Habicht-Mauche (2009) suggests that Salinas potters may have shifted from the Hansonburg ore district in the Sierra Oscuras to the Magdalena district, west of Socorro, possibly as a "response to Spanish contact" (see also Huntley and others 2007).

The Hansonburg prehistoric mines were "rediscovered" by Anglo-American prospectors in the early 1880s on the basis of information provided, interestingly, by an Isleta Pueblo native (Robert Eveleth, personal communication, March 9, 2009). Many Piro-speaking people returned to Isleta Pueblo from El Paso in the eighteenth century. A third, as yet unidentified lead source used by Rio Grande potters (Habicht-Mauche 2009; Huntley and others, Chapter 2) might be located in the Rio Abajo (Piro) district. Northrup (1959:572) refers to "some very old lead diggings [that] have been reported about 6 miles west of Alamillo," a former Piro pueblo near present San Acacia (Marshall and Walt 1984:265), and Robert Eveleth (personal communication, July 22, 2009) reports "ancient abandoned copper workings" that were assumed to be Spanish in origin in the Jerome Copper Prospects located in the same area as the "lead diggings" west of Alamillo. This focus on just a few of the many available lead sources suggests specialization in the procurement of ores by glaze ware potters (see Huntley and others, Chapter 2).

Galena crystals are reported from excavations at only seven pueblos in the Rio Grande, two of them in the Galisteo Basin: Pueblo Colorado and San Lazaro (Fenn 2004:182; Nelson 1912–1916; also see Blinman and others, Chapter 11). Galena ore also has been recovered from Tunque (Habicht-Mauche 2002), Paa-ko (Habicht-Mauche, personal communication, September 28, 2009), Pueblo del Encierro (Warren 1976), Gran Quivira (Hayes and others 1981:130), Quarai (Huntley and others 2007:1137), and Pottery Mound (Maxwell Museum of Anthropology Accession #46). The Tunque and Paa-ko galena fragments have been sourced to the Cerrillos Hills (Habicht-Mauche, personal communication, September 28, 2009), while the Quarai galena probably came from the Magdalena Mountains (Huntley and others 2007). The paucity of examples is surprising in view of Nelson's excavations of more than 1,100 rooms in Rio Grande pueblos occupied during the glaze ware period. In addition, a cache of galena crystals, in a small gray ware jar (location undisclosed), proved to be from the Hansonburg district (Eveleth, personal communication, March 3, 2009; Weber 1999).

Seventeenth-century New Mexico was one of "troublous times" for Pueblo people (Scholes 1938). Struggles for control of Indian souls and labor by Spanish missionaries and secular administrators provoked the 1680 Pueblo Revolt (Knaut 1995; Kessell 2008). Requirements for Pueblo labor surely disrupted the *imponderabilia* of daily Pueblo lives. The allotment for Pueblo labor in 1620, for example, was set at 2 percent of each pueblo's population, a number that was increased at missions (and in Santa Fe for use by the colonial administration) to 8 percent during periods of sowing and harvesting (Scholes 1936–1937).

Ten to as many as thirty to forty persons from a pueblo of "fifty or sixty houses" were required on a rotating basis for daily tasks to serve the Franciscans as bakers, servants, herders of mission cattle, collecting firewood and pinyon nuts, weaving stockings and mantas, and obtaining, preparing, and painting deer, elk, and bison hides for export (Scholes 1936–1937:313). Pueblo men and women were forced to labor in *obrajes*, or manufacturing workshops, at Santa Fe and in their respective missions.

Governors, Franciscans, and *encomenderos* pressed Pueblo men into service for construction and carpentry projects. Pueblo men were forced to drive cattle and wagons to Parral, Mexico, and farther south, where frequently they were unable to collect wages in order to return. Many, apparently, never did (Scholes 1935:82).

Owing to unspecified abuses, in 1620 Governor Eulate forbade Indian women from working in Santa Fe without their husbands being present. In 1640, an unspecified epidemic is said to have reduced the Pueblo population by some 3,000 people, an estimated 10 percent of the population (Scholes 1936–1937:324; see Ramenofsky 1996 for a review of the impact of epidemic diseases in colonial New Mexico). In 1662, claims were made against Governor Lopez for 2,400 pesos he owed Pueblo workers for labor during his administration—the equivalent of more than 19,000 days, according to Scholes (1935:82), or 52 years of labor at the rate of one *real* a day.

Probably exaggerating to some extent, Governor Lopez de Mendizabal claimed to have enlisted an auxiliary force of Pueblo men, to the number of 800 "Christian [Pueblo] Indians" for an expedition to obtain captives from various Apachean groups (Hackett 1937:187). Some 600 Pueblo men were to have been mustered in 1669 for a similar purpose, and in 1670 and 1671, another 550 accompanied Spaniards against hostile Southern Plains Apaches. In 1678, 400 Pueblo auxiliaries were again gathered for service against Navajos (Kessell 2009).

How these factors might have affected the retention and transfer of the knowledge of ore sources and glaze recipes is unknown, but the increase in production of Glaze F vessels prior to 1680 is a clear indication that access to lead sources was little affected, if at all. Spanish control of lead mines during the seventeenth century is not substantiated, and mining the documents for references to such control fails to justify suggestions to the contrary.

While Franciscans extolled the mineral wealth of the province, they were critical of the inhabitants for having failed to open mines. During his New Mexico tenure in the 1620s, for example, one priest noted that the local Spaniards seem to have "made a vow of poverty, which is a great deal for being Spaniards, who because of greediness for silver and gold will enter Hell itself to obtain them" (Milich 1966:56). Said another in 1638, "up to the present no mine has been worked there because of the unfitness and poverty, not only of the Indians but also of the Spaniards" (Hackett 1937:109).

Some, if not most, of the lead needed in colonial New Mexico during the seventeenth century was imported from the mines at El Parral in Chihuahua. Charges against the governor in the 1660s, for example, claimed that lead furnished to him for the province at Crown expense, valued at 100 pesos, never made it to Santa Fe (Scholes 1938:75). During his retreat from Santa Fe in early August 1680, Governor Otermín was informed that the residents of Rio Abajo, fleeing south on learning of the Revolt, had no ammunition (lead ball) with which to defend themselves. Word of the August revolt prompted a relief column from El Paso, which donated a barrel of powder and "a slab of lead" to the Rio Abajo refugees (Hackett and Shelby 1942:163–164).

Repeated references to lead from the mines at El Parral, supplied by the Crown for use in New Mexico, indicate that local sources of galena were seldom used by New Mexico's colonists and administrators (Hackett and Shelby 1942:11; Flagler 1990:471). In 1706, Governor Cuervo y Valdes complained to the Viceroy that:

at the time and when I came to exercise this office [of governor], I purchased and spent at the Real de Minas of Parral, one hundred pesos in lead from the mines of Santa Clara and Santa Barbara, at eight pesos the hundred-weight [kgs], and it was taken to this province [Archivo General de la Nación, Mexico City (AGN), Provincias Internas 36, exp. 4–10, f. 385, author's translation].

The single reference to New Mexicans extracting lead prior to 1680 is Vargas's 1694 order for the examination of "lead mines on the hill of San Marcos," which had been worked prior to the Revolt. On examination it was reported that the Indians had worked it as an open cut, "going for the lode and lead-colored ore of the vein. Because it had been well covered up, they saw that it was impossible to work it" (Kessell and others 1998:125). Closing that open cut might simply have been a preventative measure to deny the returning Spaniards access to lead for ball. It is not known whether this was the open pit at Bethsheba Mine excavated by the Albuquerque Archaeological Society, where the majority of the sherds recovered originated at San Marcos (Bice and others 2003).

Jones (1966) has argued that settlers continued to provide powder and ball to Pueblo allies until, in 1715, the governor recalled muskets held by Pueblo allies (see also Kessell 1979:316–317), but the "swords-to-plowshares" suggestion that potters made glaze-paint from musket balls furnished them by the colonists in the early decades of the eighteenth century remains to be determined through isotopic analyses of Parral (or other Mexican) lead sources (Blinman and others, Chapter 11). The number of muskets and amount of ammunition collected by Flores Mogollon is not identified in surviving documents, nor do documents indicate such largess on the part of the settlers or authorities. Vargas did arm his Pueblo allies in 1696 in order to aid in combating the Pueblo rebels, but in 1697 he turned over to his successor the arms and munitions he had received from the viceroy, including "*15 quintales, 11 libras de plomo*," slightly more than 1,500 pounds of lead (Kessell and others 2000:95–96).

By 1705, presidial troops were themselves often lacking not only *escopetas* (guns), but powder and ball. The distribution of 200 pounds ("*ocho arrobas*") of lead ball to New Mexico's settlers and presidial troops in 1705 involved only 282 men capable of bearing arms (Snow 1998), amounting to less than one pound of shot per man. The same amount of lead ball was again distributed in 1706, all of it purchased in Mexico by the governor at his own expense (AGN, Internas 36, exp. 4–10, f. 391).

Given the increasing hostilities from Southern Athapaskans and other hostile Southern Plains groups, the continued threats and rumors of Pueblo rebellion, and the anticipated incursions by the French, who might in fact have provided musket and ball to Southern Plains groups hostile to the Spaniards, I am dubious about any decision by settlers and their Pueblo allies to relinquish scarce ammunition for the purpose of painting pots.

RIO GRANDE GLAZE PRACTICE IN DECLINE

The characterization that seventeenth-century glazes were "degenerate" (Kidder and Shepard 1936:254, referring to Glaze VI examples from Pecos Pueblo; Mera's Glaze F) because of a tendency for the glaze to run and obscure the overall design is only partially true. While that might be the case with Pecos Glaze VI (which Shepard indicated was not made there), Schleher (personal communication, December 9, 2008) notes that more than half of her Glaze F sample from San Marcos Pueblo exhibits the "typical" runniness of the glaze. Dyer (personal communication, August 17, 2009) also informs me that "well over half" of the glazed soup-plate sherds in her sample, especially from San Marcos and San Juan, exhibit runny glazes; those from Pecos, less so. More than half of the seventeenth-century Rio Grande Glaze Ware had runny paint, but a significant portion of the ware did not.

Preucel (personal communication, June 6, 2009) notes that runny glaze on Glaze F sherds is not dominant at the refugee site of Old Cochiti, occupied about 1692–1696. To investigate this, I examined 76 glaze sherds from the Laboratory of Anthropology's collections from Old Cochiti (LA 295 and LA 84). Only 11 sherds exhibit a slight tendency for the glaze to spread "off line" (not infrequently seen on Glaze E and earlier types as well; see Warren 1976, Fig. B 17b), and only two sherds show the extreme runniness generally thought to be typical of the type. Clearly, then, some seventeenth-century glaze potters were able to maintain consistent control of the glaze paint during firing, while others, apparently, were not, or did not care to. Possibly, owing to the turmoil of the period, critical steps in the preparation of the recipes, or in the firing, were not transferred to "apprentice" potters (but see Spielmann and others 2006).

Capone (2006) provides evidence that seemingly indicates hasty, or "expedient," practice by late-period Salinas glaze ware potters in preparing tempering materials. However, this type of expedient technology by potters in other late-glaze-ware-producing pueblos has yet to be determined (except at Pecos; Shepard, in Kidder and Shepard 1936:498–514). It could be argued that if sufficient numbers of master glaze ware potters were frequently absent in the employ of Franciscans and other colonial endeavors, production at some pueblos might have shifted from an open- to a closed-ability learning on the part of apprentices, resulting, perhaps, in the hasty preparation of materials (see Lyons and Clark, Chapter 3).

Briefly, open-ability apprenticeship implies learning by trial and error with extensive instruction by an accomplished potter whose specific technological practices are passed on to the apprentice in this manner. A closed-ability apprenticeship involves learning by observation and imitation with little or no verbal instruction, and might result in "clumsy emulation" and a "failure to learn" the crucial details of the processes (Lyons and Clark, Chapter 3; Van Keuran 2006:92).

Spielmann and her colleagues (2006) suggest that runny glaze on late examples of Salinas area vessels reflects "hidden transcripts," a conscious effort to obscure ritual design symbolism from Franciscan eyes. Assuming that Salinas potters or their religious hierarchy (for the influence of a pueblo's hierarchy on potters, see Brandt 1994:16; Toulouse 1977:63) altered recipes in order to hoodwink the Spaniards with such a subterfuge, why not simply eliminate painted designs? The appearance and frequency of unpainted glaze vessels (Salinas Red Ware) in the seventeenth century produced in the Salinas and other districts, I suggest, reflects just such a decision. Warren's laboratory notes (1969b), for example, identified six distinct temper types in seventeenth-century Salinas Red sherds, including Bandelier Tuff, San Marcos (augite) latite, and diabase basalt, indicating that this late unpainted type was produced widely throughout the Rio Grande.

Unpainted, red-slipped vessels produced by Salinas potters dominate the assemblages from Abó and Quarai missions, and they represent nearly 30 percent of seventeenth-century pottery from Gran Quivira's Mound 7 (Hayes and others 1981:101-102; Hurt 1990; Toulouse 1949:14–16; Warren 1981c:71). It may be, however, that undecorated red wares were produced at the insistence of the Spaniards. Kathy Deagan (personal communication, January 20, 2009) informs me that "Red-slipped wares become common on Spanish mission sites of Florida and in St. Augustine somewhere around the mid sixteenth century, maybe a bit earlier. . . . They do seem to be of Mexican origin," as are occasional examples of Cuauhtitlan Burnished and other colonial red wares from the Valley of Mexico found in New Mexican colonial sites.

Figure 12.2 shows that Glaze F pottery during the seventeenth century was produced in substantially greater numbers than were preceding glaze types (Shepard 1942; Warren 1976, 1979b). I suggest that technological "expediency" of production by potters in some centers of manufacture was the result of increased production for Franciscan mission and Spanish household requirements (see Figures 12.3a–b). Figure 12.3c also suggests that matte-painted and non-utility plain wares from the Tewa pueblos north of Santa Fe, in addition to Salinas Red Wares, might have competed with glaze ware production for Spanish domestic and other uses.

Ceramics imported from Mexico City or Puebla consistently represent less than 1 percent of all colonial assemblages in New Mexico, clearly insufficient

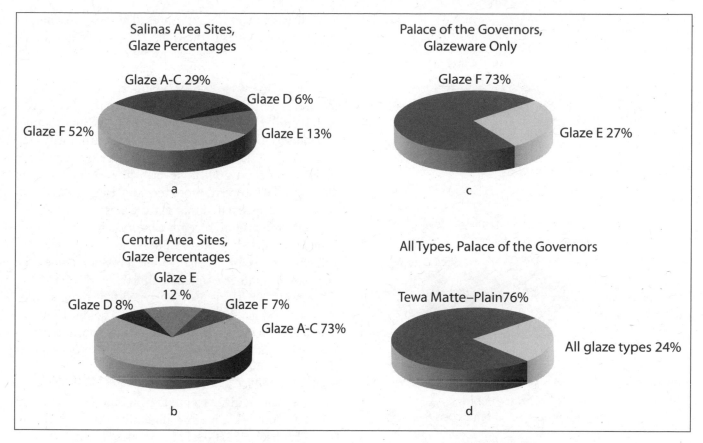

Figure 12.2. Percentages of (a) glaze ware at Salinas area sites, (b) glaze ware at Central Rio Grande sites, (c) glaze ware at Palace of Governors, and (d) all types at Palace of Governors.

to meet colonial domestic and other needs. It is likely that those needs were filled by glaze-painted and Tewa matte-painted vessels. Zia potters supplied at least one pre-Revolt colonial household with both glaze- and matte-painted vessels (Warren 1971).

I suspect that Pueblo potters were compensated for their wares, and pottery might have served as a medium of exchange with colonists and Franciscans. Although the pre-Revolt documents are silent in this regard, in 1694, Vargas remarked in his journal, *"vienen algunos Yndidos de los pecos a bender Vidriado"* ("some Indians from Pecos came to sell glaze wares"; original Spanish transcription courtesy of Rick Hendricks, July 16, 2009). Also, in December of that year, Fray Jose Diez, writing to Vargas from Tesuque Pueblo, noted that the Indians under his charge "remained without food, and for their survival it was necessary for them to support themselves . . . by making earthenware bowls and pots to sell in the villa in exchange for a little corn and meat" (Espinosa 1988:116).

MORE "TROUBLOUS TIMES" AND THE END OF THE TRADITIONS

The frequently perceived wisdom that the end of the glaze ware traditions reflects Spanish control of the sources of galena likely derives from Shepard's (1965:71) not unreasonable suggestion that "It is not surprising that the art of glaze painting was lost because this was a Time of Trouble, the time of Spanish Conquest and settlement. It is more than likely that the Spaniards gained control of the mines from which ore for glaze paint had been secured." Her statement alludes to the period following the reconquest of New Mexico under Diego de Vargas, and the permanent Spanish reoccupation of New Mexico in 1693.

Kidder (in Kidder and Shepard 1936:610), from his work at Pecos, and from Shepard's observation that Pecos Glaze VI was imported to that pueblo, concluded that glaze production had been replaced there, and in much of the Rio Grande, by Tewa matte-painted and

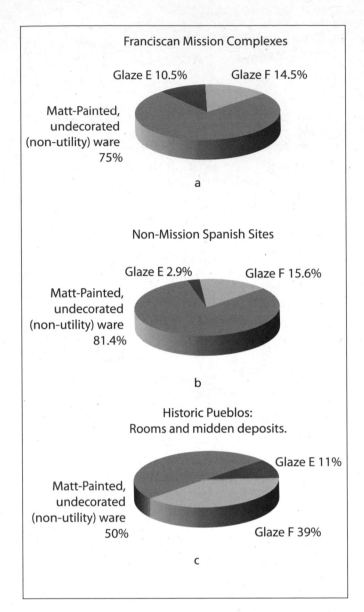

Figure 12.3. Ceramic percentages from
(a) seventeenth-century Franciscan
mission sites, (b) seventeenth-century
non-mission Spanish residential sites,
and (c) historic pueblo sites.

plain vessels by 1700. Kidder (1936:610) also noted
Nelson's (1916:176) comment on the near absence of
matte-painted Tewa pottery at pre-Revolt pueblos in the
Galisteo Basin, and its occurrence at colonial residential sites (Snow 1973). Yet, matte-painted Tewa pottery
was 36 percent of all non-utility sherds recovered from
a pre-Revolt colonial estancia at La Cienega, near Santa
Fe (Snow 2009). The remainder of the decorated types

from that site were glaze wares. The near absence of
matte-painted wares in the Galisteo Basin pueblos likely
is due to their own local glaze ware production.

Capone's analyses (Capone and Preucel 2002) indicate that glaze ware potters continued their practice at
the Keres refugee pueblo of Old Cochiti (La Cieneguilla) until it was deserted in 1695–1696. Conventional
wisdom continues to posit, somewhat arbitrarily, the
date of A.D. 1700 as the end of the Pueblo Glaze Ware
traditions (Eckert 2006). Nevertheless, Helene Warren
(1977b:2, 1979b), and more recently, Boggess and Hill
(2008) have speculated that glaze wares were produced
well into the mid-eighteenth century. The depositional
contexts reported by those authors, however, leave considerable room for alternative interpretations given the
very small number of glaze-painted sherds recovered.
Warren (1979b:191) also suggested that the Cerrillos
lead deposits had been virtually mined out by 1700.

Aside from the perceived wisdom that returning Spaniards preempted traditional Pueblo lead sources, other
factors have been offered for the failure of the glaze
traditions. Mills (2002:93), for example, suggested that
abandonment of glaze technology at Zuni was an "intentional act to mark a break with earlier ceramic production." Rothschild (2003:181) wondered whether glaze
production might not have ceased "because the basis of
identity definition changed," but she added, "or simply
because the Spanish took control of sources of lead."
In a related vein, Liebmann (2008) has suggested that
the failure of Jemez potters to continue their traditional
matte black-on-white pottery after 1680 was a conscious
effort to blur long-held precontact boundaries with their
neighbors. In any event, we should like to know how and
why intentional breaks, identity definitions, and blurring
of traditional boundaries might have been desirable or
necessary following the return of the Spaniards.

Regardless of such speculation, the simple fact that
the Salinas villages were deserted by 1675, the Rio
Abajo and Southern Tiwa pueblos by 1680–1681, and
the entire Galisteo Basin was permanently uninhabited
in 1680 (Schroeder 1979) suggests that demographic
and historical contingencies had much to do with the
end of glaze paint practice. Access to (or knowledge
of) traditional southern sources of lead (Hansonburg,
Magdalena) during the interregnum might have been
beyond the practicable reach of Middle Rio Grande or
other potters who might have been aware of those locations. Inter-pueblo hostilities while the Spaniards were
absent, as well as Apache and Navajo hostilities against

many of the pueblos, suggest that access to Cerrillos lead sources by the surviving Pueblos of the Middle Rio Grande might have made it difficult, if not impossible, to mine during the period from 1680 to 1696.

Scant attention has been focused on the pueblos of the Rio Abajo below the Southern Tiwa villages. The Piro pueblo of Sevilleta, according to charges leveled against Governor Manso, was depopulated between 1656 and 1659, the site sold, and the inhabitants transferred to Alamillo Pueblo (Hendricks and Mandell 2000:44). Senecu was destroyed early in 1675 by Apaches, and its inhabitants fled to Socorro Pueblo (Hodge and others 1945:248–259). Nevertheless, during their retreat south in response to the Pueblo Revolt, Rio Abajo colonists encountered the "friendly" inhabitants of Sevilleta, the "*pueblo del alto*" [Alamillo?], and Socorro, all of whom accompanied the retreating Spaniards to El Paso (Hackett and Shelby 1942:lxxi–lxxiv). None of those Piro pueblos was ever reestablished, and with them probably went knowledge of the southern lead ore sources at Magdalena and Hansonburg.

In 1695, the remaining Keres refugees at La Cieneguilla (Old Cochiti) left their mesa-top retreat, and most of them returned to their former pueblos (Espinosa 1988:146). Fray Sylvestre Vélez de Escalante, summarizing no-longer-extant documents, wrote that Keres Indians:

> originally from the pueblos of La Cieneguilla, Santo Domingo, and Cochiti, who had taken refuge at the Peñol of Acoma during the revolt of the year [16]96, came down, and at the end of the year [16]97 they established themselves four leagues to the north. . . . on a small river they now call Cubero. . . . about a mortar shot from La Laguna [Vélez de Escalante 1778:284].

In one of the major house-blocks in the refugee Keres village of La Cieneguilla, however, there were people from San Marcos pueblo (Kessell and others 1992:515) who subsequently disappear from the historical records. Along with their Keres neighbors, some of these San Marcos people may have moved to Laguna Pueblo, while others elected to remain at Santo Domingo where their descendants are recognized to this day (Ellis 1976).

Given that San Marcos and the Galisteo Basin pueblos are thought to have been the source of much of the lead for glaze paint, I suggest that it is not coincidence that the desertion of these settlements between 1680 and 1693 led to the near abandonment of glaze paint technology, and the concomitant loss of potters' knowledge of sources and recipes. Similarly, the Piro, or southern Rio Grande pueblos, were abandoned at the onset of the Pueblo Revolt, and the Salinas pueblos had been deserted for several years prior to the Revolt. Lacking traditional sources of lead from Rio Grande and other suppliers, potters at Zuni, and possibly Acoma, most likely also ceased production in 1680 (see Huntley and others 2007 for Zuni's use of Cerrillos and Socorro area lead sources).

Reoccupation of the Pueblo world in 1693 did not represent a tabula rasa—a clean slate reflecting more "settled" relations between Spaniards and the surviving pueblos (Dillingham 1992:129). This is clear from numerous official reports throughout the first half of the century, and later. By 1705, the population of the eight surviving Rio Grande pueblos where glaze paint formerly had been produced numbered only slightly more than 3,600 persons. That census, however, was not complete because the people were "still returning from the mountains." At Santo Domingo that year, for example, the population varied day to day between 20 and 80 persons (Hackett 1937:373–377).

Rumors of Pueblo unrest circulated as early as 1702, and a conspiracy comprising Acoma, Laguna, and Zuni prompted a detachment of soldiers to investigate, but nothing came of it (Flagler 1990:462–463). In 1704, a contingent of Hopis arrived at Taos Pueblo urging a renewed rebellion (Vélez de Escalante 1778:302); again, nothing seems to have come of the meeting. In 1708 the viceroy learned that the settlers and soldiers were causing "many extortions in their [the pueblos] women and daughters . . . taking from them what they have and not allowing them to plant and harvest" (Flagler 1990:467). Moved by "secret reports" in 1709, the viceroy issued a decree in which he noted that "the Pueblo Indians continued to be taken away all at once by the governor and alcaldes mayores of those provinces, [and] the pueblos are left with very few people, and the smaller ones without any" (Hackett 1937:431). As a result, he feared "the revolt that was being threatened every day would take place."

Because of Villasur's defeat at the hands of French and their Pawnee allies (Thomas 1935), the Pueblo auxiliaries were said have "became so overbearing" that an uprising was feared throughout the province (Jones 1966:102). In 1731, one priest was forced to once again forbid women cooks in the missions, and he instructed the priests to cease sending the Indians to work outside their missions (Archives of the Archdiocese of Santa Fe, New Mexico Records Center and Archive, Santa Fe [AASF], Loose Documents Nos. 1, 2).

Abuses by civil authorities were reported in great detail in 1749 and 1750 by various Franciscans and, again, in a lengthy diatribe in 1760 (Hackett 1937:425–430, 468–479, 488; Kelley 1941:166–168). It is clear that the familiar church and state struggles for control of Pueblo souls and backs continued virtually unabated until the later decades of the eighteenth century. As late as 1770, Fray Hinojosa issued instructions forbidding friars to employ weekly Pueblo helpers in missions for "weaving mantas, even under the pretext of keeping them busy, or in grinding grain for the Spaniards" (AASF, *Patentes* III, VI, No. 2).

As a result, it seems likely that, with the passing years and continued demands on Pueblo men and women for labor, the memory of glaze paint recipes faded, until, at Santo Domingo in 1880, Bandelier was told that the art of glaze paint "is totally lost." At Cochiti, he was informed that those who had made it "went south [and] are still living at El Paso" (Lange and Riley 1966:108, 215), and Bandelier inserted, "(Piros)," not realizing the extent of glaze practice in the Rio Grande. The following year, Lieutenant Bourke noted some pottery at Acoma that was "spotted and flecked with a green pigment" and remarked that the Acomas, and "to a very small extent the Lagunas, are the only Indians among whom I have detected any manifestations of an acquaintance" with the art of glazing (Bloom 1937:364).

CONCLUSIONS

Indigenous networks of interaction, whatever their nature during the nearly 400 years of glaze-paint production, and the communities of potters that participated in them, were severely disrupted during the seventeenth century. Although glaze-paint technology remained situated among various seventeenth-century pueblos, certainly until the Revolt of 1680, and perhaps as late as 1694–1695, evidence suggests increasingly hasty or expedient treatment by some potters. Labor requirements for Pueblo women, many of whom must have been traditional potters, might well have created "disconnects" with apprentice potters, resulting in failure of complete transmission of traditional technological knowledge.

Such "disconnects" might also have resulted from decisions by Pueblo authorities to limit or alter the contexts in which glaze technology was transmitted from "master" potter to apprentices, resulting in some instances in "closed-ability apprenticeships" (Lyons and Clark, Chapter 3). If apprentice potters, like their traditional instructors, received compensation for their products, regardless of the expediency with which their wares were produced, this might account for increased and hasty, if "faulty," production of the late glaze types. Ultimately, perhaps, production of unglazed Salinas Red Wares for mission and general colonial use signaled the near demise of Salinas district glaze ware production, and desertion of the entire district during the early years of the 1670s ended the practice entirely in that area. Increasing production and distribution of matte-painted Tewa polychrome vessels for Franciscans and colonial residents might have compensated for labor demands on glaze potters that precluded mining activities and, ultimately, decreasing production in some pueblos.

The turmoil among pueblo communities during the interregnum (1680–1693), and during the final years of the century, saw the permanent desertion of traditional suppliers of lead from the Rio Grande and the disappearance of glaze communities of practice. It can be assumed, as a result of these factors, that former networks through which lead, recipes, and other technological knowledge formerly flowed were irrevocably disrupted and had become impractical or impossible to reestablish during the eighteenth century.

CHAPTER THIRTEEN

Mineral Wealth and Value

Tracing the Impact of Early Spanish Colonial Mining on Puebloan Pigment and Glaze Paint Production

Noah Thomas

The production of glaze ware in the protohistoric Southwest was an important representation of Pueblo practice for Spanish explorers in the late sixteenth century. The recognition of glazed pots and their attendant technology fueled speculation by Spanish colonists of both the industriousness of Pueblo communities and the possibility of mineral wealth and local acumen necessary for the expansion of the Spanish mining industry into the new territory. Such practices also acted as a conduit for an exchange of cultural meanings surrounding mineral wealth and extraction at a time when cultural *doxa* for both Pueblo communities and Spanish colonists were being challenged.

For Pueblo communities, colonial incursions significantly affected daily life through the ravages of war and disease, the privations of taxation and religious persecution, and the disruption of traditional economic and resource allocation practices that accompanied the introduction of Spanish goods and new domestic plants and animals. Syncretic practices emphasizing the continuity of Puebloan traditions within colonial media or meaning frameworks emerged during this period (Farago and Pierce 2006; Lomawaima 1989; Mills 2002; Mobley-Tanaka 2002). Similarly, the Spanish colonial economy in its New Mexican context was transformed, being heavily indebted to local *encomienda* labor, women taken into households, and Pueblo resource knowledge and skilled practice. Colonial households incorporated indigenous products and tastes, and even at various times modified Spanish caste designations through the mobility of indigenous persons between pueblo and mestizo communities (Brooks 2002). Syncretic practice also intermittently affected the strictures of Catholic practice through the incorporation of Kiva spaces and imagery in mission architecture (Kessell 1979; Vivian 1979).

I argue here that the interaction of two distinct communities of practice—Spanish colonial miners and Pueblo pigment procurers—during the early colonial period (A.D. 1598–1680) produced a similarly syncretic approach to minerals and their social and economic value. I explore this syncretic practice historically through a particular reading of *entrada* documents and contemporary metallurgical treatises, and in reference to ethnographic descriptions of Pueblo mineral use. These practices are explored materially through an analysis of archaeological data recovered from the seventeenth-century metallurgical workshop found in the historic component of LA 162, the pueblo of Paa-ko (Fig. 13.1).

The archaeological material discussed here was recovered by the University of Chicago Summer Field Studies Program from 1995 to 2005, under the direction of Mark Lycett. The workshop at LA 162 was in use during the first half of the seventeenth century (as indicated by radiocarbon assays and associated ceramics) and offers a firsthand look at the types of minerals appropriated by seventeenth-century Spanish miners and the various processes used to assess and extract metallic wealth from them. As few examples of unprocessed minerals are available for this period, this analysis is valuable for assessing the types of ore bodies that were available to Pueblo potters. The syncretic practice indicated by the workshop assemblage also sheds light on similar practices incorporated in contemporary and antecedent Pueblo glaze ware technology.

The mineral assemblage and suite of technologies practiced at the metallurgical workshop at LA 162 is representative of the historical development of Puebloan mineral procurement and use practices, and the appropriation of mineral resources under Spanish colonialism, during the late sixteenth and early seventeenth centuries.

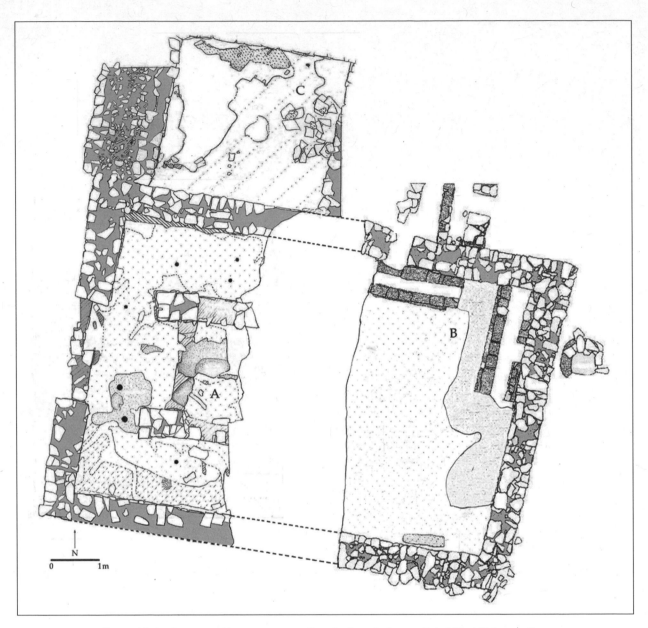

Figure 13.1. Seventeenth-century metallurgical workshop at LA 162: (A) base of smelting furnace; (B) linear bin furnaces, possibly for metal refining and forge work; (C) charcoal concentration and roasting platform. The workshop was unfortunately bisected by a pothunter's trench excavated in the 1950s. Map by Noah Thomas.

This provides an example of a process of commodification of mineral resources under colonialism (Kopytoff 1986). Minerals used as pigment and paint were centrally incorporated within Pueblo meaning frameworks in a variety of media involved with religious paraphernalia and social categories of identity. Puebloan value designations intersected with Spanish colonial meaning frameworks for the assessment of mineral worth

through color. From the *entradas* of the 1580s through the Pueblo Revolt of 1680, the interaction between miners and indigenous procurers of minerals shaped the "biography" of minerals as a class of objects, shaping their assessed value and use through economic and cultural pressure.

The appropriation of mineral resources by Spanish colonists transformed a material that was important for the creation of symbolically charged objects, or inalienable goods, to a commodity valued for its exchangeability as precious metal. This transformation reorganized indigenous labor and practice through the taxation of goods and labor, and the introduction of workshop production contexts. It is clear from entrada documents that the practice of assessing mineral value was more than just an assay process determining material content. Mineral value was assessed in reference to social parameters, particularly labor requirements, and deeper cultural regimes of value involving color designations.

COLOR SIGNIFICANCE AND THE DETERMINATION OF VALUE

Spanish mining was the premier industry in the creation of value in the colonial world of the seventeenth century. Spanish conceptions of value related to mining and the production of minerals intersected Puebloan practices that created value from painted objects. Colored minerals were used extensively in Puebloan ritual in the Pueblo IV period to paint katsina masks, prayer sticks, and ceramic vessels. Minerals were involved in extensive systems of exchange, linking communities across broad regions to specific places, helping to create and recreate the memory of origins and migrations (Duff 2002; Eckert 2006; Fenn and others 2006; Graves and Eckert 1998; Habicht-Mauche 1993, 2006; Habicht-Mauche and others 2000; Huntley and others 2007). An example of this is provided in Chapter 6, in Eckert's discussion of the color symbolism of Heshotauthla and Kwakina Polychrome. In recent periods, minerals were often a medium for expressing the color designations that reference social distinctions, geographic associations, and spiritual connections to temporal processes (Cushing 1979; Ferguson and Hart 1985; Ortiz 1969; Parsons 1966).

The interaction between Spanish colonial metallurgists and Puebloan pigment procurers, despite the distinct histories, created an overlay of practice. This was particularly true for each community's approach to the valuation of materials and the cultural categories of meaning within which color played a significant part. Both communities of practice included a common language of color that indicated the value of minerals, the divisions between color types, and the potential of landscapes. Rather than assessing the value of an ore body based on its mineral components, as is done in prospecting today, Spanish colonial prospectors used color as the primary indicator of metallic content.

In the mining industry of New Spain, technologies of metal extraction were organized based on the characterization of the ore body exploited as either "red" (*colorados*) or "black" (*negrillos*) ores, where color indicated internal properties. Both colorados and negrillos ores could equally be rich in silver or other metals, but the processing technologies required of each were quite distinct. Accompanying color designations were determinations of the internal qualities of ores as either "dry" or "wet," referencing alchemical notions of how metals formed within the earth. Red ores were considered "dry" ores and amenable to mercury amalgam processing. Red coloring is repeatedly used as a reference for silver deposits in landscape descriptions of the period. In color associations of the sixteenth and seventeenth centuries, green copper ores could be indicative of red ore internal qualities, through their association with gossan (weathered surface ore) deposits that were typically red owing to the presence of iron hydroxides (Barba 1923:97). Copper was also understood as "the origin or foundation of all silver mines," in that copper "gives the color to the silver ore known as negrillos," a possible recognition of primary mineralization involving copper sulfides (Barba 1923:72–73). Black ores were typically sulfide ores and required additional processes, such as roasting or calcination, that were more appropriate for smelting technologies. Color designations therefore had a direct influence on the practice of mining, determining the scale of operations, ranging from the capital-intensive mercury amalgamation processes to the smaller-scale smelting facilities. Color thus affected the potential profitability of an operation based on access to other resources needed for successful metal extraction.

A Spanish prospector's conceptualization of red and black ores placed value on newly encountered landscapes in terms of their wealth-bearing potential. In contrast, color and landscape attributes in traditional Puebloan practice indicated the values inherent in a moral economy, an inalienable "wealth" associated with the inherent directionality of sacred beings or the cosmological reference points of a socialized universe. Ethnographic work among Pueblo communities suggests that color references social organization and core cosmological concepts. Ortiz's (1969) ethnography of San Juan Pueblo emphasizes the importance of color distinctions in moiety divisions, referencing basic cosmological divisions between summer and winter seasonal cycles. Color designations are rooted to the origin of socialized people in the Tewa worldview, linked to the creation of six pairs of brothers who explored and defined the boundaries of the Tewa universe from the Tewa place of origin.

Some significant areas of overlap are also present when one looks at how color informed practice for Spanish and Puebloan communities. Colors, and the internal properties that they represented, were manipulated within the domain of "medicine" both by seventeenth-century Spanish colonial metallurgists and by Puebloan ritual practitioners. For Spanish metallurgists, transformations of color indicated a transformation of the character of an ore. Embedded within metallurgical color terminology was a discourse concerning the link between spiritual transformation and the transformation of matter, derived from European medieval alchemical traditions. Alchemical and metallurgical processes were often conceptualized as healing processes, through work engaged in balancing the internal properties of a substance in order to perfect it (Barba 1923; Holmyard 1957). There is a general blurring of distinctions between that which is "healing" in the transformation of metals and those substances deemed efficacious for the curing of ailments. Materials such as sulfur, alum, and verdigris, used in metallurgical processes, are listed as medicines in the Salazar inspection of the Oñate colony in 1598 (Hammond and Rey 1953:220, 255). Litharge (lead oxide) was used as an ingredient in many of the medicines available in the Spanish colonies in the sixteenth century (Simpson 1937). Litharge was necessary for the refining of silver, drawing parallels between techniques for the curing of the metallic body and of the human body.

Within the healing practices of the Northern Tewa, Pueblo communities that probably had direct contact with Spanish mining efforts, color is an indicator of identity through its association with moiety divisions and seasonal qualities. This is distinct from the process of transformation that was assumed in Spanish metallurgical practices. The use of specific colors in ritual practice, such as the use of colored corn at sodality initiations, indicates both communal identities related to village and moiety and individual identities related to becoming members of ritual sodalities (Ford 1992:226). Color is one of a series of identity-establishing attributes for medicines used to heal ailments based on "hot" or "cold" imbalances (Ford 1992:132–134).

Cultural perspectives on the meaning of color in Spanish and Puebloan communities of practice form the negotiative context within which value designations were determined by Spanish prospectors. The value of minerals for both communities of practice during the late sixteenth and early seventeenth centuries ranged on a continuum from a commodity used to produce wealth within a global economy to a material referencing identity, symbolic process, and social value. Spanish miners used color designations to determine landscape worth, triggering the commodification of landscape resources. Color designations were also embedded in other meaning frameworks involved with metallurgical practice that referenced internal qualities of materials not easily commodified. Color referenced character in terms of process, in what Gage has called a "language of movement" (Gage 1999). This formed a common ground between value designations of both communities. The Pueblo valuation of minerals linked color to internal qualities of identity that referenced inalienable aspects of cultural patrimony.

From this perspective, the historical record of early prospecting and ore assays suggests the importance given to Puebloan mineral knowledge by Spanish miners. Early historic exchange of minerals appears to have centered on copper carbonate and copper sulfide ores, despite Spanish colonial preferences for mining lead sulfide bearing silver ores. Copper minerals appear to have been accepted as potentially silver-rich ores. In 1581, Gallegos accepted "samples of a copperish steel-like metal," probably chalcopyrite, thought to be rich in silver. In 1582, Luján and Espejo were taken to copper deposits, which Espejo (but not Luján) claimed were silver-rich (Bolton 1963; Hammond and Rey 1953, 1966). Following in their path, Farfan de Godos in 1598 was taken to the same mines and was impressed with the deep blue color of the ores. A recent translation of the Farfan account by the Office of Ethnohistoric Research, Arizona State Museum, indicates that Farfan identified these minerals as smalt, a synthetic pigment created as a by-product of cobalt-silver ore processing in Europe. These historical records show how value was negotiated in an early colonial context, and document that copper minerals, particularly those exhibiting blue-green coloration, became a medium of exchange.

At the seventeenth-century metallurgical workshop at LA 162, distinctions between red ores and black ores, and the value of blue-green minerals, provided a strong structuring framework for ore acquisition and the organization of the technology. Copper carbonate ores, particularly malachite and azurite minerals, dominate the assemblage, despite historical preferences for lead and silver sulfide ores in the mining industry of New Spain. Lead sulfide and carbonate ores are present in the vicinity of the pueblo and were a component of the technology at LA 162, as well. The focus on copper ores may be an extension of the negotiations of ore value initiated in the initial *entrada* prospecting accounts.

Puebloan practice emphasizing the value of blue-green minerals overlapped with Spanish values positioning copper as "giving the color" to silver ores. Three smelting facilities from the seventeenth century have been excavated in New Mexico. All of these facilities reflect a technology with a significant use of copper ores, despite their being located adjacent to lead ores with a profitable silver content in the Cerrillos and New Placers mining districts (Vaughan 2001, 2006; Warren and Weber 1979). The smelting facilities at San Marcos Pueblo (LA 98) and Paa-ko (LA 162) were located within pueblos that had a long history of occupation. This differs from the strategy of Spanish colonists who developed the mining industry in northern New Spain (such as Zacatecas and Parral), where mining operations were often newly-formed communities. The three major mining communities in the New Mexican colony were La Cienega, San Marcos, and El Tuerto, and these were all occupied pueblos at the time of the New Mexican colony was established (Barrett 2002; Milford and Swick 1995).

The incorporation of pueblos, and presumably pueblo inhabitants, into early mining endeavors in New Mexico suggests a context in which indigenous labor, knowledge, and skill were viewed as vital to the success of mining practices. The assessment of mineral value in the early colony triggered a kind of double assay, evident in the coupling of mineralogical assessments (based on internal qualities) with assessments of the character of indigenous communities in terms of docility and industriousness.

The determination of material value in this early period occurred within contexts where indigenous practice involving resource knowledge and skilled labor played a central role. These contexts facilitated future appropriations of resources under Spanish colonial rule. Establishment of a mining industry in New Mexico hinged on continuing the exploitation of mineral resources that were important in precolonial mineral exchange. Other industries of the early colony had similar roots. For example, the trade in hides by Rio Grande Pueblos and Plains tribes, and the production and trade of textiles, were important elements of precolonial exchange systems that figured prominently in the effort of colonial elites to obtain wealth (Pierce 2006; Webster 1997, 2000).

PRODUCING VALUE: ORE PROCUREMENT AND PROCESSING AT LA 162

The ore assemblage and technology of ore preparation at the workshop at LA 162 is representative of the value negotiations just outlined. Ore acquisition and processing in the incipient Spanish colonial mining industry in New Mexico can be viewed as a syncretic practice during this period. In this regard, the composition of ore recovered from the excavations of the workshop is of particular interest to the discussion of mineral types incorporated in ceramic glaze and paint recipes. Ores used in the metallurgical workshop at LA 162 appear to have been predominantly treated by Spanish metallurgists as negrillos ores, in that roasting played a large part in the pre-smelting processing treatments for both copper and lead ores. Both lead and copper ores were smelted in a furnace regime consisting of a reducing atmosphere in temperatures exceeding 1100° C achieved with a forced draft system utilizing bellows, using wood charcoal as fuel. High-temperature, oxidizing furnace operations also appear to have been employed but are not as well represented based on the volumes of metallurgical material recovered. The metallic content of the ore was obtained through smelting operations, and further refining processes including cupellation and possibly a cementation process involving sulfur (Thomas 2008).

The assemblage has two aspects that are relevant to the discussion of minerals in relation to ceramic production: (1) mineral choice, and how those choices reflect local knowledge and exploitation of sources, and (2) ore processing technologies for minerals, and how those technologies reflect continuity and innovation in Pueblo practice that may have become incorporated within ceramic production. Ore recovered from the workshop at LA 162 exhibits a wide variety of compositions but can be grouped into four basic types. Petrographic analyses of ores obtained from the facility, coupled with SEM-EDS and XRF quantitative and semi-quantitative analysis of element composition, suggest that a variety of copper, lead, and zinc ores were used (see Thomas 2008 for a more complete description of element composition). The copper ores are (1) gossan ores that are primarily malachite [$Cu_2CO_3(OH)_2$] but also iron hydroxides (limonite, $FeO(OH)_nH_2O$) produced by weathering of iron sulfide minerals; (2) ores that are primarily chrysocolla [$(Cu,Al)_2H_2Si_2O_5(OH)_4 \cdot nH_2O$], with remnant copper sulfides such as chalcopyrite ($CuFeS_2$) and covellite (CuS); and (3) sulfide ores, primarily chalcopyrite with some occurrence of covellite and malachite. The lead ores recovered from the facility contain primary minerals of galena (PbS), sphalerite (ZnS), and calcite ($CaCO_3$); carbonates of lead and zinc, such as cerrusite ($PbCO_3$) and smithsonite ($ZnCO_3$); and sulfates of lead such as anglesite ($PbSO_4$). A zinc silicate is also associated with this ore and is most likely hemimorphite [$Zn_4Si_2O_7(OH)_2 \cdot H_2O$], which commonly occurs with smithsonite (Nesse 2000). Both the lead and copper ores suggest that colonial miners at Paa-ko exploited the oxidized zones of primary ore deposits associated with iron, copper, zinc, and lead sulfides, such as chalcopyrite, pyrite, sphalerite, and galena, with calcite and quartz as the primary gangue minerals.

The fact that gossan ores are the primary ores used at the facility suggests that mineral procurement for the workshop took advantage of near-surface deposits, probably as extensions of precolonial mineral procurement localities. Excavations at the Bethsheba mine near Cerrillos suggest the Spanish workings followed ore exposures initially mined by Pueblo mineral procurers (Bice and others 2003). A similar strategy may have been employed by prospectors using ore sources in proximity to LA 162, such as those found in the Tijeras, New Placers, or Placitas mining districts. The overlapping of precolonial and colonial mining tend to blur the distinction between early colonial mining operations and seventeenth-century Puebloan mineral procurement. In fact, the mining in both cases may be a continuation of precolonial practices augmented by iron tools in certain circumstances. This may contribute to the negative assessment of Spanish mining provided in contemporary records of the industry and by ethnohistorians and archaeologists (see Snow, Chapter 12).

Ore composition, particularly the lead ores found at the pueblo, may address some of the questions posed by Blinman and others (Chapter 11) concerning the use of either galena or cerrusite as primary fluxing minerals for Pueblo glaze. The workshop ores contain both minerals, with petrographic analysis demonstrating their crystalline intergrowth (Fig. 13.2). If LA 162 ores are representative of a source or sources used in glaze production, then both minerals were probably

incorporated into glaze compositions. The composition of the ores also may address questions concerning the co-occurrence of coloring agents for glaze production, namely manganese, iron, and copper. Although manganese is present in minor concentrations in at least one ore sample analyzed from the workshop, copper, iron, calcium, and zinc minerals are nearly always present in significant percentages. This compositional variance is carried through the production process at LA 162, with slag compositions containing metallic copper, calcium, and iron silicates, and furnace refractory exhibiting concretions of zinc mineralization from its volitization during furnace operation.

Aspects of the mineral assemblage and associated features at LA 162 suggest that Pueblo mineral processing procedures continued to be practiced while the metallurgical workshop was in operation, and may have been incorporated in the technology at the workshop. Ore appears to have been processed during the colonial occupation of the pueblo, ancillary to other activities on the plaza, as indicated by the processed malachite found in plaza surfaces (Lycett 2004). Similarly, recent survey and excavation of an early colonial period field house in the floodplain adjacent to San Pedro arroyo recovered malachite fragments and what appeared to be a tool kit for ore processing incorporated within the floor assemblage. The volume of ore represented by each of these two contexts is small compared with that found in the workshop, but they suggest that ore processing was

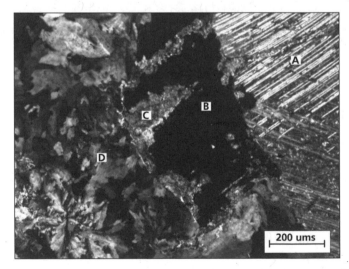

Figure 13.2. Photomicrograph of lead ore sample from the metallurgical workshop at LA 162, in transmitted, cross-polarized light (XPL). A = calcite; B = galena; C = cerrusite; D = anglesite. Photo by Noah Thomas.

Figure 13.3. Northern exterior area of the metallurgical workshop at LA 162: (A) concentration of charcoal and burned earth, (B) tabular sandstone platforms. Photo by Noah Thomas.

conducted in traditional Puebloan workspaces as well as the metallurgical workshop.

A low-temperature reduction process was used at the workshop, similar to Pueblo ceramic firing technologies. Feature 90E/-163N/F1 (Fig. 13.3) is reminiscent of ceramic firing features described by Orcutt at San Lazaro (Blinman and others, Chapter 11) and consists of small cobble "tripods" associated with a dense charcoal accumulation capped in layers by a burned silt-loam. Although this feature may be the remnant of a firing platform for ceramic production, it is located at the base of deposits for the metallurgical workshop, and the lead ore found in the charcoal matrix suggests that it functioned at some point as an ore roasting facility for the smelting operations. Both lead ores and copper ores were roasted in similar features across the workshop, often incorporating fragments of mold-made adobe block (possibly a Spanish-introduced technology) rather than cobble elements, placed in proximity to smelting furnaces. One such feature contains a ventilation system similar to those found in kivas and may represent the incorporation of Pueblo roasting technology within the facility.

The analysis of the lead slag produced at the workshop as a by-product may provide a historically contextual "experimental" case study for the effects of firing regimes on local lead minerals. Lead slag recovered from the workshop is predominantly glassy with some mineralization, including the formation of lead, calcium, and iron silicates. It also often contains a fine dispersal of metallic copper and lead droplets and crushed parent rock material. It is interesting to note in reference to the possible effect of manganese on glaze color that although manganese was not recognized as a significant compositional element in the XRF analysis of lead ore, it does appear in significant weight percentages in the XRF data for the lead slag material (0.33% to 0.9%). This suggests that it may be concentrated as part of the reduction process, or it is a component of refractory, flux, or fuel composition. Fuel and refractory composition do influence other glassy lead materials present at the site, such as the glassy components of litharge cakes in their contact with ash-lined refractory material. The glassy slag from the workshop was produced at high temperatures (above 1100° C) and in highly reducing atmospheres made possible by the combined use of charcoal and forced draft. Although this exceeded what was possible with Pueblo firing technology (utilizing oxidizing atmospheres with natural draft), the slag is consistently black or greenish black, similar to Pueblo glaze colors.

The refining operations and the copper and iron forge work at the workshop used wood as the primary fuel source. All other metallurgical activities appear to have relied on charcoal. The colonial introduction of charcoal as a fuel source, distinct from raw wood fuel, may be a significant contribution to Pueblo pyrotechnology. Charcoal production was a separate technology involving the combustion of wood fuel in a low-oxygen environment, necessary for the highly reducing atmospheres of smelting operations. Interestingly, charcoal also appears to have been used exclusively for open-air roasting operations at the workshop. The charcoal was made predominantly from ponderosa pine, with an unidentified species of oak also used in small quantities (Kathleen Morrison, personal communication 2007). This corresponds to historical preferences within the metallurgical industry for charcoal made from hardwoods (Bakewell 1971). The availability of this new fuel source may have contributed to some of the changes recognized in glaze appearance during this period.

DISRUPTION OF TRADITIONAL PRODUCTION PRACTICES THROUGH COMMODIFICATION

The incorporation of Puebloan mineral procurement practices in the metallurgical technology at LA 162 had the potential to disrupt the historical link between mineral procurement and social production through disruption of the practices involved with the production of ritual paraphernalia. The manufacture of other items to accommodate colonial tribute demands and work regimes, such as mantas and hides, entailed a shift in the way traditional production activities were scheduled and organized in Pueblo productive practices. For textile production, Webster (2000) documents that by the mid-seventeenth century demands for tribute resulted in rescheduling seasonal cloth production, changing traditional gendered divisions of labor, and shifting the production of cloth from ritual spaces to household and workshop contexts. New technologies were introduced through tribute demands and contexts of mission indoctrination, with wool and knitting techniques becoming increasingly important toward the end of the seventeenth century. A similar trajectory can be traced with other goods, such as hides prepared for trade to the mining centers of Parral and Zacatecas (Pierce 2006).

The commodification of materials involved with important social exchange in precolonial contexts of production was realized through the appropriation of Pueblo labor within these new contexts of production. In the decades following the initial colonization, various governors instituted workshop production as a way to generate personal wealth through the production of a higher volume of tribute goods. Hide painting and textile manufacture were conducted in such contexts under Governors Juan de Eulate (1618–1625) and Luis de Rosas (1637–1641). Workshop contexts for textile production included both Pueblo and Mexican Indian workers (Pierce 2006:139). Goods produced were traded in the mining centers of northern New Spain, especially Parral.

One way to look at workshop production is to view it as a strategy of colonial elites to reconfigure indigenous labor in order to break traditional production practices through the formation of commodity production. Materials whose value was closely tied to Pueblo moral economies were transformed through appropriated labor into instruments of colonial wealth acquisition. The facility at LA 162 provides an archaeological example of a workshop context, formally delimited by the terraces of masonry construction. The metallurgical workshop constituted a new social context for work that supplanted earlier production in households, kivas, or plazas. Metallurgical facilities, particularly those involved with time-dependent processes such as smelting and forging, are often highly structured in order to both limit and facilitate productive action within their spaces (Keller and Keller 1996). The highly structured space of the facility at LA 162, built adjacent to the historic plaza and the adjoining room block, would have entailed a similar restrictive structuring of action.

The internal organization of the facility was related to other structuring activities in the pueblo and surrounding landscape that entailed wood gathering, charcoal preparation, mining, and ore sorting. As with textile production, these activities may have impacted the traditional organization of production and social structures of action, including the gendered divisions of labor and, particularly for mining and the appropriation of minerals, the tasks under the direction of ritual sodalities.

Producing value in workshops divorced value from its precolonial contexts because the appropriation of labor undercut traditional practice, and the appropriation of resources limited the kinds of materials that were acquired for traditional uses and the forms of exchange within which they participated. The pressures of the mining industry on Pueblo mineral use went beyond just replacing that use with colonial elite appropriation; these pressures could be systemically disruptive to the moral economy within which mineral pigments played a significant part.

CONCLUSION

The technology of the metallurgical workshop at LA 162 was syncretic because it incorporated Pueblo resource knowledge and ore processing practices. Spanish colonists appropriated Pueblo labor and resources, and attempted to commodify a resource traditionally used to establish or reference inalienable possessions and cultural patrimony.

At the same time, the intersection of communities of practice in the technology at LA 162 opened avenues for the appropriation of Spanish colonial resources by Pueblo practitioners, such as metals used as objects of adornment, and this is evident at the workshop (Thomas 2008). Copper sheets produced from refined copper ingots were cut into trapezoidal and circular shapes, stamped, incised, and perforated for suspension. This appropriation of metallic worth as objects of adornment may be interpreted, in part, as a re-emphasis of mineral value as referencing social value. Such re-appropriations are evident in the nineteenth and twentieth centuries with the production of silver jewelry from silver coin, and the associated value of these items beyond their metallic worth as collateral for the funding of feasts and ritual occasions (Adair 1944; Ostler and others 1996). The production of copper "jewelry" at LA 162 is an antecedent practice possibly with similar goals, prefiguring the development of Pueblo and Navajo silverwork.

In concert with the themes addressed in this volume, it is informative to view the production of glaze ware as lying between the two extremes of commodity appropriation and the recovery of signification. The intersection of Puebloan mineral use with Spanish colonial valuation of mineral resources highlights the cultural tensions of signification present in the use of minerals that held a common value between both communities of practice. On the one hand, the use of lead ores for the production of ceramic glaze allowed for the continuation of traditionally significant imagery within mission contexts, despite their attempted repression by missionaries. Spielmann and others (2006) suggest that glaze ware became a ceramic form associated with mission contexts, enabling Pueblo potters to mask ritually significant imagery with simplified designs and runny glaze during the early colonial period in the Salinas district. On the other hand, glaze ware vessels became the bearers of colonial practice through the production of new ceramic forms associated with missionization, such as candlesticks and baptismal fonts (Dyer, Chapter 14; Mills 2002). The rejection of glaze-painted ceramics as an appropriate medium for social identification in the post-Revolt period may be tied to the tensions developed in the process and contestation of commodification and missionization.

The vitrification of minerals within glaze technology was perhaps too close to Spanish colonial metallurgical determinations of value for the practice to continue in the post-Revolt period. Glaze paint may have symbolized the transformative properties of ore minerals and the industry that undercut traditional mineral procurement and use. Spanish mineral appropriation appears to have "piggy-backed" on Puebloan mineral procurement strategies. Owing to the appropriative nature of the process, once mining practices were instituted, Puebloan mineral procurers may have had restricted access to lead minerals that were available only in conjunction with Spanish mining practices and demands. As part of a syncretic technological system, lead mineral procurement and associated processing technologies may have left the domain of traditional practice (through the instigation of colonial work regimes) to be subsumed under the suite of practices applied to such minerals under the Spanish mining industry. The continuation of glaze ware ceramics throughout the colonial period may in effect be an artifact of the overlay of practices between each community made possible by the shared suite of practices. Rather than a continuation of precolonial practice, seventeenth-century glaze technology may be a syncretic colonial practice. Shared practices between Spanish miners and Puebloan mineral procurers may have compensated for a break in the continuity of traditional knowledge owing to population loss and other factors, in effect reinstituting resource networks disrupted by colonial appropriation and population reduction (see Snow, Chapter 12).

The revitalization movements instigated in the wake of the Revolt called for the painting of katsina masks, perhaps re-appropriating mineral color as a signifier of identity in contrast to the Spanish colonial recognition of color as an indication of the transformative processes producing wealth. The distinction between color as indicative of identity and color as indicative of process may have been drawn more fully in the attempt at cultural preservation, in effect drawing a sharp distinction between each community of practice. Such cultural distinctions could have made certain technologies inappropriate, perhaps including the pyrotechnology of glaze that became associated with the extractive metallurgy, or smelting, introduced by Spanish colonists. Although Puebloan smiths became proficient in iron, copper, and silver fabrication in subsequent periods, they ceased to use Spanish techniques of extractive metallurgy.

CHAPTER FOURTEEN

Glaze-painted Colono Wares

Continuity or Innovation?

Jennifer Boyd Dyer

Colono wares signal Spanish contact across the Spanish Empire. Because colono wares are low-fired, locally produced ceramics that take on European shapes (Deagan and Cruxent 1993; Ferguson 1980; Hume 1962), this hybrid pottery can be used to address native change or persistence during the early colonial period (defined as initial contact through the seventeenth century). Colono wares appear in low frequencies at many settlements in New Mexico, and elsewhere, beginning in the seventeenth century. Vessel shape is usually considered a highly conservative technological variable (Reina and Hill 1978). However, in the case of colono wares, this empirical generalization does not hold. In fact, vessel shape changes are one of the most visible markers of the contact horizon. The appearance of colono wares suggests that Pueblo potters copied European vessel forms readily and without difficulty, just as design styles can be copied easily between groups without direct learning. However, because colono wares in New Mexico have not been the subject of sustained research, unlike in Florida or the Caribbean (Boyd and others 1951; Deagan 1983, 1985, 1987, 1990a, 1990b, 1995; Ewen 1990; Garcia-Arevalo 1990; Henry 1992; Rolland and Ashley 2000; Saunders 2000; Singleton and Bograd 2000; Smith 1995; South and others 1988; Vernon and Cordell 1991, 1993), we do not know whether shape was the only attribute to change or whether other technological variables also changed, signaling a new ceramic tradition.

An operating assumption behind this study is that technological style (Lechtmann 1977) underlies variation in artifacts and includes all of the decisions that an individual makes during the production of an artifact, whether compositional, formal, or decorative (Schiffer and Skibo 1987). This concept is particularly useful for investigating complex technologies, such as ceramics, that require shared recipes and learning networks within a group (Habicht-Mauche and others 2006; Rice 1987). Potters share a set of manufacturing techniques constrained by local tradition, which are taught to each successive generation, creating bounded social units (Crown 2001; Eckert 2008) or communities of practice (Silliman 2009; Stark 2006; Van Keuren 2006). Because ceramics are physical manifestations of cultural learning and group identity, I use them to elucidate change and continuity in Pueblo groups during the early colonial period.

My research on glaze-painted colono wares in New Mexico is the first systematic technological analysis of colono wares in the Southwest (Dyer 2010). In this chapter, I present results from my colono ware analysis that show considerable continuity between precolonial and early colonial ceramics, with some subtle technological differences in colono wares. The results are significant because they indicate that the early colonial period in New Mexico was characterized by Pueblo resilience and innovation, with little evidence of disruption by the Spaniards. Additionally, I show that there is significant variability in soup plates produced throughout the colony of New Mexico, which suggests that these new vessel forms were not manufactured with strict guidelines using a "Spanish mold," nor were they produced under heavy-handed Spanish control.

COLONO WARES IN NEW MEXICO

Rim forms of Rio Grande glaze-painted ceramics change through time. The most dramatic change occurs during the early colonial period when Pueblo potters adopt new, Spanish-inspired vessel forms, known as

Figure 14.1. Several Colono Ware Forms. From left to right: Candlestick, from Pecos Pueblo; glaze-on-orange soup plate, from San Marcos Pueblo; and glaze-on-red teacup (runny glaze), from San Gabriel del Yunque Pueblo. Photographs by Shawn Penman (left) and Ann Ramenofsky (middle, right), reproduced courtesy of the Robert S. Peabody Museum of Archaeology, Phillips Academy (left), the American Museum of Natural History (middle), and the Maxwell Museum of Anthropology, University of New Mexico (right).

colono wares. These forms include candlesticks, teacups, pitchers, baptismal fonts, and soup plates (Fig. 14.1).

Soup plates are by far the most common colono ware form found in early colonial period assemblages in New Mexico (Penman 2002). Glaze-painted soup plates, which are small, shallow bowls, are thought to have been smaller versions of glaze-painted traditional bowls; both likely were used for food service at the household level (Capone 2004; Nelson and Habicht-Mauche 2006; Warren 1979b). However, these vessel forms were not functionally equivalent. Traditional bowls likely were used to serve stews or porridges in which all ingredients were mixed together, whereas soup plates may have been for serving individual components of a meal (Deetz 1977) or European-introduced foods, which may have been associated with higher status. Additionally, glaze-painted soup plates were individual serving vessels (Vernon and Cordell 1991, 1993), whereas glaze-painted traditional bowls were much larger, likely used as communal serving vessels, which probably did not appeal to Spanish sensibilities. In fact, soup plates may be a physical manifestation of a shifting focus on the individual, within the context of the rise of modernism in Europe (Deetz 1977).

Many assumptions have been made regarding colono ware production and consumption, but because of the lack of work on colono wares in New Mexico, they are not empirically based. Common assumptions are that colono wares in New Mexico were produced by Pueblo potters under the direction of local Spanish religious or secular personnel, and that colono wares were substitutes for preferred, but difficult to obtain, European pottery, including *majolicas* (Deagan 1990a; Goggin 1968; McEwan 1990; Saunders 2000; Vernon 1988). However, the idea that colono wares were exclusively used by Spaniards is questionable because soup plates have been found in purely native contexts in New Mexico, such as in field houses on mesa tops in the Jemez Mountains (Boyd and Constan 2002; Kulisheck 2001, 2002, 2005). In terms of production, the mechanism of technology transfer of colono wares from the Spaniards to Pueblo potters is unknown. For instance, it is not known whether the Spaniards dictated the forms, or whether Pueblo potters chose to make these new forms in response to a new market demand.

METHOD OF INVESTIGATION

I begin with three questions: (1) Was there technological continuity or change in glaze-painted ceramics during the early colonial period? (2) Was the technology of glaze-painted colono wares as different as their

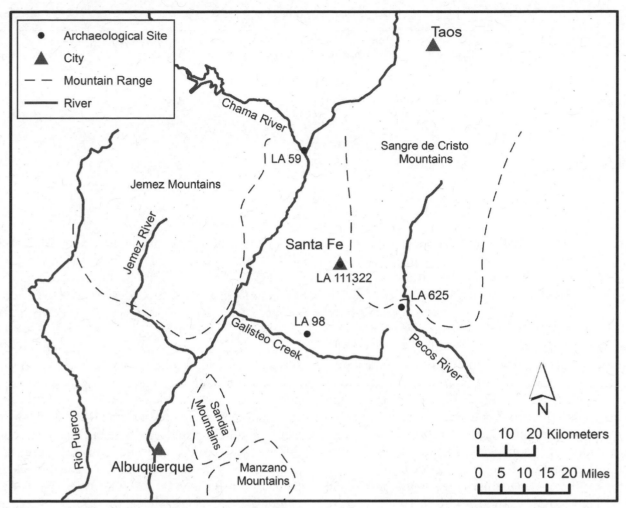

Figure 14.2. Study Area showing San Gabriel del Yunque (LA 59), San Marcos Pueblo (LA 98), Pecos Pueblo (LA 625), and Palace of the Governors (LA 111322). Map produced by Audrey Al-Ali.

morphology, constituting the beginning of a new modern Pueblo ceramic tradition? (3) What was the range of variability in glaze-painted colono wares? To address these questions, multiscalar analyses are conducted to compare microscopic and macroscopic variation. Microscopic variables are measured to determine whether glaze-painted traditional bowls changed in composition during the early colonial period, and whether or not soup plates were distinct compositionally. Variability in soup plates is measured through a systematic analysis of macroscopic variables related to morphology, decoration, surface treatments, and vessel construction.

Rio Grande Glaze C bowls (A.D. 1425–1490) and Glaze D bowls (A.D. 1490–1515), both produced before contact, are used as a baseline for comparisons with early colonial period Glaze E bowls (A.D. 1515–1650/1700) and Glaze F bowls and soup plates (A.D. 1625–1700) (McKenna and Miles 1991). One caveat is that the cross-dates for glaze ceramics may not accurately address the production span of each type (Ramenofsky, Chapter 9). The production dates of Glaze A Yellow are especially problematic, but they are not used in this study. Even though the bounding dates may be off, rim shapes provide strong temporal signals, and Glaze C through Glaze F ceramics were produced sequentially, albeit with some overlap.

Ceramics from mission and non-mission settings are analyzed, including two mission pueblos, San Marcos and Pecos; the first Spanish capital, San Gabriel del Yunque; and the Palace of the Governors in Santa Fe, the first Spanish villa or town, which was also the second Spanish capital of New Mexico (Fig. 14.2). The site

Table 14.1. Ceramic Sample

Temper Type	Pueblo	Province	Glaze C	Glaze D	Glaze E	Glaze F	Glaze SP	Plain SP	Total
Augite Monzonite	San Marcos	Eastern	23	17	14	29	29	3	115
Hornblende Latite Rock	Other Galisteo Basin	Eastern	8	12	9	48	28	2	107
Sand/Siltstone	Pecos	Eastern	22	24	56	13	59	1	175
Vitric Tuff	Yunque	Northern	0	4	4	113	69	0	190
Pajarito Andesite	Other Rio Arriba	Northern	0	4	3	33	16	0	56
All			53	61	86	236	201	6	643

selection provides a broad lens for studying ceramic change or continuity in New Mexico during the early colonial period, and also allows colono wares to be compared throughout the colony of New Mexico to determine if these new vessel forms were made uniformly, which might reflect Spanish control over colono ware production, tribute demands, or possibly forced labor.

I separated glaze-painted pottery from different production locales based on differences in temper type. Using Anna Shepard's (1942) work, I was able to assign ceramic thin-sections to production areas, or glaze districts. Because certain tempers were likely exclusively used by potters of certain pueblos, the associations were sometimes to the spatial scale of a pueblo. Here, I discuss the results of five temper types: augite monzonite used in San Marcos ceramics (Warren 1969a, 1979b), hornblende latite in other Galisteo Basin ceramics (such as Pueblo Blanco and San Lazaro) (J. Habicht-Mauche, personal communication 2009), sand/siltstone in Pecos ceramics (Shepard 1942), vitric tuff in Yunque ceramics (see discussion below), and Pajarito andesite in other Rio Arriba or Northern Pajarito ceramics (Table 14.1).

For the tempers from the northern Rio Arriba and Pajarito Plateau province, Gary Smith (Earth and Planetary Sciences, University of New Mexico) helped to determine likely geologic sources (see Dyer 2010 for more information on these temper types). According to Smith, the vitric tuff temper likely derives from the crystal-poor ash beds in the Chamita Formation, relatively close to Yunque (Gary Smith, personal communication 2007). Thus, ceramics with vitric tuff temper are likely produced at Yunque. In fact, Florence Hawley Ellis defined these ceramics as "Yunque Glaze Polychrome," a variant of San Juan Red-on-orange with a glaze paint decoration (Honea 1966). Vitric tuff may also have been used as temper for glaze-painted ceramics produced at

San Juan Pueblo, or possibly other nearby Tewa pueblos (David Snow, personal communication 2009).

Likewise, according to Smith (personal communication 2007), Pajarito andesite-tempered ceramics are potentially local to Yunque. However, the Pajarito andesite sands are probably found closer to Santa Clara and San Ildefonso pueblos than to Yunque. The Pajarito andesite temper likely derives from the andesitic-rich sands of the Puye or Tschicoma formations in the northeast corner of the Jemez Mountains, on the northern Pajarito Plateau. Tewa potters are not known for using andesite as a tempering material, preferring vitric tuff or ash. Therefore, andesite-tempered glaze-painted ceramics may represent intrusive Tano groups from the Galisteo Basin, who are known to have preferred andesites as a tempering material. If Tano potters moved into the northern Rio Arriba and Pajarito Plateau province during the early Spanish colonial period, they may have begun producing glaze-painted ceramics utilizing locally available andesitic sands.

Pajarito andesite (my term) may be the same temper type as Warren's (1979b) Jemez andesite, which she identified (albeit with no description) in glaze-painted ceramics at Otowi (LA 169), Tsirege (LA 170), Yaposhi (LA 250), and Ha'atse (LA 370). However, because of the great diversity of andesitic material in the Jemez Mountains, in terms of both composition and age, I use the term Pajarito andesite to distinguish it from vitreous andesite (Kidder and Shepard 1936; Shepard 1942), which is present in the southeast Jemez Mountains (Gary Smith, personal communication 2009).

COMPOSITIONAL ANALYSIS

Based on point-counting data from 340 ceramic thin-sections, I use ternary diagrams to examine ceramic constituents and amount of clay processing through time and between vessel forms within each production area or pueblo. Ceramic components are examined by calculating frequencies of clay, aplastics or temper, and voids. The amount of clay processing is inferred using the proxy of void frequencies, where high frequency of voids reflects little time spent processing or kneading clay to remove air bubbles.

San Marcos Pueblo Ceramics

The compositions of precolonial and colonial period bowls produced at San Marcos Pueblo appear to be similar (Fig. 14.3). The ternary diagram shows continuity in frequencies of clay to aplastics to voids in precolonial and colonial period ceramics. This finding indicates stability in the composition of San Marcos ceramics during the early colonial period.

In terms of void frequencies, there is no difference between precolonial bowls (C–D) and colonial period bowls (E–F); both have 4.3 percent voids. ANOVA confirms that time is not an important factor with regard to void frequencies, with a *p*-value of 0.350. Thus, the amount of clay preparation does not appear to change during the early colonial period.

In contrast, when comparing the composition of San Marcos soup plates and Glaze F bowls, there is evidence for different compositions, with some of the soup plates having more voids than the Glaze F bowls (Fig. 14.4).

The San Marcos soup plates have an average of 8 percent voids, whereas the Glaze F bowls have an average of 4.8 percent voids. ANOVA confirms that the San Marcos soup plates have significantly more voids than the Glaze F bowls, with a *p*-value of 0.005. This result suggests that San Marcos soup plates were produced using an expedient technology—that is, less time was spent processing (kneading and wedging) the wet clay-temper mix before vessels were formed.

Other Galisteo Basin Ceramics

The compositions of precolonial and colonial period bowls produced at other Galisteo Basin pueblos appear to be similar. The ternary diagram shows significant overlap in frequencies of clay, aplastics, and voids in precolonial and colonial period ceramics, with slightly more voids in colonial period ceramics (Fig. 14.5).

The slight increase in void frequency is from 6.7 to 9.1 percent in traditional bowls during the early colonial period. However, ANOVA indicates that time is not a significant factor for void frequency in traditional bowls, with a *p*-value of 0.268. Thus, these results indicate no significant changes in composition (frequencies of clay, aplastics, and voids) or clay preparation (void frequencies) of traditional vessels during the early colonial period.

In contrast, when comparing other Galisteo Basin soup plates to Glaze F bowls, there is a significant difference in composition, in which soup plates have much fewer voids than the Glaze F bowls (Fig. 14.6). In fact, the other Galisteo Basin soup plates have an average of 4.4 percent voids, whereas the Glaze F bowls have an average of 9.2 percent. ANOVA confirms that the other Galisteo Basin soup plates have significantly fewer voids than Glaze F bowls, with a *p*-value of 0.000. Thus, other Galisteo Basin soup plates are technologically distinct from Glaze F bowls in terms of composition and clay preparation.

For both San Marcos and other Galisteo Basin ceramics, there is a significant difference in overall composition, specifically in void frequency, between soup plates and Glaze F bowls. However, they show the exact opposite patterns. San Marcos soup plates have more voids than their Glaze F counterparts, whereas other Galisteo Basin soup plates have fewer voids than Glaze F bowls. Thus, there is evidence that less time was spent processing clay when manufacturing soup plates at San Marcos than for bowls, but the opposite trend is evident for soup plates manufactured in the other Galisteo Basin pueblos where there was higher craftsmanship in the soup plates than in the bowls.

Pecos Pueblo Ceramics

The ratio of clay to aplastics to voids in Pecos ceramics before and after contact shows major overlap in percentages (Fig. 14.7), indicating no significant compositional differences in Pecos bowls through time. There are subtle changes in void frequency through time. However, ANOVA confirms that time is not a significant factor with regard to void frequency in Pecos bowls, with a *p*-value of 0.271. Thus, there is no evidence, for significant differences in bowls through time in overall composition or clay preparation (void frequencies).

Unfortunately, I was unable to make a formal comparison between Pecos soup plates and Glaze F bowls owing to the small sample of Glaze F bowls (*n* = 7), which reflects the dramatic decrease at Pecos in production of traditional bowls at this time.

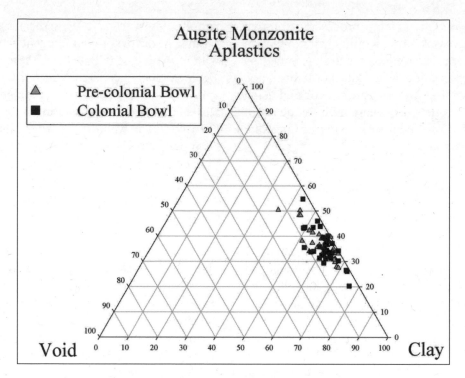

Figure 14.3. Composition of San Marcos
precolonial and colonial period bowls.

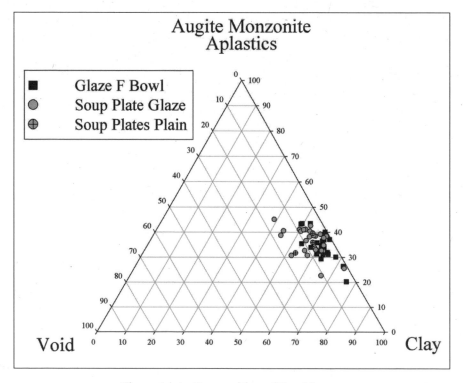

Figure 14.4. Composition of San Marcos
soup plates and Glaze F bowls.

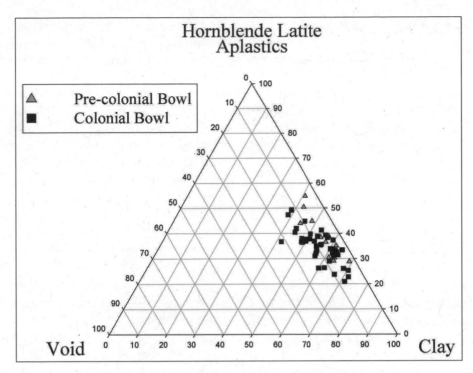

Figure 14.5. Composition of other Galisteo
Basin precolonial and colonial period bowls.

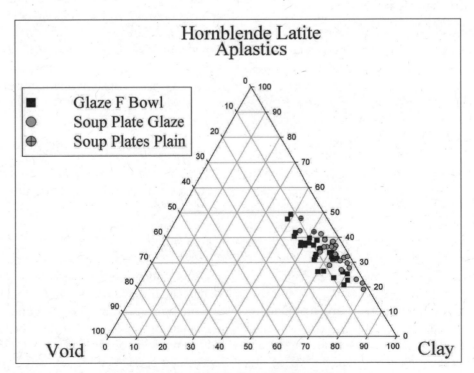

Figure 14.6. Composition of other Galisteo
Basin soup plates and Glaze F bowls.

San Gabriel del Yunque Ceramics

Last, we turn to San Gabriel del Yunque ceramics. Unfortunately, the sample size for vitric tuff-tempered ceramics prior to Glaze F is inadequate to test whether or not there are compositional differences in ceramics produced during the precolonial and colonial periods. The sample sizes of thin-sections for Glaze D and Glaze E bowls are three each, as compared with 17 Glaze F bowls and 32 glaze-painted soup plates.

When comparing the soup plates with Glaze F bowls, it is clear that they have different compositions (Fig. 14.8). The differences between Yunque soup plates and bowls relate to frequencies of both voids and aplastics. For Yunque ceramics, there are fewer voids and aplastics in soup plates than in Glaze F bowls. Specifically, the Yunque soup plates have an average of 2.3 percent voids and 25 percent aplastics, whereas the Glaze F bowls have an average of 4.3 percent voids and 32 percent aplastics.

Thus, the Yunque soup plates have fewer voids and aplastics (that is, they are more clay-rich) as compared with Glaze F bowls. ANOVA confirms that the Yunque soup plates have fewer voids and aplastics than the Glaze F bowls, with p-values of 0.001 and 0.003, respectively.

Component Analysis Discussion

Overall the results of the compositional analysis show that precolonial and colonial period traditional bowls are the same technologically in terms of composition (that is, ingredients) and clay preparation (that is, void frequencies). This striking continuity is clearly demonstrated for San Marcos, other Galisteo Basin pueblos, and Pecos ceramics, reflecting remarkable stability in the ceramic tradition during the early colonial period. The consistency of this pattern suggests that Spanish contact did not cause overall disruption in Pueblo ceramic production techniques. Yunque ceramics were not included in this comparison because production of glaze-painted ceramics did not begin in earnest until the seventeenth century with Glaze F ceramics. Overall, there is strong evidence for stability in ceramic production after contact.

Colono wares and traditional bowls are significantly different in composition, specifically in terms of time spent processing clay. Thus, colono wares are both morphologically and compositionally different. All of the temper types except for augite monzonite exhibit similar trends in that soup plates have fewer voids and aplastics

than the Glaze F bowls. Only San Marcos ceramics reverse these trends. These results suggest that more time was spent in clay preparation for the other Galisteo Basin and Yunque soup plates than for Glaze F bowls (the opposite of what was found for San Marcos soup plates).

Table 14.2 summarizes the results of analysis of variances (ANOVA) run to compare void frequencies of glaze-painted ceramics before and after contact as well as between vessel forms. For all ceramics examined, there are no statistical differences in void frequencies between precolonial and colonial period traditional vessels, with p-values ranging from 0.268 to 0.350, but there are significant statistical differences in void frequencies between colono wares and traditional bowls, with p-values all below 0.005.

Because compositional differences vary among the pueblos or production areas, it seems likely that potters experimented with these new vessel forms. Potters likely tried out new recipes when making colono wares. They mixed different ratios of clay to aplastics, and they spent more or less time processing clay. These innovations were distinctive for each production area. In sum, the compositional analysis indicates that soup plates were technologically distinct from Glaze F bowls.

Despite these compositional differences, colono wares are similar enough to traditional bowls, as seen in the somewhat overlapping data clouds on the ternary diagrams, to be considered the same ware as other Rio Grande glaze-painted ceramics. Given the pattern, it is reasonable to suggest that Pueblo potters manufactured the new vessel forms, not Spaniards or other newcomers to New Mexico.

MACROSCOPIC ANALYSIS

Next, I examine the variability among soup plates. To do so, I analyze 643 ceramic rim sherds, measuring eight macroscopic variables related to vessel construction, morphology, surface treatment, and decoration (Table 14.3).

However, before discussing variability among soup plates, I address overall trends in soup plates (Table 14.4), which may be explained by their common function or Spanish preferences, or both. For instance, soup plates tend to have vessel walls that range from 5.12 to 5.49 mm thick, and rims that are 5.77 to 6.21 mm thick (except for sand/siltstone-tempered soup plates, which have thinner vessel walls and thicker rims than the other soup plates). In terms of morphology, soup plates are

Table 14.2. Void Frequency ANOVA Results: Summary of *p*-Values

Pueblo or Province	Precolonial vs. Colonial Traditional Vessels	Colono Wares vs. Traditional Vessels
San Marcos	0.350	0.005
Other Galisteo Basin	0.268	0.000
Pecos	0.271	--
Yunque	--	0.001

all relatively small, with mean rim diameters ranging from approximately 20 to 22 cm. In terms of surface treatments, most soup plates have medium-to-low polish intensity (that is, luster) except for sand/siltstone-tempered soup plates that mostly have high polish. In terms of decoration, glaze-painted decorations consist primarily of simple designs or motifs, which are usually confined to the rim. Common glaze-painted designs are zigzag lines, parallel lines (similar to tick marks), and cross motifs. Finally, many soup plates have brown (and runny) or black glaze paint on red/orange slip (except for sand/siltstone-tempered soup plates). By contrast, most traditional bowls are decorated with tan slip. These differences may indicate that soup plates were produced primarily for Spanish consumption or used in different contexts than traditional bowls, or both.

Finally, regardless of production locale, soup plates rarely have green glaze paint (4%–12%), which is a relatively common glaze paint color on Glaze F bowls (12.5%–37%). Differences in glaze paint color may indicate compositional (recipe) differences (Blinman and others, Chapter 11; Schleher and others, Chapter 10). Because glaze-paint recipes are a product of direct learning, glaze paint color differences may have significance regarding the groups producing soup plates. For instance, differences in glaze paint color between soup plates and traditional bowls suggest differences in potting groups—possibly a subset of potters exclusively manufactured soup plates.

Despite this uniformity, soup plates exhibit striking pueblo-specific differences, which suggest that Spaniards did not control soup plate production, and that potters had flexibility to innovate when manufacturing these new forms. For instance, soup plates from each pueblo have different color schemes. Yunque (vitric tuff-tempered) soup plates commonly have a brick-red slip, San Marcos (augite monzonite-tempered) soup plates have an orangish slip, and Pecos (sand/siltstone-tempered) soup plates

have tan and buff slips. Of these, Pecos soup plates are the most visually distinctive, especially in terms of their light slip colors (buff and tan), high polish intensity on interior and exterior surfaces, thick rims, and thin vessel walls. It seems that potters at each pueblo were striving for their own aesthetic, likely related to signaling group or place (Wobst 1977).

Soup plates also exhibit variability by province related to vessel construction, morphology, and decoration. Specifically, soup plates in the northern Rio Arriba and Pajarito Plateau province tend to have thicker walls, shorter and thinner rims, smaller rim angles, larger vessel size, and more red/orange slips than their counterparts in the eastern Pecos and Galisteo Basin province. Even though all of these differences are not statistically significant (Table 14.5), comparison of soup plate variability by province suggests that potters from different communities of practice exercised creative license within a set of known stylistic or technological norms when manufacturing these new vessel forms.

Table 14.3. Macroscopic Variables in Relation to Ceramic Production Steps

Ceramic Production Step	Macroscopic Variables
Vessel construction	Sherd thickness Rim thickness
Morphology	Rim diameter Rim angle Rim length
Surface treatments	Polish intensity
Decoration	Glaze-paint color Slip color

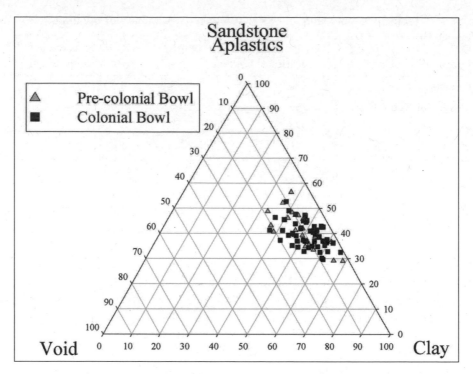

Figure 14.7. Composition of Pecos Pueblo precolonial and colonial period bowls.

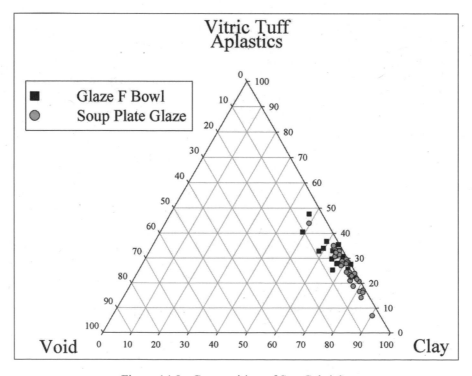

Figure 14.8. Composition of San Gabriel del Yunque soup plates and Glaze F bowls.

Table 14.4. Overall Trends for Soup Plates

Variable	Overall Trend	Comments
Sherd Thickness	All similar except sand/siltstone-tempered (which is thinner)	All (except sand/siltstone-tempered): 5.12–5.49mm, sand/siltstone-tempered): 4.75mm
Rim Thickness	All similar except sand/siltstone-tempered (which is thicker)	All (except sand/siltstone-tempered): 5.77–6.21mm, sand/siltstone-tempered): 7.26mm
Rim Diameter	All similar (when augite monzonite-tempered is removed due to poor sample size)	All (except ugite monzonite-tempered): 19.98–22.07cm, augite monzonite-tempered: 14cm
Polish Intensity	All similar except sand/siltstone-tempered (which is more highly polished)	All: mostly medium to low polish sand/siltstone-tempered: mostly high polish
Slip Color	Mostly red slips except sand/siltstone-tempered, which is mostly buff and tan slips	All (except and/siltstone-tempered): 47-86% red slips; sand/siltstone-tempered: 42% buff slips, 40% tan slips
Glaze paint	Mostly brown; black next most common. Green relatively uncommon	All: 35-69% brown glaze All: 4-12% green glaze

Table 14.5. Soup Plate Variability by Province

Variable	Northern	Eastern	Statistical Significance
Sherd Thickness	Thicker	Thinner	Significant difference between vitric tuff-tempered and sand/siltstone-tempered soup plates
Rim Thickness	Thinner	Thicker	Sand/siltstone-tempered soup plates are significantly thicker than all others
Rim Diameter	Larger	Smaller	None
Rim Angle	Smaller	Larger	Significant difference between vitric tuff-tempered and sand/siltstone-tempered soup plates ($p=0.003$)
Rim Length	Shorter	Longer	Yes ($p=0.000$)
Slip Color	More red/orange	Less red/orange	Yes ($p=0.000$)

CONCLUSION

In sum, because ceramics represent a complex and conservative technology passed down from generation to generation within communities of practice, they provide a powerful means to elucidate how Pueblo peoples and their traditions were impacted by Spanish contact. This study demonstrates striking stability in the glaze-painted ceramic tradition in north-central New Mexico during the early colonial period, which indicates Pueblo resilience in response to Spanish contact. The most dramatic change in the glaze-painted ceramic tradition after contact is the adoption of new, Spanish-influenced vessel forms, with some subtle technological changes that indicate Pueblo innovation. However, despite these subtle differences, all of the production steps appear to be the same for both glaze-painted colono wares and traditional bowls.

These patterns are elucidated more fully in my dissertation (Dyer 2010), where I provide more in-depth analyses of the technology of colono wares versus traditional bowls. Finally, significant variability in colono wares suggests that the Spaniards did not impose strict criteria on many aspects of colono ware manufacture. Pueblo potters were in control of colono ware production, and they had the flexibility to experiment with these new vessel forms within a range of norms specific to each production locale or community of potters. In sum, Pueblo potters were innovating when manufacturing colono wares within the context of a relatively stable glaze-painted ceramic tradition.

Acknowledgments

This study has been enhanced by the feedback and comments I received from Dr. Ann Ramenofsky. I also would like to thank Drs. Linda Cordell and Judith Habicht-Mauche for their insightful editorial comments and for the opportunity to participate in the 2009 SAA symposium from which this volume evolved. This study is based upon work supported by the National Science Foundation under Grant No. 0530158, a Hibben Legacy Dissertation Scholarship, and an American Fellowship from the American Association for University Women.

CHAPTER FIFTEEN

Thinking about Pottery Production as Community Practice

Rosemary A. Joyce

The contributions to this volume are distinguished by the care taken to consider often small details, and the consequent way the work as a whole begins to construct an understanding of linked fields of practice among people in a social network that was constituted by the making of specific things: polychrome and glaze-decorated pottery in the Southwestern United States.

Kari Schleher, Deborah Huntley, and Cynthia Herhahn (Chapter 10) make clear why these particular pots are so good to think about:

> potters intentionally attempted to produce certain colors, luster, and mechanical characteristics when preparing [paints]. . . . Glaze paint production entails an intentionality and complexity that provides information about the nature of the organization of production and the community of practice for pottery manufacture at particular villages and across wider areas.

Similar logic underlies Suzanne Eckert's (Chapter 6) convincing study of two glaze ware types in the Zuni region. She argues that the "similarity of exterior designs suggests a conscious attempt by the painters of these bowls to make them indistinguishable from one another when viewed at a distance."

"Intention," "conscious attempt": with these papers we are dealing with the realm of at least potentially self-conscious practices that are critical to the formation and reproduction of social worlds. Treating patterns of production and consumption as evidence of practices changes the kinds of questions we can ask and the kinds of answers we can get. Linda Cordell and Judith Habicht-Mauche, in their introduction to this volume (Chapter 1), suggest these pottery types are an ideal case study for this approach because their "production, distribution,

and use involved activating social networks at various scales. These networks [they continue] can be thought of as 'communities of practice' that both encompassed and crosscut various social groups and boundaries and, thus, can effectively be studied using a practice theory approach."

COMMUNITIES OF PRACTICE AND SITUATED LEARNING

The concept of a "community of practice" draws explicitly on the work of anthropologist Jean Lave, who, with sociologist Elliot Wenger, outlined a model of "situated learning" that both depended on and reproduced communities of practice (Lave and Wenger 1991). Rooted in ethnographic studies of apprenticeship, the model of situated learning identifies successful learning as being promoted when beginning practitioners undertake tasks that are *legitimately* part of production processes—that is, not artificial or make-work tasks. While legitimate participation allows learners to gain competence in skills they actually need and will actually use, giving them real roles in production puts the novice at risk. In the metaphor of this model, beginning learners are located on the *periphery* of mastery, and this social, embodied location or situation must be taken into account. This is where the *situated* nature of situated learning comes in: tasks assigned are legitimate but also are appropriate, requiring skills that learners at a specific stage have, and involving steps they can succeed in carrying out. Such situated learning—or *legitimate peripheral participation*—allows the learner to progress with confidence while making real contributions to the shared goal.

Models of situated learning and communities of practice are exceptionally promising for archaeologists already interested in theories of practice but concerned with such issues as the apparent stasis and automaticity of some views of practice (Joyce and Lopiparo 2005). Situated learning and communities of practice should be critical to archaeologists thinking about how crafting is structured as embodied practices transmitted over generations. The dynamic and temporal nature of learning allows us to understand the development of skills and their incorporation as embodied skill, or *hexis*. For Bourdieu (1977:93) "bodily hexis is political mythology *em-bodied*, turned into a permanent disposition, a durable manner of standing, speaking, and thereby of feeling and thinking." Yet this formulation obscures the fact that bodily dispositions are not inborn, but learned. As an explicit learning environment takes form, and explicit shared goals about the production of specific target products are reproduced, the process of becoming a skilled crafter also involves gradually becoming less consciously aware of the shared practices that define a community of practice, while never losing the potential of calling these practices into conscious consideration (Roddick 2009:83–85).

A community of practice is defined as a network of relations among people and objects mediated by actions they conduct, taking place in relation to other communities of practice and continuing over time (Lave and Wenger 1991:98). A particular way of doing things is learned within a community of practice, and reproduced by community members as they enact their own practices. Because of the repetition of practices in a certain manner learned by and reproduced by community members, communities of practice persist in time.

To use this new framework, we will need to be very certain how the material phenomena we can observe and describe correspond to the abstract aspects of the overall model. Perhaps we might want to borrow from another anthropologically trained student of technology and society, Bruno Latour (2005), and consider the networks activated by production, distribution, and use of specific objects that we retrace as the *evidence* of past assembly of "the social" *by* communities of practice, rather than treat them *as* the community of practice itself. A network being assembled is something more open, more contingent, and more in process than the community of practice that is part of what is assembled. The network being assembled is not completely described by specifying the human actors and social relations between them that make up the community of practice. Also assembled in the network, as is amply evident in these chapters, are non-human actors:

the ores, firing facilities, and even existing pots whose painting served as historical precedents when communities of practice went into action anew.

FROM THEORY TO PRACTICE

These perspectives require us to move away from some of our traditional ways of talking about things, their genesis, and their movement, to talking about the people who produced things. For example, Ann Ramenofsky (Chapter 9) summarizes a discussion of the seriation of Glaze A Yellow types from San Marcos Pueblo by saying "despite the disruptions of leaving and returning, San Marcos potters continued to produce [Cieneguilla Glaze-on-yellow]." What is critical here is the overall shift from talking about sherds to talking about potters—specifically, potters whose practices ran counter to the expectations of seriation models.

Shifting our way of thinking about produced similarities allows us to glimpse a practice-based model that underpins the successful use of seriation as well. Seriation depends on the expectation that novel things are subject to regular patterns of increasing popularity followed by replacement by other, new, things. So things that form series rely "on the maintenance of certain modes of co-participation" for their continued similarity over time (Roddick 2009:79). Potters, in other words, periodically innovate, and at some points their innovations are acceptable to users, who encourage sustained production, and may attract emulation by other potters, leading new practices to spread. These are statements about action and its repetition, and they have implications for how practices change as well as persist. It is this kind of shift from agent-free change and continuity to change and continuity linked to more and less conscious action that practice theories unleash. Within the range of practice theories, communities of practice provide us with a formalized framework to talk about the groups of people who maintain similarities of things through more or less conscious action.

Looking at glaze wares as products of communities of practice gives us Cynthia Herhahn's (2006) shift to thinking of compositional differences as "recipes"— human practices—rather than simply as a more neutral "composition." Schleher, Huntley, and Herhahn (Chapter 10) note that potters "appear to have worked within a system that communicates information about what has to go into a glaze, but variety in colorants and experimentation in the addition of these colorants is acceptable."

Deborah Huntley, Thomas Fenn, Barbara Mills, and Judith Habicht-Mauche (Chapter 2) take this kind of contemplation of preferences for pigments, and their relationships to communities of practice, in yet another interesting direction. They suggest that before we simply treat minerals as "raw materials" for a singular community of practice centered on pottery production, we need to think about how pigments were part of wider communities of practice centered around painting of a much larger range of things—wood, textiles, stone, ritual architecture, and people. Here we might want to employ the concept of "constellations of practice" (Wenger 1998:127–133, 168–169, 256–260) that may come about through the articulation of separate communities of practice that share common historical roots, or have members in common, or share certain things, or engage in overlapping styles or related discourses. As Roddick (2009:80) argues, constellations of practice, which may emerge with less intentionality than communities of practice, can provide us with a way to think about the sorts of regional-scale identities that archaeologists often recognize, but that we might hesitate to tie to specific peoples.

CONSTELLATIONS OF PRACTICE, TRADITION, AND INNOVATION

The utility of considering overlapping communities of practice, or constellations of practice, is illustrated by Dennis Gilpin and Kelley Hays-Gilpin's (Chapter 5) study of Hopi yellow wares, where they note the presence of shared motifs in pottery and kiva murals, the murals further implying the existence of textiles with these same motifs that have not survived archaeologically. We can imagine the painters, weavers, and potters each as communities of practice and recognize their articulation around the use of selected motifs, and in some cases materials, as forming a constellation of practice, without having to assume a uniformity of practice in what was most likely a heterogeneous network of crafters.

Diane Curewitz and Sheila Goff (Chapter 8) follow a related line of argument in their consideration of the use by potters on the Pajarito Plateau of lead from the same sources used by potters in other parts of a broader regional network. Having first established through temper studies that potters in the Pajarito area were making their own glaze-ware pottery from largely local materials, they ask how closely these Pajarito glaze ware

producers were tied to the production and exchange networks of glaze paint ware in the rest of the Rio Grande Valley. This is a question explicitly about the constellations of practice articulating different communities of practice. Rather than answer that question simply in terms of economic exchange of materials, they discuss the likely symbolic significance of the lead sources, a discursive element of the kind Wenger (1998) notes can be the product of a constellation of practices.

Implicitly, these contributors point to the significance of widely shared underlying understanding of how to do things that is a critical part of any theory of practice, whether described as *doxa* (Bourdieu 1977:159–169) or in other terms. Pajarito potters, Curewitz and Goff write, were part of a larger community of potters sharing the practice of using lead ores. They discern regionwide regularities in vessel size, use of slip color, and width and placement of framing lines, further supporting these potters' participation in a regional constellation of practice while also raising the question of how such participation can be understood in terms of human action, or practices. Curewitz and Goff (Chapter 8) suggest regional voluntary conformity was "based on technological, traditional, or even ritual reasons, that indicate shared belief systems."

How can we understand motivations like "shared belief systems" under theories of practice? The often-cited concept of *habitus,* the "durably installed generative principle of regulated improvisations" (Bourdieu 1977:78), was actually developed in relation to the historical writing of art historian Erwin Panofsky about the link between medieval thought and the production of Gothic architecture (Holsinger 2005:96–102). Panofsky used habitus to identify specific times and places as having a character or sensibility that was the product of a particular shared way of doing things and thinking about things, and in turn structured the way things were done. Holsinger (2005:99–100) argues that what attracted Bourdieu to Panofsky's concept was the way it mediated between the individual creators of Gothic cathedrals and the cultural "forms and dispositions" that structured their creativity. Panofsky, of course, has also heavily influenced archaeological thought through the incorporation of his ideas by art historian George Kubler (1962), who explicitly tied long-term historical patterns of innovation, rise in popularity, and decline of new practices to learning in workshops by apprentices and the periodic innovation within traditions of crafting. "Inventions," Kubler (1962:63) writes, "are actually one with the humble substance of everyday behavior, whereby we exercise the freedom to vary our actions a little." What makes some small variation appear innovative in the historical long-term is the way it is taken up by others in a community of practice.

Eric Blinman, Kari Schleher, Tom Dickerson, Cynthia Herhahn, and Ibrahim Gundiler (Chapter 11) explicitly make arguments related to those advanced by Kubler (1962) when they discuss the possibility that later, runnier lead glazes, possibly resulting from use of lead bullets as a source of raw material, were likely reproduced over three generations. Blinman and colleagues note that glaze composition alone does not guarantee the outcome of the production of specific glaze effects; indeed, they argue that in keeping with "glaze principles that are taught in contemporary studio pottery texts," glaze colors were strongly dependent on firing regime. They invoke a model more in keeping with a universe of innovators and apprentices than with the more mechanical vision that has traditionally been the archaeological understanding of type continuity over time. We might thus want to think about what Blinman and colleagues call "artist perspectives" in ways rooted in Kubler's and Panofsky's work, considering the agency of the individual maker embedded in a network of others who formed his or her communities of practice.

COMMUNITIES OF PRACTICE AND THE POSSIBILITIES FOR CHANGE

Jennifer Dyer (Chapter 14), extending discussion into the colonial period, employs what has become one of the more productive routes to "seeing" communities of practice: watching what happens in a known situation of culture contact or other dramatic transformation. It is in this kind of context that Steve Silliman (2001) and others have argued that the unreflective nature of practice may come into conscious contemplation, and new practices may be produced or old practices reproduced self-consciously rather than as part of a process of automatic intergenerational traditional transmission. Noah Thomas (Chapter 13) explicitly considers Spanish-Pueblo engagement over the use of lead minerals as an opportunity for the renegotiation of doxa about mineral extraction and wealth. Treating Spanish miners and Puebloans in search of pigment procurers as members of two communities of practice, Thomas shows how discourse about mineral color provided a common ground for articulation between these two communities of practice.

Dyer discusses the production of new shapes of vessels in Puebloan villages that realized Spanish shape categories through traditional Puebloan means. This is a good example of hybrid practices produced in the confrontation between different communities of practice. On one side were people who belonged to a completely internalized tradition, using a taken-for-granted suite of techniques that we recognize as a technical style, which was learned through legitimate peripheral participation. In this case, the community of practice produced and reproduced in this manner faced another such community of practice, outside any existing constellation of practice. In Thomas's (Chapter 13) discussion of the colonial Puebloan workshop at LA 162, he describes ore processing technologies that he argues reflected "continuity and innovation in Pueblo practice that may have become incorporated within Pueblo ceramic production." The hybrid technology was made possible, he proposes, because the indigenous Pueblo understanding of ores and the Spanish approach to them were each mediated by color classifications understood to reference value. While the values referenced were radically different, the overlapping practices of using color to select ores mobilized values that allowed the formation of a new or at least altered community of practice.

It did not take the presence of Europeans for such juxtapositions of communities of practice to take place, as David Phillips (Chapter 4) shows in his discussion of innovation in the Sierra polychrome tradition. Demonstrating a repeated practice of painting red and black pigments without letting the zones touch, he refers to this as the "Babícora rule." He contrasts this with a "Ramos rule," in which "when red paint is present it must be outlined in black." This recalls William Sewell's discussion of rules in structuration theory, in which the American sociologist envisions the reproduction of practices not in the fully embodied and largely unreflective way it is presented by Bourdieu (1977), but as tacitly enacting a potentially articulable schema that can be applied to novel cases (Sewell 1992). Phillips makes it clear that this is the domain of practice he is referencing, when he describes the "Ramos rule" as "a conscious break" with the "regional *habitus*." Phillips uses the concept of a "rule" in a way that foregrounds an emphasis on the conscious innovator, for whom what had been an unexamined practice becomes a "rule" at the moment it is violated and a new practice is adopted. This moment of rupture is not unlike, and may indeed be identical to, Bourdieu's (1977:168–169) concept of the moments when doxa—unexamined taken-for-granteds—comes to consciousness, always in contrast to other practices, and is either reified as orthodoxy or rejected and reconfigured in heterodoxy.

The potentially productive nature of such ruptures is implicit in Thomas's argument that glaze ware ceramics were produced in the colonial period, not as a product of continuity of preceding communities of practice, but through the production of a new colonial community of practice. His argument complements David Snow's (Chapter 12) study of the final stages of glaze production in the seventeenth century, also under colonial dominance. Snow notes that previous explanations have linked this to such factors as Spanish colonial prohibition of potters obtaining ore, deliberate alteration of traditional glaze recipes by potters to conceal knowledge, the adoption of "expedient" technological practices, or the purposeful repudiation of glaze wares in the aftermath of Spanish reoccupation of the area. Instead, he argues that demographic collapse provides "an alternative and adequate explanation for the disruption of Pueblo learning and production networks." Specifically, he pinpoints the loss of traditional connections to lead ore suppliers with the abandonment of San Marcos and other Galisteo Basin pueblos, breaking the transmission of knowledge of lead sources.

Snow demonstrates that there was variability in the degree to which seventeenth-century potters consistently control glaze paint during firing, with some keeping it from running. Others, he suggests, could not "or did not care to." He suggests that in some cases apprentice potters may not have learned critical steps in the process owing to disruption of residence and everyday practice. In terms of communities of practice and situated learning, we can restate his suggestion as a possible shift from "open-ability apprenticeship" (the model case of situated learning with legitimate peripheral participation encouraged by those with greater mastery) to "closed-ability apprenticeship" (based on imitation with little fostering of greater learning).

AVENUES FOR FUTURE DEBATE

The contributions to this volume clearly show the utility of trying to think about a well-studied technology that is the product of a community or communities of practice engaged over time in producing and reproducing

practices that become traditional through their more-or-less knowing reproduction. They also show us how difficult it is to not lose track of the people, and so they underline the urgency of our finding a way to talk about both people and things as active participants in practice.

What we need to watch for are accounts in which polychromes appear to beget polychromes, or glaze wares appear to have their own inherent animating principles that lead their popularity to grow and decline. Does it matter if we are still slipping back and forth between language rooted in talking about things as products of more and less intentional human action, or as pieces in chains made entirely of things? I think it does—and I think these authors are helping us to see why. When they focus on the innovations, the communities of practice, the rules followed or broken, we see convincing evidence of the kinds of potters who experimented with lead derived from different minerals and with firing facilities that produced different effects with these pigments. So in closing, I want to identify a few continuing challenges all of us face in making this important shift and some of the routes pointed out for us in these papers.

Patrick Lyons and Jeffrey Clark (Chapter 3) note that it has become common to assume that "a particular item of material culture can passively reflect and, at the same time, actively signal different aspects of social identity." Increasingly, though, we see that our tradition of treating objects as passive reflections of identity or even as tokens of identity fails to satisfy. We need to move forward with understandings of practice in which things themselves are actors (Gosden 2005). There are fascinating hints in these papers about the active role that the materiality of glazes and the nature of firing facilities had in the outcome of production, and thus potentially in ruptures of doxa or innovations beyond rules and schema.

We also need to attend explicitly to the intersecting communities of practice that might make up constellations of practice. We have traditional means at our disposal to talk about such large-scale patterning, of course. Hayward Franklin and Kari Schlerer (Chapter 7) describe distributions of ceramics in terms of exchange, including, possibly, the exchange of materials contained in otherwise redundant utilitarian pots. Exchange is a useful and traditional way of talking about the movement of pots. As Huntley, Fenn, Mills, and Habicht-Mauche's suggest in Chapter 2, it can also be understood in terms of communities of practices—in this case, practices of consumption. Roddick (2009:88–91) suggests we consider the communities of learned practices of consumption as co-producing the patterns of materials that we see archaeologically. Both communities of production and communities of consumption, viewed from the perspective of practice, are dependent on other practices of world-making that required certain material ways of engaging with communities that may overlap, or simply articulate, with communities of production and consumption. We need to place all of these in play to account for the complexity of structuring of regional-scale production of objects like the pots that form the focus of the researchers in this volume.

Moving further from traditional discussion of the movement of pots as exchange to concentrate on the social relations and social networks that are constituted by these exchanges, Lyons and Clark (Chapter 3) add to our vocabulary the notion of brokers and boundary objects. These would be *mediators* in Bruno Latour's vocabulary: people and things that are actors facilitating the assembly of new social networks (Latour 2005:38–40). In this case, the assembly of social networks took place in diasporic histories, which, like colonization, are, of course, situations of culture contact when embodied dispositions may be actively reconsidered and intentionally reworked.

Dyer's (Chapter 14) discussions of the continuity in production of glaze-ware bowls—which as a whole these papers show manifest a regional constellation of practice—and the diversity of new colonial wares in Spanish-introduced shapes—where she notes pueblo-specific variation in a local community of practice—is a fascinating example of how the same potters might participate in different communities of practice even of what we see today as a single activity, pottery making, at the same time. Her discussion of the more localized Spanish shapes, in contrast to the regionally consistent glaze-painted bowls, to me seems to provide support for a running theme in other papers, suggesting that the regional constellation of practice responsible for glaze ware and polychrome pots was in part oriented not just toward making pots, but toward making pots for particular, perhaps sacred or ritual, purposes.

Another difficulty, how to think about change—as innovation within a tradition or the rejection of tradition—can be understood as the emergence of different communities of practice out of what had been a single community of practice. As Gilpin and Hays-Gilpin (Chapter 5) put it, the development of Hopi yellow ware "may have involved a fusion of earlier red ware and white ware traditions or a radical replacement of the earlier pattern by innovation or by influence from other media." Gilpin and Hays-Gilpin offer a refreshingly direct peopling of the social assemblage that gives explicit form to the human actors in these networks, writing that it is "plausible that much of [Hopi yellow ware] was painted by male sodality initiates, by older women who had ritual knowledge and responsibilities, by women potters who had specialized roles in craft production and 'non-feminine' ritual roles . . . or by males who did some women's work in addition to special ritual roles."

As they and other authors show or imply, trying to think about potters as parts of communities of practice requires us to think about people as participants in very different communities of practice. I don't think it is merely my innate ceramic chauvinism that makes me want to endorse the idea that pottery is an index of much more central social participation than simply the efficient fulfillment of utilitarian needs. Eckert's (Chapter 6) brilliant suggestion that the use of two interior colors in late Zuni bowls indexes two migration histories is a particularly inspiring example of peopling our pottery by engaging with multiple overlapping communities of practice. It is no accident that studies of ceramics have been the leading edge of archaeological engagement with the concept of communities of practice (Bowser and Patton 2008; Lopiparo 2006; Roddick 2009; Sassaman and Rudolphi 2001; but see also Minar 2001).

The multiple and overlapping communities of practice sketched out cumulatively by these chapters give us the much richer vision of social life that is necessary for us to understand the histories of long term change that we can see archaeologically. The authors of these chapters are pointing the way forward for all of us working on pottery as a social phenomenon. By using technical analyses in concert with sophisticated social theory, occasionally taking bold leaps, and remaining firmly rooted locally and connected regionally, they offer a model for all of us to follow.

References

Abbott, David R.
  2000   *Ceramics and Community Organization among the Hohokam.* University of Arizona Press, Tucson.
  2006   Hohokam Ritual and Economic Transformation: Ceramic Evidence from the Phoenix Basin, Arizona. *North American Archaeologist* 27(4):285–310.
  2008   The Process, Location, and History of Hohokam Buff Ware Production: Some Experimental and Analytical Results. *Journal of Archaeological Science* 35:388–397.

Abbott, David R. (editor)
  1994   *Ceramics and the Production and Exchange of Pottery in the Central Phoenix Basin.* The Pueblo Grande Project, Vol. 3. Publications in Archaeology 20. Soil Systems, Phoenix.

Abbott, David R., Susan L. Stinson, and Scott Van Keuren
  2001   The Economic Implications of Hohokam Buff Ware Exchange during the Early Sedentary Period. *Kiva* 67:7–29.

Abbott, David R., Alexa M. Smith, and Emiliano Gallaga
  2007   Ballcourts and Ceramics: The Case for Hohokam Marketplaces in the Arizona Desert. *American Antiquity* 72:461–484.

Abbott, David R., Joshua Watts, and Andrew D. Lack
  2007   The Provenance and Concentrated Production of Hohokam Red-on-buff Pottery: Implications for an Ancient Arizona Economy. *Journal of Anthropological Research* 63:331–357.

Adair, John
  1944   *The Navajo and Pueblo Silversmiths.* University of Oklahoma Press, Norman.

Adams, E. Charles
  2002   *Homol'ovi: An Ancient Hopi Settlement Cluster.* University of Arizona Press, Tucson.
  2004   Homol'ovi: A 13th–14th-Century Settlement Cluster in Northeastern Arizona. In *The Protohistoric Pueblo World, A.D. 1275 to 1600,* edited by E. Charles Adams and Andrew I. Duff, pp. 119-127. University of Arizona Press, Tucson.

Adams, E. Charles, and Andrew I. Duff
  2004   Settlement Clusters and the Pueblo IV Period. In *The Protohistoric Pueblo World, A.D. 1275 to 1600,* edited by E. Charles Adams and Andrew I. Duff, pp. 3–16. University of Arizona Press, Tucson.

Adams, E. Charles, Vincent M. LaMotta, and Kurt Dongoske
  2004   Hopi Settlement Clusters Past and Present. In *The Protohistoric Pueblo World, A.D. 1275 to 1600,* edited by E. Charles Adams and Andrew I. Duff, pp. 128-136. University of Arizona Press, Tucson.

Ambler, J. Richard
  1983   Kayenta Craft Specialization and Social Differentiation. In *Proceedings of the Anasazi Symposium, 1981,* edited by Jack E. Smith, pp. 75–82. Mesa Verde Museum Association, Mesa Verde National Park, CO.

Amsden, Monroe
  1928   *Archaeological Reconnaissance in Sonora.* Southwest Museum Papers 1. Los Angeles.

Anderson, Keith M.
  1969   *Archaeology on the Shonto Plateau, Northeast Arizona.* Technical Series 7. Southwest Monuments Association, Globe, AZ.

Andrews, Michael J.
  1978   *St. Michaels Pueblo: Pueblo III Subsistence and Adaptation in Black Creek Valley, Arizona.* Arizona Archaeologist 13. Arizona Archaeological Society, Phoenix.

Appadurai, Arjun
 1986   Introduction: Commodities and the Politics of Value. In *The Social Life of Things: Commodities in Cultural Perspective,* edited by A. Appadurai, pp. 3–63. Cambridge University Press, Cambridge.

Arnold, Dean E.
 1985   *Ceramic Theory and Cultural Process.* Cambridge University Press, Cambridge.

Arnold, Dean E., and Alvaro L. Nieves
 1992   Factors Affecting Ceramic Standardization. In *Ceramic Production and Distribution: An Integrated Approach,* edited by George J. Bey and Christopher A. Pool, pp. 93–113. Westview Press, Boulder.

Bakewell, P. J.
 1971   *Silver Mining and Society in Colonial Mexico: Zacatecas, 1546–1700.* Cambridge University Press, Cambridge.

Bamforth, Douglas B., and Nyree Finlay
 2008   Introduction: Archaeological Approaches to Lithic Production Skill and Craft Learning. *Journal of Archaeological Method and Theory* 15:1–27.

Barba, Alvaro Alonso
 1923   *El Arte de los Metales.* Translated by Ross E. Douglass and Edward Payson Mathewson. John Wiley & Sons, New York.

Barrett, Elinore M.
 1997   *The Geography of the Rio Grande Pueblos Revealed by Spanish Explorers, 1540–1598.* Latin American Research Institute Research Papers Series 30. University of New Mexico Press, Albuquerque.
 2002   *Conquest and Catastrophe: Changing Rio Grande Pueblo Settlement Patterns in the Sixteenth and Seventeenth Centuries.* University of New Mexico Press, Albuquerque.

Baumann, Martin
 1995   Conceptualizing Diaspora: The Preservation of Religious Identity in Foreign Parts, Exemplified by Hindu Communities outside India. *Temenos* 31:19–35.

Beals, Ralph L., George W. Brainard, and Watson Smith
 1945   *Archaeological Studies in Northeast Arizona: A Report on the Archaeological Work of the Rainbow Bridge–Monument Valley Expedition.* University of California Publications in American Archaeology and Ethnology 44(1). Berkeley.

Benco, Nancy L.
 1988   Morphological Standardization: An Approach to the Study of Craft Specialization. In *A Pot for All Reasons: Ceramic Ecology Revisited,* edited by Charles C. Kolb and Louana M. Lackey, pp. 57–72. Temple University, Philadelphia.

Bernardini, Wesley
 1998   Conflict, Migration, and the Social Environment: Interpreting Architectural Change in Early and Late Pueblo IV Aggregations. In *Migration and Reorganization: The Pueblo IV Period in the American Southwest,* edited by Katherine A. Spielmann, pp. 91–114. Anthropological Research Papers 51. Department of Anthropology, Arizona State University, Tempe.
 2009   *Hopi Oral Tradition and the Archaeology of Identity.* University of Arizona Press, Tucson.

Bice, Richard A., Phyllis S. Davis, and William M. Sundt
 2003   *Indian Mining of Lead for Use in Rio Grande Glaze Paint: Report of the AS-5 Bethsheba Project near Cerrillos, New Mexico.* Albuquerque Archaeological Society, Albuquerque.

Binford, Lewis R.
 1979   Organization and Formation Processes: Looking at Curated Technologies. *Journal of Anthropological Research* 35:255–273.

Blenkinsop, J., and W. F. Slawson
 1967   Geophysical Evidence of the Zuni Lineament. *Earth and Planetary Science Letters* 3:75–80.

Blinman, Eric
 1989   Pottery. In *Kayenta Anasazi Archeology and Navajo Ethnohistory on the Northwestern Shonto Plateau: The N-16 Project,* Vol. 2, edited by Alan R. Schroedl, pp. 599–629. Cultural Resources Report 412-01-8909. P-III Associates, Salt Lake City.

Blinman, Eric, and Clint Swink
 1997   Technology and Organization of Anasazi Trench Kilns. In *The Prehistory and History of Ceramic Kilns,* edited by Prudence Rice, pp. 85–102. Ceramics and Civilization, Vol. 7. American Ceramic Society, Westerville, OH.

Bloom, Lansing B.
 1937   Bourke on the Southwest, part XII. *New Mexico Historical Review* 12:337–379.

Boggess, Douglas, and David Hill
 2008   LA 149323: Evidence for the Production of Rio Grande Glazeware during the Early Eighteenth Century. *Pottery Southwest* 26(4):2–11.

Bohannon, Paul
 1967   The Impact of Money on an African Subsistence Economy. In *Tribal and Peasant Economies,* edited by George Dalton, pp. 123–135. Natural History Press, Garden City, New York.

Bolton, H. E. (editor)
 1963   *Spanish Exploration in the Southwest.* Barnes and Noble, New York.

Boone, Elizabeth H.
2003   A Web of Understanding: Pictorial Codices and the Shared Intellectual Culture of Late Postclassic Mesoamerica. In *The Postclassic Mesoamerican World,* edited by Michael E. Smith and Francis F. Berdan, pp. 207–221. University of Utah Press, Salt Lake City.

Bourdieu, Pierre
1977   *Outline of a Theory of Practice.* Translated by Richard Nice. Cambridge University Press, Cambridge.
1990   *The Logic of Practice.* Stanford University Press, Stanford.

Bouse, Robin M., Joaquin Ruiz, Spencer R. Titley, Richard M. Tosdal, and Joseph L. Wooden
1999   Lead Isotope Compositions of Late Cretaceous and Early Tertiary Igneous Rocks and Sulfide Minerals in Arizona: Implications for the Sources of Plutons and Metals in Porphyry Copper Deposits. *Economic Geology and the Bulletin of the Society of Economic Geologists* 94:211–244.

Bower, Nathan W., Steve Faciszeweski, Stephen Renwick, and Stewart Peckham
1986   A Preliminary Analysis of Rio Grande Glazes of the Classic Period using Scanning Electron Microscopy with X-ray Fluorescence. *Journal of Field Archaeology* 13:307–315.

Bowser, Brenda J.
2000   From Pottery to Politics: An Ethnoarchaeological Case Study of Political Factionalism, Ethnicity, and Domestic Pottery Style in the Ecuadorian Amazon. *Journal of Archaeological Method and Theory* 7:219–248.
2002   *The Perceptive Potter: An Ethnoarchaeological Study of Pottery, Ethnicity, and Political Action in the Ecuadorian Amazon.* Ph.D. dissertation, Department of Anthropology, University of California, Santa Barbara. University Microfilms, Ann Arbor.

Bowser, Brenda J., and John Q. Patton
2004   Domestic Spaces as Public Places: An Ethnoarchaeological Case Study of Houses, Gender, and Politics in the Ecuadorian Amazon. *Journal of Archaeological Method and Theory* 11:157–181.
2008   Learning and Transmission of Pottery Style: Women's Life Histories and Communities of Practice in the Ecuadorian Amazon. In *Cultural Transmission and Material Culture: Breaking Down Boundaries,* edited by Miriam T. Stark, Brenda J. Bowser, and Lee Horne, pp. 105–129. University of Arizona Press, Tucson.

Boyd, Jennifer Esche, and Connie Irene Constan
2002   *Ceramics on Lower Virgin Mesa, Jemez Mountains, New Mexico.* Cultural Resources Report 1999-10-28E. Santa Fe National Forest, Santa Fe.

Boyd, Mark Frederick, Hale G. Smith, and John W. Griffin
1951   *Here They Once Stood: The Tragic End of the Apalachee Missions.* University of Florida Press, Gainesville.

Bradley, Richard
2000   *An Archaeology of Natural Places.* Routledge, London.

Bradley, Vicki L.
2004   "What If We Are Doing This All Wrong?" Sequestering and a Community of Practice. *Anthropology and Education Quarterly* 35:345–367.

Brand, Donald D.
1935   The Distribution of Pottery Types in Northwest Mexico. *American Anthropologist* 37:287–305.

Brandt, Elizabeth A.
1985   Internal Stratification in Pueblo Communities. Paper presented at the Annual Meeting of the American Anthropological Association, Washington, D.C.
1994   Egalitarianism, Hierarchy, and Centralization in the Pueblos. In *The Ancient Southwestern Community: Models and Methods for the Study of Prehistoric Social Organization,* edited by W. H. Wills and Robert D. Leonard, pp. 9–24. University of New Mexico Press, Albuquerque.

Braniff, Beatriz C.
1974   Oscilación de la Frontera Septentrional Mesoamericana. In *The Archaeology of West Mexico,* edited by Betty Bell, pp. 40–50. Sociedad de Estudios Avanzados del Occidente de México, Ajijic, Jalisco.

Breternitz, David A.
1966   *An Appraisal of Tree-Ring Dating in the Southwest.* University of Arizona Anthropological Papers 10. University of Arizona Press, Tucson.

Breternitz, David A., Arthur H. Rohn, Jr., and Elizabeth A. Morris
1974   *Prehistoric Ceramics of the Mesa Verde Region.* Museum of Northern Arizona Ceramic Series 5. Northern Arizona Society of Science and Art, Flagstaff.

Brew, J. O.
1943   On the Pueblo IV and the Katchina-Tlaloc Relations. In *El Norte de México y el Sur de los Estados Unidos: Tercera Reunión de Mesa Redonda sobre Problemas Antropológicas de México y Centro América,* pp. 241–245. Sociedad Mexicana de Antropología, México.

Brody, J. J.
  1964   Design Analysis of the Rio Grande Glaze Pottery of Pottery Mound, New Mexico. Unpublished Master's thesis, Department of Art History, University of New Mexico, Albuquerque.
  1977   *Mimbres Painted Pottery.* School of American Research, Santa Fe, and University of New Mexico Press, Albuquerque.
Brooks, James F.
  2002   *Captives and Cousins: Slavery, Kinship, and Community in the Southwest Borderlands.* University of North Carolina Press, Chapel Hill.
Broxton, David E., and Steven L. Reneau
  1996   Buried Early Pleistocene Landscapes beneath the Pajarito Plateau, Northern New Mexico. In *The Jemez Mountains Region: New Mexico Geological Society Guidebook, Forty-Seventh Annual Field Conference, September 25–28, 1996,* edited by Fraser Goff, Barry S. Kues, Margaret A. Rogers, Leslie D. McFadden, and Jamie N. Gardner, pp. 325–334. New Mexico Geological Society, Socorro.
Broxton, David E., Fraser Goff, and Kenneth Wohletz
  2008   The Geology of Los Alamos National Laboratory as a Backdrop for Archaeological Studies on the Pajarito Plateau. In *The Land Conveyance and Transfer Data Recovery Project: 7000 Years of Land Use on the Pajarito Plateau, Vol. 1: Baseline Studies,* edited by Bradley J. Vierra and Kari M. Schmidt, pp. 7–30. LAUR-07-6205. Ecology and Air Quality Group, Los Alamos National Laboratory, U.S. Department of Energy, National Nuclear Security Administration, Los Alamos, NM.
Bunzel, Ruth L.
  1972   *The Pueblo Potter.* Dover, New York.
  1984   *Zuni Kachinas.* Rio Grande Press, Glorieta, NM.
Burton, Jeffery F.
  1990   *Archeological Investigations at Puerco Ruin, Petrified Forest National Park, Arizona.* Publications in Anthropology 54. Western Archeological and Conservation Center, National Park Service, Tucson.
Capone, Patricia W.
  1995   Mission Pueblo Ceramic Analyses: Implications for Protohistoric Interaction Networks and Cultural Dynamics. Unpublished Ph.D. dissertation, Department of Anthropology, Harvard University, Cambridge.
  2004   Culture Contact Viewed through Ceramic Petrography at the Pueblo Mission of Abó, New Mexico. In *The Archaeology of Contact in Settler Societies,* edited by Tim Murray, pp. 78–90. Cambridge University Press, Cambridge.
  2006   Rio Grande Glaze Ware Technology and Production: Historic Expediency. In *The Social Life of Pots,* edited by Judith A. Habicht-Mauche, Suzanne L. Eckert, and Deborah L. Huntley, pp. 216–232. University of Arizona Press, Tucson.
Capone, Patricia W., and Robert W. Preucel
  2002   Ceramic Semiotics: Women, Pottery, and Social Meanings at Kotyiti Pueblo. In *Archaeologies of the Pueblo Revolt: Identity, Meaning, and Renewal in the Pueblo World,* edited by Robert W. Preucel, pp. 99–113. University of New Mexico Press, Albuquerque.
Carey, Henry A.
  1931   An Analysis of the Northwestern Chihuahua Culture. *American Anthropologist* 33:325–374.
Carlson, Roy L.
  1970   *White Mountain Redware, A Pottery Tradition of East-Central Arizona and Western New Mexico.* Anthropological Papers of the University of Arizona 19. University of Arizona Press, Tucson.
  1982   The Polychrome Complexes. In *Southwest Ceramics: A Comparative Review,* edited by Albert H. Schroeder, pp. 201–234. Arizona Archaeologist 15. Arizona Archaeological Society, Phoenix.
Carpenter, John, and Guadalupe Sánchez
  2008   Entre la Sierra Madre y el Mar: La Arqueología de Sinaloa. *Arqueología* 39:21–45.
Carr, Christopher
  1995a   Building a Unified Middle-Range Theory of Artifact Design: Historical Perspectives and Tactics. In *Style, Society, and Person: Archaeological and Ethnological Perspectives,* edited by Christopher Carr and Jill E. Neitzel, pp. 151–170. Plenum Press, New York.
  1995b   A Unified Middle-Range Theory of Artifact Design. In *Style, Society, and Person: Archaeological and Ethnological Perspectives,* edited by Christopher Carr and Jill E. Neitzel, pp. 171–258. Plenum Press, New York.
Christenson, Andrew L.
  1991   Identifying Pukis or Potters' Turntables at Anasazi Sites. *Pottery Southwest* 18(1):1–6.
  1994   Perforated and Unperforated Plates as Tools for Pottery Manufacture. In *Function and Technology of Anasazi Ceramics from Black Mesa, Arizona,* edited by Marion F. Smith, Jr., pp. 55–65. Center for Archaeological Investigations Occasional Paper 15. Southern Illinois University, Carbondale.
Clark, Jeffery J.
  2001   *Tracking Prehistoric Migrations: Pueblo Settlers among the Tonto Basin Hohokam.* Anthropological Papers of the University of Arizona 65. University of Arizona Press, Tucson.

Clark, Jeffery J., and Patrick D. Lyons (editors)
2012 *Migrants and Mounds: Classic Period Archaeology of the San Pedro Valley, Arizona.* Anthropological Papers 45. Center for Desert Archaeology, Tucson, AZ, in press.

Clifford, James
1994 Diasporas. *Cultural Anthropology* 9:302–338.

Cogswell, James W., David R. Abbott, Elizabeth J. Miksa, Hector Neff, Robert J. Speakman, and Michael D. Glascock
2005 A Provenance Study of Hohokam Schist-Tempered Pottery and Raw Materials from the Middle Gila River Valley, Arizona: Techniques and Prospects. In *Laser Ablation-ICP-MS in Archaeological Research,* edited by Robert J. Speakman and Hector Neff, pp. 105–115. University of New Mexico Press, Albuquerque.

Cohen, Robin
1997 *Global Diasporas: An Introduction.* University of Washington Press, Seattle.

Colton, Harold S.
1955 *Check List of Southwestern Pottery Types.* Museum of Northern Arizona Ceramic Series 2. Northern Arizona Society of Science and Art, Flagstaff.
1956 *Pottery Types of the Southwest 3C.* Museum of Northern Arizona Ceramic Series 3. Northern Arizona Society of Science and Art, Flagstaff.
1958 *Pottery Types of the Southwest 3D.* Museum of Northern Arizona Ceramic Series 3. Northern Arizona Society of Science and Art, Flagstaff.
1965 *Check List of Southwestern Pottery Types,* revised. Museum of Northern Arizona Ceramic Series 2. Northern Arizona Society of Science and Art, Flagstaff.

Colton, Harold S., and Lyndon L. Hargrave
1937 *Handbook of Northern Arizona Pottery Wares.* Museum of Northern Arizona Bulletin 11. Northern Arizona Society of Science and Art, Flagstaff.

Cordell, Linda S.
1979 *Cultural Resources Overview of the Middle Rio Grande Valley, New Mexico.* USDA Forest Service, Albuquerque, and USDI Bureau of Land Management, Santa Fe.
1997 *Archaeology of the Southwest. 2nd ed.* Academic Press, New York.
2006 Rio Grande Glaze Paint Ware in Southwestern Archaeology. In *The Social Life of Pots: Glaze Wares and Cultural Dynamics in the Southwest, AD 1250–1680,* edited by Judith Habicht-Mauche, Suzanne L. Eckert, and Deborah L. Huntley, pp. 253–271. University of Arizona Press, Tucson.

Cordell, Linda S. (editor)
1980 *Tijeras Canyon: Analyses of the Past.* Maxwell Museum of Anthropology and University of New Mexico Press, Albuquerque.

Cordell, Linda S., Suzanne L. Eckert, and Hayward H. Franklin
2008 Profiles at Pottery Mound: The 1979 UNM Test Units. In *Chasing Chaco and the Southwest: Papers in Honor of Joan Mathien,* edited by Regge N. Wiseman, Thomas C. O'Laughlin, Cordelia T. Snow, and Cathy Travis, pp. 67–82. Papers of the Archaeological Society of New Mexico 34. Albuquerque.

Costin, Cathy L.
1991 Craft Specialization: Issues in Defining, Documenting, and Explaining the Organization of Production. In *Archaeological Method and Theory,* Vol. 3, edited by Michael B. Schiffer, pp. 1–56. Academic Press, New York.
2001 Craft Production Systems. In *Archaeology at the Millennium: A Sourcebook,* edited by Gary M. Feinman and T. Douglas Price, pp. 273–327. Kluwer Academic/ Plenum Publishers, New York.

Creamer, Winifred, and Lisa Renken
1994 Testing Conventional Wisdom: Protohistoric Ceramics and Chronology in the Northern Rio Grande. Paper presented at the 59th Annual Meeting of the Society for American Archaeology, Anaheim, CA.

Creamer, Winifred, David Burdick, Patrick Hamlen, Jonathan Haas, Lisa Renken, Aaron Wenzel, and Kit Nelson
2002 Ceramic Analysis of Intra- and Intersite Occupation at Protohistoric Pueblos in the Northern Rio Grande. In *Traditions, Transitions and Technologies: Themes in Southwestern Archaeology,* edited by Sarah H. Schlanger, pp. 59–69. University Press of Colorado, Boulder.

Crotty, Helen K.
1983 *Honoring the Dead: Anasazi Ceramics from the Rainbow Bridge-Monument Valley Expedition.* Monograph Series 22. Museum of Cultural History, University of California, Los Angeles.
2007 Western Pueblo Influences and Integration in the Pottery Mound Painted Kivas. In *New Perspectives on Pottery Mound Pueblo,* edited by Polly Schaafsma, pp. 85–107. University of New Mexico Press, Albuquerque.

Crown, Patricia L.
1994 *Ceramics and Ideology: Salado Polychrome Pottery.* University of New Mexico Press, Albuquerque.

1996   Change in Ceramic Design Style and Technology in the Thirteenth to Fourteenth-Century Southwest. In *Interpreting Southwestern Diversity: Underlying Principles and Overarching Patterns*, edited by Paul R. Fish and J. Jefferson Reid, pp. 241–247. Anthropological Research Papers 48. Department of Anthropology, Arizona State University, Tempe.

1999   Socialization in American Southwest Pottery Decoration. In *Pottery and People: A Dynamic Interaction,* edited by James M. Skibo and Gary M. Feinman, pp. 25–43. University of Utah Press, Salt Lake City.

2001   Learning to Make Pottery in the Prehispanic Southwest. *Journal of Anthropological Research* 57:451–469.

2002   Learning and Teaching in the Prehispanic American Southwest. In *Children in the Prehistoric Puebloan Southwest,* edited by Kathryn A. Kamp, pp. 108–124. University of Utah Press, Salt Lake City.

2007a   Life Histories of Pots and Potters: Situating the Individual in Archaeology. *American Antiquity* 72:677–691.

2007b   Learning about Learning. In *Archaeological Anthropology: Perspectives on Method and Theory,* edited by James M. Skibo, Michael W. Graves, and Miriam T. Stark, pp. 198–217. University of Arizona Press, Tucson.

Crown, Patricia L., and Wirt H. Wills

1995   The Origins of Southwestern Containers: Women's Time Allocation and Economic Intensification. *Journal of Anthropological Research* 51:173–186.

Curewitz, Diane C.

2008   Changes in Northern Rio Grande Ceramic Production and Exchange, Late Coalition through Classic (A.D. 1250–1600). Unpublished Ph.D. dissertation, Department of Anthropology, Washington State University, Pullman.

Cushing, Frank Hamilton

1896   Outlines of Zuni Creation Myths. In *Thirteenth Annual Report of the Bureau of Ethnology,* pp. 321–447. U.S. Government Printing Office, Washington D.C.

1979   *Zuni: Selected Writings of Frank Hamilton Cushing.* Edited by Jesse Green. University of Nebraska Press, Lincoln.

David, Nicholas, Judy Sterner, and Kodzo Gavua

1988   Why Pots Are Decorated. *Current Anthropology* 29:365–389.

Deagan, Kathleen

1983   *Spanish St. Augustine: The Archaeology of a Colonial Creole Community.* Academic Press, New York.

1985   Spanish-Indian Interaction in Sixteenth Century Florida and the Caribbean. In *Cultures in Contact: The European Impact on Native Cultural Institutions in Eastern North America, A.D. 1000-1800,* edited by William Fitzhugh, pp. 281–318. Smithsonian Institution Press, Washington D.C.

1987   *Artifacts of the Spanish Colonies of Florida and the Caribbean, 1500–1800.* Smithsonian Institution Press, Washington, D.C.

1990a   Accommodation and Resistance: The Process and Impact of Spanish Colonization in the Southeast. In *Columbian Consequences 2: Archaeological and Historical Perspectives on the Spanish Borderlands East,* edited by David Hurst Thomas, pp. 297–314. Smithsonian Institution Press, Washington D.C.

1990b   Sixteenth-Century Spanish-American Colonization in the Southeastern United States and the Caribbean. In *Columbian Consequences 2: Archaeological and Historical Perspectives on the Spanish Borderlands East,* edited by David Hurst Thomas, pp. 225–250. Smithsonian Institution Press, Washington D.C.

1995   *Puerto Real: The Archaeology of a Sixteenth-Century Spanish Town in Hispaniola.* University Press of Florida, Gainesville.

Deagan, Kathleen, and José Maria Cruxent

1993   From Contact to Criollos: Archaeology of Spanish Colonization in Hispaniola. In *Meeting of Two Worlds: Europe and the Americas, 1492–1650,* edited by Warwick Bray, pp. 67–104. Oxford University Press, Oxford.

Dean, Jeffrey S., Alexander J. Lindsay, Jr., and William J. Robinson

1978   Prehistoric Settlement in the Long House Valley, Northeastern Arizona. In *Investigations of the Southwestern Anthropological Research Group: The Proceedings of the 1976 Conference,* edited by Robert C. Euler and George J. Gumerman, pp. 25–44. Museum of Northern Arizona, Flagstaff.

De Atley, Suzanne P.

1986   Mix and Match: Traditions of Glaze Paint Preparation at Four Mile Ruin, Arizona. In *Ceramics and Civilization, Vol. II: Technology and Style,* edited by William D. Kingery and Esther Lense, pp. 297–329. American Ceramic Society, Columbus, OH.

De Atley, Suzanne P., M. James Blackman, and Jacqueline S. Olin

1982   Comparison of Data Obtained by Neutron Activation and Electron Microprobe Analyses in Ceramics. In *Archaeological Ceramics,* edited by Jacqueline S. Olin and Alan D. Franklin, pp. 79–87. Smithsonian Institution Press, Washington, D.C.

Deetz, James
1977   *In Small Things Forgotten: An Archaeology of Early American Life.* Anchor Books, Doubleday, New York.

Dick, Herbert W.
1965   Picuris Pueblo Excavations. Manuscript on file, National Park Service, Southwest Region, Santa Fe.

Dietler, Michael
2001   Theorizing the Feast: Rituals of Consumption, Commensal Politics, and Power in African Contexts. In *Feasts: Archaeological and Ethnographic Perspectives on Food, Politics, and Power,* edited by Michael Dietler and Brian Hayden, pp. 65–114. Smithsonian Institution Press, Washington, D.C.

Dietler, Michael D., and Ingrid Herbich
1998   Habitus, Techniques, Style: An Integrated Approach to the Social Understanding of Material Culture and Boundaries. In *The Archaeology of Social Boundaries,* edited by Miriam T. Stark, pp. 232–263. Smithsonian Institution Press, Washington, D.C.

Dillingham, Rick
1992   *Acoma and Laguna Pottery.* School of American Research Press, Santa Fe.

Di Peso, Charles C.
1958   *The Reeve Ruin of Southeastern Arizona: A Study of Prehistoric Western Pueblo Migration into the Middle San Pedro Valley.* Publication 8. Amerind Foundation, Dragoon, AZ.
1974   *Casas Grandes, A Fallen Trading Center of the Gran Chichimeca,* Vols. 1–3. Amerind Foundation 9. Northland Press, Flagstaff.

Di Peso, Charles C., John B. Rinaldo, and Gloria C. Fenner
1974   *Casas Grandes, A Fallen Trading Center of the Gran Chichimeca,* Vols. 4–8. Amerind Foundation 9. Northland Press, Flagstaff.

Doyel, David E.
1974   *Excavations in the Escalante Ruin Group, Southern Arizona.* Archaeological Series 37. Arizona State Museum, University of Arizona, Tucson.
1981   *Late Hohokam Prehistory in Southern Arizona.* Contributions to Archaeology 2. Gila Press, Scottsdale, AZ.

Duff, Andrew I.
1996   Ceramic Micro-Seriation: Types of Attributes? *American Antiquity* 61:89-101.
1998   The Process of Migration in the Late Prehistoric Southwest. In *Migration and Reorganization:*

The Pueblo IV Period in the American Southwest, edited by Katherine A. Spielmann, pp. 31–52. Anthropological Research Papers 51. Department of Anthropology, Arizona State University, Tempe.
1999   *Regional Interaction and the Transformation of Western Pueblo Identities, A.D. 1275–1400.* Ph.D. dissertation, Department of Anthropology, Arizona State University, Tempe. University Microfilms, Ann Arbor.
2002   *Western Pueblo Identities: Regional Interaction, Migration, and Transformation.* University of Arizona Press, Tucson.

Dunbar, Nelia W.
2005   Quaternary Volcanism in New Mexico. In *New Mexico's Ice Ages,* edited by S. G. Lucas and K. E. Ziegler, pp. 95–106. New Mexico Museum of Natural History and Science Bulletin 28. Albuquerque.

Dunnell, Robert C.
1970   Seriation Method and Its Evaluation. *American Antiquity* 35:305–319.

Duwe, Samuel Gregg
2005   Communities of Practice and Ancient Apprenticeship in the American Southwest: Pigment Analyses of Pueblo IV Period Ceramics from Bailey Ruin, East-Central Arizona. Unpublished Master's thesis, Department of Anthropology, University of Arizona, Tucson.

Duwe, Samuel, and Hector Neff
2007   Glaze Pigment Analyses of Pueblo IV Period Ceramics from East-Central Arizona using Time-of-Flight Laser Ablation-Inductively Coupled Plasma-Mass Spectrometry (TOF-LA-ICP-MS). *Journal of Archaeological Science* 34:404–414.

Dyer, Jennifer Boyd
2010   Colono Wares in the Western Spanish Borderlands: A Ceramic Technological Study. Unpublished Ph.D. dissertation, Department of Anthropology, University of New Mexico, Albuquerque.

Eckert, Suzanne L.
2003   Social Boundaries, Immigration and Ritual Systems: A Case Study from the American Southwest. Unpublished Ph.D. dissertation, Department of Anthropology, Arizona State University, Tempe.
2005   Zuni Demographic Structure, A.D. 1300–1600: A Case Study on Spanish Contact and Native Population Dynamics. *Kiva* 70:207–226.
2006   The Production and Distribution of Glaze-Painted Pottery in the Pueblo Southwest: A Synthesis. In *The Social Life of Pots: Glaze Wares and Cultural Dynamics in the Southwest, AD 1250–1680,*

Eckert, Suzanne L. (*continued*)

   edited by Judith A. Habicht-Mauche, Suzanne L. Eckert, and Deborah L. Huntley, pp. 34–59. University of Arizona Press, Tucson.

2007   Understanding the Dynamics of Segregation and Incorporation at Pottery Mound through Analysis of Glaze-Decorated Bowls. In *New Perspectives on Pottery Mound Pueblo*, edited by Polly Schaafsma, pp. 55–74. University of New Mexico Press, Albuquerque.

2008   *Pottery and Practice: The Expression of Identity at Pottery Mound and Hummingbird Pueblo*. University of New Mexico Press, Albuquerque.

Ellis, Florence H.

1976   The Basis for Santo Domingo Pueblo's Claim to the Turquoise Mine Area (Plaintiff's Exhibit 1, Indian Claims Commission, Docket 355, *Pueblo of Santo Domingo v United States of America*). Manuscript on file, Catalogue No. 2010.41.1976g, Maxwell Museum of Anthropology, University of New Mexico, Albuquerque.

1981   Comments on Four Papers Pertaining to the Protohistoric Southwest. In *The Protohistoric Period in the North American Southwest, A.D. 1400-1700*, edited by David R. Wilcox and W. Bruce Masse, pp. 410–413. Anthropological Research Papers 24. Arizona State University, Tempe.

Espinosa, J. Manuel (editor and translator)

1988   *The Pueblo Indian Revolt of 1696 and the Franciscan Missions in New Mexico: Letters of the Missionaries and Related Documents*. University of Oklahoma Press, Norman.

Ewen, Charles R.

1990   The Rise and Fall of Puerto Real. In *Columbian Consequences 2: Archaeological and Historical Perspectives on the Spanish Borderlands East*, edited by David Hurst Thomas, pp. 261–268. Smithsonian Institution Press, Washington D.C.

Ewing, Thomas E.

1979   Lead Isotope Data from Mineral Deposits of Southern New Mexico: A Reinterpretation. *Economic Geology* 74:678–684.

Farago, Claire, and Donna Pierce (editors)

2006   *Transforming Images: New Mexican Santos In-between Worlds*. Pennsylvania State University Press, University Park.

Fenn, Forrest

2004   *The Secrets of San Lazaro Pueblo*. One Horse Land and Cattle Company, Santa Fe.

Fenn, Thomas R., Barbara J. Mills, and Maren Hopkins

2006   The Social Contexts of Glaze Paint Ceramic Production and Consumption in the Silver Creek Area. In *The Social Life of Pots: Glaze Wares and Cultural Dynamics in the Southwest, AD 1250–1680*, edited by Judith A. Habicht-Mauche, Suzanne L. Eckert, and Deborah L. Huntley, pp. 60–85. University of Arizona Press, Tucson.

Fenn, Thomas R., Barbara J. Mills, John T. Chesley, and Joaquin Ruiz

2012   Technology and Materials Transference in the prehistoric American Southwest: Isotopic and Elemental Analyses of Glaze Paints from the Mogollon Rim Region, East-Central Arizona. Manuscript on file, School of Anthropology, University of Arizona, Tucson.

Fenner, Gloria J.

1974   Design Analysis of Medio Period Painted Pottery Types. In *Casas Grandes: A Fallen Trading Center of the Gran Chichimeca, Vol. 6, Ceramics and Shell*, edited by Charles C. Di Peso, John B. Rinaldo, and Gloria J. Fenner, pp. 92–105. Amerind Foundation, Dragoon, Arizona.

Ferguson, Leland

1980   Looking for the "Afro" in Colono-Indian Pottery. In *Archaeological Perspectives on Ethnicity in America, Afro-American and Asian American Culture History*, edited by Robert L. Schuyler, pp. 14–28. Baywood, New York.

Ferguson, T. J.

2007   Zuni Traditional History and Cultural Geography. In *Zuni Origins: Toward a New Synthesis of Southwestern Archaeology*, edited by David A. Gregory and David R. Wilcox, pp. 377–406. University of Arizona Press, Tucson.

Ferguson, T. J., and E. Richard Hart

1985   *A Zuni Atlas*. University of Oklahoma Press, Norman.

Fewkes, Jesse W.

1973   *Designs on Prehistoric Hopi Pottery*. Reprinted. Dover, New York. Originally published 1919, in *Thirty-third Annual Report of the Bureau of American Ethnography*, pp. 207–284. Government Printing Office, Washington, D.C.

Flagler, Edward K.

1990   Governor Jose Chacon, Marques de la Penuela: An Andalusian Nobleman on the New Mexico Frontier. *New Mexico Historical Review* 65:455–476.

Ford, James A.

1962   *A Quantitative Method for Deriving Cultural Chronology*. Technical Manual 1. Pan American Union, Washington D.C.

Ford, Richard I.

1992   *An Ecological Analysis Involving the Population of San Juan Pueblo, New Mexico*. Garland, New York.

Fowler, Andrew P.
1988   Ceramics from Bidahochi Pueblo. Manuscript on file, Zuni Archaeology Program, Zuni, NM.

Franklin, Hayward H.
1980   *Excavations at Second Canyon Ruin, San Pedro Valley, Arizona.* Contribution to Highway Salvage Archaeology 60. Arizona State Museum, University of Arizona, Tucson.
1997   Valencia Pueblo Ceramics. In *Excavations at Valencia Pueblo (LA 953) and a nearby Hispanic Settlement (LA 67321), Valencia County, New Mexico,* edited by Kenneth L. Brown and Bradley J. Vierra, pp. 125–246. Office of Contract Archeology, University of New Mexico, Albuquerque.
2007   *The Pottery of Pottery Mound: A Study of the 1979 UNM Field School Collection, Part 1: Typology and Chronology.* Maxwell Museum Technical Series 5. University of New Mexico, Albuquerque.
2008   *New Dates from Pottery Mound, New Mexico.* Maxwell Museum Technical Series 7. University of New Mexico, Albuquerque.
2010a *The Pottery of Pottery Mound: A Study of the 1979 UNM Field School Collection, Part 2: Ceramic Materials and Regional Exchange.* Maxwell Museum Technical Series 12. University of New Mexico, Albuquerque.
2010b Montaño Site Complex (LA 33223) Ceramic Analysis. In *Report on 1988 Data Recovery at the Montaño Site Complex, LA 3322, City of Albuquerque, New Mexico, and Subsequent Analysis of Collections,* edited by Gerry Raymond, pp. 5-1 to 5-79. Submitted to the City of Albuquerque by Criterion Environmental Consulting, Albuquerque.

Friedrich, Margaret Hardin
1970   Design Structure and Social Interaction: Archaeological Implications of an Ethnographic Analysis. *American Antiquity* 35:332–343.

Futrell, Mary E.
1998   Social Boundaries and Interaction: Ceramic Zones in the Northern Rio Grande Pueblo IV Period. In *Migration and Reorganization: The Pueblo IV Period in the American Southwest,* edited by Katherine A. Spielmann, pp. 285–292. Anthropological Research Papers 51. Department of Anthropology, Arizona State University, Tempe.

Gage, John
1999   *Color and Culture: Practice and Meaning from Antiquity to Abstraction.* University of California Press, Berkeley and Los Angeles.

Gallagher, Marsha V.
1986   Ceramic Analysis. In *The Kayenta Anasazi: Archaeological Investigations along the Black Mesa Railroad Corridor, Vol. 1: Specialists'* *Reports,* by Sara Stebbins, Bruce Harrill, William D. Wade, Marsha V. Gallagher, Hugh Cutler, and Leonard Blake, pp. 30–52. Museum of Northern Arizona Research Paper 30. Flagstaff.

Garcia-Arevalo, Manuel
1990   Transculturation in Contact Period and Contemporary Hispaniola. In *Columbian Consequences 2: Archaeological and Historical Perspectives on the Spanish Borderlands East,* edited by David Hurst Thomas, pp. 269–280. Smithsonian Institution Press, Washington D.C.

Garrett, Elizabeth M.
1976   A Petrographic Analysis of Thirty Pottery Mound Polychrome, San Clemente Polychrome, and Glaze C Sherds from Pottery Mound, New Mexico. *Pottery Southwest* 3(1):4–8.

Gerald, Rex E.
1958   Davis Ranch Site (ARIZ:BB:11:7 AF). Manuscript on file, Amerind Foundation, Dragoon.
1975   *Drought Correlated Changes in Two Prehistoric Pueblo Communities in Southeastern Arizona.* Ph.D. dissertation, Department of Anthropology, University of Chicago. ProQuest, Ann Arbor.

Giddens, Anthony
1979   *Central Problems in Social Theory: Action, Structure and Contradiction in Social Analysis.* University of California Press, Berkeley and Los Angeles.
1984   *The Constitution of Society: Outline of the Theory of Structuration.* University of California Press, Berkeley and Los Angeles.

Gifford, James C.
1980   *Archaeological Explorations in Caves of the Point of Pines Region, Arizona.* Anthropological Papers of the University of Arizona 36. University of Arizona Press, Tucson.

Gilroy, Paul
1997   Diaspora and the Detours of Identity. In *Identity and Difference,* edited by Kathryn Woodward, pp. 299–343. Sage, London.

Ginn, Sarah, and Judith Habicht-Mauche
2005   Lead Isotope Analysis and Sourcing of Glaze Plaints on Shepard's Glaze Ware Sherds from the Northern and Southern Pajarito Districts. Manuscript on file, Ceramic Materials Research Laboratory, Department of Anthropology, University of California, Santa Cruz.

Gladwin, Harold S.
1928   *Excavations at Casa Grande, Arizona, February 12–May 1, 1927.* Southwest Museum Papers 2. Southwest Museum, Los Angeles.

Gladwin, Winifred, and Harold S. Gladwin
1929   *The Red-on-buff Culture of the Gila Basin.* Medallion Papers 3. Gila Pueblo, Globe.

1930　*Some Southwestern Pottery Types: Series I.* Medallion Papers 8. Gila Pueblo, Globe.

1931　*Some Southwestern Pottery Types: Series II.* Medallion Papers 10. Gila Pueblo, Globe.

1935　*The Eastern Range of the Red-on-buff Culture.* Medallion Papers 16. Gila Pueblo, Globc.

Goff, Sheila

1993　Brief Analysis of Two Hopi Yellow Ware Sherds and Two Bidahochi Sherds. Manuscript on file, University of Colorado Museum, Boulder.

2009　Pajarito Plateau Glaze Paint Ware Production Earlier and More Widespread than Previously Thought. *Kiva* 74:371–392.

Goggin, John M.

1968　*Spanish Majolica in the New World.* Yale University Publications in Anthropology 72. Yale University Press, New Haven.

Gosden, Chris

2005　What Do Objects Want? *Journal of Archaeological Method and Theory* 12:193–211.

Gosselain, Olivier P.

1992　Technology and Style: Potters and Pottery among the Bafia of Cameroon. *Man* 27:559–586.

2000　Materializing Identities: An African Perspective. *Journal of Archaeological Method and Theory* 7:187–217.

2008　Mother Bella Was Not a Bella: Inherited and Transformed Traditions in Southwestern Niger. In *Cultural Transmission and Material Culture: Breaking Down Boundaries,* edited by Miriam T. Stark, Brenda J. Bowser, and Lee Horne, pp. 150–177. University of Arizona Press, Tucson.

Gossett, Cye W., and William J. Gossett

1988　*Preliminary Report for Final Excavations at Montaño Pueblo, LA 33223.* Rio Abajo Archaeological Services, Socorro.

Graves, Michael W.

1984　Temporal Variation in White Mountain Redware Design Styles. *The Kiva* 50:3–24.

Graves, William M.

1996　Social Power and Prestige Enhancement among the Protohistoric Salinas Pueblos, Rio Grande Valley, New Mexico. Unpublished M.A. thesis, Department of Anthropology, Arizona State University, Tempe.

Graves, William M., and Suzanne L. Eckert

1998　Decorated Ceramic Distributions and Ideological Developments in the Rio Grande Valley, New Mexico. In *Migration and Reorganization: The Pueblo IV Period in the American Southwest,* edited by Katherine Spielmann, pp. 263–284.

Anthropological Research Papers 51. Department of Anthropology, Arizona State University, Tempe.

Graves, William M., and Katherine A. Spielmann

2000　Leadership, Long-Distance Exchange, and Feasting in the Protohistoric Rio Grande. In *Alternative Leadership Strategies in the Prehispanic Southwest,* edited by Barbara J. Mills, pp. 45–59. University of Arizona Press, Tucson.

Green, David

1979　*A Handbook of Pottery Glazes.* Watson-Guptill, New York.

Gregory, David A., and David R. Wilcox (editors)

2007　*Zuni Origins: Toward a New Synthesis of Southwestern Archaeology.* University of Arizona Press, Tucson.

Guernsey, Samuel J.

1931　*Explorations in Northeastern Arizona: Report on the Fieldwork of 1920–1923.* Papers of the Peabody Museum of American Archaeology and Ethnology 22(1). Harvard University, Cambridge.

Guthe, Carl E.

1925　*Pueblo Pottery Making: A Study at the Village of San Ildefonso.* Published for the Phillips Academy, Andover, by Yale University Press, New Haven.

Haas, Wm. Randall, Jr.

2006　The Social Implications of Basketmaker II Cordage Design Distribution. *Kiva* 71:275–298.

Habicht-Mauche, Judith A.

1991　Evidence for the Manufacture of Southwestern-Style Culinary Ceramics on the Southern Plains. In *Farmers, Hunters, and Colonists: Interaction between the Southwest and the Southern Plains,* edited by Katherine A. Spielmann, pp. 51–70. University of Arizona Press, Tucson.

1993　*The Pottery from Arroyo Hondo Pueblo, New Mexico: Tribalization and Trade in the Northern Rio Grande.* Arroyo Hondo Archaeological Series 8. School of American Research Press, Santa Fe.

1995　Changing Patterns of Pottery Manufacture and Trade in the Northern Rio Grande Region. In *Ceramic Production in the American Southwest,* edited by Barbara J. Mills and Patricia L. Crown, pp. 167–199. University of Arizona Press, Tucson.

1998　The Production and Exchange of Rio Grande Glaze-Painted Pottery: New Approaches to Old Questions. Paper presented at the 63rd Annual Meeting of the Society for American Archaeology, Seattle.

2000　Pottery, Food, Hides, and Women: Labor, Production, and Exchange across the Protohistoric Plains-Pueblo Frontier. In *The Archaeology* of *Regional Interaction: Religion, Warfare, and Exchange across the American Southwest and Beyond*, edited by Michelle Hegmon, pp. 209–231. University Press of Colorado, Boulder.

2002 Stable Lead Isotope Analysis of Rio Grande Glaze Paints and Ores Using ICP-MS: A Comparison of Acid Dissolution and Laser Ablation Techniques. *Journal of Archaeological Science* 29: 1043–1054.

2006 The Social History of the Southwestern Glaze Wares. In *The Social Life of Pots: Glaze Wares and Cultural Dynamics in the Southwest, AD 1250–1680,* edited by Judith A. Habicht-Mauche, Suzanne L. Eckert, and Deborah L. Huntley, pp. 4–16. University of Arizona Press, Tucson.

2009 Studying Glaze-Paint Production and Exchange in the American Southwest Using Lead Isotope Analysis. Paper presented at the 74th Annual Meeting of the Society for American Archaeology, Atlanta.

Habicht-Mauche, Judith A., and Sarah Ginn
2004 The Origins of Glaze Painted Pottery in the Central Rio Grande. Paper presented at the 69th Annual Meeting of the Society for American Archaeology, Montreal.

Habicht-Mauche, Judith A., Suzanne L. Eckert, and Deborah L. Huntley (editors)
2006 *The Social Life of Pots: Glaze Wares and Cultural Dynamics in the Southwest, A.D. 1250-1680.* University of Arizona Press, Tucson.

Habicht-Mauche, Judith A., Stephen T. Glenn, Homer Milford, and A. Russell Flegal
2000 Isotopic Tracing of Prehistoric Rio Grande Glaze-Paint Production and Trade. *Journal of Archaeological Science* 27:709–713.

Habicht-Mauche, Judith A., Stephen T. Glenn, Mike P. Schmidt, Rob Franks, Homer Milford, and A. Russell Flegal
2002 Stable Lead Isotope Analysis of Rio Grande Glaze Paints and Ores Using ICP-MS: A Comparison of Acid Dissolution and Laser Ablation Techniques. *Journal of Archaeological Science* 29:1043–1053.

Hackett, Charles Wilson
1937 *Historical Approaches Relating to New Mexico, Nueva Vizcaya, and Approaches Thereto, to 1773,* Vol. III. Carnegie Institution of Washington, Washington, D.C.

Hackett, Charles Wilson, and Charmion C. Shelby
1942 *Revolt of the Pueblo Indians of New Mexico and Otermín's Attempted Reconquest, 1680–1682.* University of New Mexico Press, Albuquerque.

Hagstrum, Melissa B.
1985 Measuring Prehistoric Ceramic Craft Specialization: A Test Case in the American Southwest. *Journal of Field Archaeology* 12:65–75.

Hall, Stuart
1990 Cultural Identity and Diaspora. In *Identity: Community, Culture, Difference,* edited by Jonathan Rutherford, pp. 222–237. Lawrence and Wishart, London.

Hammond, George P., and Agapito Rey
1953 *Don Juan de Oñate, Colonizer of New Mexico, 1595–1628.* University of New Mexico Press, Albuquerque.

1966 *The Rediscovery of New Mexico, 1580–1594.* University of New Mexico, Albuquerque.

Hardin, Margaret A.
1984 Models of Decoration. In *The Many Dimensions of Pottery: Ceramics in Archaeology and Anthropology,* edited by S. E. van der Leeuw and A. C. Pritchard, pp. 573–607. University of Amsterdam Press, Amsterdam.

Harlow, Francis H.
1965 Acoma Glazed Pottery. Manuscript on file, Laboratory of Anthropology, Museum of New Mexico, Santa Fe.

1968 Fourteenth-Century Painted Pottery from near Cliff, New Mexico. Manuscript on file, Office of Archaeological Studies, Museum of New Mexico, Santa Fe.

1973 *Matte-Paint Pottery of the Tewa, Keres, and Zuni Pueblos.* Museum of New Mexico Press, Santa Fe.

Harry, Karen G., Paul Fish, and Suzanne Fish
2002 Production, Distribution, and Consumption of Tanque Verde Red-on-brown Ceramics in Two Hohokam Communities. In *Ceramic Production and Circulation in the Greater Southwest: Source Determination by INAA and Complementary Mineralogical Investigations,* edited by Donna Glowacki and Hector Neff, pp. 99–109. The Cotsen Institute of Archaeology Monograph 44. UCLA Press, Los Angeles.

Hart, E. Richard
1984 Zuni Mining. Paper presented at the Annual Meeting of the American Society for Ethnohistory, New Orleans.

Hart, E. Richard (editor)
1995 Zuni and the Courts. CD-ROM produced by the Institute of the North American West. In *Zuni and the Courts: A Struggle for Sovereign Land Rights,* by E. Richard Hart. University of Kansas Press, Lawrence.

Haury, Emil W.

1931   Showlow and Pinedale Ruins. In *Recently Dated Pueblo Ruins in Arizona,* by Emil Haury W. and Lyndon L. Hargrave, pp. 4–79. Smithsonian Miscellaneous Collections 82(11).

1934   *The Canyon Creek Ruin and the Cliff Dwellings of the Sierra Ancha.* Medallion Papers XIV. Gila Pueblo, Globe.

1945   *The Excavation of Los Muertos and Neighboring Ruins in the Salt River Valley, Southern Arizona, Based on the Work of the Hemenway Southwestern Archaeological Expedition of 1887–1888.* Papers of the Peabody Museum of American Archaeology and Ethnology 24(1). Harvard University, Cambridge.

1950   *The Stratigraphy and Archaeology of Ventana Cave.* University of Arizona Press, Tucson.

1958   Evidence at Point of Pines for a Prehistoric Migration from Northern Arizona. In *Migrations in New World Culture History,* edited by Raymond H. Thompson, pp. 1–6. University of Arizona Bulletin 29(2), Social Science Bulletin 27. University of Arizona Press, Tucson.

Hawley, Florence M.

1928   Pottery and Culture Relations in the Middle Gila. Unpublished Master's thesis, Department of Anthropology, University of Arizona, Tucson.

Hawley, Fred G.

1938   *The Chemical Analysis of Prehistoric Southwestern Glaze-Paint, with Components.* University of New Mexico Bulletin, Anthropological Series 2:15–27. Albuquerque.

Hawley, Fred G., and Florence M. Hawley

1938   *Classification of Black Pottery Pigments and Paint Areas.* University of New Mexico Bulletin 321, Anthropological Series 2(4). Albuquerque.

Hayden, Brian

2001   Fabulous Feasts: A Prolegomenon to the Importance of Feasting. In *Feasts: Archaeological and Ethnographic Perspectives on Food, Politics, and Power,* edited by Michael Dietler and Brian M. Hayden, pp. 23–64. Smithsonian Institution, Washington, D.C.

Hayden, Brian, and Aubrey Cannon

1984   Interaction Inferences in Archaeology and Learning Frameworks of the Maya. *Journal of Anthropological Archaeology* 3:325–367.

Hayes, Alden C., Jon Nathan Young, and A. Helene Warren

1981   *Excavations of Mound 7.* Gran Quivira National Monument Publication 16. National Park Service. Government Printing Office, Washington, D.C.

Hays-Gilpin, Kelley A.

2000   Gender Ideology and Ritual Activities. In *Women and Men in the Prehispanic Southwest: Labor, Power, and Prestige,* edited by Patricia L. Crown, pp. 91–135. School of American Research Press, Santa Fe.

2008a   Pottery Style. In *Archaeological Investigations along the Navajo Mountain Road,* edited by Phil Geib, pp. 3.1–3.24. Navajo Nation Archaeology Department, Flagstaff. Submitted to Navajo Nation Historic Preservation Department, Window Rock, AZ. Electronic document, http://content.lib.utah.edu/cdm4/document.php?CISOROOT=/upoa&CISOPTR=106&REC=6, accessed May 14, 2012.

2008b   Painted Pottery: Analysis and Interpretation. In *Prehistory of the Northern Kayenta Anasazi Region: Archaeological Excavations along the Navajo Mountain Road (N16), Vol. 5: Analyses and Interpretation,* edited by Phil R. Geib and Kimberly Spurr, pp. 3.1–3.33. Navajo Nation Archaeology Department Report 02-48. Flagstaff, AZ.

2010   Sikyatki Style: Origins, Iconography, Cross-media Comparisons, and Organization of Production. Manuscript on file at Department of Anthropology, Northern Arizona University, Flagstaff.

Hays-Gilpin, Kelley A., and Steven LeBlanc

2007   Sikyatki Style in Regional Context. In *New Perspectives on Pottery Mound Pueblo,* edited by Polly Schaafsma, pp. 109–136. University of New Mexico Press, Albuquerque.

Hays-Gilpin, Kelley A., Trixi D. Bubemyre, and Louise M. Senior

1996   The Rise and Demise of Winslow Orange Ware. In *River of Change: Prehistory of the Middle Little Colorado River Valley, Arizona,* edited by Charles E. Adams, pp. 53–74. Arizona State Museum Archaeological Series 185. University of Arizona, Tucson.

Hays-Gilpin, Kelley A., Elizabeth Newsome, and Emory Sekaquaptewa

2010   *Siitalpuva,* "Through the Land Brightened with Flowers": Ecology and Cosmology in Mural and Pottery Painting, Hopi and Beyond. In *Painting the Cosmos: Metaphor and Worldview in Images from the Southwest Pueblos and Mexico,* edited by Kelley Hays-Gilpin and Polly Schaafsma, pp. 120–137. Museum of Northern Arizona Bulletin 67. Flagstaff.

Hays-Gilpin, Kelley A., and Eric Van Hartesveldt (editors)

1998   *Prehistoric Ceramics of the Puerco Valley: The 1995 Chambers-Sanders Trust Lands Ceramic Conference.* Museum of Northern Arizona Ceramic Series 7. Flagstaff.

Heckman, Robert A., Barbara K. Montgomery, and Stephanie M. Whittlesey
2000 *Prehistoric Painted Pottery of Southeastern Arizona.* Technical Series 77. Statistical Research, Tucson.

Hegmon, Michelle
1992 Archaeological Research on Style. *Annual Review of Anthropology* 21:517–536.
1998 Technology, Style, and Social Practices: Archaeological Approaches. In *The Archaeology of Social Boundaries,* edited by Miriam T. Stark, pp. 264–279. Smithsonian Institution Press, Washington, D.C.

Hegmon, Michelle, and Wenda R. Trevathan
1996 Gender, Anatomical Knowledge, and Pottery Production: Implications of an Anatomically Unusual Birth Depicted on Mimbres Pottery from Southwestern New Mexico. *American Antiquity* 61:747–754.

Heidke, James M.
1996a Production and Distribution of Rincon Phase Pottery: Evidence from the Julian Wash Site. In *A Rincon Phase Occupation at the Julian Wash Site, AZ BB:13:17 (ASM),* by Jonathan B. Mabry, pp. 47–71. Technical Report 96-7. Center for Desert Archaeology, Tucson.
1996b Ceramic Artifacts from the Cook Avenue Locus. In *Archaeological Data Recovery Project at the Cook Avenue Locus of the West Branch Site, AZ AA:16:3 (ASM),* by Allen Dart and Deborah L. Swartz, pp. 53–76. Technical Report 96-8. Center for Desert Archaeology, Tucson.
2004 Utilitarian Ceramic Production and Distribution in the Prehistoric Tonto Basin. In *2000 Years of Settlement in the Tonto Basin: Overview and Synthesis of the Tonto Creek Archaeological Project,* edited by Jeffery J. Clark and James M. Vint, pp. 77–138. Anthropological Papers 25. Center for Desert Archaeology, Tucson.

Helms, Mary W.
1988 *Ulysses' Sail: An Ethnographic Odyssey of Power, Knowledge, and Geographical Distance.* Princeton University Press, Princeton, NJ.
1993 *Craft and the Kingly Ideal: Art, Trade, and Power.* University of Texas Press, Austin.

Hendricks, Rick, and Gerald J. Mandell
2000 Juan Manso, Frontier Entrepreneur. *New Mexico Historical Review* 75:339–368.

Henry, Susan L.
1992 *Physical, Spatial, and Temporal Dimensions of Colono Ware in the Chesapeake, 1600–1800.* South Carolina Institute of Archaeology and Anthropology, University of South Carolina, Columbia.

Hensler, Kathy Niles, and Eric Blinman
2002 Experimental Ceramic Technology, or The Road to Ruin(s) Is Paved with Crack(ed) Pots. In *Traditions, Transitions, and Technologies: Themes in Southwestern Archaeology,* edited by Sarah H. Schlanger, pp. 366–385. University Press of Colorado, Boulder.

Herhahn, Cynthia L.
1995 An Exploration of Technology Transfer in the Fourteenth-Century Rio Grande Valley, New Mexico: A Compositional Analysis of Glaze Paints. Unpublished M.A. thesis, Department of Anthropology, Arizona State University, Tempe.
2006 Inferring Social Interactions from Pottery Recipes: Rio Grande Glaze Paint Composition and Cultural Transmission. In *The Social Life of Pots: Glaze Wares and Cultural Dynamics in the Southwest, AD 1250–1680,* edited by Judith A. Habicht-Mauche, Suzanne L. Eckert, and Deborah L. Huntley, pp. 177–196. University of Arizona Press, Tucson.

Herhahn, Cynthia L., and Eric Blinman
1999 Materials Science Meets the Artisan: A Look at Innovation through Experiments with Lead-glazed Paints from the American Southwest. Paper presented at the 64th Annual Meeting of the Society for American Archaeology, Chicago.

Herhahn, Cynthia L., and Deborah L. Huntley
1996 Technology, Ideology, and the Development of Rio Grande Valley Craft Specialization. Manuscript on file with the authors.

Hibben, Frank C.
1955 Excavations at Pottery Mound, New Mexico. *American Antiquity* 21:179–180.
1975 *Kiva Art of the Anasazi at Pottery Mound.* KC Publications, Las Vegas, NV.

Hill, J. Brett, Jeffery J. Clark, William H. Doelle, and Patrick D. Lyons
2004 Prehistoric Demography in the Southwest: Migration, Coalescence, and Hohokam Population Decline. *American Antiquity* 69:689–716.

Hill, James N.
1970 *Broken K Pueblo: Prehistoric Social Organization in the American Southwest.* Anthropological Papers of the University of Arizona 18. University of Arizona Press, Tucson.

Hodge, Frederick Webb, George P. Hammond, and Agapito Rey
1945 *Fray Alonso de Benavides' Revised Memorial of 1634.* University of New Mexico Press, Albuquerque.

Holmyard, E. J.
1957 *Alchemy.* Dover, New York.

Holsinger, Bruce W.
2005   *The Premodern Condition: Medievalism and the Making of Theory.* University of Chicago Press, Chicago.

Honea, K. H. (compiler)
1966   *Eighth Southwestern Ceramic Seminar, Rio Grande Glazes.* Museum of New Mexico, Santa Fe.

Hume, Ivor N.
1962   An Indian Ware of the Colonial Period. *Quarterly Bulletin of the Archeological Society of Virginia* 17:1–14.

Huntley, Deborah L.
2004   *Technological Style, Exchange, and the Organizational Scale of Pueblo IV Zuni Society.* Ph.D. dissertation, Arizona State University, Tempe. University Microfilms, Ann Arbor.
2006   From Recipe to Identity: Exploring Zuni Glaze Ware Communities of Practice. In *The Social Life of Pots: Glaze Wares and Cultural Dynamics in the Southwest, AD 1250–1680,* edited by Judith A. Habicht-Mauche, Suzanne L. Eckert, and Deborah L. Huntley, pp. 105–123. University of Arizona Press, Tucson.
2008   *Ancestral Zuni Glaze-Decorated Pottery: Viewing Pueblo IV Regional Organization through Ceramic Production and Exchange.* Anthropological Papers of the University of Arizona 72. University of Arizona Press, Tucson.

Huntley, Deborah L., and Cynthia L. Herhahn
1996   Technological Change and the Development of Rio Grande Craft Specialization. Paper presented at the 1996 Chacmool Conference, Calgary, Canada.

Huntley, Deborah L., and Keith W. Kintigh
2004   Archaeological Patterning and Organizational Scale of Late Prehistoric Settlement Clusters in the Zuni Region of New Mexico. In *The Protohistoric Pueblo World, A.D. 1275–1600,* edited by E. Charles Adams and Andrew I. Duff, pp. 62–74. University of Arizona Press, Tucson.

Huntley, Deborah L., Katherine A. Spielmann, Judith A. Habicht-Mauche, Cynthia L. Herhahn, and A. Russell Flegal
2007   Local Recipes or Distant Commodities? Lead Isotope and Chemical Compositional Analysis of Glaze Paints from the Salinas Pueblos, New Mexico. *Journal of Archaeological Science* 34:1135–1147.

Hurt, Wesley R.
1990   *The 1939–1940 Excavation Project at Quarai Pueblo and Mission Building, Salinas Pueblo Missions National Monument, New Mexico.* National Park Service, Southwest Cultural Resources Center Professional Paper 29. Santa Fe.

Jenkins, Richard
1997   *Rethinking Ethnicity.* Sage, London.

Jennings, Calvin H.
1965   Excavations at the Puerco Site. Manuscript on file, Museum of Northern Arizona, Flagstaff.

Jones, Deborah L.
1995   Identifying Production Groups within a Single Community: Rio Grande Glaze-decorated Ceramics at Quarai Pueblo. Unpublished Master's thesis, Department of Anthropology, Arizona State University, Tempe.

Jones, Okah L., Jr.
1966   *Pueblo Warriors & Spanish Conquest.* University of Oklahoma Press, Norman.

Joyce, Rosemary A., and Jeanne Lopiparo
2005   Doing Agency in Archaeology. *Journal of Archaeological Method and Theory* 12:365–374.

Judd, Neil M.
1930   *The Excavation and Repair of Betatakin.* Proceedings of the United States National Museum 2828. Smithsonian Institution, Washington, D.C.
1954   *The Material Culture of Pueblo Bonito.* Smithsonian Institution, Washington, D.C.
1959   *Pueblo del Arroyo Chaco Canyon, New Mexico.* Smithsonian Institution, Washington, D.C.

Judge, W. James
1989   Chaco Canyon–San Juan Basin. In *Dynamics of Southwest Prehistory,* edited by Linda S. Cordell and George J. Gumerman, pp. 209–261. Smithsonian Institution Press, Washington, D.C.

Kanes, Clive, and Stephen Lerman
2007   Analyzing Concepts of Community of Practice. In *New Directions for Situated Cognition in Mathematics Education,* edited by Anne Watson and Peter Winbourne, pp. 303–328. Springer, New York.

Keller, Charles M., and Janet Dixon Keller
1996   *Cognition and Tool Use: The Blacksmith at Work.* Cambridge University Press, New York.

Kelley, Henry W.
1941   Franciscan Missions of New Mexico, 1740–1760. *New Mexico Historical Review* 16(2):148–183.

Kelley, Jane Holden
2008   *El Zurdo: A Small Prehistoric Village in West-Central Chihuahua, Mexico, Part 1: Introduction and 1991 Field Studies.* Maxwell Museum Technical Series 9(1). Maxwell Museum of Anthropology, University of New Mexico, Albuquerque.
2009   *El Zurdo: A Small Prehistoric Village in West-Central Chihuahua, Mexico, Part 3: Material Culture and Conclusions.* Maxwell Museum Technical Series 9(3). Maxwell Museum of Anthropology, University of New Mexico, Albuquerque.

Kelley, J. Charles, and Howard D. Winters
1960 A Revision of the Archaeological Sequence in Sinaloa, Mexico. *American Antiquity* 25:547–561.

Kelley, Vincent C.
1977 *Geology of the Albuquerque Basin, New Mexico.* New Mexico Bureau of Mines and Mineral Resources Memoir 33. Socorro.

Kelly, Isabel
1938 *Excavations at Chametla, Sinaloa.* Ibero-America 14. University of California, Berkeley.

Kelly, Sophia E.
2009 The Role of Zuni Glaze Wares in Pueblo IV Period Social Interaction. Manuscript on file with author.

Kessell, John L.
1979 *Kiva, Cross, and Crown: The Pecos Indians and New Mexico, 1540–1840.* National Park Service, Washington, D.C.
2008 *Pueblos, Spaniards, and the Kingdom of New Mexico.* University of Oklahoma Press, Norman.
2009 A Long Time Coming: The 17th Century Pueblo-Spanish War. Manuscript on file with author.

Kessell, John L., Rick Hendricks, and Meredith Dodge (editors)
1992 *By Force of Arms: The Journals of Don Diego de Vargas, 1691–1693.* University of New Mexico Press, Albuquerque.
1998 *Blood on the Boulders: The Journals of Don Diego de Vargas, New Mexico, 1694–1697.* University of New Mexico Press, Albuquerque.

Kessell, John L., Rick Hendricks, Meredith D. Dodge, and Larry D. Miller (editors)
2000 *That Disturbances Cease: The Journals of Don Diego de Vargas, New Mexico, 1697–1700.* University of New Mexico Press, Albuquerque.

Kidder, Alfred V.
1915 *Pottery of the Pajarito Plateau and Some Adjacent Regions in New Mexico.* American Anthropological Association Memoir 2(6):407–462.
1917 Notes on the Pottery of Pecos. *American Anthropologist* 19:325–360.
1927 Southwestern Archaeological Conference. *Science* 66:489–491.

Kidder, Alfred V., and Anna O. Shepard
1936 The Glaze-Paint, Culinary, and Other Wares. In *The Pottery of Pecos,* Vol. 2. Phillips Academy Papers of the Southwest Expedition 7. Yale University Press, New Haven.

Kintigh, Keith W.
1994 Chaco, Communal Architecture, and Cibolan Aggregation. In *The Ancient Southwestern Community,* edited by W. H. Wills and Robert D. Leonard, pp. 131–140. University of New Mexico Press, Albuquerque.
2000 Leadership Strategies in Protohistoric Zuni Towns. In *Alternative Leadership Strategies in the Prehispanic Southwest,* edited by Barbara J. Mills, pp. 95–116. University of Arizona Press, Tucson.
2007 Late Prehistoric and Protohistoric Settlement Systems in the Zuni Area. In *Zuni Origins: Toward a New Synthesis of Southwestern Archaeology,* edited by David A. Gregory and David R. Wilcox, pp. 361–376. University of Arizona Press, Tucson.

Knaut, Andrew L.
1995 *The Pueblo Revolt of 1680: Conquest and Resistance in Seventeenth-Century New Mexico.* University of Oklahoma Press, Norman.

Kopytoff, Igor
1986 The Cultural Biography of Things. In *The Social Life of Things: Commodities in Cultural Perspective,* edited by Arjun Appadurai, pp. 64–91. Cambridge University Press, Cambridge.

Kreiger, Alex D.
1944 The Typological Concept. *American Antiquity* 9:271–288.

Kroeber, Alfred L.
1916 *Zuni Potsherds.* American Museum of Natural History, Anthropological Papers 18(1):1–36.

Kubler, George
1962 *The Shape of Time: Remarks on the History of Things.* Yale University Press, New Haven.

Kulisheck, Jeremy
2001 Settlement Patterns, Population, and Congregacion on the 17th Century Jemez Plateau. In *Following Through: Papers in Honor of Phyllis S. Davis,* edited by Regge N. Wiseman, Thomas C. O'Laughlin, and Cordelia T. Snow, pp. 77–101. Papers of the Archaeological Society of New Mexico 27. Albuquerque.
2002 Mobility as Resistance: Pueblo Responses to Spanish Colonization in Seventeenth Century New Mexico, USA. Paper presented at the 67th Annual Meeting of the Society for American Archaeology, Denver.
2005 The Archaeology of Pueblo Population Change on the Jemez Plateau, A.D. 1200 to 1700: The Effects of Spanish Contact and Conquest. Unpublished Ph.D. dissertation, Department of Anthropology, Southern Methodist University, Dallas.

Lange, Charles H., and Carroll L. Riley
1966 *The Southwestern Journals of Adolph F. Bandelier, 1880–1882.* University of New Mexico Press, Albuquerque, and School of American Research Press and Museum of New Mexico Press, Santa Fe.

Lange, Richard C.
1992 Pots, People, Politics, and Precipitation: Just Who or What Are the Salado Anyway? In *Proceedings*

Lange, Richard C. (*continued*)
    of the Second Salado Conference, Globe, AZ, 1992, edited by Richard C. Lange and Stephen Germick, pp. 325–333. Arizona Archaeological Society Occasional Paper. Phoenix.

Larkin, Karin Burd
  2006 Community Reorganization in the Southern Zone of the Casas Grandes Culture Area of Chihuahua Mexico. Unpublished Ph.D. dissertation, Department of Anthropology, University of Colorado, Boulder.

Larkin, Karin Burd, Jane H. Kelley, and Mitchel J. Hendrickson
  2004 Ceramics as Temporal and Spatial Indicators in Chihuahuan Cultures. In *Surveying the Archaeology of Northwest Mexico,* edited by Gillian E. Newell and Emiliano Gallaga, pp. 177–204. University of Utah Press, Salt Lake City.

Latour, Bruno
  2005 *Reassembling the Social: An Introduction to Actor-Network Theory.* Oxford University Press, Oxford.

Lave, Jean
  1996 The Practice of Learning. In *Understanding Practice: Perspectives on Activity and Context,* edited by Seth Chaiklin and Jean Lave, pp. 3–32. Cambridge University Press, Cambridge.

Lave, Jean, and Etienne Wenger
  1991 *Situated Learning: Legitimate Peripheral Participation.* University of Cambridge Press, Cambridge.

LeBlanc, Steven
  1998 Settlement Consequences of Warfare during the Late Pueblo III and Pueblo IV Periods. In *Migration and Reorganization: The Pueblo IV Period in the American Southwest,* edited by Katherine A. Spielmann, pp. 115–136. Anthropological Research Papers 51. Department of Anthropology, Arizona State University, Tempe.

Lechtman, Heather
  1977 Style in Technology--Some Early Thoughts. In *Material Culture: Styles, Organization, and Dynamics of Technology,* edited by Heather Lechtman and Robert S. Merrill, pp. 3–20. West, St. Paul, MN.

Lekson, Stephen H.
  1990 Sedentism and Aggregation in Anasazi Archaeology. In *Perspectives on Southwestern Prehistory,* edited by Paul R. Minnis and Charles L. Redman, pp. 333–340. Westview Press, Boulder.

Lemonnier, Pierre
  1986 The Study of Material Culture Today: Towards an Anthropology of Technical Systems. *Journal of Anthropological Archaeology* 5:147–186.

Leonard, Robert D.
  2001 Evolutionary Archaeology. In *Archaeological Theory Today,* edited by Ian Hodder, pp. 65–97. Polity Press, Cambridge.

Leplat, Jacques
  1988 Les habiletes cognitives dans le travail. In *Les Automatismes Cognitifs,* edited by Pierre Perruchet, pp. 139–172. Pierre Mardaga Editeur, Liege.

Levine, Frances E.
  1999 *Our Prayers Are in This Place: Pecos Pueblo Identity over the Centuries.* University of New Mexico Press, Albuquerque.

Li, Linda C., Jeremy M. Grimshaw, Camilla Nielsen, Maria Judd, Peter C. Coyte, and Ian D. Graham
  2009 Evolution of Wenger's Concept of Community of Practice. *Implementation Science* 4:11 Available online at http://www.implementationscience.com/content/4/1/11.

Liddell, Donald M. (editor)
  1945 *Handbook of Nonferrous Metallurgy. 2nd* ed. McGraw-Hill, New York.

Liebmann, Matthew
  2008 The Innovative Materiality of Revitalization Movements: Lessons from the Pueblo Revolt of 1680. *American Anthropologist* 110:360–372.

Lindsay, Alexander J., Jr.
  1969 The Tsegi Phase of the Kayenta Cultural Tradition in Northeastern Arizona. Unpublished Ph.D. dissertation, Department of Anthropology, University of Arizona, Tucson.
  1987 Anasazi Population Movements to Southeastern Arizona. *American Archaeology* 6:190–198.
  1992 Tucson Polychrome: History, Dating, Distribution and Design. In *Proceedings of the Second Salado Conference, Globe, AZ, 1992,* edited by Richard C. Lange and Stephen Germick, pp. 230–237. Arizona Archaeological Society Occasional Paper. Phoenix.

Lindsay, Alexander J., Jr., and Calvin H. Jennings (compilers)
  1968 *Salado Red Ware Conference: Ninth Southwestern Ceramic Seminar, October 13–14, 1967.* Museum of Northern Arizona Ceramic Series 4. Northern Arizona Society of Science and Art, Flagstaff.

Lindsay, Alexander J., Jr., J. Richard Ambler, Mary Anne Stein, and Philip M. Hobler
  1968 *Survey and Excavations North and East of Navajo Mountain, Utah, 1959–1962.* Museum of Northern Arizona Bulletin 45. Glen Canyon Series 8. Northern Arizona Society of Science and Art, Flagstaff.

Lister, Robert H.
 1958   *Excavations in the Northern Sierra Madre Occidental, Chihuahua and Sonora, Mexico.* University of Colorado Studies, Series in Anthropology 7. University of Colorado Press, Boulder.

Lomawaima, Hartman H.
 1989   Hopification: A Strategy for Cultural Preservation. In *Columbian Consequences, Vol. I: Archaeological and Historical Perspectives on the Spanish Borderlands West,* edited by David Hurst Thomas, pp. 93–99. Smithsonian Institution Press, Washington, D.C.

Longacre, William A.
 1970   *Archaeology as Anthropology: A Case Study.* Anthropological Papers of the University of Arizona 17. University of Arizona Press, Tucson.

Lopiparo, Jeanne
 2006   Crafting Children: Materiality, Social Memory, and the Reproduction of Terminal Classic House Societies in the Ulúa Valley, Honduras. In *The Social Experience of Childhood in Ancient Mesoamerica,* edited by Traci Ardren and Scott Hutson, pp. 133–168. University Press of Colorado, Boulder.

Lycett, Mark T.
 2004   Report of Archaeological Excavations at LA 162, Bernalillo County, New Mexico, conducted by the University of Chicago Archaeological Field Studies Program between June 15 and August 1, 2002. Manuscript on file, New Mexico Historic Preservation Division, Santa Fe.

Lyons, Patrick D.
 2003   *Ancestral Hopi Migrations.* Anthropological Papers of the University of Arizona 68. University of Arizona Press, Tucson.
 2004a Cliff Polychrome. *Kiva* 69:361–400.
 2004b José Solas Ruin. *Kiva* 70:143–181.
 2012a Ceramic Typology, Chronology, Production, and Circulation. In *Migrants and Mounds: Classic Period Archaeology of the San Pedro Valley, Arizona*, edited by Jeffery J. Clark and Patrick D. Lyons. Anthropological Papers No. 45. Center for Desert Archaeology, Tucson, in press.
 2012b By Their Fruits Ye Shall Know Them: The Pottery of Kinishba Revisited. In *Kinishba Lost and Found: Mid-Century Excavations and Contemporary Perspectives,* edited by John R. Welch. Arizona State Museum Archaeological Series. University of Arizona, Tucson, in press.

Lyons, Patrick D., and Jeffery J. Clark
 2008   Interaction, Enculturation, Social Distance, and Ancient Ethnic Identities. In *Archaeology without Borders: Contact, Commerce, and Change in the U.S. Southwest and Northwestern Mexico*, edited by Laurie D. Webster and Maxine McBrinn, pp. 185–207. University Press of Colorado, Boulder, and Conaculta/INAH, Chihuahua, Mexico.

Lyons, Patrick D., and Alexander J. Lindsay, Jr.
 2006   Perforated Plates and the Salado Phenomenon. *Kiva* 72:5–54.

Lyons, Patrick D., and Anna A. Neuzil
 2006   Research on the Mills Collection. *Archaeology Southwest* 20(2):17.

Lyons, Patrick D., Jeffery J. Clark, and J. Brett Hill
 2011   Ancient Social Boundaries Inscribed on the Landscape of the Lower San Pedro Valley. In *Contemporary Archaeologies of the Southwest*, edited by William H. Walker and Kathryn Venzor, pp. 175–196. University Press of Colorado, Boulder.

Lyons, Patrick D., Kelly A. Hays-Gilpin, and
Louise M. Senior
 2001   Homol'ovi III Ceramics. In *A Pueblo Hamlet in the Middle Little Colorado River Valley*, edited by E. Charles Adams, pp. 137–226. Arizona State Museum Archaeological Series 193. University of Arizona, Tucson.

Lyons, Patrick D., J. Brett Hill, and Jeffery J. Clark
 2008   Demography, Agricultural Potential, and Identity among Ancient Immigrants. In *The Social Construction of Communities: Agency, Structure, and Identity in the Prehispanic Southwest,* edited by Mark D. Varien and James Potter, pp. 191–213. AltaMira Press, Lanham, MD.
 2011   Irrigation Communities and Communities in Diaspora. In *Movement, Connectivity, and Landscape Change in the Ancient Southwest*, edited by Margaret C. Nelson and Colleen A. Strawhacker, pp. 375–401. University Press of Colorado, Boulder.

Marshall, Hannah Meara
 1972   Structural Constraints on Learning: Butchers' Apprentices. In *Learning to Work,* edited by Blanche Geer, pp. 39–48. Sage, Beverly Hills.

Marshall, Michael P.
 1987   *Archaeological Investigations in a 16th–Early 17th century Piro Pueblo in the Village of San Antonio.* Office of Contract Archeology, University of New Mexico, Albuquerque.

Marshall, Michael P., and Henry J. Walt
 1984   *Rio Abajo: Prehistory and History of a Rio Grande Province.* New Mexico Historic Preservation Program, Santa Fe.

Mathien, Frances Joan
 1985   *Ornaments and Minerals from Chaco Canyon.* Division of Cultural Research, National Park Service, Santa Fe.

1997   Ornaments of the Chaco Anasazi. In *Ceramics, Lithics, and Ornaments of Chaco Canyon, Vol. III,* edited by Frances Joan Mathien, pp. 1119–1220. Publications in Archeology 18G, Chaco Canyon Studies, National Park Service, Santa Fe.

2001   The Organization of Turquoise Production and Consumption by the Prehistoric Chacoans. *American Antiquity* 66:103–118.

Mauss, Marcel

2006   Techniques of the Body. Translated by Ben Brewster and reprinted. In *Techniques, Technology and Civilization,* edited by Nathan Schlanger, pp. 77–95. Berghahn Books, New York. Originally published, 1935, *Journal de Psychologie* 31:271–293.

McEwan, Bonnie G.

1990   The Role of Ceramics in Spain and Spanish America during the 16th Century. *Historical Archaeology* 26:92–108.

McGuire, Randall H., and María Elisa Villalpando C.

1993   *An Archaeological Survey of the Altar Valley, Sonora, Mexico.* Arizona State Museum Archaeological Series 184. University of Arizona, Tucson.

McKenna, Peter J., and James. A. Miles

1991   Archaeological Survey Ceramic Manual. Manuscript on file, Branch of Cultural Resources, Southwest Regional Office, National Park Service, Santa Fe, NM.

Mera, Harry P.

1933   *A Proposed Revision of the Rio Grande Glaze-Paint Sequence.* Technical Series of the Laboratory of Anthropology, Bulletin 5. Santa Fe.

1935   *Ceramic Clues to the Prehistory of North Central New Mexico.* Technical Series of the Laboratory of Anthropology, Bulletin 8. Santa Fe.

1940   *Population Changes in the Rio Grande Glaze-Paint Area.* Technical Series of the Laboratory of Anthropology, Bulletin 9. Santa Fe.

Milford, Homer E., and Mike E. Swick

1995   *Cultural Resource Survey for Real de Los Cerrillos Project, Santa Fe County, New Mexico, Vol. 1: Historic Survey of the Los Cerrillos Area and Its Mining History.* New Mexico Abandoned Mine Land Bureau Report, 1994-2. New Mexico Mining and Minerals Division, Santa Fe.

Milich, Alicia Ronstadt

1966   *Relaciones, by Zarate Salmeron.* Horn and Wallace, Albuquerque.

Miller, Daniel

1998   Why Some Things Matter. In *Material Cultures: Why Some Things Matter,* edited by D. Miller, pp. 3–20. University College London Press, London.

Mills, Barbara J.

1995   The Organization of Protohistoric Zuni Ceramic Production. In *Ceramic Production in the American Southwest,* edited by Barbara J. Mills and Patricia L. Crown, pp. 200–230. University of Arizona Press, Tucson.

1999   Ceramics and Social Contexts of Food Production in the Northern Southwest. In *Pottery and People: A Dynamic Interaction,* edited by James M. Skibo and Gary M. Feinman, pp. 99–114. University of Utah Press, Salt Lake City.

2000   Gender, Craft Production, and Inequality. In *Women and Men in the Prehispanic Southwest: Labor, Power, and Prestige,* edited by Patricia L. Crown, pp. 301–343. School of American Research Press, Santa Fe.

2002   Acts of Resistance: Zuni Ceramics, Social Identity, and the Pueblo Revolt. In *Archaeologies of the Pueblo Revolt,* edited by Robert W. Preucel, pp. 85–98. University of New Mexico Press, Albuquerque.

2003   Multicrafting, Migration, and Identity in the American Southwest. Paper presented at the 68th Annual Meeting of the Society for American Archaeology, Milwaukee.

2004   The Establishment and Defeat of Hierarchy: Inalienable Possessions and the History of Collective Prestige Structures in the Puebloan Southwest. *American Anthropologist* 106:238–251.

2007a   A Regional Perspective on Ceramics and Zuni Identity, A.D. 200–1630. In *Zuni Origins: Toward a New Synthesis of Southwestern Archaeology,* edited by David A. Gregory and David R. Wilcox, pp. 210–238. University of Arizona Press, Tucson.

2007b   Performing the Feast: Visual Display and Suprahousehold Commensalism in the Puebloan Southwest. *American Antiquity* 72:210–239.

2011   Themes and Models for Understanding Migration in the Southwest. In *Movement, Connectivity, and Landscape Change in the Ancient Southwest,* edited by Margaret C. Nelson and Colleen A. Strawhacker, pp. 345–359. University Press of Colorado, Boulder.

Mills, Barbara J., and Patricia L. Crown

1995   Ceramic Production in the American Southwest: An Introduction. In *Ceramic Production in the American Southwest,* edited by Barbara J. Mills and Patricia L. Crown, pp. 1–29. University of Arizona Press, Tucson.

Mills, Barbara J., and Patricia L. Crown (editors)

1995   *Ceramic Production in the American Southwest.* University of Arizona Press, Tucson.

Mills, Barbara J., and T. J. Ferguson
2008   Animate Objects: Shell Trumpets and Ritual Networks in the Greater Southwest. *Journal of Archaeological Method and Theory* 15:338–361.

Mills, Jack P., and Vera M. Mills
1972   The Dinwiddie Site: A Prehistoric Salado Ruin on Duck Creek, Western New Mexico. *The Artifact* 10(2):1–50.

Minar, C. Jill
2001   Motor Skills and the Learning Process: The Conservation of Cordage Final Twist Direction in Communities of Practice. *Journal of Anthropological Research* 57:381–405.

Minar, C. Jill, and Patricia L. Crown
2001   Learning and Craft Production: An Introduction. *Journal of Anthropological Research* 57:269–280.

Mobley-Tanaka, Jeanette L.
2002   Crossed Cultures, Crossed Meanings: The Manipulation of Ritual Imagery in Early Historic Pueblo Resistance. In *Archaeologies of the Pueblo Revolt: Identity, Meaning, and Renewal in the Pueblo World,* edited by R. W. Preucel, pp. 77–84. University of New Mexico Press, Albuquerque.

Montgomery, Barbara K., and J. Jefferson Reid
1990   An Instance of Rapid Ceramic Change in the American Southwest. *American Antiquity* 55:88–97.

Montgomery, Ross, Watson Smith, and J. O. Brew
1949   *Franciscan Awatovi: The Excavation and Conjectural Reconstruction of a 17th-century Spanish Mission Establishment at a Hopi Indian Town in Northeastern Arizona.* Papers of the Peabody Museum of American Archaeology and Ethnology 36. Harvard University, Cambridge.

Morris, Earl
1939   *Archaeological Studies in the La Plata District.* Carnegie Institution, Washington, D.C.

Motsinger, Thomas N.
1992   The Rise and Fall of a Village Industry: Specialized Ceramic Production in Protohistoric New Mexico. Unpublished Master's thesis, Department of Anthropology, Northern Arizona University, Flagstaff.
1997   Tracking Protohistoric Glaze-Paint Ceramic Specialization in the Upper Rio Grande Valley, New Mexico. *Kiva* 63(2):101–116.

Mount, James E., Stanley J. Olsen, John W. Olsen, George A. Teague, and B. Dean Treadwell
1993   *Wide Reed Ruin, Hubbell Trading Post National Historic Site.* Professional Papers 51. Division of Anthropology, Southwest Cultural Resources Center, National Park Service, Santa Fe.

Naranjo, Tessie
1995   Thoughts on Migration by Santa Clara Pueblo. *Journal of Anthropological Archaeology* 14:247–250.

Nelson, Ben A., and Steven A. LeBlanc
1986   *Short-Term Sedentism in the American Southwest: The Mimbres Valley Salado.* Maxwell Museum of Anthropology and University of New Mexico Press, Albuquerque.

Nelson, Kit, and Judith A. Habicht-Mauche
2006   Lead, Paint, and Pots: Rio Grande Intercommunity Dynamics from a Glaze Ware Perspective. In *The Social Life of Pots: Glaze Wares and Cultural Dynamics in the Southwest, AD 1250–1680,* edited by Judith A. Habicht-Mauche, Suzanne L. Eckert, and Deborah L. Huntley, pp. 197–215. University of Arizona Press, Tucson.

Nelson, Nels C.
1912–1915   Field Notes of the Excavations at San Marcos Pueblo. On file, American Museum of Natural History, New York.
1916   Chronology of the Tano Ruins, New Mexico. *American Anthropologist* 18:159–180.
1912–1916   Excavation field notes, Pueblo Colorado, Pueblo Lazaro, and Tunque Pueblo. Manuscript on file, Archaeological Records Management Section, Laboratory of Anthropology, Santa Fe.

Nesse, William D.
2000   *Introduction to Mineralogy.* Oxford University Press, Oxford.

Neuzil, Anna A.
2008   *In the Aftermath of Migration: Renegotiating Ancient Identity in Southeastern Arizona.* Anthropological Papers of the University of Arizona 73. University of Arizona Press, Tucson.

Neuzil, Anna A., and Patrick D. Lyons
2006   *An Analysis of Whole Vessels from the Mills Collection Curated at Eastern Arizona College, Thatcher, Arizona.* Technical Report 2005-001. Center for Desert Archaeology, Tucson.

New Mexico Energy, Minerals, and Natural Resources Department
2008   Report on the Galisteo Basin. Electronic document, *http://www.emnrd.state.nm.us/MAIN/documents/ Galisteo.Basin.Report.pdf,* accessed March 13, 2012.

New Mexico Geological Society
1982   *New Mexico Highway Geologic Map.* New Mexico Bureau of Mines and Mineral Resources, Socorro.

Northrup, Stuart A.
1959   *Minerals of New Mexico.* Revised ed. University of New Mexico Press, Albuquerque.

Odegaard, Nancy, and Kelley Hays-Gilpin
  2002   Technology of the Sacred? Painted Basketry in the Southwest. In *Traditions, Transitions, and Technologies: Themes in Southwestern Archaeology,* edited by Sarah H. Schlanger, pp. 307–331. University Press of Colorado, Boulder.

O'Donovan, Maria
  2002   *New Perspectives on Site Function and Scale of Cerro de Trincheras, Sonora, Mexico: The 1991 Surface Survey.* Arizona State Museum Archaeological Series 195. University of Arizona, Tucson.

Orcutt, Janet D.
  1999   Chronology. In *The Bandelier Archaeological Survey,* Vol. I, edited by Robert P. Powers and Janet D. Orcutt, pp. 85–116. Intermountain Cultural Resources Management Professional Paper 57. National Park Service, Santa Fe.

Ortiz, Alfonso
  1969   *The Tewa World: Space, Time, Being and Becoming in a Pueblo Society.* University of Chicago Press, Chicago.

Ortner, Sherry B.
  1984   Theory in Anthropology since the Sixties. *Comparative Studies in Society and History* 26:126–166.

Ostler, James, Marian E. Rodee, and Milford Nahohai
  1996   *Zuni: A Village of Silversmiths.* Zuni A:Shiwi Publishing and the University of New Mexico Press, Albuquerque.

Ownby, Mary F.
  2012   Temper and Petrographic Analysis of Perforated Plate CCS 66. Manuscript on file, Desert Archaeology, Tucson.

Parekh, Bhikhu
  1994   Some Reflections on the Hindu Diaspora. *New Community* 20:603–620.

Parsons, Elsie Clews
  1933   Some Aztec and Pueblo Parallels. *American Anthropologist* 25:611–631.
  1966   *Pueblo Indian Religion.* University of Nebraska Press, Lincoln.

Pauketat, Timothy R. (editor)
  2001   *The Archaeology of Traditions: Agency and History before and after Columbus.* University Press of Florida, Gainesville.

Penman, Shawn L.
  2002   The Role of Acculturation in Colonoware Production: Pecos Pueblo, New Mexico. Unpublished Ph.D. dissertation, Department of Anthropology, University of New Mexico.

Pepper, George H.
  1996   *Pueblo Bonito.* Reprinted. University of New Mexico Press, Albuquerque. Originally published 1920, Anthropological Papers of the American Museum of Natural History, Vol. 27. New York.

Peterson, Jane D.
  1994   Salado Polychrome from Pueblo Grande: Indices of Ceramic Production Systems. In *The Pueblo Grande Project, Vol. 3: Ceramics and the Production and Exchange of Pottery in the Central Phoenix Basin,* edited by David R. Abbott, pp. 371–406. Soil Systems Publications in Archaeology No. 20. Soil Systems, Inc., Phoenix.

Phillips, David A., Jr.
  2008   The End of Casas Grandes. Paper presented at the 73rd Annual Meeting of the Society for American Archaeology, Vancouver.

Phillips, David. A., Jr., and John P. Carpenter
  1999   The Robles Phase of the Casas Grandes Culture. In *The Casas Grandes World,* edited by Curtis F. Schaafsma and Carroll Riley, pp. 55–60. University of Utah Press, Salt Lake City.

Phillips, David A., Jr., Christine S. VanPool, and Todd L. VanPool
  2006   The Horned Serpent Tradition in the North American Southwest. In *Religion in the Prehispanic Southwest,* edited by Christine S. VanPool, Todd L. VanPool, and David A. Phillips, Jr., pp. 17–29. AltaMira Press, Lanham, MD.

Pierce, Christopher D.
  1992   Effects of Pocket Gopher Burrowing on Archaeological Deposits: A Simulation Approach. *Geoarchaeology* 7:185–208.

Pierce, Christopher D., and Ann F. Ramenofsky
  2000   Report on Archaeological Research at Pueblo San Marcos (LA 98) during 1999 by the University of New Mexico, SE-272. Submitted to the New Mexico Historic Preservation Division, Santa Fe.

Pierce, Donna
  2006   Hide Paintings in New Mexico: New Archival Evidence. In *Transforming Images: New Mexican Santos in-between Worlds,* edited by Claire Farago and Donna Pierce, pp. 138–44. Pennsylvania State University Press, University Park.

Pingitore, Nicholas E., Jr., David Hill, Joshua Villalobos, Jeff Leach, and John A. Peterson
  1997   ICP-MS Isotopic Signatures of Lead Ceramic Glazes, Rio Grande Valley, New Mexico, 1315–1700. *Proceedings of the Materials Research Society Symposium* 462:217–227.

Pinson, Ariane Oberling
  2008   The Geology of Mission San Marcos, New Mexico (combined 1999 and 2000 field seasons). Manuscript on file, American Museum of Natural History, New York.

Plog, Stephen
2003 Exploring the Ubiquitous through the Unusual: Color Symbolism in Pueblo Black-on-White Pottery. *American Antiquity* 68:665–695.

Post, Stephen S., and Steven A. Lakatos
1995 Santa Fe Black-on-white Pottery Firing Features of the Northern Rio Grande Valley, New Mexico. In *Of Pots and Rocks: Papers in Honor of A. Helene Warren*, edited by Meliha S. Duran and David T. Kirkpatrick, pp. 141–154. Papers of the Archaeological Society of New Mexico 21. Albuquerque.

Potter, James M.
1997a *Communal Ritual, Feasting, and Social Differentiation in Late Prehistoric Zuni Communities.* Ph.D. dissertation, Arizona State University. University Microfilms, Ann Arbor.
1997b Communal Ritual and Faunal Remains: An Example from the Dolores Anasazi. *Journal of Field Archaeology* 24:353–364.
2000 Pots, Parties, and Politics: Communal Ritual in the American Southwest. *American Antiquity* 65:471–492.

Powers, Robert P., and Janet D. Orcutt (editors)
1999 *The Bandelier Archeological Survey,* 2 vols. Intermountain Cultural Resources Management Professional Paper 57. National Park Service, Washington, D.C.

Preucel, Robert W., and Patricia W. Capone
2002 Ceramic Semiotics: Women, Pottery, and Social Meanings at Kotyiti Pueblo. In *Archaeologies of the Pueblo Revolt: Identity, Meaning and Renewal in the Pueblo World,* edited by Robert W. Preucel, pp. 99–113. University of New Mexico Press, Albuquerque.

Rakita, Gordon F. M., and Gerry R. Raymond
2003 The Temporal Sensitivity of Casas Grandes Polychrome Ceramics. *Kiva* 68:153–184.

Ramenofsky, Ann F.
1996 The Problem of Introduced Infectious Diseases in New Mexico: A.D. 1540–1680. *Journal of Anthropological Research* 52:161–184.
1998 The Illusion of Time. In *Unit Issues in Archaeology: Measuring Time, Space, and Material*, edited by Ann F. Ramenofsky and Anastasia Steffen, pp. 74–84. University of Utah Press, Salt Lake City.
2001 Summary Report of the 2000 Season of Archaeological Research at San Marcos Pueblo (LA 98) by the University of New Mexico (Permit SE-155, ABE-427). Submitted to the Archaeological Conservancy and the New Mexico Historic Preservation Division, Santa Fe.

Ramenofsky, Ann F., and James K. Feathers
2002 Documents, Ceramics, Tree-Rings, and Luminescence: Estimating Final Native Abandonment from the Lower Rio Chama. *Journal of Anthropological Research* 58:121–159.

Ramenofsky, Ann F., Fraser Neiman, and Christopher D. Pierce
2009 Measuring Time, Population and Residential Mobility from the Surface at San Marcos Pueblo, North Central New Mexico. *American Antiquity* 74:505–530.

Ramenofsky, Ann F., C. David Vaughan, and Michael Spilde
2008 Seventeenth-Century Metal Production at San Marcos Pueblo. *Historical Archaeology* 42(4):105–131.

Raymond, Gerry (editor)
2010 *Report on 1988 Data Recovery at the Montaño Site Complex, LA 3322, City of Albuquerque, New Mexico, and Subsequent Analysis of Collections.* Submitted to the City of Albuquerque by Criterion Environmental Consulting, Albuquerque.

Reed, Erik K.
1954 Test Excavations at San Marcos Pueblo. *El Palacio* 61:323–343.
1955 Painted Pottery and Zuni History. *Southwestern Journal of Anthropology* 11:178–193.

Reed, Lori Stephens
1990 X-Ray Diffraction Analysis of Glaze-Painted Ceramics from the Northern Rio Grande Region, New Mexico. In *Economy and Polity in Late Rio Grande Prehistory,* edited by Steadman Upham and Barbara Diane Staley, pp. 90–149. University Museum Occasional Papers 16. New Mexico State University, Las Cruces.

Reina, Ruben E., and Robert M. Hill II
1978 *The Traditional Pottery of Guatemala.* University of Texas Press, Austin.

Reneau, Steven L., and David P. Dethier
1996 Pliocene and Quaternary History of the Rio Grande, White Rock Canyon and Vicinity, New Mexico. In *The Jemez Mountains Region: New Mexico Geological Society Guidebook, Forty-seventh Annual Field Conference, September 25–28, 1996,* edited by Fraser Goff, Barry S. Kues, Margaret A. Rogers, Leslie D. McFadden, and Jamie N. Gardner, pp. 317–324. New Mexico Geological Society, Socorro.

Reneau, Steven L., Eric V. McDonald, Jamie N. Gardner, Thomas R. Kolbe, John S. Carney, Paula M. Watt, and Patrick A. Longmire
1996 Erosion and Deposition on the Pajarito Plateau, New Mexico, and Implications for Geomorphic

Reneau, Steven L., Eric V. McDonald, Jamie N. Gardner, Thomas R. Kolbe, John S. Carney, Paula M. Watt, and Patrick A. Longmire (*continued*)

        Responses to Late Quaternary Climatic Changes. In *The Jemez Mountains Region: New Mexico Geological Society Guidebook, Forty-seventh Annual Field Conference, September 25–28, 1996,* edited by Fraser Goff, Barry S. Kues, Margaret A. Rogers, Leslie D. McFadden, and Jamie N. Gardner, pp. 391–398. New Mexico Geological Society, Socorro.

Rhodes, Daniel

  1973   *Clay and Glazes for the Potter.* Krause Publications, Iola, WI.

Rice, Prudence M.

  1987   *Pottery Analysis: A Sourcebook.* University of Chicago Press, Chicago.

  1992   Specialization, Standardization, and Diversity: A Retrospective. In *The Ceramic Legacy of Anna O. Shepard,* edited by R. Bishop and F. Lange, pp. 257–279. University of Colorado Press, Boulder.

Riley, Carroll L.

  1975   The Road to Hawikuh: Trade and Trade Routes to Cibola-Zuni During the Late Prehistoric and Early Historic Times. *The Kiva* 41:137–159.

  1995   *Rio del Norte: People of the Upper Rio Grande from Earliest Times to the Pueblo Revolt.* University of Utah Press, Salt Lake City.

Riley, Carroll L., and Joni L. Manson

  1983   The Cibola-Tiguex Route: Continuity and Change in the Southwest. *New Mexico Historical Review* 58:350–363.

Rinaldo, John B.

  2008   Notes on the Historic Origins of Zuni Culture. *Kiva* 74:129–140.

Roddick, Andrew

  2009   *Communities of Pottery Production and Consumption on the Taraco Peninsula, Bolivia, 200 BC–AD 300.* Ph.D. dissertation, University of California, Berkeley. Proquest, Ann Arbor.

Rolland, Vicki L., and Keith H. Ashley

  2000   Beneath the Bell: A Study of Mission Period Colonoware from Three Spanish Missions in Northeastern Florida. *Florida Anthropologist* 53(1):36–61.

Roscoe, Will

  1991   *The Zuni Man-Woman.* University of New Mexico Press, Albuquerque.

Rothschild, Nan A.

  2003   *Colonial Encounters in a Native American Landscape: The Spanish and Dutch in North America.* Smithsonian Books, Washington, D.C.

Roux, Valentine

  2003   Ceramic Standardization and Intensity of Production: Quantifying Degrees of Specialization. *American Antiquity* 68:768–782.

Sackett, James R.

  1982   Approaches to Style in Lithic Archaeology. *Journal of Anthropological Archaeology* 1:59–112.

Safran, William

  1991   Diasporas in Modern Societies: Myths of Homeland and Return. *Diaspora* 1:83–99.

  1997   Comparing Diasporas: A Review Essay. *Diaspora* 8:255–291.

  2004   Deconstructing and Comparing Diasporas. In *Diaspora, Identity and Religion: New Directions in Theory and Research,* edited by Waltraud Kokot, Kachig Tölölyan, and Carolin Alfonso, pp. 9–29. Routledge, London.

Sassaman, Kenneth, and Wictoria Rudolphi

  2001   Communities of Practice in the Early Pottery Traditions of the American Southeast. *Journal of Anthropological Research* 57:407–425.

Sauer, Carl, and Donald Brand

  1932   *Aztatlán: Prehistoric Mexican Frontier on the Pacific Coast.* Ibero-America 1. University of California Press, Berkeley.

Saunders, Rebecca

  2000   *Stability and Change in Guale Indian Pottery, A.D. 1300–1702.* University of Alabama Press, Tuscaloosa.

Sayles, E. B.

  1936   *An Archaeological Survey of Chihuahua, Mexico.* Medallion Paper 22. Gila Pueblo, Globe, Arizona.

Schaafsma, Curtis F.

  2007   Appendix D: Compilation of Excavated and Previously Reported Ceramics from Pottery Mound. In *New Perspectives on Pottery Mound Pueblo,* edited by P. Schaafsma, pp. 277–293. University of New Mexico Press, Albuquerque.

Schaafsma, Polly

  1994   The Prehistoric Kachina Cult and Its Origins as Suggested by Southwestern Rock Art. In *Kachinas in the Pueblo World,* edited by Polly Schaafsma, pp. 63–79. University of New Mexico Press, Albuquerque.

Schaafsma, Polly (editor)

  2007   *New Perspectives on Pottery Mound Pueblo.* University of New Mexico Press, Albuquerque.

Schaafsma, Polly, and Curtis F. Schaafsma

  1974   Evidence for the Origins of the Pueblo Kachina Cult as Suggested by Southwestern Rock Art. *American Antiquity* 39:535–545.

Schaafsma, Polly, and Karl A. Taube

2006   Bringing the Rain: An Ideology of Rain Making in the Pueblo Southwest and Mesoamerica. In *A Pre-Columbian World,* edited by Jeffrey Quilter and Mary Miller, pp. 232–285.

Schachner, Gregson

2006   The Decline of Zuni Glaze Ware Production in the Tumultuous Fifteenth Century. In *The Social Lives of Pots: Glaze Wares and Cultural Dynamics in the Southwest, AD 1250–1680,* edited by Judith A. Habicht-Mauche, Suzanne L. Eckert, and Deborah L. Huntley, pp. 124–141. University of Arizona Press, Tucson.

Schiffer, Michael B., and James Skibo

1987   Theory and Experiment in the Study of Technological Change. *Current Anthropology* 28:595–622.

Schiffer, Michael B., with Andrea R. Miller

1999   *The Material Life of Human Beings: Artifacts, Behavior, and Communication.* Routledge, London.

Schleher, Kari L.

2005   Standardization in Pottery: An Ethnoarchaeological and Archaeological Comparison. Paper presented at the 70th Annual Meeting of the Society for American Archaeology, Salt Lake City.

2007   Thin Sections of Time: Petrographic Analysis of Northern Rio Grande Glaze Paint Wares from San Marcos Pueblo, New Mexico. Poster presented at the 72th Annual Meeting of the Society for American Archaeology, Austin.

2010a   Petrographic Analysis of Ceramics from the Montaño Site Complex, LA 33223. In *Report on 1988 Data Recovery at the Montaño Site Complex, LA 3322, City of Albuquerque, New Mexico, and Subsequent Analysis of Collections*, edited by Gerry Raymond, pp. 6-1 to 6-23. Submitted to the City of Albuquerque by Criterion Environmental Consulting, Albuquerque.

2010b   Petrographic Analysis of Pottery Mound Ceramics. In *The Pottery of Pottery Mound, A Study of the 1979 UNM Field School Collections, Part 2: Ceramic Materials and Regional Exchange*, by Hayward H. Franklin, pp. 66-71. Maxwell Museum of Anthropology Technical Series 12. University of New Mexico, Albuquerque.

2010c   The Role of Standardization in Specialization of Ceramic Production at San Marcos Pueblo, New Mexico. Unpublished Ph.D. dissertation, Department of Anthropology, University of New Mexico.

Schleher, Kari L., and Jennifer E. Boyd

2005   Petrographic Analysis of Glaze-Painted Ceramics. In *Across the Caja del Rio Plateau, III: Hunters and Farmers in the Northern Rio Grande,* edited by Peggy A. Gerow and Patrick Hogan, pp. 153–165. Office of Contract Archeology, University of New Mexico, Albuquerque.

Schmidt, Erich F.

1927   A Stratigraphic Study in the Gila-Salt Region, Arizona. *Proceedings of the National Academy of Sciences of the United States of America* 13(5):291–298.

1928   *Time-Relations of Prehistoric Pottery Types in Southern Arizona.* Anthropological Papers of the American Museum of Natural History 30(5). New York.

Schoenwetter, James

1965   Pollen Studies at Reeve Ruin and the Davis Ranch Site: Preliminary Report. Manuscript on file, Arizona State University Libraries, Tempe.

Scholes, France V.

1935   Civil Government and Society in New Mexico in the Seventeenth Century. *New Mexico Historical Review* 10:71–111.

1936–1937   Church and State in New Mexico, 1659-1670. *New Mexico Historical Review* 11:9–76, 145–78, 283–94, 297–349.

1938   Troublous Times in New Mexico, 1659–1670. *New Mexico Historical Review* 13:63–84.

1944   Correction. *New Mexico Historical Review* 19:243-246.

Schroeder, Albert H.

1979   Pueblos Abandoned in the Historic Times. In *Southwest,* edited by Alfonso Ortiz, pp. 235–255. Handbook of North American Indians, Vol. 9, William C. Sturtevant, general editor. Smithsonian Institution, Washington, D.C.

Scott, Stuart D., and Michael S. Foster

2000   The Prehistory of Mexico's Northwest Coast: A View from the Marismas Nacionales of Sinaloa and Nayarit. In *Greater Mesoamerica: The Archaeology of West and Northwest Mexico,* edited by Michael S. Foster and Shirley Gorenstein, pp. 107–135. University of Utah Press, Salt Lake City.

Self, Stephen, Grant Heiken, Martha L. Sykes, Kenneth Wohletz, Richard V. Fisher, and David P. Dethier

1996   *Field Excursions to the Jemez Mountains, New Mexico.* New Mexico Bureau of Mines and Mineral Resources Bulletin 134. Socorro.

Seventh Southwestern Ceramic Seminar

1965   Acoma-Zuni Pottery Types. September 24–25. Research Center, Museum of Northern Arizona, Flagstaff.

Sewell, William H.

1992   A Theory of Structure: Duality, Agency, and Transformation. *American Journal of Sociology* 98:1–29.

Shafer, Harry J.
1999   The Mimbres Classic and Postclassic: A Case for Discontinuity. In *The Casas Grandes World,* edited by Curtis F. Schaafsma and Carroll L. Riley, pp. 121–133. University of Utah Press, Salt Lake City.

Sheffer, Gabriel
1986   A New Field of Study: Modern Diasporas in International Politics. In *Modern Diasporas in International Politics,* edited by Gabriel Sheffer, pp. 1–15. Croom Helm, London.

Shepard, Anna O.
1936   The Technology of Pecos Pottery. In *The Pottery of Pecos,* Vol. 2, by Alfred Vincent Kidder and Anna O. Shepard, pp. 389–587. Phillips Academy, Yale University Press, New Haven.

1939   Technology of La Plata Pottery. In *Archaeological Studies in the La Plata District: Southwestern Colorado and Northwestern New Mexico,* by Earl H. Morris, pp. 249–287. Carnegie Institution of Washington Publication 519. Washington, D.C.

1942   *Rio Grande Glaze Paint Ware: A Study Illustrating the Place of Ceramic Technological Analysis in Archaeological Research.* Carnegie Institution of Washington, Publication 528, Contribution 39. Washington, D.C.

1965   Rio Grande Glaze Paint Pottery: A Test of Petrographic Analysis. In *Ceramics and Man,* edited by Frederick R. Matson, pp. 62–87. Aldine, Chicago.

1985   *Ceramics for the Archaeologist.* Reprinted. Braun-Brumfield, Ann Arbor. Originally published 1956 [revised 1965], Carnegie Institution Publication 609. Washington, D.C.

Silliman, Stephen W.
2001   Agency, Practical Politics, and the Archaeology of Culture Contact. *Journal of Social Archaeology* 1:190–209.

2009   Change and Continuity, Practice and Memory: Native American Persistence in Colonial New England. *American Antiquity* 74:211–230.

Simpson, Lesley Byrd
1937   The Medicine of the Conquistadores: An American Pharmacopoea of 1536. *Osiris* 3:142–164.

Sinclair, Anthony
2000   Constellations of Knowledge: Human Agency and Material Affordance in Lithic Technology. In *Agency in Archaeology,* edited by Marcia-Anne Dobres and John Robb, pp. 196–212. Routledge, London.

Singleton, T. A., and M. Bograd
2000   Breaking Typological Barriers: Looking for the Colono in Colonoware. In *Lines That Divide: Historical Archaeologies of Race, Class, and Gender,* edited by J. A. Delle, S. A. Mrozowski, and Robert Paynter, pp. 3–21. University of Tennessee Press, Knoxville.

Slawson, William F., and Carl F. Austin
1960   Anomalous Leads from a Selected Geological Environment in West-Central New Mexico. *Nature* 187(4735):400–401.

1962   A Lead Isotope Study Defines a Geological Structure. *Economic Geology* 57:21–29.

Smith, Greg C.
1995   Indians and Africans at Puerto Real: The Ceramic Evidence. In *Puerto Real: the Archaeology of a Sixteenth-Century Town in Hispaniola,* edited by Kathleen Deagan, pp. 335–374. University Press of Florida, Gainesville.

Smith, Monica L.
1999   The Role of Ordinary Goods in Premodern Exchange. *Journal of Archaeological Method and Theory* 6:109–135.

Smith, Watson
1952   *Kiva Mural Decorations at Awat'ovi and Kawaika-a.* Reports of the Awat'ovi Expedition No. 5. Papers of the Peabody Museum of American Anthropology and Ethnology 37. Harvard University, Cambridge.

1971   *Painted Ceramics of the Western Mound at Awatovi.* Reports of the Awatovi Expedition 8, Papers of the Peabody Museum of American Archaeology and Ethnology 38. Harvard University, Cambridge.

Smith, Watson, Richard B. Woodbury, and Natalie F. S. Woodbury
1966   *The Excavation of Hawikuh: Report of the Hendricks-Hodge Expedition.* Museum of the American Indian, Heye Foundation, New York.

Snow, David H.
1973   Some Economic Considerations of Historic Rio Grande Pueblo Pottery. In *The Changing Ways of Southwestern Indians: A Historical Perspective,* edited by Albert H. Schroeder, pp. 55–72. Rio Grande Press, Glorieta, NM.

1981   Protohistoric Rio Grande Pueblo Economies: A Review of Trends. In *The Protohistoric Period in the North American Southwest, A.D. 1450–1700,* edited by David R. Wilcox and W. Bruce Masse, pp. 354–377. Anthropological Research Papers 24. Arizona State University, Tempe.

1982   The Rio Grande Glaze, Matte-paint, and Plainware Tradition. In *Southwest Ceramics: A Comparative Review,* edited by Albert H. Schroeder, pp. 235–278. *Arizona Archaeologist* 15. Arizona Archaeological Society, Phoenix.

1983   A Note on Encomienda Economics in Seventeenth-Century New Mexico. In *Hispanic Arts & Ethnohistory in the Southwest: New Papers Inspired by the Works of E. Boyd,* edited by M. Weigle, pp. 347–358. Ancient City Press, Santa Fe.

1997   *"Por alli no ay losa, ni se hace,"* Gilded Men and the Glazed Pottery on the Southern Plains. In *The Coronado Expedition to Tierra Nueva: The 1540–1542 Route across the Southwest,* edited by Richard Flint and Shirley Cushing Flint, pp. 344-364. University Press of Colorado, Boulder.

1998   1705 Santa Fe Muster Roll. *Herencia* 6(3):39–42.

2009   Ceramics from LA 20000: A 17th Century Estancia near Santa Fe. *Pottery Southwest* 28(2): 12–18.

Sökefeld, Martin

2002   Alevi Dedes in the German Diaspora: The Transformation of a Religious Institution. *Zeitschrift für Ethnologie* 127(2):163–186.

2004   Religion or Culture? Concepts of Identity in the Alevi Diaspora. In *Diaspora, Identity and Religion: New Directions in Theory and Research,* edited by Waltraud Kokot, Kachig Tölölyan, and Carolin Alfonso, pp. 133–155. Routledge, London.

Solometo, Julie

2008   The Context and Process of Pueblo Mural Painting in the Historic Era. Unpublished manuscript in the author's possession.

South, Stanley, Russell K. Skowronek, and Richard E. Johnson

1988   *Spanish Artifacts from Santa Elena.* Anthropological Studies 7. Occasional Papers of the South Carolina Institute of Archaeology and Anthropology. University of South Carolina, Columbia.

Spielmann, Katherine A.

1998   Ritual Influences on the Development of Rio Grande Glaze A Ceramics. In *Migration and Reorganization: The Pueblo IV Period in the American Southwest,* edited by Katherine A. Spielmann, pp. 253–261. Anthropological Research Papers 51. Department of Anthropology, Arizona State University, Tempe.

2002   Feasting, Craft Specialization, and the Ritual Mode of Production in Small-Scale Societies. *American Anthropologist* 104:195–207.

2004a   Clusters Revisited. In *The Protohistoric Pueblo World, A.D. 1275–1600,* edited by E. Charles Adams and Andrew I Duff, pp. 137–144. University of Arizona Press, Tucson.

2004b   Communal Feasting, Ceramics, and Exchange. In *Identity, Feasting, and the Archaeology of the Greater Southwest: Proceedings of the 2002 Southwest Symposium,* edited by Barbara J. Mills, pp. 210–232. University Press of Colorado, Boulder.

Spielmann, Katherine A., Jeannette L. Mobley-Tanaka, and James M. Potter

2006   Style and Resistance in the Seventeenth-Century Salinas Province. *American Antiquity* 71:621–647.

Spier, Leslie

1917   *Outline for a Chronology of Zuni Ruins.* American Museum of Natural History, Anthropological Papers 18(3):207–331.

1918   *Notes on some Little Colorado Runis.* American Museum of Natural History, Anthropological Papers 18(4):303–362.

1919   *Ruins in the White Mountains, Arizona.* American Museum of Natural History, Anthropological Papers 18(5):363–387.

Sprehn, Maria

2003   *Social Complexity and the Specialist Potters of Casas Grandes in Northern Mexico.* Ph.D. dissertation, University of New Mexico, Albuquerque. University Microfilms, Ann Arbor.

Stark, Barbara L.

1995   Problems in Analysis of Standardization and Specialization. In *Ceramic Production in the American Southwest,* edited by B. J. Mills and P. L. Crown, pp. 231–267. University of Arizona Press, Tucson.

Stark, Miriam T.

2006   Glaze Ware Technology, the Social Lives of Pots, and Communities of Practice in the Late Prehistoric Southwest. In *The Social Lives of Pots: Glaze Wares and Cultural Dynamics in the Southwest, AD 1250-1680,* edited by Judith A. Habicht-Mauche, Suzanne L. Eckert, and Deborah L. Huntley, pp. 17–33. University of Arizona Press, Tucson.

Stark, Miriam T., and James M. Heidke

1995   Early Classic Period Variability in Utilitarian Ceramic Production and Distribution. In *The Roosevelt Community Development Study, Vol. 2: Ceramic Chronology, Technology, and Economics,* edited by James M. Heidke and Miriam T. Stark, pp. 363–393. Anthropological Papers 14. Center for Desert Archaeology, Tucson.

Stark, Miriam T., Brenda J. Bowser, and Lee Horne (editors)

2008   *Cultural Transmission and Material Culture: Breaking Down Boundaries.* University of Arizona Press, Tucson.

Steen, Charlie R.

1965   Excavations in Compound A, Casa Grande National Monument, 1963. *The Kiva* 31(2):59–82.

Stein, John R., and Andrew P. Fowler
1996   Looking beyond Chaco in the San Juan Basin and Its Peripheries. In *The Prehistoric Pueblo World, A.D. 1150–1350,* edited by Michael A. Adler, pp. 114–130. University of Arizona Press, Tucson.

Stevenson, Matilda Coxe
1904   *The Zuni Indians.* Twenty-third Annual Report of the Bureau of American Ethnology, Smithsonian Institution. Washington, D.C.

Stewart, Joe D., Jane H. Kelley, A. C. MacWilliams, and Paula J. Reimer
2004   Archaeological Chronology in West-Central Chihuahua. In *Surveying the Archaeology of Northwest Mexico,* edited by Gillian E. Newell and Emiliano Gallaga, pp. 205–245. University of Utah Press, Salt Lake City.

Stimac, James
1996   Hornblende-Dacite Pumice in the Tshirege Member of the Bandelier Tuff: Implications for Magma Chamber and Eruptive Processes. In *The Jemez Mountains Region: New Mexico Geological Society Guidebook, Forty-seventh Annual Field Conference, September 25–28, 1996,* edited by Fraser Goff, Barry S. Kues, Margaret A. Rogers, Leslie D. McFadden, and Jamie N. Gardner, pp. 269–274. New Mexico Geological Society, Socorro.

Tanner, Clara Lee
1976   *Prehistoric Southwestern Craft Arts.* University of Arizona Press, Tucson.

Thomas, Alfred Barnaby
1935   *After Coronado: Spanish Exploration Northeast of New Mexico, 1696–1727.* University of Oklahoma Press, Norman.

Thomas, David H.
2000   Excavations at Mission San Marcos, New Mexico: SE-143 and BE-022, Summer 1999. Report submitted to the New Mexico Historic Preservation Office, Santa Fe. Manuscript on file, American Museum of Natural History, New York.

Thomas, Noah
2008   Seventeenth-century Technology on the Spanish Colonial Frontier: Transformations of Technology, Value and Identity. Unpublished Ph.D. Dissertation, Department of Anthropology, University of Arizona.

Tölölyan, Kachig
1996   Rethinking Diaspora(s): Stateless Power in the Transnational Moment. *Diaspora* 5:3–36.

Toulouse, Betty
1977   *Pueblo Pottery of the New Mexico Indians.* Museum of New Mexico Press, Santa Fe.

Toulouse, Joseph H., Jr.
1949   *The Mission of San Gregorio de Abo: A Report on the Excavation and Repair of a Seventeenth-Century New Mexico Mission.* Monographs of the School of American Research 13. University of New Mexico Press, Albuquerque.

Triadan, Daniela
1997   *Ceramic Commodities and Common Containers: Production and Distribution of White Mountain Red Ware in the Grasshopper Region, Arizona.* Anthropological Papers of the University of Arizona 61. University of Arizona Press, Tucson.
1998   Socio-Demographic Implications of the Pueblo IV Ceramic Production and Circulation: Sourcing White Mountain Red Ware from the Grasshopper Region, Arizona. In *Migration and Reorganization: The Pueblo IV Period in the American Southwest,* edited by Katherine A. Spielmann, pp. 233–252. Anthropological Research Papers 51. Department of Anthropology, Arizona State University, Tempe.

Triadan, Daniela, Barbara J. Mills, and Andrew I. Duff
2002   From Compositional to Anthropological: Fourteenth-Century Red Ware Circulation and Its Implications for Pueblo Reorganization. In *Ceramic Production and Circulation in the Greater Southwest: Source Determination by INAA and Complementary Mineralogical Investigations,* edited by Donna M. Glowacki and Hector Neff, pp. 85–97. Monograph 44. Cotsen Institute of Archaeology, University of California, Los Angeles.

Upham, Steadman
1982   *Polities and Power: An Economic and Political History of the Western Pueblo.* Academic Press, New York.

van der Veer, Peter, and Steven Vertovec
1991   Brahmanism Abroad: On Caribbean Hinduism as an Ethnic Religion. *Ethnology* 30:149–166.

Van Dyke, Ruth M.
1997   The Andres Great House Community: A Ceramic Chronometric Perspective. *Kiva* 63:139–154.

Van Hoose, Jonathan E.
2008   Learning Lineages as Reflected in Ceramic Production in Early Historic Northwestern New Mexico. Unpublished Ph.D. dissertation, Department of Anthropology, University of New Mexico, Albuquerque.

Van Keuren, Scott
2006   Decorating Glaze-Painted Pottery in East-Central Arizona. In *The Social Life of Pots: Glaze Wares and Cultural Dynamics in the Southwest, AD 1250–1680,* edited by Judith A. Habicht-Mauche,

Suzanne L. Eckert, and Deborah L. Huntley, pp. 86–104. University of Arizona Press, Tucson.

VanPool, Christine S.
2003   The Shaman-Priests of the Casas Grandes Region, Chihuahua, Mexico. *American Antiquity* 68:696–717.

VanPool, Christine S., Todd VanPool, and
Marcel Harmon
2008   Plumed and Horned Serpents in the American Southwest. In *Touching the Past: Ritual, Religion, and Trade of Casas Grandes,* edited by Glenna Nielsen-Grimm and Paul Stavast, pp. 47–58. Popular Series 5. Museum of Peoples and Cultures, Brigham Young University, Provo.

VanPool, Todd L., Christine S. VanPool, and
David A. Phillips, Jr.
2006   The Casas Grandes and Salado Phenomena: Evidence for a Religious Schism in the Greater Southwest. In *Religion in the Prehispanic Southwest,* edited by Christine S. VanPool, Todd L. VanPool, and David A. Phillips, Jr., pp. 235–251. AltaMira Press, Lanham, MD.

Vare, Paul
2008   From Practice to Theory: Participation as Learning in the Context of Sustainable Development Projects. In *Participation and Learning: Perspectives on Education and the Environment, Health and Sustainability,* edited by Alan Reid, Bjarne Bruun Jensen, Jutta Nikel, and Venka Simovska, pp. 128–143. Springer, New York.

Varien, Mark D., William D. Lipe,
Michael A. Adler, Ian Thompson, and
Bruce A. Bradley
1996   Southwestern Colorado and Southeastern Utah Settlement Patterns: A.D. 1100–1300. In *The Prehistoric Pueblo World, A.D. 1150–1350,* edited by M. A. Adler, pp. 86–113. University of Arizona Press, Tucson.

Vaughan, Charles David
2001   *Investigating Spanish Colonial Mining and Metallurgy.* Archaeological Conservancy and the New Mexico Historic Preservation Division, Santa Fe.
2006   Taking the Measure of New Mexico's Colonial Miners, Mining, and Metallurgy. Unpublished Ph.D. dissertation, University of New Mexico, Albuquerque.

Vélez de Escalante, Silvestre
1778   *Extractos de Noticias.* Translated by Eleanor B. Adams. Eleanor B. Adams Papers, MSS 826 BC, Box 13, Folder 21. Center for Southwest Research, University of New Mexico, Albuquerque.

Vélez-Ibáñez, Carlos G.
1988   Networks of Exchange among Mexicans in the U.S. and Mexico: Local Level Mediating Responses to National and International Transformations. *Urban Anthropology* 17:27–51.

Vélez-Ibáñez, Carlos G., and James B. Greenberg
1992   Formation and Transformation of Funds of Knowledge among U.S.-Mexican Households. *Anthropology and Education Quarterly* 23:313–335.

Vernon Richard
1988   17th Century Apalachee Colono-Ware as a Reflection of Demography, Economics, and Acculturation. *Historical Archaeology* 22(1):76–83.

Vernon, Richard, and Ann S. Cordell
1991   Distribution and Technological Study of Apalachee Colono-Ware from San Luis de Talimali. *Florida Anthropologist* 44:316–330.
1993   A Distributional and Technological Study of Apalachee Colono-Ware from San Luis de Talimali. In *The Spanish Missions of La Florida,* edited by Bonnie G. McEwan, pp. 418-442. University Press of Florida, Gainesville.

Vertovec, Steven
1991   Inventing Religious Tradition: *Yagnas* and Hindu Renewal in Trinidad. In *Religion, Tradition, and Renewal,* edited by Armin W. Geertz and Jeppe Sinding Jensen, pp. 79–97. Aarhus University Press, Aarhus.
1994   "Official" and "Popular" Hinduism in Diaspora: Historical and Contemporary Trends in Surinam, Trinidad and Guyana. *Contributions to Indian Sociology* 28:123–147.

Vint, James M.
1999   Ceramic Artifacts. In *The Bandelier Archeological Survey,* edited by Robert P. Powers and Janet D. Orcutt, pp. 389–468. Intermountain Cultural Resources Management Professional Paper 57. National Park Service, Washington, D.C.

Vint, James M., and Jeffery F. Burton
1990   Ceramics. In *Archeological Investigations at Puerco Ruin, Petrified Forest National Park, Arizona* by Jeffery F. Burton, pp. 97–126. Publications in Anthropology 54. Western Archeological and Conservation Center, National Park Service, Tucson.

Vint, James M., and Jeffery J. Clark
2004   An Overview of the Tonto Creek Ceramic Analyses: General Trends and Vessel Function. In *2000 Years of Settlement in the Tonto Basin: Overview and Synthesis of the Tonto Creek Archaeological Project,* edited by Jeffery J. Clark and James M. Vint, pp. 43–76. Anthropological Papers 25. Center for Desert Archaeology, Tucson.

Vivian, Gordon
  1979   *Gran Quivira: Excavations in a Seventeenth Century Jumano Pueblo.* Archaeological Research Series 8. National Park Service, Washington, D.C.

Voll, Charles
  1961   The Glaze Paint Ceramics of Pottery Mound, New Mexico. Unpublished Master's thesis, Department of Anthropology, University of New Mexico, Albuquerque.

Walker, William H.
  2008   Practice and Nonhuman Social Actors: The Afterlife Histories of Witches and Dogs in the American Southwest. In *Memory Work: Archaeologies of Material Practices,* edited by Barbara J. Mills and William H. Walker, pp. 137–157. School for Advanced Research Press, Santa Fe.

Walker, William H., and Michael B. Schiffer
  2006   The Materiality of Social Power: The Artifact-Acquisition Perspective. *Journal of Archaeological Method and Theory* 13:67–88.

Wallaert-Pêtre, Hélène
  2001   Learning How To Make the Right Pots: Apprenticeship Strategies and Material Culture, A Case Study in Handmade Pottery from Cameroon. *Journal of Anthropological Research* 57:471–493.
  2008   The Way of the Potter's Mother: Apprenticeship Strategies among Dii Potters from Cameroon, West Africa. In *Cultural Transmission and Material Culture: Breaking Down Boundaries,* edited by Miriam T. Stark, Brenda J. Bowser, and Lee Horne, pp. 178–198. University of Arizona Press, Tucson.

Ward, Albert E.
  1975   *Inscription House: Two Research Reports.* Museum of Northern Arizona Technical Series 16. Northern Arizona Society of Science and Art, Flagstaff.

Warren, A. Helene
  1968   Petrographic Notes on Glaze-paint Pottery. In *The Cochiti Dam Archaeological Salvage Project, Part I: Report on the 1963 Season,* assembled by Charles H. Lange, pp. 184-197. Museum of New Mexico Research Records 6. Museum of New Mexico Press, Santa Fe.
  1969a   Tonque: One Pueblo's Glaze Pottery Industry Dominated Middle Rio Grande Commerce. *El Palacio* 76(2):36–42.
  1969b   Notes on Historic Plainwares Tempering Materials (8/69). Manuscript on file with David H. Snow, Albuquerque, New Mexico.
  1970   Notes on the Manufacture and Trade of Rio Grande Glazes. *The Artifact* 8(4):1–7.
  1971   Notes on Pottery and laboratory analysis forms from Casa Quemada (LA 4955). Manuscript on file, Laboratory of Anthropology, Santa Fe.
  1976   The Ceramics and Mineral Resources of LA 70 and the Cochiti Area. In *Archaeological Excavations at Pueblo del Encierro, LA 70, Cochiti Dam Salvage Project, Final Report, 1964–1965.* Laboratory of Anthropology Note 78. Santa Fe.
  1977a   Early Redwares of the Middle Rio Grande Valley. *Pottery Southwest* 4(2):2–3.
  1977b   Eighteenth Century Historic Pottery of the Cochiti District. *Pottery Southwest* 4(1):2–3.
  1979a   The Glaze Paint Wares of the Upper Middle Rio Grande. In *Archaeological Investigations at Pueblo del Encierro, LA 70, Cochiti Dam Salvage Project, Cochiti, New Mexico,* edited by David H. Snow, pp. B1–B184. Laboratory of Anthropology Note 78. Museum of New Mexico, Santa Fe.
  1979b   The Glaze Paint Wares of the Upper Middle Rio Grande. In *Archaeological Investigations in Cochiti Reservoir, New Mexico, Vol. 4: Adaptive Change in the Northern Rio Grande Valley,* edited by Jan V. Biella and Richard C. Chapman, pp. 187–216. Office of Contract Archeology, University of New Mexico, Albuquerque.
  1980   Prehistoric Pottery of Tijeras Canyon. In *Tijeras Canyon: Analyses of the Past,* edited by Linda S. Cordell, pp. 149–168. University of New Mexico Press, Albuquerque.
  1981a   *The Micaceous Pottery of the Rio Grande.* Archaeological Society of New Mexico Anthropological Papers 6. Albuquerque.
  1981b   A Petrographic Study of the Ceramics at Four Historic Sites of the Galisteo Basin, New Mexico. *Pottery Southwest* 8(2):2–4.
  1981c   A Petrographic Study of the Pottery of Gran Quivira. In *Contributions to Gran Quivira Archeology,* edited by Alden C. Hayes, pp. 57–74. National Park Service Publications in Archeology 17. Washington, D.C.

Warren, A. Helene, and Frances J. Mathien
  1985   Prehistoric and Historic Turquoise Mining in the Cerrillos District: Time and Place. In *Southwestern Culture History: Collected Papers in Honor of Albert H. Schroeder,* edited by Charles L. Lange, pp. 93–127. Papers of the Archaeological Society of New Mexico 10. Ancient City Press, Santa Fe.

Warren, A. Helene, and Robert H. Weber
  1979   Indian and Spanish Mining in the Galisteo and Hagan Basins. In *Archaeology and History of Santa Fe County,* edited by Raymond V. Ingersoll,

pp. 7–11. Special Publication 8. New Mexico Geological Society, Albuquerque.

Washburn, Dorothy K.
1977   *A Symmetry Analysis of Upper Gila Area Ceramic Design.* Papers of the Peabody Museum of Archaeology and Ethnology 68. Harvard University, Cambridge.
1978   A Symmetry Classification of Pueblo Ceramic Designs. In *Discovering Past Behavior: Experiments in the Archaeology of the American Southwest,* edited by Paul Grebinger, pp. 101–121. Gordon and Breach, London.
2001   Remembering Things Seen: Experimental Approaches to the Process of Information Transmittal. *Journal of Archaeological Method and Theory* 8:67–99.

Wasley, William W., and David E. Doyel
1980   Classic Period Hohokam. *The Kiva* 45:337–352.

Waterworth, Robert M. R.
1988   Glaze Painted Ceramics in Dolores Archaeological Program Collections. In *Dolores Archaeological Program: Supporting Studies: Additive and Reductive Technologies,* compiled by Eric Blinman, Carl J. Phagan, and Richard H. Wilshusen, pp. 437–447. U.S. Bureau of Reclamation, Engineering and Research Center, Denver.

Weaver, Donald E., Jr.
1972   A Cultural-Ecological Model for the Classic Hohokam Period in the Lower Salt River Valley, Arizona. *The Kiva* 38:43–52.
1973   Excavations at Pueblo del Monte and the Classic Period Hohokam Problem. *The Kiva* 39:75–87.
1976   Salado Influences in the Lower Salt River Valley. *The Kiva* 42:17–26.

Weber, Robert H.
1999   Two Lithic Caches from the Rio Grande Valley near Socorro, New Mexico. In *La Frontera: Papers in Honor of Patrick H. Beckett,* edited by Meliha S. Duran and David T. Kirkpatrick, pp. 197–203. Papers of the Archaeological Society of New Mexico 25.

Webster, Laurie D.
1997   Effects of European Contact on Textile Production and Exchange in the North American Southwest: A Pueblo Case Study. Unpublished Ph.D. dissertation, Department of Anthropology, University of Arizona.
2000   Pueblo Textile Production and Exchange. In *Beyond Cloth and Cordage: Archaeological Textile Research in the Americas,* edited by Penelope B. Drooker, pp. 179–204. University of Utah Press, Salt Lake.

Weigand, Phil C., and Garman Harbottle
1993   The Role of Turquoises in Mesoamerican Trade Structure. In *The American Southwest and Mesoamerica: Systems of Prehistoric Exchange,* edited by Jonathan E. Ericson and Timothy G. Baugh, pp. 159–177. Plenum Press, New York.

Welch, John R., and Daniela Triadan
1991   The Canyon Creek Turquoise Mine, Arizona. *Kiva* 56:145–164.

Welker, Eden A.
1997   *Attributes of Aggregation at Pueblo San Marcos and Pecos Pueblo in the Northern Rio Grande.* Ph.D. dissertation, University of Colorado. University Microfilms, Ann Arbor.

Wellmeier, Nancy J.
1998   *Ritual, Identity, and the Mayan Diaspora.* Garland, New York.

Wendorf, Fred
1950   *A Report on the Excavation of A Small Ruin near Point of Pines, East Central Arizona.* University of Arizona Bulletin XXI(3). Social Science Bulletin 19. Tucson.

Wendrich, Willeke (editor)
2012   *Archaeology and Apprenticeship: Body Knowledge, Identity, and Communities of Practice.* University of Arizona Press, Tucson.

Wenger, Etienne
1990   *Toward a Theory of Cultural Transparency: Elements of a Social Discourse of the Visible and the Invisible.* Ph.D. dissertation, Department of Information and Computer Science, University of California, Irvine. ProQuest, Ann Arbor.
1998   *Communities of Practice: Learning, Meaning, and Identity.* Cambridge University Press, Cambridge.

Wenger, Etienne, and William M. Snyder
2000   Communities of Practice: The Organizational Frontier. *Harvard Business Review* (January–February):139–145.

Wenger, Etienne, Richard McDermott, and William M. Snyder
2002   *Cultivating Communities of Practice: A Guide to Managing Knowledge.* Harvard Business School Press, Cambridge.

Whalen, Michael E., and Paul E. Minnis
2001   *Casas Grandes and Its Hinterland: Prehistoric Regional Organization in Northwest Mexico.* University of Arizona Press, Tucson.

Wiessner, Polly
1983   Style and Social Information in Kalahari San Projectile Points. *American Antiquity* 48:253–276.
1984   Reconsidering the Behavioral Basis for Style: A Case Study among the Kalahari San. *Journal of Anthropological Archaeology* 3:190–234.

Wilcox, David R., David A. Gregory, and J. Brett Hill
  2007   Zuni in the Puebloan and Southwestern Worlds. In *Zuni Origins: Toward a New Synthesis of Southwestern Archaeology,* edited by David A. Gregory and David R. Wilcox, pp. 165–209. University of Arizona Press, Tucson.

Willey, Gordon R., and Phillip Phillips
  1958   *Method and Theory in American Archaeology.* University of Chicago Press, Chicago.

Wilson, Gordon P. (editor)
  2005   *Guide to Ceramic Identification: Northern Rio Grande Valley and Galisteo Basin to 1700 AD.* Laboratory of Anthropology, Technical Series Bulletin 12. Santa Fe.

Windes, Thomas C., and Dabney Ford
  1992   The Nature of the Early Bonito Phase. In *Anasazi Regional Organization and the Chaco System,* edited by David E. Doyel, pp. 75–86. Maxwell Museum of Anthropology, Anthropological Papers 5. University of New Mexico, Albuquerque.

Wobst, H. Martin
  1977   Stylistic Behavior and Information Exchange. In *For the Director: Research Essays in Honor of James B. Griffin,* edited by Charles E. Cleland, pp. 317–342. Anthropological Papers of the Museum of Anthropology 61. University of Michigan, Ann Arbor.

Woodbury, Richard B., and Nathalie F.S. Woodbury
  1966   Decorated Pottery of the Zuni Area. In *The Excavation of Hawikuh by Frederick Webb Hodge: Report of the Hendricks-Hodge Expedition,* by Watson Smith, Richard B. Woodbury, and Nathalie F.S. Woodbury, pp. 302–336. Contributions from the Museum of the American Indian, Heye Foundation 20. Museum of the American Indian, New York.

Woodson, M. Kyle
  1999   Migrations in Late Anasazi Prehistory: The Evidence from the Goat Hill Site. *Kiva* 65(1):63–84.

Woosley, Anne I., and Bart Olinger
  1993   The Casas Grandes Ceramic Tradition: Production and Interregional Exchange of Ramos Polychrome. In *Culture and Contact: Charles C. Di Peso's Gran Chichimeca,* edited by Anne I. Woosley and John C. Ravesloot, pp. 105–32. Amerind Foundation New World Studies Series 2. University of New Mexico Press, Albuquerque.

Yunker, Brian, and Richard H. Wilshusen
  2000   The Dolores Legacy: Data from the Dolores Archaeological Program. CD-ROM (accompanies revised User's Guide to the DAP Data). On file, Anasazi Heritage Center, Dolores, Colorado.

Zedeño, María Nieves
  1994   *Sourcing Prehistoric Ceramics at Chodistaas Pueblo, Arizona: The Circulation of People and Pots in the Grasshopper Region.* Anthropological Papers of the University of Arizona 58. University of Arizona Press, Tucson.

  2002   Artifact Design, Composition, and Context: Updating the Analysis of Ceramic Circulation at Point of Pines, Arizona. In *Ceramic Production and Circulation in the Greater Southwest: Source Determination by INAA and Complementary Mineralogical Investigations,* edited by Donna M. Glowacki and Hector Neff, pp. 74–84. Monograph 14, The Cotsen Institute of Archaeology, University of California, Los Angeles.

Index

ABSTRACT

This volume examines dynamic social networks among Ancestral Pueblo potters and potting communities between about A.D. 1250 and 1700 as manifest in their polychrome and glaze-paint decorated wares. These centuries saw dramatic changes in ways of life for Ancestral Pueblo peoples. The period began with migrations from the northern and western portions of Pueblo territory to the south and east where very large villages were established. Some of these villages integrated both newcomers and older residents, while others may have housed newcomers from different homelands. Still other villages may have housed local peoples who came together in aggregated settlements. The period ends at about the time of the Pueblo Revolt of 1680 when many of the social ties among villages were torn asunder in the wake of Spanish colonization and concomitant massive population decline and reorganization. After about 1680, production of Pueblo glaze-paint decorated pottery ceased, although matte-painted yellow and polychrome pottery types continued to be produced.

The introduction of polychrome pottery, including glaze-decorated types, marked a dramatic change in pottery technology as well as in color schemes. Clays and tempers were probably obtained close to the potter's village by members of her household or the potter herself. Slips, pigments and fluxes, however, often had to be acquired from more distant sources, with their procurement likely embedded in diverse social interaction networks. The contributors to this volume present details of compositional studies—including lead isotope and instrumental neutron activation analyses (INAA), petrography, electron microprobe analysis, scanning electron microscopy, and experimentation—to identify where raw materials were acquired and how they were handled, mixed and processed at Pueblo villages over these four centuries. The authors use inferences derived from practice theory to describe how social networks were constituted among the people who created, distributed and used polychrome and glaze-paint decorated pottery. Some of the authors also refer to situated learning theory as a means of informing themselves about social relationships between teachers and apprentices within communities of practice formed around pottery production and distribution.

RESUMEN

En este volumen se presenta un análisis de las redes de dinámicas sociales entre las ceramistas de los Pueblos Ancestrales y las comunidades alfareras entre los años 1200 A.D. y 1700, como se puede observar en sus tipos cerámicos policromos y de pintura vidriada. Aquellos siglos fueron testigos de importantes cambios en el estilo de vida de la gente de los Pueblos Ancestrales. El período comenzó con migraciones desde las partes norte y occidente de los territorios de los Pueblos, hacia el sur y el este, en donde se establecieron grandes aldeas. Algunas de estas aldeas integraron tanto a los recién llegados como a los antiguos residentes, mientras otras solamente alojaron a recién llegados de distintas tierras originarias. De cualquier modo, algunas de esas aldeas pudieron ser viviendas de las gentes locales que se juntaron en asentamientos agregados. El período termina al rededor de la época de la Revuelta de los Pueblos en 1680 A.D. cuando muchos de los lazos sociales entre las aldeas se rompieron al alba de la colonización española, con las decadencias y reorganizaciones poblacionales concomitantes. Más o menos después de 1680, cesó la producción de la cerámica decorada vidriada, aunque continuaron los tipos amarillo mate y policromo.

La introducción de la cerámica policroma, incluyendo los tipos decorados-vidriados, marcaron un cambio muy fuerte, tanto en la tecnología cerámica, como en los esquemas de color. Las arcillas y los desgrasantes eran probablemente obtenidos en fuentes cercanas a las aldeas de las ceramistas, ya fuera por miembros de su familia, o por ellas mismas. Sin embargo, los engobes, pigmentos y fundentes, a menudo se tenían que adquirir desde fuentes más distantes, lo cual significaba que su obtención derivaba en diversas redes de interacción social. Quienes contribuyen en este volumen, presentan detalles de estudios de composición —incluyendo el isótopo de plomo y el análisis instrumental de activación de neutrones (INAA), la petrografía, el análisis de micropruebas de protones, el escaneo microscópico de electrones o microscopía de escáner de electrón, y la experimentación— para identificar las fuentes de obtención de materias primas, el cómo los manejaban, mezclaban y procesaban en los Pueblos durante esos cuatro siglos. Los autores utilizan inferencias derivadas de la teoría práctica para describir cómo se constituían las

The volume begins with a chapter introducing the domain of this research and its historic and theoretical contexts (Linda S. Cordell and Judith Habicht-Mauche). The second chapter provides the detailed compositional data shared in this research and the theoretical and methodological perspectives guiding data collection (Deborah Huntley, Thomas Fenn, Judith Habicht-Mauche and Barbara J. Mills). Each of the following chapters is a case-study exploring the communities of practice developed by potters who produced polychrome and glaze-paint decorated pottery over two hundred years and suggesting how, and perhaps why these pottery traditions were introduced, continued or discontinued in different places. These chapters examine Roosevelt Red ware of Central Arizona (Patrick Lyons and Jeffrey Clark), Chihuahuan polychromes of Northwest Mexico (David Phillips), Hopi polychrome pottery (Dennis Gilpin and Kelley-Hays Gilpin), Zuni polychromes and glaze-painted pottery (Suzanne Eckert), glaze-painted pottery from the Central Rio Grande sites of Pottery Mound and Montaño Bridge Pueblo (Hayward Franklin and Keri Schleher), glaze-paint decorated pottery from the Pajarito Plateau (Diane Curewitz and Sheila Goff), glaze-paint decorated pottery from San Marcos Pueblo, Galisteo Basin, New Mexico (chapter by Ann Ramenofsky and chapter by Schleher, Deborah Huntley, and Cynthia Herhan), and production of Rio Grande glaze-paint decorated pottery (Eric Blinman and others). Four chapters explore the contexts in which glaze-paint was used and discontinued during the Spanish Colonial period (chapter by Eric Blinman and others, chapter by Noah Thomas, chapter by David Snow, and chapter by Jennifer Boyd Dyer). The final chapter, by Rosemary Joyce, is a masterful commentary and overview of the implications of practice theory, situated learning theory, and the contents of this book.

redes sociales entre las personas que crearon, distribuyeron y usaron la cerámica decorada vidriada y policroma. Algunos autores también hacen referencia a la teoría de aprendizaje en sitio como un medio para informarse acerca de las relaciones sociales entre maestros y aprendices dentro de las comunidades de práctica formadas al rededor de la producción cerámica y la distribución.

El volumen comienza con un capítulo que introduce el ámbito de esta investigación y sus contextos históricos y teóricos (Linda S. Cordell y Judith Habicht-Mauche). El segundo capítulo proporciona los datos composicionales detallados que se comparten en este trabajo, así como la recopilación de datos en los que se basan las perspectivas teóricas y metodológicas (Deborah Huntley, Thomas Fenn, Habicht-Mauche y Barbara J. Mills). Cada uno de los capítulos siguientes es un caso de estudio que explora las comunidades con prácticas desarrolladas por alfareros que produjeron las cerámicas policromas y decoradas vidriadas por más de dos siglos, y sugiere el cómo y, tal vez el por qué, surgieron estas tradiciones cerámicas, se continuaron o se descontinuaron en distintos sitios. Estos capítulos examinan los tipos "Roosevelt Red" del centro de Arizona (Patrick Lyons y Jeffrey Clark), los policromos Chihuahuenses del noroeste de México (David Phillips), la Cerámica Hopi Policroma (Dennis Gilpin y Kelley-Hays Gilpin), los policromos y vidriados Zuni (Suzanne Eckert), la cerámica vidriada de los sitios centrales del Río Grande "Pottery Mound" y "Montaño Bridge Pueblo" (Hayward Franklin y Keri Schleher), la cerámica vidriada decorada de la Cuenca del Pajarito (Diane Curewitz y Sheila Goff), la cerámica vidriada decorada del Pueblo San Marcos, en la Cuenca del Galisteo, Nuevo México (un capítulo por Ann Ramenofsky, y un capítulo por Keri Schleher, Deborah Huntley y Cynthia Herhan), y la producción de la cerámica vidriada decorada Rio Grande (Eric Blinman y otros). Cuatro de los capítulos exploran los contextos en los cuales la pintura vidriada estuvo en uso y luego se descontinuó durante el período colonial hispano (un capítulo por Eric Blinman y otros, uno por Noah Thomas, uno por David Snow y uno por Jennifer Boyd Dyer). El capítulo final por Rosemary Joyce, es un magistral comentario y revisión acerca de las implicaciones de la teoría práctica, la teoría de aprendizaje en sitio, y del contenido de este libro.

ANTHROPOLOGICAL PAPERS OF THE UNIVERSITY OF ARIZONA

Anthropological Papers listed as O.P., D are available as Docutech reproductions (high quality xerox) printed on demand. They are tape or spiral bound and nonreturnable.